PELHAM GRENVILLE WODEHOUSE

VOLUME 3
"The Happiness of the World"

PAUL KENT

Praise for Volumes 1 & 2

"Despite Wodehouse's antipathy towards critics, Kent's first volume demonstrates just how much the thick-skinned of us have to explore in his work. It is therefore excellent news that we await two more volumes of his work that can help us to unpick that poetry and try to better understand the source of that "sunlit perfection".
Eliza Easton in the Times Literary Supplement (TLS)

"I have been enthralled while reading it . . . [Kent's] accounts of Plum himself, and so many of his major characters, are consistently masterful and compelling, bringing time and again new and fascinating insights into their backgrounds, characters and motivations. The book is indeed a masterpiece".
Sir Edward Cazalet, PGW's grandson

"Kent displays an encyclopaedic knowledge of the minutiae of Wodehouse's oeuvre and presents his arguments in a lively and engaging prose style that treads a delicate balance between academic rigour and readability. We read Wodehouse because he was a master of words. We can read Kent for the same reason".
Stewart Ferris, *Wooster Sauce*, December 2020

"[A] whole new perspective on Wodehouse".
Peter van Nieuwenhuizen, The Netherlands Wodehouse Society

"Brilliant. The breadth of Wodehouse and wider references [Kent brings] in is staggering. And again, it's about the writing: hooray! Kent is forging the new path in the way I hope writing about Wodehouse will go".
Tim Andrew, Chairman, The P.G. Wodehouse Society (UK)

"Some fascinating insights into Plum's work. Tends to make you think about Wodehouse; what you have read and what you think/thought you know/knew. As Abbie Hoffman said: "Steal this book".
Ken Clevenger, Fans of PG Wodehouse Facebook site

"Vol. 2, which I have just finished has really blown me away. It gave me a warm glow of happiness".
David Salter, The P.G. Wodehouse Society (UK) member

PELHAM GRENVILLE WODEHOUSE

VOLUME 3
"The Happiness of the World"

PAUL KENT

Leapfrog Press
New York and London

PELHAM GRENVILLE WODEHOUSE

P.G. WODEHOUSE 1881-1975
HUMOURIST
NOVELIST
LYRICIST
PLAYWRIGHT

So reads the simple inscription on the memorial stone unveiled in London's Westminster Abbey in 2019, honouring the greatest comic writer of the 20th century. Sir Pelham Grenville Wodehouse KBE was all these things, writing more than 70 novels, 300 short stories, over 200 song lyrics and more than 20 plays in a career spanning eight decades. Over 40 years after his death, Wodehouse is not just surviving but thriving all over the world, so far being translated into 33 languages from Azerbaijani

to Ukrainian via Hebrew, Italian, Swedish and Chinese. There are also established Wodehouse societies in the UK, the USA, Belgium, Holland and Russia. His books are demonstrating the staying power of true classics, and are all currently in print, making him as relevant – and funny – as he ever was.

About the Author

Vice-Chairman of the P G Wodehouse Society (UK), Paul Kent began reading Wodehouse at the age of 12, and is now much older than that. He has published works on Montaigne, Voltaire and Shakespeare, and a guide to creative writing *How Writers Write*. He is currently compiling *What Ho!*, a series of short essays on Wodehouse; laying the foundations for Volume 4 of his trilogy, *Plum's Literary Heroes;* and Volume 5, *Showbiz Wodehouse.*

Pelham Grenville Wodehouse
Volume 3: "The Happiness of the World"

9 8 7 6 5 4 3 2 1

Published in the United States by Leapfrog Press, 2024
Leapfrog Press, Inc
www.leapfrogpress.com

First published by TSB, 2022
TSB is an imprint of:
Can of Worms Enterprises Ltd
7 Peacock Yard, London SE17 3LH
United Kingdom
www.canofworms.net

Cover design: James Shannon
Typesetting: Tam Griffiths and James Shannon
Index: Rebecca Zipper

Printed and bound in the United Kingdom

ISBN: 978-1-948585-59-0

British Library Cataloguing in Publication Data
A catalogue record for this book is available from the British Library

Library of Congress Cataloging-in-Publication Data
A catalog record for this book is available from the Library of Congress

June 1936

Dear Mr Wodehouse,

In recognition of your outstanding and lasting contribution to the happiness of the world, it gives me much pleasure to offer you the Mark Twain medal.

With all good wishes,

Yours sincerely,

Cyril Clemens

A POTTED LIFE OF P.G. WODEHOUSE

1881	October 15	Birth of Pelham Grenville Wodehouse at 1 Vale Place, Guildford, Surrey
1894		PGW first attends Dulwich College, London
1900		Receives his first payment for writing: from *Public School Magazine* for an article entitled 'Some Aspects of Game-Captaincy'
1900	September	Starts work at the Hong Kong and Shanghai Bank, London
1901	July	First real short story published in *Public School Magazine*, entitled 'The Prize Poem'
1901	August 16	First contribution to *Globe* newspaper
1902	September 9	Resigns from the HS Bank
1902	September 17	First article for *Punch* magazine, entitled 'An Unfinished Collection'
1902	September 19	First book published, *The Pothunters*
1904	April 16	First visit to the USA
1904	August	Appointed Editor of the 'By The Way' column at the *Globe*
1904	December 10	First published lyric, 'Put Me In My Little Cell', sung in *Sergeant Brue* at the Strand Theatre, London
1906	March 6	Employed by Seymour Hicks as the resident lyricist at the Aldwych Theatre
1906	March 19	First meets future collaborator Jerome Kern
1906	August	First novel for adults, *Love Among the Chickens*, published
1907	December 6	Joins Gaiety Theatre as lyricist
1909		Second visit to USA, where he sells short stories to *Collier's* and *Cosmopolitan*
1911	August 24	First play, *A Gentleman of Leisure*, opens in New York
1913	April 8	First play in London, *Brother Alfred*, flops
1914	August 2	Returns to New York
1914	August 3	Meets Ethel Rowley, née Newton, an English widow, at a New York party
1914	September 30	Marries Ethel Rowley and inherits her daughter Leonora
1915	March	Appointed drama critic of [US] *Vanity Fair*
1915	June 26	First appearance of Lord Emsworth and Blandings Castle in the serialisation of *Something New* (*Something Fresh* is U.K. title) in *Saturday Evening Post*
1915	September 18	Jeeves makes his first appearance, in the story 'Extricating Young Gussie' published in *Saturday Evening Post*
1916	September 25	First Bolton, Wodehouse & Kern musical comedy, *Miss Springtime* debuts in New York and is moderately successful

1919	June 7	First Oldest Member story, 'A Woman is Only a Woman', published in *Saturday Evening Post*
1923	April	First Ukridge short story, 'Ukridge's Dog College', appears in *Cosmopolitan*
1926		PGW elected a Fellow of the Royal Society of Literature
1926	July	First Mr Mulliner story, 'The Truth About George', appears in *Strand* magazine
1930	June 1	Starts first contract with MGM in Hollywood
1933	August	First instalment of the first Jeeves and Bertie Wooster novel, *Thank You, Jeeves*, published in *Strand*
1934	January 19	Successfully challenges in court the U.K. Inland Revenue's attempts to claim more income tax on his earnings
1934	June	Settles in Le Touquet, France
1935	June 3	Buys Low Wood in Le Touquet
1936	June 26	Awarded medallion by International Mark Twain Society
1939	June 2	Invested as D. Litt at Oxford University
1939	September 3	Britain declares war on Germany
1940	May 21	PGW, Ethel and animals try to leave Le Touquet in the light of the German advance, but their car twice breaks down
1940	July 21	Start of PGW internment by Germans in camps successively at Loos Prison (Lille), Liege, Huy and Tost (Upper Silesia)
1941	June 21	PGW released from internment and taken to Berlin
1941	June 26	PGW makes the first of five radio broadcasts for fans in neutral USA
1941	July 15	'Cassandra's' BBC radio broadcast of a vituperative attack on PGW, calling him a traitor
1943	September 11	PGW transferred to Paris
1944	May 16	Death of PGW's step-daughter Leonora
1947	April 27	PGW and Ethel arrive in US on SS America
1952	March	Ethel buys a house in Basket Neck Lane, Remsenburg, Long Island, New York, close to Guy Bolton's home
1955	December 16	PGW becomes an American citizen
1960	January 27	PGW elected to the *Punch* table
1961	July 15	BBC broadcasts 'An Act of Homage and Reparation' by Evelyn Waugh
1965	May 27	BBC TV series *The World of Wooster* begins transmission
1967	February 16	BBC TV series *Blandings Castle* begins transmission
1974	November	PGW's last complete novel, *Aunts Aren't Gentlemen*, published in the U.K.
1975	January 1	PGW knighted by Queen Elizabeth II, his wife Ethel taking the title Lady Wodehouse
1975	February 14	PGW dies in hospital

CONTENTS

WORLD ENOUGH
AND TIME

Preface:
World Enough and Time

On 20 September 2019, a memorial commemorating the life and work of Pelham Grenville Wodehouse was dedicated in Westminster Abbey, London. Fashioned from limestone, it is situated on a wall in the South Quire Aisle and bears the author's name and dates, bordered by the four words "Humourist", "Novelist", Playwright", "Lyricist". Compared to some of the 165 (or so) neighbouring plaques and statues, it's a small, unpretentious affair – all 708 x 500mm of it. Yet for all its simplicity, it has one attribute that sets it apart from all the others: Plum is the only out-and-out comic writer in the entire pantheon.

This notable achievement was recognized in the formal wording of the dedication ceremony, which celebrated not just the art of the humourist, but the need for laughter in our daily lives. After His Royal Highness the Duke of Kent officially delivered the stone into the safe keeping of the Abbey, the Dean (The Very Reverend Dr John Hall) remarked on "all that [Wodehouse] achieved and contributed to the joy of life"; and later in the Prayers, came this:

> O Lord God, from whom floweth all delight and at whose right hand are pleasures for evermore: we give thee thanks for P. G. Wodehouse and all thy servants whose art bringeth joy and consolation; lifting the heavy heart, and lightening the darkest day.

Quite how Plum would have reacted to all the pomp and circumstance is difficult to say. Ambivalence, most likely: extremely flattered by the honour yet discomfited by the fuss, and maybe even a little embarrassed as one who had never embraced a formal religion (the best he could commit to was "we'll have to wait and see"). He might have reflected on the way humourists and clergymen share the ambition of bringing "joy and consolation" to their respective congregations while differing somewhat in their methods. But any sober reflection would have been instantly shown the door by the spirited performances of his song lyrics 'Oh Gee! Oh Joy!' and 'My Castle in the Air' by Hal and Lara Cazalet, his great-grandchildren, and the lively readings from his novels that so good-naturedly punctured the atmosphere of high solemnity.

For some of us who were there, both lay and ordained, it did feel oddly subversive to be chortling in church; and not just any old church, but a 1,000-year-old building in which all the English and British monarchs since 1066 have been crowned, and where at least 16 of them were subsequently buried. But then, nothing was sacred to Plum, not even the Church of England, in which four of his uncles served as men of the cloth. Indeed, his stories feature the antics of well over 50 Bishops, Deans, Vicars, Rectors and Curates, most of whom are made to look as flawed and fallible as the rest of us.

The historical significance of the memorial was picked up in the speech made by the President of The P. G. Wodehouse Society (UK) Alexander Armstrong, who noted that shortly before his death, Wodehouse's likeness in wax had been commissioned by Madame Tussaud's. A sculptor had duly been dispatched from London to Plum's home on Long Island, New York complete with a tray of glass eyeballs to find the perfect match for his subject's – who was genuinely excited at the prospect of being immortalized in this way. But that immortality had proved fleeting; celebrity ebbs and flows, and Plum's effigy was eventually decapitated, removed from display and placed in storage along with all the others who had fallen by fame's wayside, possibly never to be seen in public again. The Abbey commemoration was, by contrast, in a whole different league – *that* memorial wasn't going anywhere any time soon: "Tussauds," Armstrong challenged, "We see your wax and raise it to stone". And with that, Wodehouse was finally history. In a good way.

A few weeks later, I revisited the Abbey to take some photographs of the stone, and having done so, thought I'd explore Poets' Corner and pay my respects to some of Wodehouse's fellow inmates. His personal favourites Shakespeare and Tennyson were of course present and correct, as were Chaucer, Shelley, Keats, Wordsworth, Hardy, Pope and T.S. Eliot to name just a few of the hundreds of writers Plum references in his stories and novels. But it only takes a matter of seconds for even a keen student of literature to begin wondering who some of these other honorands were: Christopher Anstey? Adam Lindsay Gordon? John Philips? William Mason? Worthy writers in *their* time, though not, as things have played out, for *all* time – and proof that neither wax nor even stone are the final arbiters in the artist's battle with posterity. At that point it struck me that the relationship between Wodehouse World and time would be a useful picklock for this third volume of ramblings; quite simply, because if those of us convinced of his genius are unable to explain how and why his work will survive long-term, the odds are considerably shortened that it won't. While Plum's advancement to the Abbey a mere 44 years on from his death is more than worthy of celebration, it doesn't follow he can claim The Man From Stratford's unassailable immortality quite yet.

Wodehouse World has a fascinating yet complex involvement with chronology, being both in and out of time simultaneously from its very earliest beginnings until the present day. Indeed, Plum's obituarist in the London *Times* (February 17, 1975) drew attention to how normal rules of ageing didn't seem to apply to his output:

> The remarkable thing about the work of his old age was that it stayed true to the formula of earlier days without seeming to date.

Wodehouse's sensibility, the anonymous writer mischievously continued, "came to a standstill" on or around "Boat Race night of Mafeking year" – which, it wasn't necessary to explain to that journal's educated readers, was in the spring of 1900 when Plum would have been 18. How could it be that Wodehouse's Eggs, Beans and Crumpets "paradoxically . . . never took on a period flavour", living as they did "in a timeless fairy land in which it was irrelevant whether transport was by Hansom cab or jet aircraft"? Well, we might respond equivocally, they do and they don't: they date horribly, only it doesn't seem to matter. Quite *why* it doesn't seem to matter is perhaps the question we should – and will – be asking in what follows.

Unlike some of his fellow authors who wrote with one eye on posterity, Plum had no grand scheme for jumping the life to come. In a 1959 magazine article, he could be found pondering how he kept getting away with pouring old wine into only slightly different bottles even as his 80th birthday loomed:

> This [redundancy] is pointed out to me every time a new
> book of mine dealing with Jeeves or Blandings Castle or
> the Drones Club is published in England. 'Edwardian!' the
> critics hiss at me. (It is not easy to hiss the word *Edwardian*,
> containing, as it does, no sibilant, but they manage it).
> And I shuffle my feet and say, 'Yes, I suppose you're right'.

It's just that they *weren't* right in the slightest.

Here's the thing: certain aspects of style and subject matter squarely
place a writer's work *in* time, while others – arguably more difficult to
define - propel it in the direction of timelessness, the tension between the
two ultimately determining the fate of this written legacy. Wodehouse
World, informed by his Edwardian and even in parts Victorian sensibility, should have been heading for the dustbin of history by 1959, but
had clearly still got legs. And still has, fully 100 years after Plum entered
his mid-season form. So just what is it *within his writing* that, against all
odds, keeps it afloat? It's a question that still begs a convincing answer.

Ultimately, I'll be exploring three possibilities in this book: whether
Wodehouse World will eventually fall into neglect like the work of some
of his neighbours in the Abbey; if it can somehow outrun Time's wingèd
chariot and evolve into classic literature; or if this has already happened.
We'll start by looking at the most time-sensitive element of his output,
satire, before moving in a steady, broadly chronological progression
towards *myth*, a state of timelessness only the greatest writing achieves.
Along the way, I'll examine a host of questions that surface from this
tension between the changing and the changeless, including the burning
issues of just how real reality is, whether Plum was a secret subversive,
the uses of innocence, the changing face of English society in the 20th
century, the evolution of Plum's writing style and the nature of his global
popularity – all of them matters that will amplify and hopefully parcel up
themes and issues arising from the first two volumes.

Before we start, though, I would like to sincerely thank everyone
who has stuck with this series from the beginning, allowing me to see
the project through to its conclusion. Having said that, I'm not entirely
sure this third instalment does mark the end of the affair, since there's
still so much left to say. But whatever transpires, I've already racked up
a massive debt of thanks to the giants of Wodehouse scholarship whose
work has made mine possible. I won't list them again but would instead
like to highlight the collective generosity of those who have thrown out
the lifebelt when necessary. No request for information or clarification,

no matter how fat-headed or just plain weird, has so far been ignored; quite the opposite, in fact, and it's gratifying to feel that despite occasional differences of opinion or emphasis, we all seem to be pulling in the same general direction – to make Wodehouse World better understood, and to promote its enjoyment by future generations.

Finally, my grateful thanks are once again due to Sir Edward Cazalet and the Trustees of the Wodehouse Estate, without whose generosity none of this could have happened.

Paul Kent, London, March 2022

P.G. WODEHOUSE,
SATIRIST

Introduction:
P.G. Wodehouse, Satirist

In these complex, hustling days, if authors are to be true to life, they must put far more into their descriptions of every-day life and action than they have dreamed of doing hitherto.
The Literature of the Future, Vanity Fair, June 1914

The 'gangs' of New York exist in fact. I have not invented them. Most of the incidents in this story are based on actual happenings.
Psmith, Journalist

As much as art can shape life, life is always the creative force behind an artist, literary or other.
M.M. Winkler, 'The Persona in Three Satires of Juvenal', 1983

"There is nothing like fury for stimulating the pen. Ask Dante. Ask Juvenal".
Cocktail Time

"He laughed at the wit. The satire didn't go so well".
Pigs Have Wings

The received wisdom about Pelham Grenville Wodehouse's literary achievement is nowhere better summed up than in David A. Jasen's 1974 biography *P.G. Wodehouse: A Portrait of a Master*:

> The wonderful world of Wodehouse into which one escapes is an elaborate but perfectly constructed, romanticized, idealistic conception which is gleefully detached from reality.

Wodehouse World as a glorious fantasy wholly separate from our own experience is a perspective encouraged by Plum himself when, in *Performing Flea*, he famously claimed to write "musical comedy without music . . . ignoring real life altogether".

This is not the most promising start to an Introduction that proposes to examine Wodehouse's use of satire. For satire without real life can't be satirical; robbed of targets that actually exist and are widely recognizable, it instantly loses its main reason for existing – to be the whistle-blower on human folly and depravity. Real bang-up-to-date human folly and depravity like this, called out by Bertie in *The Code of the Woosters*, which was published less than a year before the outbreak of the Second World War:

> "The trouble with you, Spode, is that just because you have succeeded in inducing a handful of half-wits to disfigure the London scene by going about in black shorts, you think you're someone. You hear them shouting 'Heil, Spode!' and you imagine it is the Voice of the People. That is where you make your bloomer. What the Voice of the People is saying is: 'Look at that frightful ass Spode swanking about in footer bags! Did you ever in your puff see such a perfect perisher?'"

In *Very Good, Jeeves*, Bertie confesses that "I am not frightfully up in the personnel of the political world", but here he's bang on the nail. Roderick Spode's followers, the "Saviours of Britain" or "Black Shorts", were unsubtly modelled on Oswald Mosley's real-life bunch of amateur Nazis, the Black Shirts, such that any of Plum's contemporary readers would immediately recognize the topical reference. Complete with his wonky version of the Hitler moustache, Mosley spent the 1930s clamouring for appeasement and a political alliance with Nazi Germany, and in this rare moment of political engagement, Bertie comprehensively trashes his dollar-store version of Fascism. Plum clearly intended the portrait to sting:

> About seven feet in height, and swathed in a plaid ulster which made him look about six feet across, [Spode] caught the eye and arrested it. It was as if Nature had intended to make a gorilla, and had changed its mind at the last moment.

With just a few dabs of his descriptive brush, Wodehouse successfully burlesques Fascism and its most prominent domestic apologist with a mix of observation and invention such that in retrospect it's difficult to separate the fact from the fiction. Mosley, though undeniably tall, never reached 7'0" (and certainly not 9'7" as Bertie later claims), was not particularly broad-shouldered and not remotely simian. That moustache – more laterally expansive than Hitler's – is plausibly likened to "the faint discoloured smear left by a squashed blackbeetle on the side of a kitchen sink"; and Plum dresses Spode in an Irish tartan, denoting Mosley's Anglo-Irish ancestry but which, as far as I can make out, was entirely absent from his public wardrobe – as indeed were shorts, black or otherwise. Nor are we privy to his real-life table manners, although we're told that witnessing Spode eating asparagus "alters one's whole conception of Man as Nature's last word".

Mosley would come to a sticky end just over a year after *The Code of the Woosters* was published: belatedly imprisoned in 1940, he spent most of the rest of his life in exile, and in 2005 was voted the "worst" Briton of the previous millennium by the writers of *BBC History* magazine, an award for which there was stiff competition from Jack the Ripper. Indeed, given how regularly Plum's portrayal is still quoted in books and in the press, it's interesting to speculate that it might just have contributed to Mosley's ongoing infamy. Every time Spode is mentioned in this and the three other novels in which he appears, there is usually a consummate zinger somewhere in the vicinity, of which Bertie's description "[b]ig chap with a small moustache and the sort of eye that can open an oyster at sixty paces" is undoubtedly the jewel in the crown, closely followed by "a chap who even in repose would have made an all-in wrestler pause and pick his words". Then there's the character's unattractive predisposition to violence:

> "I shall immediately beat you to a jelly. To a jelly," he repeated, rolling the words round his tongue as if they were vintage port. "Have you got that clear?"

> "I am going to thrash this man within an inch of his life."

> "Couldn't you possibly see your way to letting me do something to him, Wooster? If it was only to kick his spine up through his hat?"

Even when he's on the back foot, the man's an utter thug, and it takes the threat of being outed as a part-time designer of women's underwear to curb his loutish demeanour. As far as I'm aware, Mosley didn't dabble in ladies' nethergarments on the side. But whether he did or not is completely immaterial, for once read, it's impossible to view anything to do with Nazism in quite the same way ever again.

Yet outside this example, satire is a theme that rarely excites any lengthy discussion among the Wodehouse fraternity: it's almost as if on this single occasion, Plum had an unprecedented rush of blood to the head that never recurred. In truth however, Wodehouse channels his inner satirist all the way through his work; far more regularly – and successfully – than he has ever been credited with. And although the Spode example may be particularly notorious because (a) it's noticeably outspoken and (b) the character has a direct historical analogue, Establishment figures of every stripe – and much besides – are always finding themselves in his crosshairs.

Honourable exceptions to this scholarly neglect are Benny Green's *P.G. Wodehouse, a Literary Biography* published back in 1981, which reports several congruences between Plum's satirical sense and real life, as does chapter 3 of Brian Taves's 2006 *P.G. Wodehouse and Hollywood*. In *P.G. Wodehouse in His Own Words*, Tony Ring and Barry Day write that in the school stories, "Wodehouse the gentle satirist is already at work", and John Dawson in *P.G. Wodehouse's Early Years* agrees with Richard Usborne that "Plum could write stinging satire with the best of them". But for all these glancing mentions, I have only been able to source a single paper that confronts the subject at any length: in her 2016 reading of *The Code of the Woosters*, Françoise Dupeyron-Lafay correctly identifies a "social, satirical, parodic and subversive dimension" to Plum's writing "long ignored or unperceived, and under-researched, which deserves to be brought out". Absolutely. And this unfortunate vacancy in our appreciation of his work has distorted our understanding of his achievement to its overall detriment, serving to play down at least two significant instincts within Plum's creative imagination: his sense of mischief and sometimes even rebellion (watch out for the word "subversive" in this volume – it appears no fewer than 18 times); and his lifelong connectedness to the world he lived in, aspects of which are still identifiable in *our* world over a century on, linking the two in our imaginations.

Clearly, some recalibration is required, for satire was always hiding in plain sight in Wodehouse World, inseparable from the way its creator 'took in' humanity and its works right from the word go. For example: I noted in Volume 1 that Plum's baptism into musical theatre took place at a performance of Gilbert and Sullivan's comic opera *Patience*, where he would later describe his teenage self as "drunk with ecstasy", the show "the finest thing that could possibly be done" (p. 161). This powerful epiphany has been rightly seized on by Wodehouse scholars as one of the most significant wellsprings of Plum's theatrical sensibility; indeed, he directly quotes or alludes to the show around 40 times in his writings.

P.G. Wodehouse, Satirist

Less often remarked, however, are its subject and style; for *Patience* is, above all else, a pin-sharp satire of the aesthetic movement of the 1880s, headed in literature by such writers as Oscar Wilde, Algernon Charles Swinburne and Walter Pater. William Schwenck Gilbert, who provided the show's lyrics, was the young Wodehouse's hero and a satirist to his socks. His lampooning of the aesthetes' rallying call of "art for art's sake" clearly resonated, for down the years Plum would also delight in puncturing this brand of literary narcissism, creating dozens of arty types including Ralston McTodd (author of 'Across the pale parabola of joy'), Lancelot Mulliner ('Darkling: A Threnody'), Aileen Peavey, Rodney Spelvin, Reginald Sprockett, Aubrey Barstowe and many others whose pretentiousness far outruns their talent. Plum references Gilbert's tart, waspish lyrics on dozens if not hundreds of occasions between 1902's *The Pothunters* and 1973's *Bachelors Anonymous,* describing him as an "originator" and "a humorist of the first rank" (*New York Times*, 7 Nov 1915). Indeed, he was using that memory of *Patience* to help Bertie Wooster poke fun at notions of highbrow and lowbrow culture as late as 1963's *Stiff Upper Lip, Jeeves*, over 60 years after he'd first seen it.

Merrymaking at the world's expense is the satirist's bread and butter, a means of keeping the reader in touch with life, constantly checking for anything that puts on false airs and threatens to grow too big for its boots. And the more you read of Wodehouse's published output, the clearer it becomes that this is where he too is coming from. Virtually nothing and no-one is off-limits, including all those things he loved, and even himself. So, we might profitably begin this Introduction by asking why, Spode and his footer bags notwithstanding, this critical blind-spot exists; and why even an esteemed satirist of the calibre of Richard Ingrams, former editor of the British satirical fortnightly *Private Eye*, should categorically state in his essay 'Much Obliged, Mr. Wodehouse' that "Wodehouse is definitely not a satirist". After all, he should know, shouldn't he?

The story usually goes that satire takes no prisoners, and Plum was simply too good-natured, too full of the milk of human kindness (not to mention sweetness and light) to go for the jugular. But even if that were wholly true, we'd have to indulge in some pretty nifty sophistry to shoehorn the following song parody into our argument. Written in 1906, it is directed at the left-leaning Liberal Party M.P. (Member of Parliament) John Burns and his claim that "the man does not live who is worth a salary of five hundred pounds a year", since Burns was being paid four times that amount as a Cabinet minister:

Now you're in the Cabinet, Johnny Burns,
And two thousand pounds you get, Johnny Burns;
    But five hundred is too much
    For a single man to touch—
That was what you used to say, don't forget.

Dear old Johnny, think it over,
    'Ere your money you refuse;
Now you find yourself in clover,
    You'll hold quite different views;
You won't pay quite so much attention
    To what a fellow earns—
Stick to all that you can collar,
    Honest Johnny Burns.

There are unemployed you meet, Johnny Burns,
Cold and hungry in the street, Johnny Burns;
    Fifteen hundred pounds a year
    Would do much their lot to cheer—
Don't you want to give the poor men a treat?

Then you know the rates have grown, Johnny Burns,
And it's due to you alone, Johnny Burns;
    Your expenditure is rash
    When it's other people's cash—
But you stick like a leech to your own.

Already it's clear that Plum didn't spend his entire life lost in a fantasy world that only existed between his ears; in fact, if you're only familiar with his romantic comedies, this early acid lyric may come as something of a shock. Wodehouse's mid-season satire would usually take the form of a sly wink or occasionally a dig in the ribs; here, it's a punch in the face as he ponders the fate of the £1,500 of his £2,000 salary Burns claims no man should need. At the time Plum wrote this, the average labourer's wage was well under £50 per annum, so, he ponders, will good old Johnny pledge the surplus to the working men whose cause he champions, given that local taxes are rising on his watch ("the rates have grown")? Or is he only open-handed when it's someone else's money he's spending? The narrator of the piece strongly suspects the latter, making Burns's remark complete and utter humbug.

So where to begin with this *ad hominem* assault? First off, we need to invoke Rule 101 of Literary Criticism: we should not wilfully confuse the contents of the lyric with its writer's private political views. Plum, with his freelancer's hat on, is here working for the *Daily Express* newspaper whose editorial brief, then as now, is that of a populist right-of-centre daily – so that was the type of material he knew they'd likely pay for. It's a simple case of demand and supply. He had astutely set his words to a patriotic tune – 'Dolly Gray' – that everybody would have known, being a wildly popular Boer War anthem from five years earlier; then he had taken considered aim at the politician's Achilles' heel and let rip. Job done, fee duly banked and entered in his *Money Received for Literary Work* journal.

By the time this poem was published, Plum's journalism – satirical and otherwise – had already appeared in dozens of magazines of almost every type and complexion, from the well-known (*Punch*) to the downright obscure (*Land and Water Illustrated*). Some is credited to him, some printed anonymously or under a pseudonym: but the invaluable *Madame Eulalie* website has happily collected much of this early Wodehouse ephemera, and it makes for a fascinating browse, proving – among many other things – two important principles: that Plum had a detailed knowledge of what was going on in the world around him, right down to long-forgotten historical minutiae it now takes a forest of footnotes to explain; and that at this stage of his career he would write just about anything for anybody as long as it paid.

Wodehouse had been deadly serious about his journalism from his days at Dulwich College, where he co-edited the school magazine, *The Alleynian*. Indeed, in May 1898, prior to assuming those responsibilities, we find him writing a letter to *Chums* magazine posing the question "How can one become a journalist?", and receiving a considered, printed reply from the editor (and experienced writer of schoolboy fiction) Max Pemberton:

> One can become a journalist, Mr. Wodehouse, only if Providence has willed it. The first requisite is, not only that a man shall be able to write about the things he sees and hears, but that he shall be able to write about them in such a way that other people will be interested in his work.

Journalism, says the oracle, is about keeping your eyes and ears open to the world around you. Fine-tuning those antennae will help find the stories you need. And then comes some sound practical advice that Plum would cleave to for the rest of his life:

> [H]e should begin by studying the columns of some journal which buys the kind of work he thinks he can write best. When he begins to understand what kind of contribution the editor is in the habit of accepting, let him sit down to his article. His first efforts should be brief; they should be bright; and they should deal with some subject a little out of the common.

So: don't waste words, be upbeat and cultivate a distinct *perspective*. Above all, if you want to be successful, write what people want to read; what editors will buy; and what you're best suited to write. That was a lot of balls to keep in the air, but Plum was quick on the uptake, able and ambitious, and transferred those principles across to every-thing he wrote, including fiction. On being told by his father he would not be following his older brother Armine to Oxford University, Plum's first thoughts were to "start a paper" with two close school friends, Bill Townend and Eric George. They would do the illustrations, while he provided the words:

> 'Tis a gorgeous scheme. I have a brain that could fill 3 papers with eloquence wit & satire if need be.

Note the inclusion of "satire" in the bill of fare, which would also run to "interviews, pomes [sic], drorks [drawings] (comic & serious), an edito-rial and reviews of books". He'd even done the sums:

> For about £15 you can get 1000 copies published. We will get 1000 people to pay a yearly subscription at 6d [sixpence] a week & there you are. You clear £10 per week.

While awaiting their response he would be sending "some pomes [sic] to a few editors soon. Let us hope the boodle rolls in".

Well, at least the second half of the plan worked out well. Wodehouse would never self-publish; but after leaving school in 1900, impatient to make his name and secure sufficient funds to buy himself out of his job at the Hong Kong and Shanghai Bank, he worked like a demon. In 1901 he was recovering from a case of mumps and emerged from that convalescence with 19 short stories (as he later claimed). Hard-headed and driven (and not vague and dreamy as he's sometimes presented) he struck gold almost immediately when a prizewinning satire on game captaincy turned into a regular gig at *Public School Magazine*, where he produced a monthly column titled 'Under the Flail' from December 1900 until the paper's demise two years later. Writing anonymously as 'Jack Point' (the "strolling jester" from Gilbert and Sullivan's *The Yeomen of the Guard*), his job seems to have been the collation of news items from educational institutions around the country. It was a brief he would quickly abandon in favour of a more polished, structured essay that could at times border on the seditious, written from the point of view of the insider/subordinate – which just so happens to be the traditional perspective of the satirist. No longer "under the flail" himself, he could write about subjects he would not have dared address in the columns of *The Alleynian.*

In just six months, Plum grew the column from a space-filler to something rather more substantial, taking potshots at a wide range of familiar school-life targets. In the July number, we find parents, popular literature and end-of-term school reports in his sights:

> Every schoolboy . . . knows that a report is not worth the paper it is written upon. The average report, if it were not beneath notice, would involve its author in a suit for libel. One knows the sort of thing. "He has distinct abilities, which he neutralizes by a persistent laziness. His behaviour leaves much to be desired, and his manner is impertinent," signed, the form-master (his mark X). Then on the last line a perfectly irrelevant remark from the Head, "I am sorry to see this report".

Already, Wodehouse's ear for parody – that essential tool of the satirist – is note-perfect (my school reports from the 1970s read *exactly* like that). Come the summer vacation, he's tilting at the awfulness of school food (an easy target, admittedly). Autumn term finds him railing against having an elder brother at the same school (his brother Armine had a "glittering career" at Dulwich, according to the school's archivist Jan Piggott); and the incomprehensible textbooks on Ancient Greek written by German professors that lined the walls of every public school library in England (mine included). Bringing in the New Year, he holds forth on the correct attire to wear at University, opining that "the brighter the waistcoat, the less bright the intellect" – Psmith's and Jeeves's razor-sharp fashion critiques all ready and waiting in the wings.

Read in conjunction with his school stories, these articles paint an evocative – and accurate – picture of the schoolboy's life; indeed, some of the material, suitably repurposed, might be pressed into service by a historian of Edwardian private education, bringing colour, vividness and a sense of realism to the narrative. Most importantly however, the lightly satirical writing style and tone Plum was busy developing was one he could profitably carry forward into his adult journalism almost unchanged, with the added bonus of having a much broader canvas to work on.

As John Dawson's revelatory *P.G. Wodehouse's Early Years* continually confirms, Wodehouse began hoovering up broad swathes of experience as his horizons lengthened. By 1904, he had already published novels, travelled to America, worked in a busy newspaper office in Central London and was rubbing shoulders with theatrical and literary types in the West End. Some of this material was put to immediate use, some 'banked' for a time in the future when it might come in handy, and those who have mistakenly written that Plum led a reclusive and uneventful life must have somehow managed to skim over this insanely busy and varied period of his biography. Throughout his early journalism, everything was fair game for Plum's sceptical satirist's eye, no topic too small to catch his attention. In a single poem published in the monthly magazine *The Books of Today and the Books of Tomorrow* from April 1904, he takes swipes at:

- the downfall of the American cotton speculator Daniel J. Sully;

- the financial difficulties of the M.C.C. (Marylebone Cricket Club);

- the early stages of the Russo-Japanese War;

- the British Prime Minister Arthur Balfour's misplaced optimism;

- Rudyard Kipling's verse parodies of various poets, written as if they were motorists, which were currently being published in the *Daily Mail*.

P.G. Wodehouse, Satirist

This was a journalist who was clearly doing his homework, diligently reading the dailies from cover to cover in search of inspiration – a ritual that would continue until the end of his life. In that same month, Plum's satirical verse twice appeared in the *Daily Chronicle* (on the subjects of policemen's pay and the brain-sapping qualities of "six-shilling novels"); and he assembled an all-star cast of fictional schoolboys to debate the hot topic of corporal punishment in a piece for *Punch* entitled 'Man's Inhumanity to Boy'. These constitute a small selection of just over 100 stories, poems, one-liners and paragraphs Plum managed to place in a variety of publications in that year, many of them satirical in nature, as was a decent percentage of his daily contributions to the 'By the Way' column of the *Globe* newspaper, for which he had been working since August 16 1901, and which we'll be returning to shortly.

Sarcasm, parody, irony and burlesque – Plum could do them all, and while not earning quite as much as Johnny Burns, he didn't do too badly. In September 1902, the month in which he resigned from the bank, he would trouser a total of £16.4/- (16 pounds, four shillings, or £16.20) from his writing, which surpassed his combined professional salary and parental allowance by a pound or so ("Record so far!" – he comments in his account book). Something was clearly working, and working well, for in the year 1904, that figure would rise (by his own, sometimes faulty reckoning) to a total of £411.14.10 (£411.74), £330 or so more than his basic pay from the 'gainful' employment he had left behind. Using the Bank of England's online inflation calculator, the 'buying power' of the £411 (before tax) equates to a shade over £51K at 2020 values. In the chips? For a single man of 23, yes, he was, at a time when his bed and full board was costing a mere guinea (£1.05) per week. The following year, 1905, he would equal Johnny Burns's maximum needful wage of £500 (£62,172 in 2020), and we must never forget that it was Plum's journalism, not his fiction, that kept him financially afloat during his early career, a parallel income stream that allowed him to pursue his dream of being a writer.

And so it was that for two decades or so, topical satire would be a staple of Wodehouse's journalistic output, a way of looking at the world that would nose its way into his novels and short stories. In *A Damsel in Distress* from 1919, he briefly ducks out of the plot to riff on the theme of London tea-shops:

> In London, when a gentlewoman becomes distressed
> . . . she collects about her two or three other distressed

gentlewomen, forming a quorum, and starts a tea-shop in the West End, which she calls Ye Oak Leaf, Ye Olde Willow-Pattern, Ye Linden-Tree, or Ye Snug Harbour, according to personal taste. There, dressed in Tyrolese, Japanese, Norwegian, or some other exotic costume, she and her associates administer refreshments of an afternoon with a proud languor calculated to knock the nonsense out of the cheeriest customer. Here you will find none of the coarse bustle and efficiency of the rival establishment of Lyons and Co., nor the glitter and gaiety of Rumpelmayer's. They rely for their effect on insufficiency of light, an almost total lack of ventilation, a property chocolate cake which you are not supposed to cut, and the sad aloofness of their ministering angels.

All these real-life references check out, and there are hundreds of others like them dotted throughout his work to the very end: Barribault's hotel and restaurant (a thinly-disguised Claridge's in Brook Street, London W1) features in eight Wodehouse plots from 1947's *Full Moon* to 1971's *Much Obliged, Jeeves*, and is described in *Frozen Assets* as "probably the best and certainly the most expensive establishment of its kind in London" catering to "men of impatient habit who want what they want when they want it and tend to become peevish if they do not get theirs quick". So, no change there, then.

And there's more – much more. In *A Gentleman of Leisure*, we are helpfully told:

> If you have the money and the clothes, and do not object to being turned out into the night just as you are beginning to enjoy yourself, there are few things pleasanter than supper at the Savoy Hotel, London.

Once again, *plus ça change*, as with chocolate vending machines that never work, one of which is situated on the platform at Market Blandings station in 1915's *Something Fresh* (although, to be fair, it has been fixed eight years later in *Leave it to Psmith*). In that latter novel, we also learn of the grim, identikit suburban villas of West Kensington, London W14:

> Situated in one of those districts where London breaks out into a sort of eczema of red brick, [the street] consists of

two parallel rows of semi-detached villas, all exactly alike, each guarded by a ragged evergreen hedge, each with coloured glass of an extremely regrettable nature let into the panels of the front door.

They're still there; I used to rent the basement flat in one of them. Lastly for now, Plum devotes a whole chapter in *Big Money* to emphasizing the tiresome banality of the social grind that is "a London Season", during which, at various evening entertainments, Ann Moon is forced to dress up as "an Agate at a Jewel Ball, a Calceolaria at a Flower Ball, [and] Mary Queen of Scots at a Ball of Famous Women Through the Ages".

Plum would always parachute a few cultural observations into his writing as a kind of knowing wink to his regular readers. Indeed, it became a lifetime's habit. In his school stories from the early 1900s, repeated references to brewing, ragging, cutting, Sherlock Holmes, Gilbert and Sullivan, toasted muffins and other commonplaces of schoolboy life would help keep his audience onside; and even in the 1970s, mentions of Marilyn Monroe, Gina Lollobrigida, Yul Brynner, protest singers, electric guitars, blue suede shoes, plane hijacking, "the fuzz", the atomic bomb, the Beatles, Interflora, Billy Graham, *Playboy* and Agatha Christie would pepper his stories and serve as nuggets of shared experience. In fact, a lack of familiarity with the outside world is deemed unusual, when, in *Quick Service*, Joss Weatherby likens it to "finding someone who had never heard of the Great War". It's not innocence but ignorance. Even into his 80s, Plum would walk to the local corner store to get his daily paper, that umbilical cord that connected him to the outside world.

Although he had been permanently domiciled in America for almost thirty years by the 1970s, Plum still kept a weather eye on what was happening three thousand miles away in the old country by reading airmailed copies of quality broadsheets (the London *Sunday Times* and the *Observer* – see Herbert Warren Wind's *The World of P.G. Wodehouse* for further details). It was this habit that would have led to Bertie getting stuck in a traffic jam caused by a protest march at the opening of 1975's *Aunts Aren't Gentlemen*. The previous year hadn't been a vintage year for U.K. labour relations, what with the introduction of the Three Day (working) Week by Edward Heath's Conservative government, and strikes by miners, rail workers, firefighters, civil servants and ambulance crews an almost daily fact of life. Here's Bertie's take on what's happening:

Whatever these bimbos were protesting about, it was obviously something they were taking to heart rather. By the time I had got into their midst not a few of them had decided that animal cries were insufficient to meet the case and were saying it with bottles and brickbats, and the police who were present in considerable numbers seemed not to be liking it much. It must be rotten being a policeman on these occasions. Anyone who has a bottle can throw it at you, but if you throw it back, the yell of police brutality goes up and there are editorials in the papers the next day.

Not Plum's finest hour, making Bertie sound like the slightly bewildered nonagenarian his creator was; but at least he was trying to stay *au courant* at an age when many of us would have long since thrown in the towel. And anyway, a fantasy writer wouldn't have bothered with any of this stuff, so how is it that this factual stratum within Wodehouse's creative imagination is given such scant attention?

First and foremost is Wodehouse's longstanding and ultimately deleterious reputation for being, as I put it in Volume 1, "cheerfully divorced from reality", which sometimes makes Plum's realism difficult to spot. Or, more likely, it's a case that you don't tend to see what you aren't looking for. Take the subject of suicide, for example. You might swear blind it can never be a part of Plum's paradisiacal world – only it is, and on several occasions. In 'Rough-Hew Them How We Will' Paul Boielle (unsuccessfully) throws himself in front of a speeding car after his girlfriend ditches him, he loses his job, and he can't offload his paintings. In both 'Mr Potter Takes a Rest Cure' and *Summer Lightning*, Plum alludes to Arthur Schopenhauer's 1851 essay 'On Suicide', and if that's not surprising enough, there's the story 'A Sea of Troubles':

> It had not been without considerable thought that Mr. Meggs had decided upon the method of his suicide. The knife, the pistol, the rope—they had all presented their charms to him. He had further examined the merits of drowning and of leaping to destruction from a height . . .
> No, poison was the thing.

Of course, Mr. Meggs doesn't top himself – this is P.G. Wodehouse after all. But the thought is there, and Plum has triumphantly managed to insert the joke "I'll be hanged if I commit suicide!" But while this untypical effort (which also involves sexual harassment in the workplace) may not rank him alongside Charles Bukowski as a high priest of dirty realism, it might lead us to suspect there's more to Wodehouse than simply a fantasist at play in his own perfectly delightful La-La-Land. Shifting our attention to Blandings for a moment, even pignapping really is a thing (c.f. *The Times*, 15 January 2020 'How to Steal Pigs and Influence People') which, at a stroke, renders the plots of *Heavy Weather, Full Moon* and *Uncle Fred in the Springtime* – in which the Empress is held captive – strictly factual (although vegan activists and Instagram don't feature in Plum's version).

So, while it's perfectly fair to propose that stylistically Plum spent most of his time eschewing real*ism* (as I argued in both previous volumes), we're equally justified in venturing that the subject matter from which he built Wodehouse World, including much of the weirder stuff, was ultimately sourced from reality. To quote the back cover of Norman Murphy's wonderfully informative and entertaining *A Wodehouse Handbook*, "many of P.G. Wodehouse's legendary characters and settings were based on fact", and a scan of the chapter titles confirms this: London Social Life, London Locations, Some Aspects of Life in the Country, Country Houses, Cricket, The Clergy, Potty Peers – and so on. In the opening chapter Norman remarks that "[Wodehouse] wrote for over seventy years and his stories reflect the background, social standards and events of his time . . . He made a point of using topical references all his life". To which we might need to add that the journey from topical references to satire is but the smallest of steps; all Plum needed to do was filter his raw experience and newspaper reading through his sideways sensibility, and . . . bingo!

Norman then leads us to the nub of the argument *à propos* these references, namely that "the first readers of his books appreciated them more than we do today". In other words, if those topical references are no longer topical, they will have fallen through the cracks in history into oblivion. *We might even mistake them for stuff he invented.* Thankfully, Norman pioneered and then triumphantly cornered the market in rescuing and explaining this shedload of material that never quite made it into the history textbooks, and a small number of other writers have since taken the hint, marking Plum down as a reporter and even a recorder of the world he lived in. Hubert O'Hearn, writing in *The London Economic* in 2017, bracketed Wodehouse and Trollope together as "writers of withering satire of English mores wrapped carefully in the softest cashmere of well-chosen words"; and Julian Fellowes, creator of period drama

Downton Abbey (and adapter of the 2004 movie version of *Piccadilly Jim*), homes in on Plum's piercing observer's eye, stating that he "remains the greatest chronicler of a certain kind of Englishness that no-one else has ever captured quite so sharply, or with quite as much wit and affection". So, what follows in this volume – indeed, the spine of its central argument – is the distinction between the *circumstantial* satire in Plum's writing, much of which has fallen into desuetude; and the longer-lasting *behavioural* satire, the enduring personality traits that animate his characters and which remain, to this day, fresh as paint.

A second reason why Wodehouse's satire might be passed over is its wonted subtlety. While the genre traditionally trades in specific points of view and clear messaging, Plum's writing, regularly eschewing both, doesn't offer the scholar much low-hanging fruit (like the Spode example) to pick off the tree. That said, towards the end of his life, he wasn't averse to letting his narrator's mask slip in order to address his readers more directly. Take this little excursion from 1967's *Company for Henry* about crusty gentlemen's clubs that refuse to move with the times:

> It was only in the last year or so that its conservative committee had reluctantly unbent to the extent of providing a small room where members could entertain their female friends . . . Its atmosphere was one of intensely respectable gloom, the furniture heavy, the windows half hidden by massive drapes and the waiters aged and tottery.

That very same club, which Plum doesn't name (but begins with 'G' and is still situated in Garrick Street, London WC2), remains notorious for its all-male membership policy, reform being voted down when the subject was last debated in 2015. It was the sort of starchy formality which, as we'll see later, our man absolutely loathed. In fact, for a gent of his advanced years, he was proving quite the feminist around this time. He had probably read in *The Times* about the drafting of the Family Law Reform Act in 1969, and had seen a potential plot mover in there, which he duly pressed into service for *a Pelican at Blandings* published late that same year. The dastardly Duke of Dunstable (whose name Plum borrowed from a character in G&S's *Patience*, by the way) tries to prevent his niece Linda Gilpin marrying the man of her dreams, John Halliday, by making her a ward of court – something he wouldn't have been able to do had she been male. This unfairness prompts Gally Threepwood to comment that "[t]hese chaps who make the law in England are pretty hardboiled blokes. No sentiment".

So here we have two actual situations, both of which are being addressed in a fictional context. Plum confronts the first with thinly disguised editorializing; the second he deftly subverts by weaving his point of view seamlessly into the plot, fixing it for Linda and John with a combination of chicanery and persuasion. Wodehouse's mid-season satire most often inclines to the latter option; and the more familiar we become with his work, the more we notice a number of recurring, real-life themes and preoccupations starting to announce themselves, alerting us that Wodehouse The Social Commentator was never too far away, even when flying his satire beneath the radar. More of which from Chapter 3 onwards.

The third and final reason Wodehouse might not immediately suggest himself as a satirist is the slipperiness of the genre itself. Satire is the Swiss Army knife in the writer's toolbox, and its use needn't be confined, as is often assumed, to a topical or political agenda, having, as I say, just as much to do with timeless facets of human behaviour as what happened yesterday in Parliament. The root of the term is thought to come from the Latin 'lanx satura', meaning "a mixed dish". All human life is here, together with many different ways of looking at it: but what unites the various branches and styles on this smorgasbord is a representation of the world using different forms and degrees of exaggeration. Given it's impossible to exaggerate something that doesn't already exist, satire, by its very nature, never quite leaves behind its original – actual – inspiration; whether fascist dictators, arty aesthetes or tea shops, the reflex towards selective hyperbole always remains the same. Sometimes the subject is so preposterous it satirizes itself; at others it needs the writer's helping hand. The distortion can be scarcely noticeable or wildly surreal, respectively resembling reportage or (almost) pure fantasy. But when looking at Plum's personal take on the genre, it's crucial that we view his (mainly) comic satire using a wide-angled lens, since down the years his stories nimbly dance through several different modes and types.

One distinction that can make our job easier is that between the so-called Juvenalian and Horatian schools of Classical satire, named after two Roman poets Plum probably studied in 1899/1900, his final academic year at Dulwich College (for the record, the curriculum stipulated Juvenal's last seven *Satires* (10-16) and the 30 poems in Horace's *Odes*, Book 3). For as we've already proved time and again in these pages, if you want to learn about Wodehouse, a good place to start is literature.

Juvenal (full name Decimus Junius Juvenalis) flourished in the late 1st and early 2nd century AD. His satire, characterized by what Plum calls its "fervour and eloquence" ('Some Aspects of Game Captaincy') and "righteous fury" (*Jeeves in the Offing*) was nursed in anger and frustration. It is hard-hitting, personal, and provocative; in the opening lines of his *Satire 1*, he comments that "Difficile est saturam non scribere" ("it is difficult *not* to write satire") for there was so much wrongdoing in Ancient Rome that needed foregrounding and putting right. "All vice is at its acme" he concludes after naming-and-shaming dozens of real-life perps whose concupiscence, stupidity, ignorance and/or corruption he doesn't approve of. And what's more, he trumpets, there's no end in sight to this decadence, for "our grandchildren will do the same things, and desire the same things, that we do". Man will always be hard-wired for sin and venality.

Although Wodehouse was usually way more even-tempered and urbane than Juvenal, his satire does occasionally stray into his predecessor's territory, as in the Johnny Burns lyric and several further examples we'll be encountering in Chapter 1. Until then, we'll make do with a short verse, 'Cacoëthes Scribendi' ('a malignant disease of writing'), whose title he borrowed from Juvenal, in which he savages upper-class lady amateurs:

> *Lady Clara Vere de Vere,*
> *I do not think a lot of you:*
> *I'll slate your novel all I know,*
> *If it is sent me to review.*

> *Lady Clara Vere de Vere,*
> *Typewriters stand within your hall:*
> *The stain of ink is on your brow,*
> *The pile of sheets is waxing tall.*
> *You hold your course without remorse:*
> *The Public you would turn from worth*
> *To works whose only merit is*
> *Their authoress's noble birth.*

> (*Vanity Fair* U.K., 1905)

"[Good] grammar is more than coronets" he continues (parodying Tennyson's maxim "Kind hearts are more than coronets"), and concludes that Lady Clara should "leave the market free for those / Who write to earn their daily bread" - meaning the likes of him, of course. A little more acidic than we are used to in Wodehouse – but threaten Plum's livelihood, and you would likely glimpse a side of the man you weren't expecting – as we'll see in Chapter 7.

The most sustained appearance of this Juvenalian streak in his mainstream work can be found in a suite of five stories based on his experiences in Hollywood published between December 1932 and June 1933 and later collected in *Blandings Castle*. From June 1 1930 through to May 1931, Plum had endured twelve frustrating months as a screenwriter for Metro-Goldwyn-Mayer, and when his contract wasn't renewed, he decided to let them have it with both barrels – or as he put it, "write some stuff knocking them good" – and didn't he! There was clearly something about the place, the studio system and some of the people he met in "Dottyville-on-the-Pacific" that got under his skin like very little else ever managed. Indeed, Juvenal would have heartily approved of the most toxic among these stories, 1933's 'The Castaways', in which a young Englishman is shanghaied by the Perfecto-Zizzbaum Motion Picture Corp., chained to a typewriter and forced to turn out "[p]owerful drama[s] of life as it is lived by the jazz-crazed, gin-crazed Younger Generation whose hollow laughter is but the mask for an aching heart". In a rare congruence of satire and Beckettian absurdism, Plum lets rip with a vengeful astringency almost unknown in the rest of his output, tonally resembling contemporary Hollywood chroniclers like Nathaniel West or F. Scott Fitzgerald. It's not a commonplace sight in Wodehouse World to witness a mob of frenzied writers feeding their scripts into a bonfire, cheering and laughing as they embrace redundancy. Or for the lovers – Bulstrode Mulliner and Mabelle Ridgway – to buy a machine gun and join a bootlegging operation. But living and working in Hollywood can do that, even to Wodehouse characters.

Plum immediately realized that going so far over the top didn't really gel with his mid-season style, telling his agent Paul Reynolds that the story "wasn't quite up to the mark" – he had perhaps let his bile get a little *too* out of control – and it remained unpublished in America until 1935. But this example highlights the main problem with Wodehouse as a Juvenalian satirist – he couldn't stay mad for long. Even more importantly, he could never tolerate those of a perpetually sour or critical disposition. Indeed, he occasionally uses Juvenal as shorthand for someone who can't see the good in anyone or anything, or is motivated by bitterness; and justly so, for his predecessor was a glass half-empty kinda guy.

In the 1902 short story 'The Adventure of the Split Infinitive', Rose

Burdock (a rather lame spoof of Sherlock Holmes) deduces the following from a newspaper cutting:

> "I will not read this to you," he said, "the style is really too painful. Not that there is not some excuse for the reporter in the present case. He was suffering from ear-ache when he wrote, and, from his curious partiality for quotations from Juvenal, I should judge that he had only recently recovered from an attack of gout".

In another early story ('Football, My Dear Sir, Why – '), Juvenal is said to focus exclusively on "the utter pettiness of life and the hollowness of all things human" - which would never be Plum's style at all. For most of the time, he was not the reforming satirist committed to changing society, preferring a watching brief; showing rather than telling and allowing his readers to make up their own minds. On more than one occasion, he highlights the damage the satirist can do if, in his zeal to change things, he doesn't address his targets with sufficient care. Even one as serious as lousy poetry.

Five years prior to the main action of 1918's *Piccadilly Jim*, Jimmy Crocker was working as an arts reviewer on the *Sunday Chronicle* and had been assigned a book of reflective verse self-published by Ann Chester, whose uncle Peter now takes up the story:

> They sent this Crocker boy to get an interview from her, all about her methods of work and inspirations and what not. We never suspected it wasn't the straight goods. Why, that very evening I mailed an order for a hundred copies to be sent to me when the thing appeared. And . . . it was just a josh from start to finish. The young hound made a joke of the poems and what Ann had told him about her inspirations and quoted bits of the poems just to kid the life out of them.

To Jimmy's younger self, Ann's poetry was "the sort of stuff that long-haired blighters read to other long-haired blighters in English suburban drawing rooms", but his satirical swipes return to haunt him when he falls in love with the slighted author further down the road. Like the jobbing journalist he was, he had tossed off his review and instantly forgotten about it, his "boy's undisciplined sense of humour . . . riot[ing] like a young colt, careless of what it bruises and crushes". The trouble was that the review had "devastated" the author, who later describes it as "cruel and heartless". Which doubtless it was: but even knowing this, the older version of Jimmy still gives himself the benefit of the doubt and even reckons he has done Ann a favour:

> [She] had admitted . . . that it was his satire that had crushed out of her the fondness for this sort of thing. If that was so the part he had played in her life had been that of a rescuer. . . It was he who had destroyed the minor poetry virus in her.

But had he done the right thing? As a stranger, he hadn't cared about Ann's feelings; now her lover, he ponders that "[t]here was no disguising the penalty of his deed of kindness".

The ambivalence here is interesting: on the one hand, Plum is letting us know that satire can be a powerful weapon in a writer's arsenal, one it's a good idea to learn how to use responsibly or it can do more harm than good; on the other, he's quite clearly implying that some things *deserve* satirizing – indeed, it's the satirist's *duty* to mock the afflicted, whatever collateral damage may result. To let offenders off the hook is to suffer fools gladly. Humour the Ralston McTodds of this world and they'll keep getting away with their fifth-rate drivellings; hence Plum's ongoing war on Modernism, blank verse and confessional poetry bound in limp, purple covers. We're not privy to the quality (or otherwise) of Ann's verse, and by the very last page of the story it still isn't clear if she intends to forgive Jimmy for his mocking criticism. But then, of course, she does, putting the past – and her poetry – conveniently behind her so that we can enjoy a happy ending. It's a close-run thing, as is the issue of whether satire is a force for good, or just plain cruel. Either way, the mature Wodehouse demonstrates a clear awareness of its double-edged nature, albeit one he had failed to convincingly resolve in that hasty conclusion.

This oscillation brings us to that second style of Classical satire, the Horatian, which fitted Wodehouse's temperament like a glove and would find its natural home in his classic, mid-season fiction.

Quintus Horatius Flaccus (c.66/5 – 8BC) was more often moved to amused irritation than bitter anger by the antics of his fellow men. Stating that in a life well-lived, "[h]umour is often stronger and more effective than harshness in solving [our] difficulties" (*Satires* 1:10, vv.14-15), he tends to address his readers as if he's talking privately to a friend rather than ranting indignantly in public. Instead of trying to bludgeon the truth into us, he prefers coaxing and cajoling us into it. Which is not to say he's more tolerant of folly and wrongdoing than Juvenal: simply that his strategies for winning an audience are more subtle.

With its informal manner couched in rhythms of everyday speech, his work had been a favourite in England for several centuries, translated, quoted and paraphrased by literally dozens of authors including several Plum had studied and enjoyed: John Dryden, Alexander Pope, Jonathan Swift and his all-time favourite poet, Alfred, Lord Tennyson. And that's just the highbrows: Horace's influence had also bled into English public school literature in the schoolboys' manner of speaking (see Volume 1 pp. 51-54 for a comparison between Wodehouse and his early mentor, the author Frederick Swainson in these matters). He was also given to quoting Horatian maxims, a favourite being "aequam memento rebus in arduis servare mentem" ("remember to keep a clear head in difficult times") which pops up in his journalism, *Money in the Bank* and *The Girl on the Boat*, where the narrator helpfully translates it "[f]or the benefit of those who have not, like myself, enjoyed an expensive classical education". But it's in his chummy, conversational yet opinionated narrative style that Plum may have gained most from the acquaintance, for it echoes Horace's voice almost exactly, both men being "sharp and rising . . . with an eye to the main chance" (J. Griffin, *Horace in the Thirties*).

Coincidence? I'd venture not. That manner of address is already present in Plum's earliest non-fiction as well as his 1902 debut novel *The Pothunters*, in which the quietly seditious littérateur 'Alderman' Charteris appears to share Horace's more softly-softly approach to satire. As editor of *The Glow Worm*, "a clever periodical" that "was a great deal more in demand than the recognized school magazine, the *Austinian*", Charteris is said to favour a "bright" but not "militant" editorial style that "chronicled school events in a snappy way" and is not sufficiently scurrilous to attract the hostile attentions of the powers that be. Plum, with his commercial author's hat on, is also at pains to tell us it's a formula that delivers a tidy profit every issue, further justifying his seal of approval. This is how to run a successful alternative news source without goading or confronting authority – by gently subverting it instead. And unlike Jimmy Crocker, Charteris is instinctively aware there are undrawn lines he shouldn't cross. And so, he doesn't – just like his creator.

Then, in the 1911 story 'Pillingshot's Paper', the journalistic status quo at St Austin's is sensationally challenged by a brash new rival, *The Rapier*. This second unofficial organ is bankrolled by the supercilious and overbearing J.G. Scott, which specializes in the Juvenalian character assassination of pupils in a rival house - 'Henry's' - its proprietor doesn't care for. While *The Glow Worm* never resorts to libel, the aptly named *Rapier* "never did anything else", a difference that leads Rudd, the head of house, to debate the newcomer's merits with Scott, not knowing he's behind it:

"I say, Scott," he said. "Seen this?"

"*The Rapier*? I did glance at it. It seemed to me to supply a long-felt want. Fill an obvious void, if you know what I mean."

"I don't like it."

Scott stared. "Don't like it? What's wrong with it?"

Rudd sat down. "Of course it's been got up by somebody in this house," he said.

"What makes you think that?"

"Well, you know we've got this row on with Henry's?"

"Row? Henry's?" Scott's face cleared. "Of course, yes." he said, "I remember. I did hear something about some row."

"This'll make it worse."

"Not a bit of it," said Scott. "By showing Henry's exhibits how they appear to the casual outside observer, the paper will lead them to reform. Once they have reformed, we shall have no objection to them. The row will cease automatically" . . .

"All the same, this thing will have to be stopped."

"Stopped!"

PELHAM GRENVILLE WODEHOUSE

"Yes. It's causing no end of disturbance already. I've stopped two fights already between our kids and Henry's."

"Why, weren't we winning?" queried Scott, interested.

The cynical, devil-take-the-hindmost Scott is here posing as the reforming satirist, claiming that a blood-letting war will cleanse the body politic and even "reform" it. In fact, he doesn't care a damn – it's all a rag to him, put on for his own amusement.

Rudd, by contrast, realizing this will upset the delicately balanced ecosystem that holds the school together, is all for taking steps to shut the paper down. Which as a responsible prefect, he does; not by edict, but, having learned of Scott's involvement, gently 'persuading' him to give it up. Deft management of the conflict may have triumphed over public confrontation and restored order; yet it's possible to detect the same sense of authorial ambivalence as in the Crocker episode. Plum presents *The Rapier* as a palpable hit, and even though he casts doubt on how long it can remain a novelty, it surfs a swell of genuine popularity among its readers. Moreover, the victorious Rudd is portrayed as something of an elitist killjoy, even a bore, "a solid, grave youth, who always looked a little mournful", living as he does "above the common things of life". This indicates, to me at least, that although Plum's Horatian narrative voice would nearly always prevail for the next 60 years, his inner Juvenal was never completely suppressed, as we'll be seeing on several occasions in what follows.

But it wasn't just Horace's voice and tone that Plum borrowed; he also took on board several aspects of his predecessor's perspective and modus operandi. As a preview of many examples we'll encounter later in this book, here's one of my personal favourites from 1933's *Heavy Weather*. By this point, Plum's satire doesn't really look like satire at all, so seamlessly is it woven into the fabric of his writing and the ethos of Wodehouse World. But all the while those perennially recurring satirical themes he has been working to establish are lying in wait just below the surface, waiting to announce themselves – and so it is here.

Lord Emsworth isn't usually one for speaking truth to power, particularly when that power is his sister; but on the rare occasions he does, he makes it count. And so, when Connie baulks at the idea of their nephew Ronnie Fish marrying lowly chorus girl Sue Brown (who Clarence is fond of), he briefly emerges from his usual fogginess to deliver some well-aimed barbs:

(Connie) "I think the whole thing deplorable. I am not a snob . . ."

"But you are," said Lord Emsworth, cleverly putting his finger on the flaw in her reasoning.

Lady Constance bridled.

"Well, if it is snobbish to prefer your nephew to marry in his own class . . ."

"Galahad would have married her mother thirty years ago if he hadn't been shipped off to South Africa".

Snobbery has always been a favourite target for the satirist, and if Clarence wasn't so perennially guileless you would swear he meant those remarks to smart. For a start, his comic timing is absolutely faultless, quietly but insistently interrupting Connie's haughty flow with just three blunt and incontestable monosyllables that stop her in her tracks. Unaccustomed to resistance, particularly from her educationally sub-optimal brother, she is brought up short and already on the back foot in her response. Sensing this, Clarence moves in for the kill with only his second utterance: if their brother Gally hadn't been the victim of the same brand of family snobbery that is being perpetuated by Connie, Sue would now be her niece – for Gally was once desperately in love with Sue's mother Dolly Henderson, also a chorus girl, whom he would have married had he not been shipped off to the colonies to cool his ardour. At which point Connie realizes she has lost the argument, petulantly remarking that "the only thing I have to say about Miss Brown's mother is that I wish she had never had a daughter". At which point Clarence sums up his own way of judging the suitability of prospective family members: Sue, despite her humble, non-U origins, is "extremely sound on pigs" – which is good enough for him. Case closed, with no real damage done, and we both marvel and rejoice and that Clarence has, for once, managed to come out on top unaided courtesy of some good old-fashioned straight talking.

In this example, Wodehouse's debt to Horatian satire lies in the way he regards Connie and the nature of her transgression. Neither writer expects too much from his fellow human beings, allowing Plum to dial down the outrage and have some fun at the transgressor's expense. As one of Horace's translators Niall Rudd informs us, his subject believed people "could spare themselves a great deal of misery by acceptance, restraint, good humour, and tolerance", and these virtues are promoted by viewing life from a healthily humorous perspective. So, what Juvenal would amplify into a crime against society prior to denouncing it, Horace would shrug off as nettlesome folly – that is, if he wasn't already mocking it.

This is the nature of Plum's mature satirical instinct in a nutshell. His satire isn't simply about roasting people he doesn't like, but, by parading their foibles, subliminally encouraging his readers not to behave like them. He doesn't encourage us to think of Connie's snobbery as a badge of honour, but neither is she wholly the pantomime villain. When Plum plays up Alaric Dunstable's ill-temper, Percy Pilbeam's oiliness, 'Beefy' Bastable's self-entitlement and Oofy Prosser's meanness, they're not 'baddies' as such, but what we might call 'the opposition', for the most part figures of fun. At their very worst, these characters are charmless busybodies whose lack of redeeming features is portrayed as its own punishment, for none of them appears particularly happy, except when they get their own way – which isn't very often, since they're nearly always denied what they want. Which means that those who stoop to folly are more to be pitied than scorned in Wodehouse World, and the absence of anything actively evil in his work allows that model to work without us having to worry too much about its ultimate viability. Lightness, as always, is triumphant. Not, I hasten to add, that Plum was being a moralizing satirist in allowing the good guys to win every time; let's just say that a unique form of Wodehousean justice has been allowed to prevail, and that his satire is on the side of the angels.

So, having coaxed satire from out of the shadows of Wodehouse scholarship, how might this affect our understanding and appreciation of his work? We should always remember that even while Plum's comic lightness was busy removing any realistic obstacles to his humour, he was quietly checking the guy ropes that were anchoring his world to the ground. We all probably know a snob like Connie, a loveable rogue like Gally Threepwood, a slightly vague Lord Emsworth type or a nice-but-dim Bertie Wooster – as will readers of Wodehouse's stories many generations into the future. These are all stylized, satirical portraits, character types extracted and exaggerated from what we might experience in our own lives; yet they are *essentially* true, drawing Wodehouse World and ours together as we recognize each in the other.

It was hardly a new technique, being old hat even by the time

P.G. Wodehouse, Satirist

Horace and Juvenal picked up the ball and ran with it: Theophrastus (371-287 BCE) was doing much the same thing rather earlier, producing line drawings of "The Authoritarian", "The Chatterer", "The Ironical Man" and a dozen other character types in what little survives of his work, and it's possible to follow the lineage of this kind of observational comedy through the Roman satirist Petronius to the stock figures of Italian *commedia dell'arte* and on through English Restoration Comedy to Oscar Wilde and, ultimately, Plum. Would that we had the time and space to do this: but very often with these humourists, we find ourselves laughing *with* their created worlds rather than simply *at* them, because we're *in* them. And *that* – quite simply – is why Wodehouse's is not a fantasy world. Moreover, it remains popular for the very same reason those classical satires continue to be entertaining two millennia after their composition, even though we may know nothing of their original inspiration. For while today's satire can be tomorrow's fish-and-chip wrapping, it can also play the longest game, talking to us across the centuries, time-bound, yet timeless.

So, as I begin to assemble a body of evidence to bolster these assertions, I'm going to quote what Plum wrote in his accounts ledger in September 1901 on learning he had successfully placed seven topical "pars" (paragraphs) in *The Globe* newspaper that month:

> Good! There is a reasonable hope of my getting this post permanently. Let the good work go forward!

He did. And it did.

P.G. WODEHOUSE,
JOURNALIST

Chapter 1:
P.G. Wodehouse, Journalist

"Write not what you like, but what editors like".

* * *

*"Study the papers, and see what they want," said my authorities.
I studied the papers. Some wanted one thing, apparently, others
another.*

* * *

*I wrote a satirical poem, full of quaint rhymes . . . That night I
sent off two sets of verses to a daily and an evening paper. Next
day both were in print, with my initials next to them. "Verse is the
thing," I said.*

Not George Washington

*He looked about him for some occupation which should combine in
happy proportions a small amount of work and a large amount of
salary, and, finding none, drifted into journalism.*

The Head of Kay's

In *Hot Water*, the narrator chimes in with the following comment:

> Your literary man is generally supposed to be a dreamy,
> absent-minded person, unequal to keeping his head in cir-
> cumstances which call for practical common sense.

Well, this chapter is going to be all about how Plum didn't fit this lazy
stereotype. Ever. And particularly during his tenure as an on-the-job
newspaperman, which almost exactly coincided with the reign of Edward VII – the "Edwardian Age" which ran from the death of Queen
Victoria in January 1901 to the king's own demise in May 1910.

Far from being "gleefully detached from reality" during this period,
Plum was a committed grafter who spent his 20s ducking and weaving
through the streets of imperial London, perpetually in search of a
subject for the next "par" or poem he could sell. This called for an
attention to detail he would recall in 1939's *Uncle Fred in the Springtime* in
the person of the writer Ricky Gilpin:

> Poets, as a class, are business men. Shakespeare describes the poet's eye as rolling in a fine frenzy from heaven to earth, from earth to heaven, and giving to airy nothing a local habitation and a name, but in practice you will find that one corner of that eye is generally glued on the royalty returns. Ricky was no exception. Like all poets, he had his times of dreaminess, but an editor who sent him a cheque for a pound instead of the guinea which had been agreed upon as the price of his latest *morceau* was very little older before he found a sharp letter on his desk.

Hence Plum's revelatory account book 'Money Received for Literary Work', in which he devoutly kept track of the dozens of *morceaux* he placed between 1900 and 1908, complete with occasional note-to-self commentary. In February 1901, for example, he opined that having rejected his first ten submissions and only paid five shillings for the eleventh, *Fun* magazine was proving no fun and "not worth the candle". By contrast, a piece for *Sandow's* on 'Physical Culture at Dulwich College' paid well and was settled promptly, occasioning the comment "I must cultivate the magazine of the great Sandow".

To describe Wodehouse as ambitious – both artistically and financially – and even a little obsessed by his work would not be to overstate the case. It's also quite clear that he relished being at the centre of things, swimming in the currents of time and history at the heart of Edwardian London. It's here he would find the raw material for his work; but while the term 'Edwardian' is liberally sprinkled around Wodehouse scholarship (often aided and abetted by the man himself), only rarely is that decade of British history examined in any detail to see how it might have shaped not just the content of his work, but the tenor of his imagination. And so here we are, ready and willing to do just that.

According to political historian Roy Hattersley in his treatise *The Edwardians*, the era is often portrayed as one "long and sunlit afternoon", a time when the nation rested on its oars, "exhausted by the activity and achievement of Victorian [times]". It's a metaphor picked up by novelist A.N. Wilson, who describes those years in *After The Victorians* as "a Golden age of peace and prosperity, of long afternoons and country house parties". Which would admirably fit both the subject and ethos of Wodehouse's mid-season World, itself seeming to hang in time, perfectly preserved in amber during one of history's intermissions. At a century's remove, it is easy for us to feel nostalgic for such a leisurely, prosperous time in which everything appears more settled and certain than in our own – and it can't be denied that for many of his readers, this ahistorical stasis is an important element of Plum's 'offer'. But it is far from being a reliable reflection of that formative period in his consciousness; the decade when Plum, thrown on his own resources, started to make his way in the world.

At that time, the American novelist Henry James, long an English resident, was full of foreboding for the future, writing that Victoria's passing would "let loose incalculable forces of possible ill", and that "the wild waters are upon us now". She had reigned for over 60 years, and many quite elderly citizens had known no other monarch. But James's foreboding wasn't necessarily reflected in the nation at large: although at the height of its power and influence in the world, Edwardian England showed itself only too keen to throw off the more irksome shackles of its Victorian inheritance. Samuel Hynes, in his comprehensive study *The Edwardian Turn of Mind* notes that the relentless "rationalism, positivism and materialism" of the previous century had taken their toll on the nation's psyche, leading to "an ossification of authority that encased and cramped the new". Forward progress of any kind seemed glacial, for "the *forms* of values had become the values; institutions had become more important than the ideas they embodied". The Establishment appeared stiff, starchy, old and merely going through the motions, and a change was long overdue.

The new king, it was hoped, would help sweep away some of this dead wood by the simple expedient of not being his mother; and although 3,000 funerary elegies were published within a month of Victoria's death, it must have come as a relief that the nation's figurehead would no longer be an 81-year-old woman who had worn nothing but black mourning clothes for the last four decades of her life. King Edward, 59 on his accession, took his royal responsibilities seriously enough while refusing to let them cramp his leisure activities which included gambling, sailing, shooting, horse racing, visiting continental spas and consorting with famous actresses. As 'modern' as a British monarch was ever likely to get in 1901, he was popular with all social classes, and there is no doubt that "Bertie", as he was affectionately known, lent a different tone and tenor to British life and represented a definite break with the past. Perhaps Plum filed that name away for future reference.

So, what was going on in Britain as Wodehouse immersed himself in the ebb and flow of Edwardian life? Some headlines might come in handy to help orientate ourselves as we start our look at his journalistic output from the period:

To begin with, there were two main political parties in 1901:

- The Conservative Party had been in power since 1895, its Parliamentary seats swollen by a group of the more traditionalist Liberals (the Unionists) who had split from the main body of the Liberal Party in 1886. This semi-permanent coalition had been influential in carrying forward several significant forward-looking social reforms, including the 1902 Education Act that standardized and upgraded the school systems of England and Wales;

- The Liberal Party itself, having long since lost its Unionist members, was a loose association of diverse, more progressive groups that embraced, according to novelist H.G. Wells, "everything that was left out by the other parties", adding that "[i]t is the party . . . of the unfailing and the untried . . . of decadence and hope".

Despite all appearances, this was no binary, left/right set-up: rather it was a rich, fluid and sometimes confusing mix of traditionalism and change. As Hattersley puts it, Edwardian England "teemed with the excitement of innovation", with even the king realizing how quickly "the old world was disappearing around him":

- All through society, from Parliament to business and sport, amateur "Gentlemen" drawn from the aristocracy were being displaced by professional middle-class "Players";

- Votes for Women and Home Rule for Ireland typified the radical spirit of a decade which also witnessed the rise of a Labour Party that promoted mass membership and wider Suffrage;

- The foundations of the modern welfare state arrived with the National Insurance Bill;

- Ernest Rutherford successfully initiated experiments in nuclear physics that would ultimately lead to the splitting of the atom. Cars and aeroplanes quickly became a fact of modern life;

- Across the arts, modernism arrived in force, of whose literary manifestations Wodehouse was so regularly dismissive.

And so on. The 'Land of Hope and Glory' celebrated in the finale of Edward Elgar's *Coronation Ode* of 1902 was already changing and changing fast.

To begin with, Plum seems perfectly familiar with the tension between nostalgia, inertia and forward movement. At the opening of 1909's *The Swoop!*, he satirizes English exceptionalism in the members of the middle-class Chugwater family living the dream of Empire, basking on a late summer afternoon in the garden of Nasturtium Villa somewhere out in rural Essex, passing the time playing fashionable parlour games such as 'diabolo', 'pop-in-taw' and cup-and-ball. As eldest brother Reggie devours the cricket news, Horace inquires of 14-year-old Clarence, dressed in his boy scout uniform, why he is snorting and sighing so much:

> "I was thinking," said Clarence, "of my country – of England."
>
> "What's the matter with England?"
>
> "*She's* all right," muttered Ralph Peabody.
>
> "My fallen country," sighed Clarence, a not unmanly tear be-dewing the glasses of his spectacles. "My fallen, stricken country!"
>
> "That kid," said Reggie, laying down his paper, "is talking right through his hat. My dear old son, are you aware that England has never been so strong all round as she is now?"

By which Reggie is referring not to England's status on the world stage, but how it is excelling in cricket, having won the Ashes (an odd assertion, since at the time of publication England hadn't held the trophy since 1905 and wouldn't win it again until the 1911/12 contest in Australia). Reggie has no sympathy for Clarence's doom and gloom, his inverted sense of priorities mirrored by the newspaper vendor's sandwich board out in the street, which reads:

SURREY
DOING
BADLY

And in small type beneath it:

GERMAN ARMY LANDS
IN ENGLAND

The travails of a county cricket team are seemingly more newsworthy than a homeland invasion by a hostile foreign power, which, as we'll see later, prompts Clarence to take the bull by the horns and try to stir the nation from its do-nothing complacency.

But the Chugwaters were not necessarily representative of the rest of the population, for elsewhere in Edwardian Wodehouse World, which was still in the earliest stages of its development, the transforma- tive influence of history was starting to announce itself. Two of the most regularly recurring themes in Plum's future plotting – social mobility and the redistribution of inherited wealth – would make their novelistic debut as early as 1910's *A Gentleman of Leisure* in whose plot new money supplants the old. But there were already a few significant hints that the times they were a-changin' in Plum's school stories, the majority of which were written during Edward's reign.

In the 1907 novel version of *The White Feather*, the town of Wrykyn – which has always returned a Conservative Member of Parliament – very nearly elects what Plum calls a "Radical" candidate, with only "one or two voters arriv[ing] at the last moment" to "turn the scale". This close shave reflects the actual result of the 1906 General Election, in which the Tories were given a mighty drubbing by the Liberals, losing 246 Parliamentary seats and ejecting them from power. At a personal level, Jack Bruce, the son of the Conservative candidate who has managed to hang on by the skin of his teeth, shows no intention of following his father into politics but intends to "take up motors" when he leaves school – a decision that shocks his classically-educated headmaster to the core:

> Nothing that he heard, nothing that he had read in the
> papers and the monthly reviews had brought home to
> him the spirit of the age and the fact that Things were
> not as they used to be so clearly as this one remark of Jack
> Bruce's. For here was Bruce admitting that in his spare time
> he drove motors. And, stranger still, that he did it not as
> a wild frolic but seriously, with a view to his future career.

At which point he asks a puzzled Bruce, "Do I look three hundred years old? . . . I feel more". It's a small but telling reminder of how "The old order changeth" yielding place to new, those words from Tennyson's poem *Morte d'Arthur* only serving to underline Plum's theme. For in that work, written 75 years before, the grievously wounded King Arthur is informed by Sir Bedivere that "the true old times are dead", and the future of England will belong to "new men, strange faces, other minds". Plum himself had briefly been a motorist, impulse-purchasing a Darracq car from theatre impresario Seymour Hicks in 1906 for an eye-watering £450 – just about all the spare cash he had at the time – which he promptly drove into a hedge on the outskirts of the village of Emsworth in Hampshire and abandoned, never to drive again.

Change was everywhere. Even Cook's, the traditional tea shop on Wrykyn's fictional High Street was having to ward off a brash new American interloper in the short story 'An International Affair' (see Volume 1 for further details); and in *Mike*, from 1909, the entire student body goes on strike for a day in response to what it understands as an abuse of executive power by the headmaster. This had actually happened at Haileybury school in 1900, one of the ringleaders being the future Prime Minister Clement Attlee, who we'll be meeting again in Chapter 5. Plum had recorded the event in an early notebook (see Norman Murphy's *A Wodehouse Handbook, Vol 1*. p.24 for the full story), and in Plum's fictionalized version, the masters can scarcely credit what's happened:

> "Do you seriously mean that the entire school has—has *rebelled*?"

> "'Nay, sire,'" quoted Mr Spence, "'a revolution!'"

"I never heard of such a thing!"

"We're making history," said Mr Seymour.

That quote from Mr Spence arrives uncredited from the Duc de la Rochefoucauld, who when asked by King Louis XVI if the storming of the Bastille prison indicated a revolt, replied with "Non, sire, c'est une révolution" – a disturbance of rather greater magnitude. It was all happening at Wrykyn, *multum in parvo*.

But for all the change both real and anticipated, the status quo had a significant ace up its sleeve: that highly influential sub-stratum of worthy citizens who ran the country whichever party happened to be in power. This comprised mayors, councillors, clergymen, army officers, scoutmasters and the head teachers of private schools who collectively believed, according to Samuel Hynes, that "they composed an established ruling class, [whose] behaviour is often comprehensible only if one sees behind each action the assumption of the right to rule". And it's no surprise to find that these are precisely the same classes of people who 'run' Wodehouse World, the minor authoritarians he pillories from the very start of his career right to the end.

A very early sally into political satire arrives courtesy of "Milord" Sir Alfred Venner, M.P. of Badgwick Hall in 1902's *The Pothunters*. While it is nowhere mentioned he is a Tory, he couldn't really belong to any other party, being rich, titled, and the owner of a large "country seat" with "great iron gates" and a long carriage drive, whose extensive grounds are patrolled by a small army of dogs and gamekeepers on the lookout for schoolboy trespassers. Two pupils, Ainsworth and Morton-Smith, have already been "sacked" for this offence, making the Venner estate "more out of bounds than any other out of bounds woods in the entire county that did *not* belong to Sir Alfred Venner". Here, the narrator's sarcasm makes it clear that he is no great fan of the rich man's sense of entitlement, and when in the longer novelized version of the story Venner calls on the headmaster of St. Austin's, it doesn't sit well that the wording on the M.P.'s *carte de visite* "almost shouted" his presence prior to his "whirl[ing]" into the room and launching into his tirade without any kind of greeting or formality:

> His manner was always dictatorial and generally rude.
> When he had risen in the House to make his maiden
> speech, calling the attention of the Speaker to what he

described as 'a thorough draught', he had addressed himself with such severity to that official, that a party of Siamese noblemen, who, though not knowing a word of English, had come to listen to the debate, had gone away with the impression that he was the prime minister.

As we'll see, this makes Venner the first of Plum's many bossy, slightly dodgy, self-important men of affairs, whether they be Members of Parliament, the heads of motion picture studios, theatre managers or press barons who delight in throwing their often considerable weight around.

Wodehouse's shorthand for these men is "Napoleonic", and here, the fussy, impatient blowhard is contrasted with the headmaster, an altogether easier-going man who wears his authority more lightly, having the kind of class that can't be conferred by title, wealth or property:

> Struggle with his feelings as he might, the Head could not endure that local potentate. The recent interview between them had had no parallel in their previous acquaintance, but the Head had always felt vaguely irritated by his manner and speech.

No-one seems to like Venner much, and if it's possible to sense a slight whiff of snobbery here, it is reinforced by the schoolboys, who refer to him as "that frantic blood" and a "bounder" with rather too much "side on him that he was all sorts of dooks". Which has him down as something of an arriviste who isn't to the manor born.

Detective Roberts of Scotland Yard, who pays St. Austin's a visit to look into the theft of two sports trophies (the "pots" of the title), also shows himself to be no fan of those, like Venner, who put fences round their property, astutely observing:

> Curious thing - don't know if it ever occurred to you -
> if there were no trespassers, there would be no need for
> keepers. To their interest, then, to encourage trespassers.

Roberts's grasp of the psychology of the individual is as sophisticated as Venner's is crude – if you enclose your land and criminalize those who intrude, you're making it an irresistible target for schoolboy adventurers. In so doing, Venner is literally inviting trouble. Wouldn't it be so much less bother, Roberts disinterestedly suggests, if the gamekeepers were put out of a job? It's an interestingly subversive aside for the 20-year-old Wodehouse to have made, throwing forward to Chapter 3, which examines Plum the Armchair Rebel.

Next on our tour of Plum's politicians, we'll pause at the 1905 novel *The Gold Bat*, where we meet Venner's fellow Conservative Sir Eustace Briggs, "Mayor of Wrykyn . . . and a hater of the Irish nation, judging by his letters and speeches". The so-called "Irish Question" – the issue whether or not Ireland, then wholly part of the United Kingdom, was capable of governing itself (what was called "Home Rule") – is perhaps an oddly contentious and weighty theme on which to pivot a plot aimed at young teenagers, despite being regular front-page news at the time. Once again, it would take a long digression to fully explain the situation, but for our purposes, all we need to know is that as a general principle, those like Briggs on the right of the political spectrum tended to favour direct rule from Westminster. However, two Wrykyn pupils of Celtic origin, O'Hara and Moriarty, have other ideas, tarring and feathering Briggs's statue that stands in a recreation ground close to the school. The local pro-Tory newspaper *The Wrykyn Patriot* righteously seizes on the story:

> Everything seems to point to party spite as the motive for the outrage. In view of the forth-coming election, such an act is highly significant, and will serve sufficiently to indicate the tactics employed by our opponents.

But Briggs, though a blusterer, is something of a paper tiger. As with Venner, Plum goes to some lengths to inform us that he isn't *quite* posh enough to be cut from proper Tory cloth, and that he disguises his want of social prestige by using unnecessarily long words, employing over-complex sentence constructions and emphasizing his 'aitches, which, it's implied, he would be prone to drop were he not trying so desperately hard to impress.

Although there's a theme starting to develop, at this stage it's a brave critic who would draw any firm conclusions about Plum's personal politics from these satirical pen-portraits. It really isn't clear whether he writes ill of these politicians because he disapproves of their party affiliations or simply that they are ill-mannered, overbearing oafs. Or, of course, both. Or indeed neither, simply needing an unsympathetic character to move his plot along. Two years later, he was to muddy the pool further: Briggs briefly pops up again in 1907's *The White Feather*, where we're told he has been forced to retire due to ill-health, and that Sir William Bruce (whom we met a couple of pages back) will be the Conservative candidate at the forthcoming election, at which, as we've already seen, he just scrapes in.

Bruce is an entirely different proposition from his predecessor, despite belonging to the same party: a former Wrykynian and a regular attendee of school matches, he is the donor of the Bruce Challenge Cup for the school mile. Moreover, his son (the future car mechanic) attends Wrykyn and is generally thought of as a rather good egg. This loyalty to the school, and the fact that Wrykyn "had always returned a Conservative member" co-opts the boys as Tories-by-proxy, considering Bruce-*père* to be "one of themselves" and once again intimating that it's personality, not labels, that counts. If you're a good chap, it doesn't matter what you call yourself; you will be judged by what you do and how you do it. As the headmaster remarks to Bruce-*fils*, "Apart from our political views, we should all have been disappointed if your father had not won". Nevertheless, it would appear that in Wodehouse World as in real life, the ethos of Wrykyn is essentially patrician, making Conservatism its default brand of politics. It certainly was at my boarding school; when I cheekily enquired of my headmaster who he intended voting for in the first of 1974's two general elections, I remember he looked at me as if I'd lost my mind.

In later years, Plum wouldn't hold back from having his characters openly criticizing politicians, being careful to tar them all, from whatever party, with the same broad brush. In 1958's *Cocktail Time*, even Uncle Fred comes out with a somewhat ill-natured and intemperate outburst:

> "[W]hy do you want a political career? Have you ever been in the House of Commons and taken a good square look at the inmates? As weird a gaggle of freaks and sub-humans as was ever collected in one spot. I wouldn't mix with them for any money you could offer me".

Of course, being a Lord who sits in the Upper Chamber as the Earl of Ickenham, Uncle Fred *doesn't* have to mix with these lower forms of life. Bertie too has an occasional pop at politicians, including the following from *Much Obliged, Jeeves* on the subject of Aunt Dahlia's cat:

I love Gus like a brother, but after years of non-stop sleep he has about as much intelligence as a cabinet minister.

Or how about this definitive Fawkesian moment from 1962's *Service with a Smile* when Lord Emsworth ponders that "the ideal way of opening Parliament would be to put a bomb under it and press the button". And this from one of its more mild-mannered country members, for by the time he wrote these and other put-downs of Her Majesty's Government, Wodehouse had suffered considerably at the hands of the powers that be. "There is nothing like fury," the narrator of *Cocktail Time* informs us, "for stimulating the pen. Ask Juvenal". And on these occasions, Plum had.

But all this was a long way in the future. Fresh from his toils at the bank, on September 9th [1902], Plum "started out on [his] wild lone as a freelance", practically taking up residence at the *Globe* newspaper's editorial offices at 367 Strand for the next seven years. This address was slap bang in the centre of the teeming imperial metropolis, just a few steps away from the real-life Savoy Hotel (q.v.), Simpson's restaurant and the Coal Hole pub, all of which he would namecheck in his fiction. Take this early example of shameless product placement from the 1915 American serialization of *Something New*:

> There are all sorts of restaurants in London, from the restaurant which makes you fancy you are in Paris to the restaurant which makes you wish you were. There are palaces in Piccadilly, quaint lethal chambers in Soho, and strange food factories in Oxford Street and Tottenham Court Road. There are restaurants which specialize in ptomaine and restaurants which specialize in sinister vegetable messes. But there is only one Simpson's. Simpson's, in the Strand, is unique. Here, if he wishes, the Briton may for the small sum of half a dollar stupefy himself with food. The god of fatted plenty has the place under his protection. Its keynote is solid comfort.

> It is a pleasant, soothing, hearty place – a restful temple of food. No strident orchestra forces the diner to bolt beef in ragtime. No long central aisle distracts his attention with its stream of new arrivals. There he sits, alone with his food, while white-robed priests, wheeling their smoking trucks, move to and fro, ever ready with fresh supplies.

That's quite some plug – and it was soon to re-appear in the English novel version of *Something Fresh* at even greater length and with added fulsomeness. And again, in *Big Money*. Either Plum was delighting in being our tour guide or was after a free lunch when he finally got back from the States four years after this was written. For the record, nothing much has changed in the intervening 100+ years (except the prices, and the gravy which you could stand a spoon in). Just a few doors down, the Coal Hole is the venue for Corky's rendezvous with Ukridge in 1923's 'The Debut of Battling Billson', for no good reason other than Plum enjoyed drinking there, perhaps with his journalist mates from the *Globe*. It remains an excellent place to sink a pint or several as you watch London bustle around you.

Plum's joyous immersion in the capital's comings and goings would shape his future fictional world so completely that, according to his biographer Robert McCrum, much of his later work would seem inaccessible without at least an appreciation of "this spendthrift society at whose revels he was an impressionable and sharp-eyed bystander" – for which read "sharp-eyed active participant". Bertie's flat, the Drones, the Senior Conservative Club, Barribault's – all these regular Wodehouse locations were within a stone's throw of one another in the real city. Yet even as the specific references tail off in his mid-season writing to just the occasional telling detail, the *ethos* of Edwardian London is always there for us to experience; and indeed Wodehouse can be classed among those other great contemporary portraitists of the bustling hub of Empire such as Arnold Bennett (*The Grand Babylon Hotel*), J.M. Barrie (*The Little White Bird*) and T.S. Eliot (*Preludes*), who can make us appreciate, even now, just what it might have *felt* like to live there in those times – something I'm going to start looking at now.

Although not a front-line news reporter, Wodehouse's responsibilities on the *Globe*'s 'By the Way' column meant he had to keep on top of everything that was happening around him, including news and politics, satisfying its relentless demand for around a dozen topically humorous paragraphs, jokes and poems each day, with only Sundays off. In his thinly disguised semi-autobiographical novel *Not George Washington* from 1908, he describes the daily routine at the 'On Your Way' office at the *Orb* newspaper, even as he was editing its real-life equivalent:

> The source of material was the morning papers, which were placed in a pile on our table at nine o'clock. The halfpenny papers were our principal support . . . We attended

first to the Subject of the Day. This was generally good for
two or three paragraphs of verbal fooling. There was a sort
of tradition that the first half-dozen paragraphs should
be topical. The rest might be topical or not, as occasion
served . . .
Gresham [the editor] had a way of seizing on any bizarre
incident reported in the morning papers, enfolding it in
"funny language," adding a pun, and thus making it his own.

Occupying a prominent position on the front page, 'By the Way' was
among the first items weary commuters would see as they unfolded their
broadsheet evening newspaper on the lookout for some light relief after
a busy day's work. The paper's circulation was a whopping 400,000
and, promoted to the editorship of the column in August 1904, Plum
would oversee this London institution until May 1909, even as he continued to publish his stories and novels.

He was both good and prolific, hence his meteoric rise through the
ranks in a little under two years. Although the column was unsigned,
Wodehouse scholars have been able to identify his distinctive writing
style in hundreds of separate paragraphs and poems, many of which
"sparkle with Wodehouse brilliance" – that's according to the '*Globe
Reclamation Project*' editor John Dawson, who knows whereof he
speaks, having painstakingly evaluated all of them with help from an
international team of scholars that published an intriguing selection of
attributions in 2015. In all, Wodehouse worked on over 1,600 columns,
honing his editorial eye, polishing up his sardonic smarts and teaching
him to live and work 'in the now'.

Such was 'By the Way's' success that the paper's owner Hildebrand
Harmsworth, brother of Alfred Harmsworth (later Lord Northcliffe,
who Plum would skewer as 'Lord Tilbury') eventually sat up and took
notice, "suggest[ing] we must put out one of those shilling [five pence]
paper-backed books to advertise our column". Co-written with his on/
off collaborator Herbert Westbrook, the resulting *Globe By The Way
Book* was published in August 1908. This self-styled "entirely new and
original work of humour" was described in the July/September issue
of *The World's Paper Trade Review* as a publication that "*whips hypocrisy*
[italics mine] and skits at the follies and fancies and foibles of the day
with a light, not to say lightning touch, which tickles a lot but never
stings" – that last phrase reminiscent of the editorial policy of *The
Glow Worm* Plum had created some years previously. A compendium of

topical humour, jokes, silly games and an excellent parody of a melo-dramatic serial entitled 'Wine, Women and Song', it received decent reviews outside the metropolitan bubble in which it was written: "Good humour, clear, clean and caustic" was the judgement of the *Macclesfield Courier*; the *Hull Daily Mail*'s reviewer noted that "[a] lot of melancholy can be got rid of for a shilling" and the *Glasgow Herald* called it "gen-uinely good clever fun", demonstrating that Wodehouse's writing style had legs beyond his regular readers in the capital.

Plum was such an able writer of this sort of light material, *Punch* magazine, to which he also made hundreds of contributions from September 1902 onwards, elected him to their prestigious inner-inner cabinet (the so-called 'Punch Table') in 1960, where he would join such legendary satirists as William Makepeace Thackeray, Mark Twain and James Thurber. As the gold standard of this kind of humorous writing in Britain, *Punch* was highly influential, and its editors during Plum's early days at the publication were suckers for the topical rhymes he was particularly good at producing to order – of the 47 pieces Wodehouse placed there in 1903, 18 were in verse. The metrical disciplines and verbal ingenuity involved in the composition of this kind of material would set him up in his later career as a stage lyricist; but it was a polit-ical satire that would end up making him the best-known anonymous versifier in the country, occupying his attention on and off for the next three years.

In the Westminster Parliament, tensions were rising to boiling point between the Free Food League, the Tariff Reform League and the sup-porters of Imperial Preference over what came to be known as "The Fiscal Question". And while the bone of contention – free trade versus economic protectionism – remains hugely relevant in the 21st-century, to detail the specifics of this particular outbreak of hostilities over 100 years ago would tax everyone's patience, so I'll keep this as short as possible.

Essentially, that first group (the so-called "Free Fooders") supported the status quo of tariff-free food imports into Britain, while the latter two called for the introduction of import duties on a range of products from countries outside Britain (the Tariff Reform League) but not from the British Empire (Imperial Preferencers). The figurehead and chief booster of that third principle was former screw manufacturer Joseph Chamberlain, a popular Birmingham M.P. who, in his early days as a politician, had had dead cats thrown at him while out campaigning, and who single-handedly demonstrated the political fluidity of the time by starting out as a radical Liberal, before transferring his allegiance to the Liberal Unionists and finally defecting to the Conservatives in 1912. On the free trade issue, he campaigned with the slogan "Tariff Reform Means Work for All": by discouraging cheap imports, he judged that the domestic food supply industry would not only flourish, but Britain and its colonies would gradually emerge as a formidable global trading bloc, with higher wages and more job opportunities offsetting any rise in the domestic price of food occasioned by the tariffs. To anyone who has followed the Brexit debate between 2016 and 2020, these principles will be all too familiar.

Nothing daunted, Plum composed 19 satirical poems on the subject, all of which appeared on the front page of the pro-tariff, pro-Chamberlain *Daily Express*. He was by no means the only writer on this assignment (all of whom contributed anonymously) but of the total of 48 verses that appeared between September 30 and December 21 1903, it's likely he wrote a greater number than anyone else. All featured an unnamed Parrot, whose regular anti-tariff refrain "Your food will cost you more" (or variations on that theme) quickly caught the popular imagination.

Wodehouse's efforts were occasioned by a wide variety of topical prompts, including a brilliant note-perfect spoof of the then-popular Scottish fictional character Wee MacGreegor who is worried lest his favourite "parritch" (porridge) is going to cost him "mair";

Wee MacGreegor's parents, going
To the Zoo one day, were showing
Him the elephants and camels
And the lions with the roar,
When a Parrot from his perch in-
Side a cage informed the urchin
As he munched his bowl of porridge,
That his Food would cost him more.

"But whit wey?" in accents eager
Cried the undersized MacGreegor,
"Will the parritch be expensif
Which I'm gettin' frae my paw?
Shall I lack that best of sweeties,
Which at present such a treat is?"
"You are right," replied the Parrot,
"For 'Your porridge will cost more'".

Then MacGreegor (who was tiny)
Felt his optics fill with briny
Tears; they quivered on each eyelid,
For the prospect grieved him sair.
But his granpaw, who had listened,
As he dried the tear that glistened,
Said, "Ma mannie, don't believe it,
That 'Your parritch will be mair'.

"He's a unco daft auld birdie",
Said sagacious Mr Purdie,
"And he blethers without thinking,
Does yon fulish cockatoo.
Though it's certainly a bore, it's
Just the way of sumphs of paurrits—
They can't keep themselves from squawking,
'Parritch wull cost mair the noo'".

Serious subject, utterly fatuous treatment - which is all the more impressive when we learn that Plum had only just turned 22 when he wrote it. Quality-wise, it's brimming with energy, ingenuity and *espièglerie*; and his ear picks up the argot ("whit wey", "unco", "sumphs") and pronunciations ("expensi_f_", "_fu_lish", and of course "paurrit") of Scottish English with pin-sharp clarity, perhaps influenced by current music-hall favourite Harry Lauder, whose 78rpm records were selling by the truckload around this time. Wee MacGreegor is perhaps the first (and certainly the youngest) of the many lugubrious, chippy Caledonians in Plum's writing, who range from the golf professional Sandy McHoots to recalcitrant gardener Angus McAllister, the subject of that famous remark from 'The Custody of the Pumpkin' that "[i]t is never difficult to distinguish between a Scotsman with a grievance and a ray of sunshine" (it's taken until Volume 3 to shoehorn Wodehouseans' favourite-ever quotation into the argument, but better late than never).

Not only must we remark on the technical facility Plum displays, but the way his poem manages to entertain, despite featuring a subject that would normally bore the bejazus out of the casual reader. Choosing a figure familiar from popular culture was an astute opening gambit, but the poem's intellectual energy is rare in popular verse of this kind, as can be witnessed through the *Madame Eulalie* website, which has helpfully published the efforts of all the other Parrot poets. Being the 27th in the series (and probably Plum's eighth), we might have expected the law of entropy to kick in – only it hadn't. Nor had it in most of Plum's other contributions, highlights from which include the 21st poem, in which he enrols 'Sunny Jim' (a character in adverts for 'Force' breakfast cereal) to assert that the Free Fooders' argument is evidence of "brain decay"; and the 22nd, in which he employs a loquacious, omnivorous cassowary to inform the Parrot that his argument "has no leg to stand on". Even Sherlock Holmes is pressed into service (poem 18), celebrating his sensational post-Reichenbach Falls 'resurrection' in the new tale Plum's friend and fellow-cricketer Sir Arthur Conan Doyle had published the previous month. All these figures are improbably engaged by this tedious subject, with the exception of a pretentious, *Patience*-like poet in his garret, who sends the Parrot packing in poem 35, having higher things on his mind:

> *Said the bard, "Ah, pray be quiet!*
> *What have I to do with diet*
> *When the myst'ries of Parnassus*
> *I am trying to explore?*
> *With this aim my soul obsessing*
> *I consider it depressing,*
> *This degrading, fleshly question*
> *Whether Food will cost us more.*

Art might have considered itself above these vulgar political issues, but Plum was only too happy to get stuck in if there was ready money for the taking. No lofty Parnassian he.

The Fiscal Question, at least to Wodehouse, turned out to be the gift that kept on giving: the antics of the Parrot *et al* had proved nice little earners, supplementing income from the five volumes of school stories he had published thus far, along with his salary from *Globe*. But in these various political poems and songs, it has been noted that he hadn't been particularly hard on the Tariff Reform League. This perceived bias has prompted both literary historian Paul Spiring and biographer Robert McCrum to go on record respectively claiming that the Parrot poems in particular "show that [Wodehouse] was conservative with a small 'c' – a supporter of Joseph Chamberlain and tariff reform" (*Guardian*, 26 July 2009). Sorry to shout, but THEY DO NOTHING OF THE SORT – and this is a canard that needs laying to rest before we proceed a single inch further.

At that stage in his career, as I've already noted, Wodehouse would have turned his hand to anything as long as it paid; so, what the Parrot poems *et al* "show" is the editorial line of the publications he was writing for, and nothing else. Wodehouse is just as likely to have subscribed to the know-nothing views he satirizes in a short poem he contributed to *Books for Today and Books for Tomorrow* for their February 1904 issue:

> *Upon the fiscal question I*
> *Hold no decided views.*
> *I sometimes read the* Daily Mail,
> *Sometimes the* Daily News,
> *And thoroughly agree with each*
> *That nought is true but what they teach.*

The *Mail* (staunchly Tory) and the *News* (a 'progressive' paper started by Charles Dickens in 1846) plied their trade at opposite ends of the political spectrum; so here, the narrator is placing himself in the position of someone who doesn't know what to think. For Plum to have declared any political allegiance would in all likelihood have limited his employability. Which is not to say that he was apolitical; as we'll see in Chapter 3, his motivations were actually quite complicated, even if he wasn't much of a joiner-in. So, all we can conclusively take away from *this* particular episode is that Plum had a professional involvement and a detailed familiarity with contemporary political debate of a kind the later readers of his Romantic Comedies might never suspect.

Which brief digression brings us to the subject Spiring and McCrum were writing about. Once the wretched Parrot had finally been pensioned off in December 1903, the *Daily Express* kept the bandwagon rolling by publishing Plum's satirical "fiscal pantomime" *The Sleeping Beauty* in its Christmas Day edition. Co-written with Bertram Fletcher Robinson (who, as the paper's editor, probably sanctioned the idea for the Parrot poems), it was to be the first of four annual panto offerings the pair would put together, both men sharing a similar sense of humour but somewhat at variance in their compositional talents. Their debut was a thin effort composed of dialogue and song lyrics, remarkable only for the wretched Parrot's final squawk in which it spectacularly (if unconvincingly) recants its former mantra, now realizing that with Imperial Preference "I know your food will cost you LESS!" Not that Plum had anything against parrots: he kept them as pets on and off in the 1920s and 30s and used them to great effect in the plots of 'Ukridge

Rounds a Nasty Corner' and 'Uncle Fred Flits By'.

Leapfrogging Panto 2 (we'll return to it in a few pages' time), an altogether more accomplished and spikier production was the pair's Panto 3, *A Winter's Tale*, published in the U.K. *Vanity Fair* two Christmases later in 1905. Once again, to those of us non-historians reading it in the 21st century, it's all much ado about nothing; but where our ears and eyes might prick up is Plum's uncharacteristically snide demolition of one Winston Spencer Churchill, later Prime Minister from 1940 to 1945 and again from 1951 to 1955, who at this protean stage in his career had just crossed the floor, switching parties from the Conservatives to the Liberals in the opposite direction from Joseph Chamberlain. This excursion into Juvenalian philippics rings like a cracked bell amid the panto's general flummery, early evidence of a lifelong animosity Wodehouse felt for a man he would later describe as "[o]ne of the few really unpleasant personalities I've come across" – and with whom he shared a literary agent for a time.

One can sense that this was no sudden-onset dislike, for Plum appeared highly suspicious of the young MP almost from the moment Churchill took his seat in Parliament in February 1901, aged 26. While he may not have been able to "hate in the plural", he appears to have been more than happy to loathe in the singular, and what follows is an urbane sounding but *very* sarky canter through Churchill's biography:

> *From my childhood I've nourished ambition,*
> *I made up my mind in my cot*
> *To climb to the highest position,*
> *Whether people approved me or not.*
> *So I cut some remarkable capers,*
> *Went out with the army to war,*
> *And wrote myself up in the papers:*
> *(That's all that the papers are for).*
>
> *With Arthur I next was connected,*
> *For Arthur was then in his prime:*
> *When greybeards in council collected,*
> *I gave them advice every time.*
> *A youth who's determined to preach is*
> *Regarded, I know, as a bore,*
> *But I got myself known by my speeches:*
> *(That's all that my speeches were for).*

For months with allegiance unaltered
I stuck to him closer than glue;
Nor ever in battle I faltered;
I fought with the vigour of two.
No fierce opposition dismayed me,
I yearned to be shedding my gore;
I fancied that loyalty paid me:
(That's all that my loyalty's for).

But my monarch is now a back number,
He seems to be quite up a tree,
And Arthur can only encumber
A pushing young fellow like me.
So, though it's a bit of a gamble,
I fancy I stand to gain more
If I throw in my lot with Sir Campbell:
(That's all that Sir Campbell is for).

Churchill had abandoned Arthur Balfour's Conservatives to join Sir Henry Campbell-Bannerman's Liberal Party in 1904, and Plum clearly wasn't impressed by this act of disloyalty – nor for that matter his youthful braggadocio, unattractively candid ambition and air of patrician entitlement. In the panto's Dramatis Personae he is described as a "conspirator" and elsewhere likened to Peter Pan, "the boy who wouldn't grow up".

It's clear that Plum had been following Churchill's rise through the ranks for some years already. The first verse pillories his *Morning Post* dispatches from South Africa during the Second Boer War (1899-1902) detailing Churchill's capture, imprisonment and escape from a Boer POW camp, adventures that were later collected into a successful book, *London to Ladysmith via Pretoria*. Verse two features the war hero's early days in Parliament as Conservative member for Oldham, during which time he gained a reputation as a compelling speech maker; but the "allegiance unaltered" Plum chronicles in verse three quickly evaporated as Churchill regularly voted with the Liberal opposition against the Conservative government, coming out as a leading voice against economic protectionism. A founder member of the Free Food League, his defection to the Liberals occurred soon afterwards, and by this point it's obvious that Plum has decided that Churchill was in politics simply to feather his own nest.

The verse itself is unusual for Wodehouse in that all his characteristic Horatian sense of play, in terms of subject, tone and rhythm is absent; the utterly regular metre, the flat, efficient language and cynical, bracketed refrains all give the impression of a lyricist writing through gritted teeth, and a timely reminder that Wodehouse was perfectly capable of stinging if he wanted to. He lets us know in no uncertain terms that he has got the measure of Churchill and can see straight through him, even if others can't. Indeed, the lyric brings to mind the article published in *Public School Magazine* from February 1901 that I quoted in Volume 1, in which Plum, barely out of footer bags, encouraged his schoolboy readers to "[t]hink of something really bad about somebody. Write it down and gloat over it. Sometimes, indeed, it is of the utmost use in determining your future career". Which was to prove prophetic in this lyric, if not generally elsewhere. Churchill is portrayed as a spoilt brat who can't get his way as a Conservative ("none pays attention to our claims/ To high advancement"), demanding of his new political allies among the Liberals that they make him leader immediately. This is laughed to scorn, and at the close of Act 1, he stomps off the stage never to return. Although he would in Plum's journalism, time and again, joining his cast of regular Aunt Sallies which included popular novelists Hall Caine and Marie Corelli, and playwright George Bernard Shaw.

But there was another, more important outcome of his Fiscal Question versifying: taking the rise out of Chamberlain got Wodehouse his second significant break in West End theatre, when a song he co-wrote with Jerome Kern – their first collaboration – was brazenly parachuted into a comedy of mistaken identity, *The Beauty of Bath*, in 1906:

> *Who is the man who's got a hand in ev'rything you see?*
> *Who is the man whose name you hear wherever you may be?*
> *He's in the papers ev'ry day as doing this or that;*
> *Last week, one learns, he gave John Burns a brand new bowler hat.*

Note the re-appearance of our old friend John Burns, whose trademark choice of headgear is here immortalized. Although Plum wasn't particularly proud of the lyric to 'Oh, Mr Chamberlain!', later judging it "a pretty poor effort", audiences didn't seem to agree. By his own admission, the song not only received "six or seven encores every night", he also spent "most of the next year writing encore verses", for which he received £2 a week until the end of the show's run of 287 perfor-

mances. This secured him further theatre work with impresario Seymour Hicks, who performed the song onstage, and with whom Plum
remained chummy until December 1907. At which point he decamped
to the Gaiety Theatre, conveniently situated only yards from *The Globe's*
offices, again as a jobbing wordsmith (or "a sort of Hey, Bill!" as he later
described himself). And so just at this point in his career, we can witness
the two central strands of Plum's later, mid-season writing style briefly moving into alignment – (a) his sideways take on the world filtered
through (b) his theatrical sensibility. And although the years 1908-14
were pretty fallow for Wodehouse the lyricist, the skills he was busy ac-
quiring while writing topical verse – with or without tunes – would pay
massive dividends ten years later on Broadway; skills that would, in their
turn, feed into his novels and stories (see Volumes 1 and 2 *passim*).

But even as The Fiscal Question grew smaller in Plum's rear-view
mirror, the massive social and political upheavals of 1906 supplied more
than enough material for *The Progressive's Progress*, his fourth, final and
most accomplished panto with Robinson which appeared in January
1907's edition of *The World* magazine. Essentially, it is a sketch-based
show that could easily have made it onto a revue stage, an end-of-year,
state-of-the-nation report that is well worth our attention, if only as a
career option Plum could have credibly pursued had he stuck to his
journalist's trade.

For a one-off feature in a weekly magazine, both men appear to
have put a disproportionate amount of effort into it, for it is head and
shoulders above its predecessors in terms of quality, sophistication and
ambition; all it needed was some decent tunes, a vacant stage and a
financial backer. Perhaps they intended it as a shop window for their
talents, for the duo's satirical smarts were showing signs of significant
evolution. The piece features only one real-life character (the Prime
Minister, Sir Henry Campbell-Bannerman), replacing his usual celebrity Aunt Sallies with broader-brushstroke *types*, encouraging us to view
the satire from a broader perspective. And although the panto kicks off
with the usual topical material, a less time-sensitive spectrum of themes
ends up being addressed, aspects of everyday life Plum could work with
in his future writing. Indeed, many of the topics we'll be looking at in
forthcoming chapters are to be found right here in embryo, making this
panto a fascinating re-discovery.

The mis-en-scène originates in the Anglo-French *Entente Cordiale* of
April 1904, a series of agreements designed to put an end to the two
countries' thousand-year history of mutually fractious behaviour. The

main protagonists are Monsieur Bonhomme ("Mister Good Man"), a fictional member of an actual delegation from the Paris Municipal Council that visited London in late 1905; and William Spender M.P., a bombastic member of the newly created London County Council and, punningly, "a prominent and most progressive wastrel" of other people's money. So, what we're presented with is two left-of-centre time-serving politicians on a walking tour of the British capital, encountering a number of different representative figures en route, structured as a series of comic sketches.

The Frenchman opens the batting by asking the loaded question, "[I]s it that all are satisfied in England?", his host "boldly" answering in the affirmative "with no uncertain voice". Of course, being a satire, Spender's Chugwater-style smugness begins to dissolve almost immediately, for British society is, in reality, one great big mess. Enter a policeman, who, in artful homage to Gilbert and Sullivan's 1879 comic song 'A Policeman's Lot' (from *The Pirates of Penzance*), reveals that far from maintaining law and order, he's constantly "hustled, harassed and flurried" by all and sundry, most notably militant Suffragettes who aren't averse to a little argy-bargy with the rozzers to help get their 'Votes for Women' message across:

> *"When I was but a lad, I told my father*
> *I meant to join the Force. Did he approve?*
> *He shook his head, as if he thought this rather*
> *A rash and injudicious kind of move.*
> *"My boy", he answered, "you shall have your will, but*
> *I fear that you will find, before you've done,*
> *How true is that remark of Mr Gilbert,*
> *'A pleeceman's lot is not a happy one'"".*

> *"I'm one, you know, as modest as they make 'em,*
> *With women I am diffident and shy:*
> *Around the waist I never wish to take 'em,*
> *I sort of rather blushes when they're by.*
> *Yet Suffragettes a-raising a commotion,*
> *I have to hug quite closely, or they run.*
> *It's dooty, simply dooty—not devotion.*
> *A pleeceman's lot is not a happy one".*

"We are all terrified of 'em" admits Spender, and as the plot progresses it gradually becomes clear that just about everyone in London is at one another's throats with the long-suffering police often caught in the middle, as they would be on Bertie's protest march nearly seventy years later.

The political disarray in Parliament – the subject of the next two songs – is mirrored in the rest of society, which is riven with factionalism, dissent and disagreement from top to bottom. Money and prestige, as in so many future Wodehouse plots, seem to be the main bones of contention in this dog-eat-dog world, with just about everyone trying to grab more while doing as little as possible to earn it, and/or climbing up the greasy pole towards 'respectability'.

We begin at the apex of society with a lament entitled 'The Respectable Peer', who bewails the fact that everyone thinks he's a rich profligate who dines off Anatole-style cuisine when in fact he lives, at least in his view, rather more frugally:

> *Plain water I take at my meals:*
> *I don't like French cooking at all.*
> *But the Radical presses*
> *Denounce my excesses*
> *In a manner designed to appal.*
> *My name in connection with "deals"*
> *Of the shadier sort you won't see.*
> *But each man shakes his head*
> *At the stories he's read,*
> *And thinks what my profits can be.*

Not all nobs are rich, and several of Plum's future aristos are forced to live the penny-pinching life, as we'll discover in Chapter 5: Lord Biddlecombe in 'Came the Dawn' ekes out a "slender income" by acting as an agent for a patented "combination mousetrap and pencil-sharpener", driven to such desperate measures, like "[m]any of the aristocracy" by "recent legislation of a harsh and Socialistic trend". Lord Hoddesdon (*Big Money*), Lord Chuffnell (*Thank You, Jeeves*), Sir Buckstone Abbott (*Summer Moonshine*), Lord Uffenham (*Money in the Bank*), Lord Shortlands (*Spring Fever*) and Lord Rowcester (*Ring for Jeeves*) are all similarly on their uppers.

To Spender, this is a fate they well deserve: in his view, all titled people are not just stinking rich but unprincipled, licentious, heartless and violent:

"In this country it is understood that all peers are dissolute
. . . All waste, wife-beating, infidelity, peculation, immorality, and mismanagement belong to the aristocracy—by
right, as it were".

This chimes with Mr. Mulliner's satirical assessment in 1931's 'The
Smile That Wins', who opines that:

"[t]he fact is . . . reluctant though one may be to admit it,
the entire British aristocracy is seamed and honeycombed
with immorality. I venture to assert that, if you took a
pin and jabbed it down anywhere in the pages of *Debrett's
Peerage*, you would find it piercing the name of someone
who was going about the place with a conscience as tender
as a sunburned neck".

Not so, says Plum's Respectable Peer, who reckons the Spenders and
Mulliners of this world are confusing the "respectable" aristocracy with
"the set that is flashy and smart" – the so-called "Smart Set" – that had
recently been one of the main targets in Wodehouse and Robinson's
Panto 2 from December 1904, *Little Red Riding Hood*.
    Then as now, a small metropolitan coterie of loaded, dissolute party
animals seemed to live solely to "gamble, motor, flirt, and feed", so out-
raging the "Upper Middle Class" of England that it couldn't get enough
of their exploits in "magazine article . . . pamphlet and book". This hypocrisy effectively neutered any attempt to shame these gallivanters, as
the lyric of Panto 2's title song shrewdly points out:

Satirists rage, but their wit, which to hurt is meant,
Somehow contrives to achieve the reverse;
Pleased and refreshed by the splendid advertisement,
Straight they proceed to grow steadily worse.

Celebrity culture is no 21st-century phenomenon, it seems. This shameless behaviour, fuelled by the oxygen of publicity and the double standards of those who consume it, puts us in mind of Sir Raymond "Beefy"
Bastable's bestselling bonkbuster *Cocktail Time* in, er . . . *Cocktail Time*, as
well as Gally Threepwood's scandalous society memoirs that feature in
Summer Lightning and *Heavy Weather*. A similar off-colour volume has been
written by Bertie's Uncle Willoughby in 'Jeeves Takes Charge', all these

publications threatening to open up the can of worms that passes for 'respectable' society, while making pots of money for the writers and the Lord Tilburys who publish and distribute them.

Everyone, it seems, is on the make or hustling in this Edwardian version of Babylon. Back in Panto 4, our next port of call is the theatre, never too far away from Plum's thoughts, and we're introduced to 'Lady Highflyer', the first of the many chorus girls in his stories who marry way above their social station. The Gaiety Theatre, where he would soon be working, was the London epicentre of this trend, and yet again riffing on W.S. Gilbert ('When I Was a Lad' from *H.M.S. Pinafore*), the lyric is a complete Rosie M. Banks plot in miniature. We never learn her Ladyship's original name, but she serves her time on "the last back row" until one of the principals storms off in a fit of pique and she inherits a speaking role (of just one line). Then along comes the "picture-postcard craze" and her face is suddenly for sale in every shop window. This massive exposure gets her the lead in a new show – and then this happens:

> *One night to supper I was taken by*
> *The elderly Earl of Peckham Rye.*
> *He simply lived in a front-row stall:*
> *He bought me bouquets, and said, "Might he call?"*
> *I played that peer so artfullee*
> *That now I'm a leader of societee.*

In his future work, Wodehouse would prove himself perfectly comfortable with the social elevation of women from humble backgrounds, celebrating (and spoofing) their success. Among these are Bertie's grand Aunt Julia, who, he tells us in 'Extricating Young Gussie', was "playing in pantomime at Drury Lane when Uncle Cuthbert saw her first"; then there's Daisy Trimble of the Gaiety, who has married one of his wealthy Knut friends, "and when I meet her now I feel like walking out of her presence backwards", such is her facility for adopting the airs and graces of a high-up; and what of Lady Pauline Wetherby, who, in *Uneasy Money*, still plies her trade as an exotic dancer after her ennoblement? As we witnessed at some length in Volume 2, Plum always had a soft spot for a plucky chorus girl who gets lucky, no matter what her age or station.

And so, from the aristocracy – respectable or not – the focus now switches to the opposite end of the social spectrum: those unfortunates Plum refers to on several future occasions as "the submerged tenth" or as Bertie calls them in *Much Obliged, Jeeves*, "the brick-bunging portion of the electorate". These gentlemen, it seems, are fond of skiving, drinking and little else:

> *Orl that we asks is liberty, so dear;*
> *Orl that we seeks is work—or else it's beer.*

Spender – cynically, one suspects – believes that "all members of the labouring classes are temperate and pure", although his creator would most likely beg to disagree. In Plum's later stories they will become the cheerily violent denizens of the fictitious London borough of Bottleton East who we'll be meeting in Chapter 4. Here, a "small and ragged body" of unemployed men are confronted by "an Amateur Socialist", who promises them a utopian future free from distinctions of rank, private ownership and bloated millionaires in a land flowing with free food and drink:

> *If you haven't got the money for to pay the weekly rent,*
> *If the butcher or the grocer-man their small accounts have sent,*
> *If the baker hints that cash is worth far more than pleasant promises,*
> *If your little Billy's suit of clothes is wearing through (as Tommy's is),*
> *If in one small room you're forced to live both stuffily and pokily,*
> *If, in short, affairs are running—shall we put it?—stoney brokily,*
> *Then a thorough alteration in your fortunes you will see,*
> *If only you have got sufficient sense to follow me.*

The only downside to the Socialist's version of the land of Cockaigne is that it involves working: "All must labour, irrespective of rank. There must be no idlers, no shirkers, no wastrels". This idea isn't enthusiastically embraced by the mob, and the do-gooder instantly morphs from being the saviour of the non-working man and "a real winner" to a "tyrant" ripe for a "bash", hastily making his exit pursued by a baying crowd of idlers after his blood.

Throughout these proceedings, M. Bonhomme is gradually getting the measure of how British society works, revealing himself to be just as duplicitous a "Progressive" as Spender. Workers *should* have to work to earn a living – but it's a principle that doesn't extend to bureaucrats like themselves, the lilies of the field who toil not. Indeed, shortly afterwards, we meet a group of London County Councillors who appear happy to borrow money on the slightest pretence:

> *Raise a loan! Raise a loan!*
> *It's the only thing to do,*
> *It's the finest mental pick-me-up that's known.*
> *If your tailor's bill's unpaid*
> *Don't be moody and dismayed:*
> *Raise a loan! Raise a loan! Raise a loan!*

And so it is that the theme of finance is introduced, which rounds off Panto 4 in an orgy of credit, loans, debt and the suspicion that Britain isn't as solvent as its elevated position on the world stage might lead one to think.

From John of Gaunt's infamous "sceptred isle" speech in Shakespeare's *Richard II*, the disjunction between the impressive front façade of England and its impecunious backstairs reality has been a recurrent theme in literature. In Gaunt's often-quoted and misunderstood soliloquy, England may be an "other-Eden and a "demi-paradise", but it is in hock up to its neck, "leased out/ Like to a tenement or pelting farm". And so, it is in this final song – and much of Wodehouse's subsequent oeuvre. England's credit, in short, is shot. Old money is either all lost, or is in the process of being transferred to a new breed of transatlantic carpetbaggers, one of the earliest being Pat McEachern in 1909's 'The Gem Collector':

> England still firmly believes that wealth accrues to every resident of New York by some mysterious process not understandable of the Briton. McEachern and his money were accepted by [English] society without question . . . He speedily made friends, among them Lady Jane Blunt, the still youthful widow of a man about town, who, after trying for several years to live at the rate of ten thousand per annum with an income of two and a half, had finally given up the struggle and drank himself peacefully into the tomb.

At which point McEachern steps in and marries her, the first of many transatlantic alliances in Plum's novels, most of them rather more happy, fortunate and less cynically engineered than this early example.

As a chorus of stockbrokers and shareholders now make clear, England, where "Socialism grows apace", is no place to make a return on your money. Bonhomme, claiming to be a man who has worked hard and saved money, clearly has no idea where it will be safe – from the extravagance of bureaucrats like himself. Hailing a passing Banker, he enquires "what has been the practical result of this Radical Government?" – and the banker's reply rounds out the show on a distinctly unpatriotic note:

> *If I had a friend with some money to spend,*
> *And he wished me to choose an investment,*
> *"My boy," I should say, "listen closely, I pray,*
> *To advice which is all for the best meant.*
> *If to get a return for your money you yearn,*
> *And if you don't wish to be bitten,*
> *I think it is best all your cash to invest*
> *In something that's outside Great Britain".*

Bonhomme, taking this advice as Solomonic, asks Spender to call him a cab to Charing Cross station, from where he will take the boat train back to Paris, a city that "seems to me the safer", at least financially. And so, as their final panto ends on a rhythmically jaunty but thematically downbeat note, Wodehouse and Robinson have successfully shone a searchlight on some of the ins and outs of British life, many of which I'll be examining in greater detail over the next four chapters. Just remember, however, that you saw them here first, in this early, long-forgotten piece of satire.

Over the next few years, Plum would try to make a new life for himself in America, succeeding on his second serious attempt in 1914. Clearly, the Old Country could not contain his ambition, and he would remain Stateside for the next five years while the Great War raged and bombs rained down on London. Almost the last thing he wrote (with collaborator Charles Bovill) before he left was another batch of lyrics roasting the state of the nation, performed in the 1914 revue *Nuts and Wine*. The closing number, 'We're Leaving England', contained a litany of minor annoyances, including buses that don't run on time, the lousy telephone system and the craze for the tango. But inserted among this first-world moaning (which Plum was of course satirizing) were a couple of piquing gripes that "however well I speak/ They forget me in a week", and that being an Englishman in America no longer had the cachet it once enjoyed, since "I wasn't all I ought to be". England was his "rotten native land", the birthright it conferred simply not "worth a damn", and by way of returning the compliment, London audiences stayed away from the show in their droves.

It was a sour end to this first period of Plum's career as a satirist; yet in the life of the writer, nothing is ever wasted, and already the balance in his writerly tone was shifting in favour of a richer, subtler tone. He was approaching his 30s, and that youthful Juvenalian zeal, occasionally evident in this chapter, was starting to have its edges knocked off. Open mockery would start to morph into Horatian deflation, and the whole focus of Wodehousean reality would start to shift away from specific examples into more timeless types, a process prefigured in that final panto. But most significant of all was the way Plum had already started *alchemizing* 'real' reality into his own brand of what we might call "ridiculous realism", in which it would be perfectly normal to plot and plan the kidnapping of an oversized pig without anyone, the reader included, thinking it the least bit odd. Yet while this synthesis of the real and scarcely credible was taking place in Plum's imagination, its inspiration originally came, and would continue to come, from the world he saw and experienced around him. Cue Chapter 2, in which Plum's satire takes a walk on the wackier side of life.

YOU COULDN'T
MAKE IT UP

Chapter 2:
You Couldn't Make It Up

*Truth may be stranger than fiction, but fiction is much
snappier and better balanced.*
Early Wodehouse notebook

*I believe this story to be fictitious. It was told me by a man, a perfect
stranger, whose eye gleamed with untruthfulness. He told it to me
in the knowledge that I would be unable to take any steps towards
verifying his statements . . .My own belief is that the man was a
novelist, and that he told me as a true story what was really nothing
but the plot of his next romance. Before using, in fact, he tried it, as
the saying is, upon the dog.*
'The Pro'

*Stop press news . . . Fry not out, 104. Surrey 147 for 8. A German
army landed in Essex this afternoon. Loamshire Handicap: Spring
Chicken, 1; Salome, 2; Yip-i-addy, 3. Seven ran.*
The Swoop!

Here's a question for when things fall silent in the bar-parlour: Is reality
always real? And is there a general consensus as to what reality actually is?
For if you're going to describe Wodehouse World as "gleefully detached
from reality", you'd better have a clear understanding of the reality you're
comparing it *with*. Your benchmark of *real* reality, as it were.

Unfortunately, there's no such thing. Reality, as it is fed to us, is
more like an account of a crime scene distilled from the testimony of
drunken, purblind eyewitnesses, many of whom were elsewhere at the
time. At least that was the opinion of my late-lamented godfather Victor
E. Neuburg, a pioneering academic in the field of British social history,
who once told me that his colleagues – at best – tended to draw their
conclusions from the doings of less than 3% of the country's total population. Hardly a representative sample, then. What the other 97% did,
thought, said and read rarely gets a look in (or didn't in the 1970s, when
this conversation took place). Moreover – he continued, warming to
his theme – no one in history, as it presented to us, laughs much. There
must always have been ludicrousness in the world, which would have
required a sense of the ridiculous to appreciate – only we rarely, if ever,
get to hear about it as the doings of the great and the good, the rich and

the famous, are paraded before us in humour-free narratives.

This, and other absent perspectives is a theme Malcolm Muggeridge confronts in his essay 'Wodehouse in Distress', detailing his involvement with Plum and Ethel immediately after the Second World War, as the British Establishment sought to get to grips with the Berlin Broadcasts Business (or BBB, as I've been abbreviating it). Was Wodehouse a traitor? In 1945, Muggeridge was mulling this over with Alfred Duff Cooper, who as Home Secretary had authorised the 'Cassandra' radio broadcast on the BBC that had torn Plum's reputation to shreds four years earlier. By then the British Ambassador in Paris (where Plum was being detained), Duff Cooper opined that Wodehouse's main fault was that he hadn't 'bought into' the war, and "had always evaded reality and his responsibilities as a citizen". Muggeridge remembers how he countered this argument by remarking that "there are different sorts of reality":

> Can we be so sure, for instance, that Hitler's ranting and Churchill's rhetoric and Roosevelt's Four Freedoms will seem any more real to posterity than Jeeves or Bertie Wooster?

A career politician like Duff Cooper probably assumed the answer was self-evident and the young liaison officer was off his onion. Yet the question was intended seriously: to Muggeridge, who later went on to become Plum's employer as editor of the satirical magazine *Punch*, life always had the potential, no matter how serious it got, to be absurd and nonsensical. Like Juvenal, he believed that there were no hierarchies within reality; nothing was more 'real' than anything else, there were just different ways of looking at life.

It was a sensibility that Muggeridge clearly shared with Wodehouse, not just for seeing the funny side of things but the potential for humour that lies at the heart of even the grimmest situations. An example: cleverly edited film footage of Nazi troops goose-stepping to the jaunty tune of 'The Lambeth Walk' had been one of the most inspired and funniest British propaganda coups of the war (it's still all over YouTube), and during his conversation with Duff Cooper, Muggeridge regaled the politician with one instance of a similarly off-the-wall "contribution by Wodehouse to the war effort":

The Germans, in their literal way, took his works as a guide to English manners and actually dropped an agent in the Fen country wearing spats. This unaccustomed article of attire led to his speedy apprehension. Had he not been caught, he would, presumably, have gone on to London in search of the Drones Club and have thought to escape notice in restaurants by throwing bread about in the manner of Bertie.

We don't unfortunately get to learn the outcome of Muggeridge's anecdote, but it illustrates perfectly how sometimes, real life can kick off its tight shoes and have some fun, even when we are least expecting it.

Wodehouse was to prove himself a connoisseur of those moments all his working life, his magpie's eye forever trained on reality's lunatic fringe. There's a lovely paragraph in William Shawcross's official biography of Her Majesty Queen Elizabeth, the Queen Mother in which he notes that Wodehouse's novels were her favourite books, in part because she considered them "so realistic". Shawcross immediately jumps on this remark, claiming that only a person of her privileged upper-class background could have come out with a statement as patently ridiculous as that. Yet the Queen Mum wasn't *actually* all that wide of the mark, for if you know where to look, it's perfectly possible to construct a weirdly plausible parallel to the real world without taxing the imagination too much – and Plum most certainly *did* know where to look.

From his time at *The Globe* onwards, he adored the sort of improbable stories that stretched credulity to its limits and kept potentially useful newspaper clippings in large scrapbooks that are now in the possession of his grandson, Edward Cazalet. The ones that survive date from the 1960s (or at least I think they do – Plum neatly cut around the stories he wanted, excising both dates and mastheads), and are full of the sort of material that found its way into the eight topical 'Our Man in America' segments recycled from his columns in *Punch* magazine, and inserted between the short stories in 1966's *Plum Pie*. These invariably chronicled the quirkier news stories of the day, including:

- an extended riff on the headline 'WOMAN WHO CAME TO DINNER DEPARTS AFTER 11-YEAR STAY';

- the case of Giuseppe Mancini, who, having netted

$150,000 in a year from robbing coin-operated parking meters, was so weighed down by the 20,000 dimes in his bulging pockets, the police easily caught up with him as he staggered up New York's 3rd Avenue;

- and the singing dog Buster, whose owner (Ernest Crowley of Watkins Glen, N.Y.) was in the habit of taking his pet to local old peoples' homes to entertain the inmates, prompting Plum to remark that this must "scare the pants off them". "I am aged myself", he went on, "and I know that if I were lying in bed and a dog came in and suddenly started singing the 'Jewel Song' from *Faust*, I would shoot straight up and through the ceiling".

Not only couldn't you make it up: Plum didn't have to.

Which brings us to *The Swoop!*, his satirical 25,000 word novella published in April 1909, a work that most of us who write about Wodehouse don't really know what to do with, but is nonetheless fascinating for all that. Completed in five frantic days, it has been described by Samuel Hynes in *The Edwardian Turn of Mind* as "the only comic contribution to Edwardian invasion literature", running counter to the fashion for paranoid tales of an England overrun by foreign (usually German) troops. These were selling like hot cakes, so Plum, with his commercial satirist's hat on, set out to take this somewhat strange publishing phenomenon to task.

As much a staging post in his literary development as Panto 4, *The Swoop!* offers Plum's readers a similar state of the nation analysis, only this time in the form of an absurdist fable. A fan of G.K. Chesterton, he might have been inspired by that writer's recent novella *The Napoleon of Notting Hill*, in which an alternative governance of England is also described. But whereas Chesterton set his tale 80 years in the future, Plum's fantasy takes place in the present and takes aim at a motley collection of high-profile, contemporary targets, including Lord Northcliffe's *Daily Mail*, General Baden-Powell's new Scouting movement, the military conspiracy theorist Field Marshal (Lord) Roberts and his bestselling literary amanuensis William Le Queux, all of whose interests were served by talking up the nation's military vulnerability. Plum's fellow journalists are also regularly lampooned, their dodgy working methods as true now as they were then:

By now the country was in possession of the main facts. Full details were not to be expected, though it is to the credit of the newspapers that, with keen enterprise, they had at once set to work to invent them, and on the whole had not done badly.

The (real) factual background was as follows: Germany had been on a military roll since the Franco-Prussian War of 1870-71, when it had crushed the French Army and declared itself a nation state (the "Second Reich"). From 1888, the newly united country was ruled by Kaiser Wilhelm II, Queen Victoria's grandson, who presided over a military build-up that included a massive expansion of the navy. Prone to bellicosity, he set out to make Germany a respected world power by force if necessary, and by 1908 24% of the national budget was being spent on ship and U-boat construction. So yes, you can see why there might be some nervousness across the North Sea. If an attack came, would Britain be ready? Absolutely not, apparently, Chugwateresque complacency being the order of the day. Incidentally, Kaiser Bill, following his exile to Holland after Germany's defeat in World War I, became a keen collector of Wodehouse first editions, regularly reading extracts to his "mystified" staff. Perhaps *The Swoop!* was among them.

Way ahead of the paranoia curve was George Tomkyns Chesney's 1871 story *The Battle of Dorking*, in which Britain is invaded by an unnamed (but tellingly German-speaking) nation which defeats the army decisively (at Dorking) and breaks up the Empire. "No book", a later paperback edition boasted, "has ever touched the public conscience more strongly than this" – which was to a certain extent true, quickly making invasion literature a lucrative publishing bandwagon to be jumped on. Until at least 1918, the pot was kept steadily boiling, and it even produced a couple of minor classics in *The Riddle of the Sands*, Erskine Childers's 1903 tale of two men on a sailing holiday who improbably thwart a German invasion of England; and John Buchan's *The Thirty-Nine Steps*, written immediately prior to the outbreak of World War I about German agents in Britain preparing the ground for an attack. Both these books are decent adventure yarns and still read today.

The same cannot be said of the work of William Le Queux (pronounced "Le Cur"), a prolific hack who produced several lurid novels a year with titles like *If Sinners Entice Thee, Who Giveth This Woman?* and *Whosoever Loveth: Being the Secret of a Lady's Maid*. Tucked in among this sub-Rosie M. Banks romantic pulp was his bestselling third novel,

The Great War in England in 1897 (published in 1894) in which a coalition of France and Russia provides the invasionary forces. Indeed, Le Queux was soon to become obsessed with the idea that every walk of British life was riddled with networks of foreign spies just waiting for their moment to break cover and plunge the land into chaos. Both the Foreign Office and the War Office were frequent recipients of his "intelligence": on one occasion, he claimed to have discovered a speech in which the Kaiser had outlined an invasion plan of Britain to the German military, complete with maps, plans, diagrams and even model weapons. Unfortunately, his evidence could not be produced – because, he claimed, it had been stolen from his publisher's office by German spies. Upon which the mandarins of the British civil service decided he was not to be taken seriously.

Nothing deterred, Le Queux formed a friendship with Lord Roberts, a grand old career soldier who had risen to the rank of Commander-in-Chief of the Forces in 1901, and was a sincere, if all too easily gulled patriot who perhaps wasn't aware he was being shamefully used by his new accomplice as a human shield of respectability. Opining in the House of Lords that "our armed forces are absolutely unfitted and unprepared for war", the message was one he never tired of repeating, and together, for very different reasons, the two men began whipping up measured concern into a paranoid fantasy.

Meanwhile, Wodehouse had been taking notes on the subject. In 'A Fable' (*Punch*, October 8 1902) he had framed the ongoing cold war between Britain and Germany as a conversation between a Lion and an Eagle; and in June 1903 in that same organ he had introduced a fictitious correspondent, Henry William-Jones (satirizing the dramatist Henry Arthur Jones) who would occasionally write to the editor with ridiculous suggestions for books or plays he might be commissioned to write. Among his proposals was an "Inspired-Prophecy kind of novel, in which England is overrun by invaders until the last few chapters". Its hero would be Julius Seeth, a real-life circus performer, who would command an army of trained rats, beating the aggressors hollow under the leadership of Winston Churchill and the Editor of the *Daily Mail*. "The hair of the reader will shoot up like a rocket", he confidently predicted; but however fantastical the story got, he would always, he promised, write with a "strict regard for the probabilities". Six years later, some of this ludicrous resumé would end up as plot material in *The Swoop!*

Meanwhile, in what passed for reality, Le Queux and Roberts were joined on the paranoia trail by press baron Lord Northcliffe, who, sniffing paydirt for his *Daily Mail*, ponied up the massive sum of £3,000 for the pair to go on a recce up the east coast of England to research strategic landing points an invading German army might choose, with a view to including them in Le Queux's new book *The Invasion of 1910* – which would of course be serialized in the *Mail*. In his biography of Wodehouse, Benny Green tells of Northcliffe's disappointment that the locations his costly sappers had identified weren't over-endowed with *Mail* readers, and would have to be changed so as to make the story more zesty and fear-inducing for the paper's subscribers. Changed they duly were, and the strategy worked: on the first day of the story's serialization in the *Mail* (19 March 1906), Northcliffe minions dressed as German soldiers could be witnessed walking along London's busy Regent Street, and the subsequent book version of the story went on to sell over one million copies in 27 languages - including German. Northcliffe, who by 1914 controlled around 40% of morning newspaper circulation in Britain, could have showed most fiction writers a thing or two about how to shape a story to gain maximum impact.

Naturally, this fear and loathing of Germans prompted an entire army of conspiracy theorists to come crawling out of the woodwork. So vocal did the hue and cry become that in March 1909, the Committee of Imperial Defence met in Westminster to examine the issue of foreign espionage. Which produced two notable outcomes: the formation of the British Secret Service (whose future employees would include James Bond); and *The Swoop!*, published the following month. Plum's choice of title, bang up to date, alludes to James Blyth's 1909 invasion novel *The Swoop of the Vulture*, which describes a surprise attack on England by forces of the "Imperial German Vulture". It's just that in Wodehouse's story, the country is invaded not just by Germany, but several other nations simultaneously. Complaining of the difficulties caused by so many competitors, the leader of the German forces, Prince Otto, blames Blyth's novel for giving everyone the same idea ("[i]t all comes of this dashed 'Swoop of the Vulture' business", he grumbled.) Such books, Plum implies, were promoting the idea that invading England would be a cinch, so why not give it a go? Come one, come all! And in *The Swoop!* they do – even the Swiss navy. But viewed in this light, what the hacks were marketing as patriotic concern could be interpreted as treason –a possibility that a reviewer of Blyth's book, in New Zealand, of all places, would also remark:

> One drawback of such books [is] that every device that
> the ingenuity of fictionists could suggest has been already
> freely placed by English writers at the disposal of possible
> invaders (Wellington *Evening Post*, 26 June 1909)

Could a fictional invasion possibly lead to an actual one? Could Life
imitate Art?

The hypocrisy of Le Queux, Blyth and their ilk was a theme Plum
shrewdly satirizes in the Preface to his own story, in which he ably
demonstrates that patriotism really is the last refuge of the scoundrel:

> It may be thought by some that in the pages which follow
> I have painted in too lurid colours the horrors of a foreign
> invasion of England. Realism in art, it may be argued, can
> be carried too far. I prefer to think that the majority of
> my readers will acquit me of a desire to be unduly sensa-
> tional. It is necessary that England should be roused to a
> sense of her peril, and only by setting down without flinch-
> ing the probable results of an invasion can this be done.
> This story, I may mention, has been written and published
> purely from a feeling of patriotism and duty. [Publisher]
> Mr Alston Rivers' sensitive soul will be jarred to its foun-
> dations if it is a financial success. So will mine. But in a
> time of national danger we feel that the risk must be taken.
> After all, at the worst, it is a small sacrifice to make for our
> country.

All this raises the intriguing possibility that the establishment of the
British Secret Service was more influenced by the fevered imaginations
of third-rate hacks than the inexorable rise of German sea power, making writers not just reporters of reality but, along with the world's mov-
ers and shakers, its co-authors.

Plum had telegraphed this habit in his 1906 story 'How Kid Brady
Joined the Press' – Tom Garth, a Wordsworth-quoting Oxford graduate
turned New York journalist, confesses that "[m]y passion for the dramatic's quite a disease": which translates as 'reality needs a bit of help if
it is to be turned into saleable stories that will catch the world's attention,
boost my paper's circulation and make my name'. Which was Plum's
outlook too: when we come to examine his various autobiographical
works in Chapters 6 and 7, we'll see that he wasn't one for letting the

truth get in the way of a good story, particularly if that good story had seeds of humour in it. So being both a journalist *and* a fiction writer, he could not be too judgmental of those who manipulated reality to suit their own ends without being hypocritical. *The Swoop* itself was, he tells us, written as "one of the paper-covered shilling books" (like *The Globe By the Way Book*) for popular consumption by a mass audience, often cashing in on some short-lived craze or another. Which is why Northcliffe and other contemporary press barons like Lord Beaverbrook of the *Daily Express* were not entirely unsympathetic to Wodehouse, quite simply because their motivations overlapped. Plum may have made his fictional Lord Tilbury an unprincipled, populist ogre and sociopathic charlatan, but in his 1964 swan song *Frozen Assets*, he allows the press baron to bow out happily engaged to his fabulously attractive blond secretary Gwendoline, indicating that Wodehouse didn't *quite* regard his creation as the devil incarnate (and doesn't that pairing remind you of Rupert Murdoch and Jerry Hall?).

That said, Plum didn't always give the benefit of the doubt to the print media and its dodgy protégés. It was Northcliffe's younger brother Harold Harmsworth, Lord Rothermere who, as well as promoting appeasement with Nazi Germany and a British alliance with Adolf Hitler in the pages of his newspapers, wrote the notorious 1934 *Daily Mail* editorial "Hurrah for the Blackshirts", praising Oswald Mosley (see the Introduction to this volume) for his "sound, commonsense, Conservative doctrine" which was in truth fascism by any other name. The "Saviours of Britain" weren't swanking around in their footer bags as a publicity stunt for a third-rate book – it was altogether more serious than that, as Plum makes clear by styling Spode as a trainee dictator. Other than sportsmen, Wodehouse had always been suspicious of those who voluntarily don a uniform which displays their knees; which brings us back to *The Swoop!* and boy scout Clarence Chugwater, who, when we last met him, was bewailing the bovine complacency of the rest of his family.

Clarence was not alone in worrying that "England's military strength at this time was practically nil", and that this was a sign the country's get up and go had got up and went. Or even worse, that Britain had entered a downward spiral into degeneracy. A lad of his serious and patriotic disposition might well have read an anonymous pamphlet which had been published in 1905, entitled *The Decline and Fall of the British Empire*, which, like Le Queux's invasion novels, purported to have been written in the future – only this time the date was 2005. With the benefit of a century's perspective, the writer (who turned out to be Elliott Mills, a young

Conservative Party activist recently down from Oxford University with a 4th class degree in history) identifies eight reasons for Britain's decline, which, he avers, paralleled that of Ancient Rome. We needn't list these here, needing only to comment that Mills viewed any kind of change as not just undesirable, but physically, spiritually and even morally bad for his fellow citizens. There had been a Golden Age in British history, but Social Darwinism had started to go into reverse, and as the 20th century dawned, decadence had begun to eat away at the national character.

This incipient national panic had been met with the suggestion that children should be trained in shooting and scouting from the very earliest age; and, ahead of the game as usual, Plum had already written an excellent satirical poem for *Punch*, 'The Infant in Arms' that imagined what might happen if this came to pass:

> *My child, away with your toys and games.*
> *No more on the floor shall roll*
> *The painted indiarubber globe,*
> *To gladden your infant soul.*
> *No more shall the rattle whirr: no more*
> *Shall the gay tin trumpet toot:*
> *My child, it is time that you learned to drill;*
> *It is time that you learned to shoot . . .*
>
> *Thus when the day of battle dawns,*
> *And merciless foes invade,*
> *When, sore oppressed, at the nursery door*
> *Your country knocks for aid,*
> *When far and wide through our pleasant land*
> *Sounds Armageddon's din,*
> *When England once again "expects,"—*
> *Why, that's where you'll come in.*
>
> *You'll take your air-gun from the shelf,*
> *Your catapult blithely seize,*
> *Gaily you'll gird your shooter on,*
> *And see that it lacks not peas.*
> *And as the hiss of your pop-gun's cork*
> *Is merged in the general roar,*
> *You'll bless the day when you left your play*
> *To practice the art of War.*

Mills's pamphlet and its contents were seized on by the British Army's Inspector-General of Cavalry, Robert Baden-Powell, who, having been effectively pensioned off and at something of a loose end, in 1908 published the first edition of his seminal work *Scouting for Boys* which would have been Clarence's Holy Bible. In amongst the information, advice and stirring anecdotes were passages of political commentary like this one:

> Recent reports on the deterioration of our race ought to act as a warning to be taken in time before it goes too far. One cause which contributed to the downfall of the Roman Empire was the fact that soldiers fell away from the standard of their forefathers in bodily strength.

Those "reports", as well as Mills's pamphlet, would have included the 1904 'Report on the Inter-Departmental Committee on Physical Deterioration' which had looked into "allegations concerning the [physical] deterioration of certain classes of the population" and concluded that degeneracy was not widespread. Baden-Powell begged to differ however, and, keen to prepare the next generation of British soldiers who would be capable of fighting enemies either at home or abroad, set about building a 'boys' army' to fill what he perceived as the growing void.

In the first edition of *Scouting for Boys*, the necessity for a second force is argued thus:

> There are always members of Parliament who try to make the Navy and Army smaller, so as to save money. They only want to be popular with the voters in England so that they and the party to which they belong can get into power. These men are called "politicians". They do not look to the good of the country.

While naming no names, it was obvious which political groupings Baden-Powell was referring to. In his satirical fantasy, Wodehouse helpfully does the job for him:

> The abolition of the regular army had been the first step. Several causes had contributed to this. In the first place, the Socialists had condemned the army system as unsocial. Privates, they pointed out, were forbidden to hob-nob with colonels, though the difference in their positions was due to

a mere accident of birth. They demanded that every man in the army should be a general. Comrade Quelch, in an eloquent speech at Newington Butts, had pointed, amidst enthusiasm, to the republics of South America, where the system worked admirably.

And yes, there was a Harry Quelch, a prominent activist later dubbed "one of the first Marxists in Great Britain", and his Socialist son Tom, both given to speechmaking and either one of whom Plum could be namechecking in this extract. Nor is it a coincidence that Plum singles out South America for his attentions: Baden-Powell had also highlighted Latin American countries as a salutary lesson in what disastrous things can happen when mere "politicians" and not proper "statesmen" rule the roost. Argentina, Honduras, Nicaragua and Venezuela had all experienced recent outbreaks of political discontent and violence, and the Mexican Revolution of 1910 was brewing nicely. Indeed, countries experiencing a change of ownership would be featuring in two Wodehouse plots from around this time: in *A Man of Means*, Roland Bleke gets himself mixed up in a revolution in the Latin American state of Paranoya, as does Benjamin Scobell in *The Prince and Betty* when the Mediterranean island of Mervo is restored to the status of a monarchy. Regime change was all the rage. But could it really happen here? In Britain?

In its promotional literature, the modern (British) Scout movement tends to distance itself from its paramilitary roots, and still heavily airbrushes aspects of its founder's imperialist politics. But even at the time, Wodehouse appeared in equal parts amused and slightly creeped out by the entire enterprise. He is quick to seize on the fledgling movement's hastily improvised uniform which, in Clarence's case, consists of "a flat-brimmed hat, a coloured handkerchief, a flannel shirt, a bunch of ribbons, a haversack, football shorts, brown boots, a whistle and a hockey stick" as both funny and strange. Rather more remarkable, however, was the exponential growth of the movement. Even as Plum was writing *The Swoop!*, the Scouts had grown to 100,000 members in a little under two years, with Baden Powell not only planning to take it international, but start the Girl Guides, who would assist the Empire by "mak[ing] themselves of practical use in case of invasion" and "prepare themselves for a Colonial life". Or, in other words, do the chores.

It only took a small leap of imagination to describe the combined movement, as Plum did, as "perhaps the most carefully-organised secret society in the world". And lo and behold, by the following year, organized Scout groups had already popped up in Sweden, Mexico, Argentina, Canada, Australia, South Africa and the United States, proving him right. They get everywhere: in *Service with a Smile*, we're told that Uncle Fred's acts of philanthropy can be put down to his mother having once "been frightened by a Boy Scout". Indeed, so widespread is their influence, Plum even envisages the Scouts as unlikely agents of Providence:

> You are a City merchant, and, arriving at the office one morning in a bad temper, you proceed to cure yourself by taking it out of the office-boy. He says nothing, apparently does nothing. But that evening, as you are going home in the Tube, a burly working-man treads heavily on your gouty foot. In Ladbroke Grove a passing hansom splashes you with mud. Reaching home, you find that the cat has been at the cold chicken and the butler has given notice. You do not connect these things, but they are all alike the results of your unjust behaviour to your office-boy in the morning. Or, meeting a ragged little matchseller, you pat his head and give him six-pence. Next day an anonymous present of champagne arrives at your address. Terrible in their wrath, the Boy Scouts never forget kindness.

Almost forty years later in *Joy in the Morning*, Edwin Craye, a boy scout who is a bit behind with his daily acts of kindness, attempts to clean the chimney of Bertie's cottage, Wee Nooke, with gunpowder and paraffin, only to burn it to the ground. Edwin, like Clarence, is one of those "thorough kids" with a "serious outlook on life" and a "grave and earnest spirit", making life for those around him "a perfect hell for man and beast". Once can't help but feel that Plum's later colonial outdoor types like Major Brabazon-Plank in *Uncle Dynamite* and *Stiff Upper Lip, Jeeves* or *Ring for Jeeves*'s Captain Cuthbert Gervaise Brabazon-Biggar are simply adult-sized versions of these boys – even sharing the same partiality for jungle-inflected jibberish. Here's Clarence's version as he makes himself known to the scout camp's sentry:

> A voice from the darkness said, "Een gonyama-gonyama".

> "Invooboo," replied the sentry argumentatively "Yah bo! Yah bo!

Invooboo".

An indistinct figure moved forward.

"Who goes there?"

"A friend".

"Advance, friend, and give the countersign".

"Remember Mafeking, and death to Injuns".

And in that password, Wodehouse lets us know that *he* knows Baden-Powell was the controversial garrison commander at the siege of Mafeking whose questionable tactics at this and other confrontations during the Second Boer War would ultimately see him removed from combat command.

Thus, it is the Boy Scouts lead the fightback, whittling the invading forces down to just two, the Germans and the Russians. Conflict is inevitable; but, as in many of Plum's stories, the climactic scenes take place off-stage – or in this case, cloaked by a dense pea-souper fog. Aiming their cannon into the murk, it's nigh-on impossible to fathom what's going on, which gives Plum another opportunity to take a few well-aimed pot shots against his colleagues in the Fourth Estate. An absence of facts, Plum reminds us, doesn't usually prevent journalists filing copy as if it is the gospel truth; nevertheless, it does seem ironic that although "London at that moment was richer than ever before in descriptive reporters", they can't actually see anything to report *on*. Were Wodehouse given full accreditation as a literary theorist, it would already have been noted that this short sequence is making a serious point about the unknowable nature of reality, his featured journalists being literally – and of course ironically – the blind leading the blind:

> It was the age . . . of vivid pen-pictures. In every newspaper office there were men who could have hauled up their slacks about that battle in a way that would have made a Y.M.C.A. lecturer want to get at somebody with a bayonet; men who could have handed out the adjectives and exclamation-marks till you almost heard the roar of the guns. And there they were—idle, supine—like careened battleships. They were helpless.

Even if they wanted to report the truth, Plum doesn't let them; and by way of example, we are presented with a wicked parody of the real-life *Daily Mail* journalist (and novelist) Bart Kennedy's staccato, accretive writing style ("Fog. Black fog. And the roar of guns. Two nations fighting in the fog"), but even he fails to conjure anything up from the yellowy miasma. Nor can the full-time war correspondents: the five Plum name-checks include Edgar Wallace, who at that point had only just started writing the detective novels that would make him a legend, having cut his teeth as a correspondent during the Second Boer War; and the utterly fascinating Bennet Burleigh, a Scottish shipping clerk who became a Confederate spy and gun-runner during the American Civil War, later escaping from prison, re-crossing the Atlantic and getting a paid gig at the *Daily Telegraph* covering the war in Sudan. Both these gentlemen become hopelessly lost in the murk, ultimately filing nothing of value.

Eventually, it emerges that the Germans have beaten the Russians, but are so exhausted they fall easy prey to Clarence's boy scouts armed only with catapults and hockey sticks. Cue Clarence's victory speech, which Prince Otto, who has caught a dreadful cold, insists on adenoidally interrupting:

> "England, thou art free! Thou hast risen from the ashes of the dead self. Let the nations learn from this that it is when apparently crushed that the Briton is to more than ever be feared."

> "Thad's bad grabbar," said the Prince critically.

> "It isn't," said Clarence with warmth.

> "It *is*, I tell you. Id's a splid idfididive".

And so the theme of writing once more invades Plum's narrative, in which it has been joined by Plum's second love, the theatre. Following this exchange, the final chapter details how Clarence, now hailed as the saviour of England, has been signed up for a tour of country's music halls at £1,000 per week, billed as "The Boy of Destiny".

It was brave (or perhaps foolhardy) of Plum to attempt a satirical treatment of this particular story, since he was swimming against a very strong tide stirred up by less able rivals like Blyth and Le Queux. Sometimes the satirist has to know when to pick his battles, and as he later commented in *Over Seventy*, *The Swoop!* hardly caught the public's imagination: "the people who read it", he claims, "if placed end to end, would have reached from Hyde Park Corner to about the top of Arlington Street" – a distance of about half a mile along Piccadilly.

Yet it remains a fascinating period piece because collectively, some of the ideas Plum addresses would find their ultimate expression in the genocidal atrocities of the Second World War. Three decades earlier in 1909, one does get the feeling he suspected *something* unpleasant was in the offing, for he would return to the bodily health/personal fitness/destiny of the nation mindset in *The White Hope* and *Bill the Conqueror*, where these themes are addressed through Eugenics, a contemporary phenomenon which actively sought to breed out mental and physical defects from the gene pool.

Modern eugenics had been a late Victorian phenomenon, a natural outgrowth from Darwinism; but in 1907, it gained further traction when the British Eugenics Education Society was formed with its stated aim of boosting the subject into a serious academic discipline. Yet again, Wodehouse was quick off the blocks. As early as 1900, he was contrasting the sportsman with the scholar in an essay published in *Public School Magazine* entitled 'Work', demonstrating at least a glancing awareness of the principles of natural selection that would find a home in the work of several writers of the period, most notably George Bernard Shaw in his 1903 drama *Man and Superman*:

> For the athlete is the product of Nature—a step towards the more perfect type of animal, while the scholar is the outcome of artificiality.

Plum's first actual eugenicist appears in *The White Hope*, written in 1910, in the person of Lora Delane Porter, who, in books such as *The Dawn of Better Things*, *Principles of Selection*, and *What of To-morrow?* – addresses mankind's destiny:

> If you are ignorant of Lora Delane Porter's books that is your affair. Perhaps you are more to be pitied than censured. Nature probably gave you the wrong shape of forehead. Mrs. Porter herself would have put it down to some atavistic tendency or prenatal influence. She put most things down to that . . .
> [Her] mind worked backward and forward. She had one

eye on the past, the other on the future. If she was strong on heredity, she was stronger on the future of the race. Most of her published works dealt with this subject.

Although her books are not widely read, Lora manages to indoctrinate her niece Ruth into the faith, who in her turn tries to persuade her horrified brother Bailey that eugenics is the goods:

> "A woman can't do a great deal, even nowadays, but she can have a conscience and feel that she owes something to the future of the race. She can feel that it is her duty to bring fine children into the world".

There's a fizzing powder keg of themes for discussion in those two sentences, both in Edwardian and modern contexts. As far as Ruth is concerned, however, it all boils down to finding a suitable physical specimen to marry and provide her with a child. Which she does; but as things turn out, her carefully controlled matching and hatching only serves to compound her life's problems.

Over the next few years, Wodehouse would steadily gnaw at this bone. In 1917, he reviewed a Broadway stage farce, *The Very Idea*, pronouncing it a "sensational hit" despite "deal[ing] with the always dangerous theme of Eugenics". By "dangerous", Plum was probably alluding to the sensational "Bollinger" case from 1915, in which a tragic instance of eugenic infanticide in Chicago had become a *cause célèbre* and was controversially filmed as *The Black Stork* two years later. The hoo-ha surrounding the release of the movie would probably not have escaped Plum's eagle eye, although, somewhat bizarrely, *The Very Idea* was actually a farce which, according to the *New York Times*, left the audience "convulsed". Plum gave it the thumbs-up too.

Still he wouldn't let it lie. In 1922's 'Scoring off Jeeves', Aunt Agatha informs Bertie that "it is young men like you who make the person with the future of the race at heart despair!" before suggesting he might like to marry a girl like Honoria Glossop, "somebody strong, self-reliant, and sensible, to counterbalance the deficiencies and weaknesses of your own character". What was perceived as post-war decadence gave eugenics an additional fillip, prompting those of a censorious nature like the formidable Mrs Gregson to at least pay lip service to its aims.

But it's in 1925's *Bill the Conqueror* that Plum really sinks his satirical teeth into the subject. This time the quack is a certain Professor

Appleby, who has been entrusted with the future of Horace French, a ghastly youth adopted by Cooley Paradene. Cooley proposes to divert the wealth he formerly spent supporting his sponging family to the boy's rehabilitation, and in this passage Appleby breaks the news to the soon-to-be-impoverished relatives:

> "[I]n certain circles, I think I may assert with all modesty, my views on Eugenics are considered worthy of attention. Mr Paradene, I am glad to say, has allowed himself to be enrolled among my disciples. I am a strong supporter of Mr Bernard Shaw's views on the necessity of starting a new race, building it with the most perfect specimens of the old. Horace here is a boy of splendid physique, great intelligence, sterling character and wonderful disposition."

Appleby would have his work cut out reforming Horace, because apart from anything else he has none of the qualities his tutor ascribes to him. Basically a re-run of *The Little Nugget*'s Ogden Ford from 1913, Horace actually turns out to be Appleby's accomplice in a heist involving valuable books from Cooley's library. Plum is simply associating Appleby's practice of eugenics with crime and deception; and, more topically, with Shaw, who by this time had embraced the more radical fringes of the quest for human perfection.

And with that, I think it's time we paused for breath, for this chapter has already had to cover a dizzying variety of subjects just to keep pace with Plum's satirical agenda. And besides, I'm just about done making my point.

Much of what we've looked at so far in this volume does not register among Wodehouse's classics and is usually passed over in studies of Wodehouse World. This isn't because it's necessarily inferior (although by his own exalted standards much of it is); rather, its *specificity* has hopelessly dated it. It's tied down in time and can't wriggle free; and, as I argued in Volume 1, it took Plum the best part of two decades to move on from this manner of addressing reality. It was only when he stopped looking at the world and started to draw his readers into *his* world, that his writing hit its mid-season form and could start freeing itself *from* time. And, as with so much else, it's 1915's *Something Fresh* that serves as the fulcrum in Plum's sensibility, the point where we can witness the transition starting to take place from his journalistic, outsider's approach to the world, and the transformation of that world *within* his imagination.

As he began writing the first of the Blandings series (although he couldn't of course know that), Plum felt he wasn't *quite* up to speed on the factual ins and outs of his country-house setting, so he commissioned some third-party research from an unnamed friend – as he reminisced in 'My World', an essay published in the January 1959 issue of the über-highbrow *Horizon* magazine:

> [I]t was essential for me to inform myself about the personnel of the Servants Hall at a place like [Blandings], my hero . . . having taken on the duties of a visiting valet. I knew a man who knew a lot of dukes and earls, and I asked him to give me the facts.

This wasn't the first time Plum had thought the particulars of an English country house might come in useful. In his second notebook, which he was using prior to 1906, he recorded the roles and arcane nomenclature of the 11 servants in a house he was visiting that belonged to a distant relative of his mother. His research unearthed some minor eccentricities, including the fact that the cook is always addressed as "Mrs" whether married or not; the footmen used their real first names upstairs but different "official" names downstairs; and, appealing to his love of theatre, staff positions within the house were called "characters". This clearly wasn't sufficient for his needs, but armed with his friend's new information (and no doubt some of his own), Plum was able to write the scene in which Ashe Marson and Joan Valentine arrive as counterfeit staff at Blandings, with the reality of life below stairs given the full-on *Downton Abbey* period-drama treatment:

> The door opened. Strong men hurried to take down the trunks, while fair women, in the shape of two nervous scullery-maids, approached . . . and bobbed curtseys. One was there to conduct Joan to the presence of Mrs Twemlow the housekeeper, the other to lead Ashe to where Beach the butler waited . . . After a short walk down a stone-flagged passage, Joan and her escort turned to the right. Ashe's objective appeared to be located to the left.

Each below stairs kingdom – the female ruled by the housekeeper, the male by the butler – is introduced as it would be in a historical drama. And then there's the various strata and sub-strata within this mysterious world, as Joan, who has previous form in this line of work, explains:

> Kitchen maids and scullery maids eat in the kitchen. Chauffeurs, footmen, under-butler, pantry boys, hall boy, odd man and steward's-room footman take their meals in the servants' hall, waited on by the hall boy. The stillroom maids have breakfast and tea in the stillroom, and dinner and supper in the hall. The housemaids and nursery maids have breakfast and tea in the housemaid's sitting-room, and dinner and supper in the hall. The head housemaid ranks next to the head stillroom maid. The laundry maids have a place of their own near the laundry, and the head laundry maid ranks above the head housemaid. The chef has his meals in a room of his own near the kitchen.

All very interesting, but these minutiae don't carry the story any further forward. Indeed, this kind of scene-setting is largely dispensed with in the later novels, a process of de-cluttering his writing had undergone before the next Blandings outing, 1923's *Leave it to Psmith*. By then, it's almost as if Beach runs the place single-handedly with just the odd boot boy, chauffeur, gardener and pig-person for company – and only then if the plot demands their presence, Plum having abandoned his pretensions of being a helpful tour guide, journalist, historian or anthropologist to focus exclusively on the plot. As with his school stories, it wasn't simply getting the detail right that mattered, but the creation of a self-sustaining world that had grown, as if organically, *out of itself*, that had its own unique *atmosphere* (a favourite word of his). But beneath all the editing, exaggeration and styling that would typify this new approach, a sub-frame of reality is still holding things together, allowing his keen satirical instinct to continue its operations in that more subtle, Horatian manner I indicated earlier – more of which in the following chapter.

Another way we can appreciate just how far Wodehouse was from abandoning reality is to look a little deeper at the information his well-connected friend delivered, and what he chose to do – and not do – with it. At this primal stage in Blandings' evolution, Plum could have imagined the castle however he wanted; humungous, medium, small, whatever, for his informant had aimed high, spilling the beans on one of the largest and strangest country houses in England – Welbeck Abbey, presided over by the Dukes of Portland. In the 'My World' essay, Plum remarkably still had his friend's 40-odd year-old statistics to hand and insists on quoting them in full – which I shan't, because they're too voluminous. Suffice to say, Plum was still marvelling all those years later at the mind-boggling scale of the place. Moreover, at this pivotal stage in his writing's evolution, the absolute weirdness of the whole operation, beside which Blandings – even in its mid-season craziness – resembles a model of sound governance, might well have served to blur the distinction in his mind between reality and what he felt he could get away with in his fiction. Once again, it's possible to see Plum, faced with limitless possibility, still wanting to keep things *just this side of real* (for the record, we are eventually told in 1969's *A Pelican at Blandings* that the castle has a modest 52 bedrooms).

If Plum had chosen to write out-and-out fantasy, it's possible to envisage how Blandings *might* have looked from a brief perusal of the stats he provides us with. The Welbeck estate totalled 17,000 acres; the permanent staff of around 220 embraced 42 separate occupations, including a vegetable maid, 40 gardeners, 6 window cleaners, 15 chauffeurs, 50 roadmen, 20 strappers (race-horse grooms), 12 laundresses, 4 firemen and "6 odd men". There were so many buildings, a network of tunnels totalling around fifteen miles was constructed to connect them – if it was raining, and it was unpleasant to ride out, the 5th Duke (1800-1879) had a vast indoor riding house built, 400 feet long and 50 feet high, and an outdoor "tan gallop" of 422 yards in length, lit by 4,000 gas jets and heated for the comfort of the horsemen and women who could use it both day and night all year round. Naturally, a gasworks was built on site to supply it. The kitchen garden alone covered 22 acres and had a "peach wall" around 1,000 feet long heated by braziers. The main house itself comprised dozens upon dozens of rooms, but its crowning glory must have been the underground picture-gallery-*cum*-ballroom that measured 163 feet long by 63 feet wide and 22 feet high.

The 5th Duke himself makes Lord Emsworth appear a shining beacon of sanity. As the main architect of this massive estate that could accommodate and entertain hundreds of people, he was – you guessed it – a recluse. He reportedly lived in just five rooms, all painted pink, and with little furniture. One of them was packed to the ceiling with hundreds of green boxes, each of which contained a single dark brown wig. His bed was wholly enclosed so no one could tell if he was occupying it. Only a few of his staff were allowed to address him, and he preferred to remain unacknowledged. He insisted on a chicken roasting at all hours of the day, and the servants sent him his food on heated trucks that ran on rails through the underground tunnels. He ventured outside mainly by night, accompanied by a lady servant who carried a lantern forty yards ahead of him, but if he did emerge into the daylight, he would don two overcoats, an abnormally tall hat, an extremely high collar, and carried a very large umbrella behind which he could hide should someone chance to speak to him.

The stories that have emerged from Welbeck down the years could tax the imagination of many a fantasist, although the most interesting is perhaps one of the least odd: a few months before Wodehouse made his enquiry about the nobility in 1914, the 6th Duke (clearly something of a socialite compared with his uncle) was entertaining Archduke Franz Ferdinand of Austria, who narrowly avoided being killed in a hunting accident during his stay when a gunloader fell and caused a rifle to go off within feet of the Archduke and his host. And all this happened just eighteen months before the assassination of this very same Archduke triggered the First World War. What if he had died on that winter day in the park at Welbeck instead of on the streets of Sarajevo? The history of Europe might have been rather different if that loader hadn't been so fortunate. But then, the Archduke was no stranger to carnage, having shot an estimated 300,000 animals during his life in the name of sport.

Once again, 'you couldn't make it up'. The list of real-life potty British aristocrats is almost endless, and characters like these blur the distinction between fantasy and reality to such a degree that it's sometimes difficult to tell which is which. Some of those "facts" I just quoted may well be apocryphal – it's difficult to tell, for the Abbey isn't open to the public that often, and most of it not at all. But whether they are verifiable doesn't really matter, because to the imagination they are just as compelling as stories – arguably more compelling for possibly being real. And so, for a writer, particularly one who specializes in humorous fiction, reality's hinterlands are great places to hang around and source material. Plum's bulletins from these strange, liminal locales between reality and fantasy were to become his stock-in-trade – as you'll appreciate when you read Norman Murphy's researches or the obituaries column of the *Daily Telegraph*. How about Lady Cardigan, who died the year *Something* Fresh was being written and lived in a house on the street Plum would move into in 1927? Her full title was Adeline Louisa Maria de Horsey Cardigan and Lancastre; she was wont to greet visitors lying in an open coffin, and could often be seen wearing her first husband's regimental trousers; she once turned down an offer of marriage from former Prime Minister Benjamin Disraeli citing his bad breath, and would regularly promenade in London's Hyde Park sporting a curly blonde wig, tri-cornered hat and leopard-skin cape, while her footman followed carrying her small dog on a pink cushion.

And there's plenty more where she came from. Who's to say that there wasn't a real-life equivalent of Plum's Lord Worplesdon in 'Jeeves Takes Charge'?

> He was the old buster who, a few years later, came down to breakfast one morning, lifted the first cover he saw, said "Eggs! Eggs! Eggs! Damn all eggs!" in an overwrought sort of voice, and instantly legged it for France, never to return to the bosom of the family.

Or how about this, from *Leave it to Psmith*, when the narrator parades Lord Emsworth's experience with lunatics:

> His lordship was no novice in the symptoms of insanity. Several of his best friends were residing in those palatial establishments set in pleasant parks and surrounded by high walls with broken bottles on them, to which the wealthy and aristocratic are wont to retire when the strain of modern life becomes too great. And one of his uncles by marriage, who believed that he was a loaf of bread, had made his first public statement on the matter in the smoking-room of this very castle. What Lord Emsworth did not know about lunatics was not worth knowing.

Only a brave man would deny that many actual aristocrats didn't have a similar set of skeletons in their wardrobes.

What I'm getting at is that ultimately, the reality or otherwise of the Wodehouse ethos is not quite the distinction we should be pondering; for as the critic Ernest Newman perceptively remarked as early as 1956, the strength of Plum's created world lies not in "invention" but "treatment" – how he alchemizes our world into his. Anyone can invent a world; but what they can't always do is make it ring true. Wodehouse's ready facility for doing this, says Newman,

> . . . accounts for the fact that we can always re-read with gusto the old Wodehouse books, while nothing on earth

would induce us to re-read the yesteryear novels of Mr X or Mr Z, though these gentlemen present us with a different set of characters and a different plot and a different series of actions in each of their books.

Newman is absolutely right, and his remarks strike deep into the heart of what makes Wodehouse World so successful: Plum's formulaic "treatment" of existing reality (what I've been calling his "lightness") is so utterly congenial, he didn't *need* to invent fantastical realities. Plum doesn't transport us elsewhere in order to work his magic; he simply tweaks where we already are – and on many occasions, as we've started seeing in this chapter, the real world went out of its way to do the job for him.

And so it is that the deeper we get into Wodehouse World, the less the boundaries between the books cease to matter, even if we can remember which is which. On several occasions during my early acquaintance with Plum I would start reading a story, only to realize about 50 pages in that I'd read it before. Or, more frustratingly, bought it before with my precious pocket money. Even now I sometimes hesitate when trying to recollect whether a particular plot came from *Thank You Jeeves* or *Much Obliged, Jeeves* – while not really caring. For Wodehouse World is a timeless one we exist *inside*, a place where we can feel we belong, however we conceive it. And as with all great fictional worlds, it's only when something violates that perfect symbiosis – a hiatus in the reader's mood or attention, a poor third-party adaptation, or those occasions where Wodehouse himself nods and lets the daylight in on magic – that the soufflé sags and the comedy loses some of its oomph. Too much reality or too much fantasy doesn't sit well with Plum; but once he had finally gained the confidence to tease both the real and fantastical elements he needed *out of* life, and, most critically, to play them off against one another, he had finally found the means by which his comic talent could truly thrive. And satire, that tool of the armchair rebel, was truly where Wodehouse World began.

Let's see what he made with it next.

ARMCHAIR
REBEL

Chapter 3:
Armchair Rebel

Nobody ever wants to do anything except what
they are not allowed to do.
A Prefect's Uncle

When Mike was pleased with life, he always found a difficulty
in obeying Authority and its rules.
Mike at Wrykyn

My friends, it is the rotten way this world's run. I would give some-
thing to manage matters for five minutes. Just five minutes. Yes, sir!
'Under the Flail'

"Do you take an active interest in world politics?"
"Not very active . . . What with cleaning the silver and
brushing the dog".
Cocktail Time

"Rebellion" and "P.G. Wodehouse" are not words that have traditionally been associated with one another. And yet they should be, for even the
most cursory inspection of Wodehouse World reveals it to be a seething
hotbed of agitation, some of it not so polite, from beginning to end. Or
as Richard Usborne sagely noted,

> [Wodehouse] backed young against old, prisoner against mag-
> istrate, nephew against aunt, chorus girl against star, curate
> against bishop, best-selling female novelist against precious pas-
> tels-in-prose writer or willowy poet.

Confrontation is everywhere. Take, for example, the disgraceful way
Wodehouse treats the forces of law and order, the thin blue line that
separates civilization from anarchy.

As early as 1903, in an article written for *Punch* entitled 'Our
Magistrates', a Knut is hauled before the beak for kicking a policeman
in the stomach ("jolly hard, too"), and is let off with a half-crown ($12\frac{1}{2}$
pence) fine and the most perfunctory caution. The same offence is committed in 1919's *A Damsel in Distress* by Lord Belpher, and in 1926's 'The
Inferiority Complex of Old Sippy' George Sipperly recollects how he

"punch[ed] a policeman in the stomach on Boat-Race night", attracting 30 days without the option. But did this exemplary sentence deter future assaults on that notoriously riotous evening? Hardly: Bertie is famously fined "five of the best" at Bosher Street Magistrates Court "for trying to separate a policeman from his helmet", a badge he wears with pride in several novels and stories. As does our old friend Roderick Spode in *The Code of the Woosters*. As late as 1958 in 'The Right Approach', we are informed that Augustus Mulliner has had no fewer than three fines for similar disorderly conduct on the night of the contest. Not to be left out, even the senior clergy – in the person of the Bishop of Stortford – plugs Constable Booker in the eye in 'Gala Night' following a dose of Buck-U-Uppo.

But not all the assault and battery on the boys in blue can be put down to youthful high jinks warmed by alcohol and patent remedies; indeed, there seems to be an escalation in the severity of the attacks as Wodehouse grew older: 1948's *Uncle Dynamite* has Constable Harry Potter (!) pushed into a duck pond and his eye blackened; in 1949's *The Mating Season*, that pillar of respectability Jeeves strikes Constable Ernest Dobbs from behind with a rubber cosh, knocking him senseless, and in *Do Butlers Burgle Banks* from 1968 Charlie Yost even shoots Sergeant Claude Potter of Scotland Yard "in the fleshy part of the right upper arm". Women are not left out of the fun, and pitch in with the best of them; in 1970's *The Girl in Blue*, Bernadette "Barney" Claybourne somehow manages to push the 16-stone Constable Ernest Simms into a convenient brook without him being aware of her identity, getting away scot-free with the serious felony of attempted drowning.

Plum had no obvious beef with the rozzers, and quite why he's so down on the forces of law and order is difficult to fathom. Most are either slow-witted comic figures given to communicating in monosyllables ("Ho!" being a favourite), or mean-spirited types after an easy collar – that is, when they're not being used as punchbags. But this is all part of a general undercurrent of sticking it to the man that is welcomed and even celebrated from the start to finish of Wodehouse's writing career. Take Gally Threepwood, a loveable old buster who was arrested so often in his prime that he got to be on first-name terms with most West End policemen; more, we are told, than any other other man in London. But is he ashamed of his erstwhile excesses? Absolutely not; in *Summer Lightning* he is planning to immortalize his misdemeanours in his memoirs. Although nine out of his ten sisters consider him a "deplorable" waster, Plum presents him as a clubland hero, a generous, optimistic and unreformable lord of mischief who demonstrates a Pavlovian distrust of authority.

Rebellion can take many forms, even inside an ethos as rigidly controlled as Plum's. Some are so discreet they don't always announce themselves. As we witnessed in the previous volume, the prevailing dynamic of a Wodehouse plot is a battle between the forces of change and the status quo: whether the agents of revolution are human troublemakers like Gally, Uncle Fred and Psmith, or something as ubiquitous and miasmic as love, the rhythms of disruption and resolution are almost endemic, shaking things up prior to re-ordering them by the story's end. And we might even argue that the way Wodehouse quietly destabilizes reality is itself mutinous, offering us alternative ways of looking at our own world – for this is one of the ways his satirical sense found an outlet once he'd left journalism behind. Wodehouse World isn't merely a distillation of reality, but a wholesale subversion of it.

For example, he uses the very act of writing as a metaphor for sedition in his first published novel. We have already met "Alderman" Charteris from 1902's *The Pothunters*, the schoolboy proprietor of an underground magazine; and in a story from the following year, 'The Manoeuvres of Charteris', we find him debating another manifestation of his rebellious instinct – bunking off to a nearby village:

> "My dear chap, what does it matter? The worst that can happen to you for breaking bounds is a couple of hundred lines, and I've got a capital of four hundred already in stock. Besides, things would be so slow if you always kept in bounds. I always feel like a cross between Dick Turpin and Machiavelli when I go to Stapleton. It's an awfully jolly feeling. Like warm treacle running down your back. It's cheap at two hundred lines".

Whilever he's at school, Charteris will be at war with the headmaster's authority, not for any particular reason, but simply because it's there to be resisted, like Marlon Brando's character in *The Wild One* who, when asked what he's rebelling against, replies "Whaddya got?". Rebellion is such a fixity in Charteris's life, he even prepares his lines in advance, knowing he'll be needing them when he's caught and punished. As he later explains, he doesn't hate the headmaster on a personal level, it's just that the authority the "Old Man" represents tends to cramp his style, preventing him from indulging one or two harmless activities, such as breaking bounds, that he clearly enjoys. And the risk of some collateral damage in the form of lines isn't enough of a threat to stop him relishing that "awfully jolly feeling" of warm, oozing treacle. Rebellion for Charteris is not an adrenaline rush, but something more akin to a comfort blanket he can wrap himself up in, a cross between the exploits of a highwayman (Dick Turpin) and a courtly intellectual cabalist (Machiavelli).

Is he Wodehouse, or someone Plum would like to have been had he the chutzpah? We'll probably never know; but it's no doubt significant that very few of Plum's leading schoolboys are goody two shoes, actively relishing the illegal delights of "breaking out" after the 10 o'clock curfew, climbing out of windows and down drainpipes to freedom. In *The White Feather*, they indulge in after-hours billiards and smoke Turkish cigarettes, and in *Mike*, we're told that when Mike Jackson "was pleased with life he always found a difficulty in obeying Authority and its rules", even sneaking downstairs to listen to gramophone records in his housemaster's study in the middle of the night. As responsible adults, they can quickly re-connect with their inner schoolboy renegade by the simple application of alcohol or Buck-U-Uppo. In 'The Bishop's Move', Lord Hemel of Hempstead's statue is painted pink by the titular clergyman ("Boko") and a public-school headmaster ("Catsmeat"), proving that you can take a boy out of school, but you can't take the schoolboy out of a grown man – even in the case of lofty Establishment figures.

If school life is a series of small-time power struggles between the forces of authority and those lower down the pecking order – well, that is what Plum's later, adult plots become too. In his romantic comedies, these small wars are fought between the armies of youth and age, family tussles in which nephews and nieces are pitted against uncles and aunts. Only occasionally do things threaten to take a more serious turn when parents and children clash. But in the first two post-school Psmith novels, tussles between the rulers and the ruled move outwards from families and small-scale institutions and into society at large, embracing much broader principles and even party politics. 1910's *Psmith in the City*, which began life as a six-part serial in *The Captain* magazine, is something more than a schoolboy story, for although working in a bank was a career many of the paper's readers would pursue in later life, the plot is really an extended and quite detailed disquisition on the nature of authority and how to get round it. It could even be used as a manual on 'How (but Mainly How Not) to Be a Manager', or even 'How to Manage Your Manager.' As Jeeves would later put it in 'Bertie Changes

His Mind', "[e]mployers are like horses. They want managing. Some of us have the knack of managing them, some haven't". Jeeves and Psmith both have.

Psmith in the City features four senior figures at the New Asiatic Bank, three junior and one senior. Of the junior managers, there is Mr Rossiter of Postage, who, according to one of his subordinates, is a "[f]ussy little brute. Won't leave you alone. Always trying to catch you on the hop". To Mike, the non-too-bright cricket ace who is on the receiving end of these attentions, "the restraint of the business was irksome. He had been used to an open-air life, and a life, in its way, of excitement". And so the more Rossiter's over-particular management style clips his wings, the angrier and more downcast he gets:

> "What's the good of it all? You go and sweat all day at a desk, day after day, for about twopence a year. And when you're about eighty-five, you retire. It isn't living at all. It's simply being a bally vegetable".

The gloom intensifies when he moves on to Mr Gregory's very different but equally dreadful kingdom in Fixed Deposits. The "crimson and wrathful" Gregory is a bank veteran with a bad liver and a foul mouth whose default mode of address is to shout "as if he were competing against a high wind". The daily "fountain of abuse" further deepens Mike's gloom, for he "hated being shouted at. It confused him".

But a sympathetic manager, such as our third incumbent Mr Waller, is able to bring out the best in him – such as it is. The bank veteran takes time not only to be courteous but to show him the ropes, and to Mike, "it was a pleasant change to find someone who really seemed to care what happened to him"; indeed, "his heart warmed to the benevolent man". At one o'clock on his first day in the office, Waller takes him to a local lunch counter and engages him in conversation, and once again we are told that Mike was "genuinely grateful to the cashier for troubling to seek him out and be friendly to him", for "[g]ratitude for any good turn done to him was a leading characteristic of Mike's nature".

A little kindness goes a long way, particularly with someone who is of a similarly generous disposition; and yet in two of the three junior managers, it appears to be in short supply. Mr Rossiter is by nature one of life's fussers, forever sweating the small stuff. But the bullying Gregory is the sadder case, for Plum gives us the impression that the Bank probably turned him this way – a case of nurture to Rossiter's nature. For the bank's City branch, we learn, is merely a way station where clerks are given three years' training before being shipped out to the Far East, "where you're the dickens of a big pot straight away, with a big screw and a dozen native Johnnies under you". Some of Mike's colleagues, like the fresh-faced Bannister, can't wait to leave to start their new lives as expat tin-pot potentates, lording it over the locals ("Bit of all right, that"). Perhaps Gregory was like this once: young and eager, but now bitter and twisted, his browbeating manner and dependence on alcohol a legacy of those times when he could abuse what power he had and get away with it more easily. But Mike, in a rare moment of foresight, is not remotely enamoured by the prospect before him:

> "What's the good of going out East? [You] end by getting some foul sort of fever . . and being booted out as no further use to the bank".

Not dissimilar, then, to his creator, for whom the thought of life in the Orient "scared the pants off me" (*Over Seventy*).

So: three managers, three types, who we might call the nitpicker, the bully and the sympathizer. Mike, an uncomplicated, generous soul can only respond to the last of them, someone who treats him with a modicum of respect. And he responds in kind, taking a big fall for Waller when the latter mistakenly cashes a dud cheque, getting himself the sack to protect the older family man by claiming the gaffe as his own. It doesn't seem to occur to Mike to rebel in any way; he will always do his best within his limited capabilities, lacking both the initiative and the nous to better his downtrodden situation. He is one of those staff members the system will ultimately chew up and spit out.

Psmith, however, could not be more different: an instinctive rebel, he knows that on the first day in a new job, you have to make a start on the long and sometimes tedious process of managing your manager – that is, if you are going to escape with your sanity intact and not end up a liverish time server. His default weapon is his motor mouth – he can talk anyone into silence; and from his very first encounter with Rossiter, he starts messing with his new manager's mind. Here's the second of three long and brilliant paragraphs that bludgeon his new boss into an early submission:

> "I am now a member of the staff of this bank. Its interests are my interests. Psmith, the individual, ceases to exist, and

there springs into being Psmith, the cog in the wheel of the New Asiatic Bank; Psmith, the link in the bank's chain; Psmith, the Worker. I shall not spare myself", he proceeded earnestly. "I shall toil with all the accumulated energy of one who, up till now, has only known what work is like from hearsay. Whose is that form sitting on the steps of the bank in the morning, waiting eagerly for the place to open? It is the form of Psmith, the Worker. Whose is that haggard, drawn face which bends over a ledger long after the other toilers have sped blithely westwards to dine at Lyons' Popular Café? It is the face of Psmith, the Worker".

Although Psmith's soliloquy is utter horse gas, it certainly does the trick. "Two minutes later", we are told, "Mr Rossiter was sitting at his desk with a dazed expression, while Psmith, perched gracefully on a stool, entered figures in a ledger". For anyone who comes into contact with Psmith has to bow to the demands of his world rather than the other way round. He cannot be managed, and having successfully disorientated his superior by claiming that work is an exciting new discovery, he then reels the dizzy Rossiter in.

Learning that his boss is a Manchester United supporter, Psmith loses no opportunity in engaging him on his favourite topic of conversation – having done some prior research into an activity of which he has no prior knowledge and precious little interest. Plum, no mean sports writer himself, has also done his homework, satirizing the columns of his fellow back-page journalists:

> The football editions of the evening papers are not reticent about those who play the game: and Psmith drank in every detail with the thoroughness of the conscientious student. By the end of the fortnight he knew what was the favourite breakfast-food of J. Turnbull; what Sandy Turnbull wore next his skin; and who, in the opinion of Meredith, was England's leading politician. These facts, imparted to and discussed with Mr Rossiter, made the progress of the *entente cordiale* rapid.

All these names were genuine Man U. players of the Edwardian era, the newspapers' obsession with sports trivia identical with that of our own time. But more important is the end product of this new-found camaraderie, with the Postage department becoming "quite a happy family", its former staff "amazed at the change that had come over Mr Rossiter", no longer the "pouncing panther" who would grass up his staff to senior management at the drop of a hat. Once again, kindness and understanding are the key to a brighter future for everyone, something that Psmith instinctively understands – while making life easier for himself now his boss isn't shadowing his every move: "I do not despair" says the Machiavellian clerk, "of training Comrade Rossiter one of these days to jump through paper hoops".

Now Rossiter has been brought to heel, Psmith is free to move on to his sternest challenge – our fourth panjandrum, the branch manager Mr Bickersdyke, whose very surname suggests a bruising argument. This is a very different kind of confrontation, for Bickersdyke is a nasty piece of work, at least by Wodehouse standards. We know right from the start he's a bad 'un, for his uncouth and ignorant act of walking across the sight screen while a cricket match is in progress leads to Mike being clean bowled, the momentary distraction depriving him of his century in "what was, to date, the best innings of his life" (the invading Russian army was soon to commit the identical crime at the Surrey Oval in *The Swoop!*). What's worse, Bickersdyke is both unaware of what he's done, and not only unrepentant but aggressively defensive when his misdemeanour is pointed out. The next time we meet him, he's Mike and Psmith's boss, a short, stout man with a thin-lipped mouth, slightly protruding eyes and, sin of sins in Wodehouse World, a ragged moustache. You can tell Plum *really* doesn't like him.

It's been conjectured (by Barry Phelps, Robert McCrum and others) that Plum's model for Bickersdyke was Sir Ewen Cameron (British ex-Prime Minister David Cameron's great-great grandfather), with whom the young clerk overlapped at the H.S.B. This is entirely possible, given that both men were from humble backgrounds and worked their way up through the ranks. However, unlike Cameron who stuck to banking for his entire life, Bickersdyke has got himself selected as a Parliamentary candidate – but one with a guilty secret:

> He had stood for Parliament once before, several years back, in the North. He had been defeated by a couple of thousand votes, and he hoped that the episode had been forgotten. Not merely because his defeat had been heavy. There was another reason. On that occasion he had stood as a Liberal. He was standing for Kenningford as a

Unionist. Of course, a man is at perfect liberty to change his views, if he wishes to do so, but the process is apt to give his opponents a chance of catching him (to use the inspired language of the music-halls) on the bend.

Oo-er, missus. Like Churchill and Chamberlain before him, Bickersdyke, has already crossed the floor. But his political odyssey stretches even further back than that – to a time when, in his youth, he embraced Socialism – and a quite Radical form of Socialism at that, as Psmith informs us:

> "About twenty years ago, when [Waller] and Comrade Bickersdyke worked hand-in-hand as fellow clerks at the New Asiatic, they were both members of the Tulse Hill Parliament, that powerful institution. At that time Comrade Bickersdyke was as fruity a Socialist as Comrade Waller is now. Only, apparently, as he began to get on a bit in the world, he altered his views to some extent as regards the iniquity of freezing on to a decent share of the doubloons. And that, you see, is where the dim and rusty past begins to get mixed up with the live, vivid present".

The politically pliable Bickersdyke is now revealed as having travelled almost the full distance from left-wing (Socialism) via the sort-of-centre (Liberal) to right-wing (Unionism), so Psmith has indeed caught his boss "on the bend" and puts this sensitive information to good use – as we'll see in a moment. The branch manager was never sufficiently well-born to be a shoo-in for high office, and his sin – at least in Plum's insinuation – is to have serially changed his political allegiances to suit his social and financial ambitions. The higher he climbs, the more right-wing he becomes. Waller, by contrast, has never been tempted to follow him up the greasy pole, so a Socialist he remains, and a useful foil for alerting us to his boss's many shortcomings. Essentially, Waller is true to himself; Bickersdyke doesn't appear to have a self to be true *to*. And in the Wodehousean scheme of things, this pliable embrace of contingency counts against him.

Bickersdyke's stump speech early in the novel expresses a hearty rightist contempt for some of the topical issues we looked at earlier: Free Trade (making him an ally of Chamberlain); the proposed budget cuts in the Royal Navy and "Alien Immigration". But even the briefest glance at the minutes of the Tulse Hill Parliament – helpfully provided by Waller – provides Psmith with this smoking gun, and as he leafs through the ledger in Bickersdyke's presence he remarks, "I like the bit where you call the Royal Family blood-suckers" before litotically adding "Your political views have changed a great deal since those days, have they not?" Were this to make the papers, Bickersdyke's political ambitions would instantly be toast. But Psmith makes him an offer he can't refuse, those secrets are kept hidden, and he squeezes home with a slender majority of 157, the election punctuated by cheery violence from the many-headed of Kenningford:

> Psmith, who went down on the polling-day to inspect the revels and came back with his hat smashed in, reported that, as far as he could see, the electors of Kenningford seemed to be in just that state of happy intoxication which might make them vote for Mr Bickersdyke by mistake.

Plum would have read, and probably greatly enjoyed Charles Dickens's hilarious account of the Eatanswill by-election in *The Pickwick Papers*, in which the town's brandy supply is laced with laudanum to keep its voters from exercising their democratic right. But his satire stops somewhat short of his fellow writer's brutally inventive cynicism, for at this stage in his career, Plum was still trying to keep things real. Well, real-ish.

But although Wodehouse quite clearly loathes the Bickersdykes of this world, that doesn't make him necessarily more sympathetic to Waller's Socialism, which is both subversive and revolutionary, advocating the abolition of plutocrats, the House of Lords and even the aforementioned Royal Family. Indeed, like many a satirist, Plum seems to have no firm allegiances of his own, giving everyone from whatever branch of politics the gimlet eye. On the left, bypassing the fundamentally decent Waller, he sharpens his wit on Comrade Prebble, an arrogant windbag with whom he has considerable fun. At a Sunday tea party held in Waller's parlour, Prebble holds forth on his favourite subject, causing Mike to realize that "till now, he had never known what boredom meant. There had been moments in his life which had been less interesting than other moments, but nothing to touch this for agony". On moving into the drawing room, Mike is once again singled out for one-to-one indoctrination, with Prebble "like the Ancient Mariner, [holding] him with a glittering eye", having apparently "only touched the fringe of his subject in his [previous] lecture".

This is an early rehearsal for Bertie's awkward tea party in 1922's 'Comrade Bingo', which mercilessly impales the left-wing rhetoric of Old Rowbotham, who is keen on massacring the bourgeoisie, sacking Park Lane and disembowelling the hereditary aristocracy, even daring to criticize Jeeves to his face as "an obsolete relic of an exploded feudal system". Similarly, when Rowbotham's fellow traveller Comrade Pott tears Bertie off a strip for providing a lavish afternoon tea ("I wonder the food didn't turn to ashes in our mouths! Eggs! Muffins! Sardines! All wrung from the bleeding lips of the starving poor!"), it becomes evident on his departure that not only has he "pretty well finished the ham", but "if you had shoved the remainder of the jam into the bleeding lips of the starving poor it would hardly have made them sticky". Someone lacking an ear for the cadences of political rhetoric – or an understanding of political hypocrisy – simply couldn't have written that.

Like those of his creator, Psmith's politics remain a mystery. Addressing all and sundry as "Comrade", and confessing to Bickersdyke that "I incline to the Socialist view" are simply smoke screens to conceal – what, exactly? On one occasion, he finds his adopted convictions challenged not by ideology, but his colleague Bristow's choice of garish waistcoat:

> "It's discouraging, this sort of thing. I try always to think well of my fellow man . . . I do my best to see the good that is in him, but it's hard. Comrade Bristow's the most striking argument against the equality of man I've ever come across".

Things aren't always so jokey, however. Back at school, the first time Psmith mentions Socialism (in 1908's 'The Lost Lambs'), he shows himself to be both astute and cynical about his new hobby, proclaiming it to be "a great scheme . . . You work for the equal distribution of property, and start by collaring all you can and sitting on it". Later in the story, he impresses on Mike that in grabbing one of the prized two-man studies before anyone else, they should have no guilt in "stak[ing] out our claims. This is practical Socialism".

By the following year, however, this cynicism has altered somewhat. Back in Volume 2, I labelled Psmith one of Plum's "Fixers", along with Uncle Fred and Gally Threepwood, characters who duck and weave their way through life in their attempts to distribute sweetness and light as widely as possible. Their methods aren't always orthodox – or sometimes even legal – but their instinct is to leave the world a better place than they found it. And this, accompanied by an eye for bettering his own position, is Psmith's take on political philanthropy, his "Socialism", which, as he informs Bickersdyke, "is rather of the practical sort" rather than the endless windbaggery of Comrade Prebble. By the end of *Psmith in the City*, he has not only transformed the Postage department into a pleasant place to work, he has also managed to free Mike (and himself) from Bickersdyke's bullying attentions and gained them both places at Cambridge University, following which Mike's future will be assured when he becomes the land agent of Mr Smith senior's estate. Having "solved all [his friend's] difficulties and smoothed out all the rough places which were looming in [his] path", Psmith has made a solid start in his Fixer's career, conveniently bankrolled by his wealthy father.

His next brush with 'real' politics occurs in *Psmith, Journalist*. Stewart Waring is a high-ranking Commissioner of Buildings in New York City, whose slum tenements become the focus of Psmith's attentions as the temporary sub-editor of *Cosy Moments* magazine. Waring is a grafter, who, in return for large bungs from property developers, rubber stamps the construction of "rotten [tenement] buildings . . . a strong breeze would have knocked down" which quickly degenerate into slums. Once again, it's easy to tell that Plum doesn't like him, for Waring has supervised the construction of a music hall built with "material about as strong as a heap of meringues" which has led to its collapse "kill[ing] half the audience". Like Bickersdyke, Waring is seeking higher office – as an Alderman, one of the city's lawmakers, while secretly owning some of these dingy tenements on which he collects sizeable rents. Armed with this information, Psmith catches another high-up on the bend; if it were to be revealed in *Cosy Moments* that Waring was a slum landlord, his chance of election would suffer a damaging blow.

Surviving several cack-handed attempts to rub him out, Psmith eventually manages to extract $5003 dollars from Waring to refurbish the properties, or as he puts it, "making those tenements fit for a tolerably fastidious pig to live in" (the odd $3 will buy him a new hat, replacing a titfer that was ruined by a stray bullet). And after Psmith has won the upper hand, Plum includes a short homiletic remark that wouldn't sound out of place in one of his more sententious public school scenarios:

> The Waring type is dangerous when it is winning, but it is
> apt to crumple up against strong defence.

And so it is here; Psmith has once again (metaphorically) punched the bully on the nose and won. The payment made, he agrees to keep schtum about Waring's property portfolio, dismissing the grafter with a slice of convincing *realpolitik*:

> "I have been studying the papers of late, and it seems to me that it doesn't much matter who gets elected . . . the other candidates appear to be a pretty fair contingent of blighters. If the People are chumps enough to elect you, then they deserve you".

When Plum is writing politics, only the least suitable appear to seek office, giving the would-be rebel plenty to rebel against. But squirrel away that pay-off about the People being "chumps", for it will be receiving deeper scrutiny in Chapter 4.

As we'll see momentarily, the likes of Waring aren't exactly typical of Wodehouse World, more a sort of early aberration that disappeared once Plum's lightness had started to work its magic. By the next time we meet Psmith, the nature of rebellion in Wodehouse novels has also changed, and we can conveniently turn to Psmith's final novelistic outing as an illustration of the new improved order at work.

From 1909 to 1923, our hero took an extended vacation, returning in re-workings of earlier material until 1915 but then disappearing off the radar until *Leave it to Psmith*. During the crucial intervening period, Wodehouse's world mushroomed in his imagination and his writing style came close to being perfected. The only thing that's happened to Psmith is that he no longer has his father's fortune to aid and abet his philanthropy. He's still a practical Socialist, but the canny Wodehouse, now on top of his craft, has limited his character's ambitions so that they are now more proportionately tailored to his unique talents and newly straitened circumstances. Instead of taking on the violently-inclined slum landlords of New York or even uppity bank managers, he brings about his version of social justice by the more roundabout strategy of purloining umbrellas in London's clubland. Obviously.

Psmith's first encounter with his future fiancée Eve Halliday is brought about by a sudden impulse to play Robin Hood with The Honourable Hugo Walderwick's brolly, which he steals and silently presents to her as she shelters from the rain under a shop awning. Only later that day does the theft become apparent:

"Do you mean to say you gave me somebody else's umbrella?"

"I had unfortunately omitted to bring my own out with me this morning".

"I never heard of such a thing!"

"Merely practical Socialism. Other people are content to talk about the Redistribution of Property. I go out and do it".

Then, of course, there's "Comrade" Walderwick to be appeased. But being a Drone of "a very C3 [low] intelligence", it doesn't prove one of Psmith's greatest challenges:

"You have lost your umbrella, Comrade Walderwick, but in what a cause! In what a cause, Comrade Walderwick! You are now entitled to rank with Sir Philip Sidney and Sir Walter Raleigh. The latter is perhaps the closer historical parallel. He spread his cloak to keep a queen from wetting her feet. You – by proxy – yielded up your umbrella to save a girl's hat. Posterity will be proud of you, Comrade Walderwick. You will go down with legend and song. Children in ages to come will cluster about their grandfather's knees, saying: 'Tell us how the great Walderwick lost his umbrella, grandpa!' And he will tell them, and they will rise from the recital better, deeper, broader children".

Plum is here playing down the Politics and introducing Literature into the equation in the form of two of the Elizabethan era's most revered love poets, Sidney and Raleigh, both of them swashbucklers and word-smiths. Fame of an eternal stripe awaits Walderwick not in the annals of politics but in "legend and song", immortalizing his selfless if wholly unintended act of generosity in endless art. All of which is vintage Psmithian applesauce – and yet not altogether so, for here we are nearly one hundred years on celebrating the part Walderwick and his brolly have played in one of Plum's finest novels.

Despite this being his swansong, Psmith's socialism was apparently set to continue in this helpful, philanthropic vein: in his preface to a 1968 American edition of *Mike and Psmith*, Plum tells us that the monocled one "inevitably" becomes a "prosperous counsellor at the bar like Perry Mason, specializing, like Perry, in appearing for the defense" – still fighting for the underdog against the world's bullies, still being of service. In *Leave it to Psmith*, however, his public-facing acts of rebellion with their accompanying big themes have disappeared.

And yet somehow, they haven't, for isn't human kindness itself quite a big theme? Even when it manifests itself in the tiniest things of life? Small increments, not big gestures, turn out to be the agents of change in Wodehouse World, and from the very start, dissent was as much about *who* was being rebelled against as *what*, the individual him/herself rather than what that individual represents. The point or principle at issue (the *what*) sometimes threatened to be more important than its human agent (the *who*), and when this happened the results would never truly mesh with Plum's approach to comedy. The stakes were simply too big, the scope too spacious; too much confrontation, too little accommodation, we might say – or even too much Juvenal, too little Horace. In the case of Waring, a single, sketchily-drawn character is being called on to embody massive themes of greed and corruption that were endemic throughout New York governance, and frankly, he's not up to the job. That said, Plum did have one decent stab at a 3D villain who might make the grade in a hard-boiled crime novel: in some of the many versions of *A Gentleman of Leisure*, John McEachern adeptly plays the system, and almost makes the grade.

Expelled from Eton, the erstwhile John Forrest crosses the Atlantic, adopts an Irish surname and re-invents himself as a policeman in the Big Apple. In Chapter 3 of the 1910 novel version, Plum provides us with a long and detailed account of his ascent up the ladder of corruption, making sure we know that the infrastructure is well established within New York's Finest to help him on his way. Graft is portrayed as the most natural thing in the world, and in the earliest version of the story ('The Gem Collector'), it's hinted that McEachern will go all the way and seek election as the city's Mayor. Starting out as a humble beat cop, he extracts small sums from bars that want to stay open later than their licence allows. Soon he has the $3,000 necessary to buy his promotion to detective-sergeant, which gives him greater scope. Word gets around, and the city now seems full of "philanthropists" prepared to "dress his front" in return for looking the other way, and he quickly amasses the $15,000 he requires to make him a captain. At this point, he discovers that "El Dorado was no mere poet's dream" and has to keep records of his holdings in "house property, railroad shares, and a dozen other profitable things". He is "like Moses on the mountain, looking down into the Promised Land" – albeit a promised land built entirely on sleaze. The American Dream, early Wodehouse style; and not a million miles away from the theme of *The Great Gatsby* that Plum's future neighbour, F. Scott Fitzgerald, would publish 15 years later.

But although Wodehouse is keen to let us know that *he* knows how the system works, he was never cut out to be a social crusader. Moreover, none of this is particularly funny, and these three proto-villains we've been looking at (Bickersdyke, Waring, McEachern) generally sour the atmosphere of the stories they appear in. Comic novels were never going to advance the cause of freedom and fair play in any radical way, as Plum himself acknowledges when he proposes that Waring will more than likely get elected, Bickersdyke actually does, and McEachern doesn't end up in jail. Nor did opening large cans of actual worms mix too well with love stories of the kind that graces *A Gentleman of Leisure*. Best leave that campaigning stuff to out-and-out realists like Upton Sinclair, whose sensational 1906 novel *The Jungle*, set in the Chicago meat-packing industry, had recently caused a massive outcry and would ultimately lead to the creation of the Food and Drug Administration (F.D.A.). In order to do that Sinclair had had to shock, and Plum wasn't in the business of having his characters fall into mincing machines or children being eaten alive by rats. It was far easier (and lighter) to make his satire arise naturally out of his characters' individual behaviour, and not anything bigger and more overwhelming that they might represent. Therefore, any future Bickersdyke would not be a Unionist first and a bully second, but the other way about – that is, if his political affiliation was mentioned at all. Plum first had to ditch the labels, or at least play them down, switching the focus from issues to personalities. While not everyone would be interested in seeing a Unionist defeated, just about everyone loves it when a bully gets his just deserts or at least has the wind taken out of his sails. So having flirted with big subjects, Plum didn't quite show them the door; rather he cut them down to a size where he could convincingly subvert them with humour. As I noted just now, when mid-season Wodehouse World hove into view, it was not so much *what* there was to rebel against but *who*.

Characters of this new mid-season kidney are physically and temperamentally not that dissimilar from their predecessors, differing only in how Plum writes *about* them. Invariably florid male aristocrats or businessmen who enjoy throwing their considerable weight around, their sour, suspicious, misanthropic dispositions tend to be exacerbated by a variety of intestinal disorders linked to a ballooning BMI. Though they may be successful, Plum is already punishing them by blighting their lives not just with poor health, but a general dissatisfaction with their lot in life, the world never *quite* living up to their lofty, entitled expectations.

There's a good, generic description of their caste to be found in the opening of 1924's *Bill the Conqueror*, with the spotlight on Sir George Alexander "Stinker" Pyke, soon to become the press and publishing baron Lord Tilbury:

> It is the custom nowadays to describe all successful men who are stumpy and about twenty pounds overweight as Napoleonic. But, hackneyed though the adjective is, it must be admitted that there was indeed something suggestive of Napoleon in the port of Sir George Pyke as he strode up and down his office. His generously-filled waistcoat and the habit he dropped into in moments of meditation of thrusting the fingers of his right hand in between its first and second buttons gave at any rate a superficial resemblance to the great Corsican—and this resemblance was accentuated by the gravity of his plump, determined face. He looked like a man fond of having his own way: nor in the last twenty years of his life had he often failed to get it.

So – not a Conservative Unionist, but "Napoleonic", a historical reference all his readers would recognize, since by the early 20th century the adjective, along with its negative connotations, had already entered the language. It's an epithet Plum uses frequently for vertically-challenged, overbearing, selfish types who have absolutely no thought for the well-being of others. Once again, notice the shift from issue to character in the way Plum alchemizes unpleasantness within his created vision. He isn't implying the whole world's unpleasant, just this person. The effect is local, not general – and hence fixable, one grump at a time.

An early prototype of this formula, one that Plum had yet to perfect, is the financier Benjamin Scobell from 1912's *The Prince and Betty* who is also described "a goblin in fairyland . . . somewhat below the middle height . . . lean of body and vulturine of face" with "a greedy mouth, a hooked nose, liquid green eyes and a sallow complexion". Quite a catch, then. But Scobell is ugly on the inside as well. He is another Big Apple slum landlord, a man who knows the price of everything, the value of nothing, is tone deaf to poetry and purblind to the beauties of the natural world. His tragedy, as we learn from the 1931 rewrite *A Prince for Hire* is that while he is stinking rich, he has never learned how to enjoy spending his money. For Plum's Napoleons are almost invariably misers too, financially as well as spiritually parsimonious.

Another example from this era of prototypes is the *soi-disant* "Napoleon of Finance" Geoffrey Windlebird (sometimes Windleband) from the *A Man of Means* stories who sells shares in gold mines short on gold, with a sideline in get-rich-quick schemes. For a man who supposedly lived with his head in the clouds, Plum absolutely understands how the scam works – and not only that, is able to explain it crisply and efficiently in words of one syllable:

> Say, for instance, that the Home-grown Tobacco Trust, founded by Geoffrey in a moment of ennui, failed to yield those profits which the glowing prospectus had led the public to expect. Geoffrey would appease the excited shareholders by giving them Preference Shares (interest guaranteed) in the Sea-gold Extraction Company, hastily floated to meet the emergency. When the interest became due, it would, as likely as not, be paid out of the capital just subscribed for the King Solomon's Mines Exploitation Association, the little deficiency in the latter being replaced in its turn, when absolutely necessary and not a moment before, by the transfer of some portion of the capital just raised for yet another company. And so on, *ad infinitum.* There were moments when it seemed to Mr Windlebird that he had solved the problem of Perpetual Promotion.

Plum would rarely parade such in-depth knowledge of dodgy finance again; in the future when a scam is in the offing, the mechanics are kept far, far simpler than this. Take "Soapy" Molloy's substantial oeuvre dating between 1925 and 1972, or "Oily" Carlisle's attempts in *Big Money* to sell bogus shares in an Australian gold mine which either doesn't exist, or if it does, is entirely deficient in gold. A scam is still a scam, but the mechanism has either been simplified or forcibly evicted in the interests of lightness.

But even as he approached 40, Plum still hadn't quite perfected his ideal comedy villains; there was still too much negativity curdling that milk of human kindness whenever they appeared. When they did finally arrive, they would be more the comedy grump and less the career asshole, and a move in the right direction was evident in Plum's lyric to 'Napoleon', a song that first appeared in his 1917 stage musical *Have a Heart*:

> *Napoleon was a fat gazook*
> *He never took to banting* [dieting]
> *And every time he walked upstairs*
> *He had to stand there panting,*
> *But gee! That did not worry him*
> *When up against the foeman*
> *He knew that it's the brains that count*
> *And not a guy's abdomen.*

This Napoleon was modelled on theatre impresario Abraham Lincoln Erlanger (short, fat, bald, no-neck), who had employed Plum the previous year on the Broadway show *Miss Springtime*. Notorious for his hectoring manner and installing a punchbag in his office, he would re-surface as the bullying theatre producer Blumenfield in three Jeeves and Bertie yarns from 1918-34. But really, he is more ridiculous, or perhaps if we're going to be charitable, *colourful* than threatening – and so things would remain in the characters Plum cut from this cloth. Sure, his Napoleons remain unpleasant, arrogant and domineering, but malice aforethought is for the most part ruled out of the equation. Lord Tilbury turns a coin catering to (some might say exploiting) the general public's undeveloped literary tastes. But this is not a crime against humanity, or even a crime: it in fact brings a good deal of pleasure to his readers. What he has become, rather than a villain, is a symbol of a rich and privileged class that mimics the behaviour of feudal barons towards those beneath them in life's pecking order. Power and influence should be accompanied by a sense of *noblesse oblige* – only with these guys, it isn't.

King of the new breed is surely Alaric Pendlebury-Davenport, 6th Duke of Dunstable, whose presence joyously blights 1939's *Uncle Fred in the Springtime*, 1961's *Service with a Smile* through to *A Pelican at Blandings* in 1969 – thirty years he spends tarnishing the reputation of the English Establishment. Think of Lord Emsworth's evil twin and you won't go far wrong – not difficult, since both men are contrasted in all three novels, and we are told that Clarence has disliked the Duke "in a dreamy way for forty-seven years". Indeed, "one-way pockets" Dunstable (Eton, Cambridge and the Guards) has made being objectionable his life's passion and something of an art form, being blackballed by members of the Pelican Club, and breaking off his engagement to a young Connie Threepwood when he judges her marriage settlement insufficient. Not that he's without a bob or two – once again he's just tight, abruptly terminating his wooing of Vanessa Polk on discovering she is not, as he thought, the daughter of a millionaire.

Already minted, he's constantly looking for ways to get richer: "He never misses a trick," says Gally, and "[i]f the opportunity presents itself of running a mile in tight shoes to chisel someone out of twopence, he springs to the task". Dunstable's winning ways also embrace mental instability and vandalism, having a tendency to set about perfectly innocent sitting-room furniture with a poker if any little thing isn't to his liking. As the compilers of *Who's Who in Wodehouse* have it, he is "opinionated, arbitrary and autocratic", his standing among his Wiltshire neighbours being "roughly that of a shark at a bathing resort". During his extended, unwelcome and usually self-invited stays up at Blandings, he plots to kidnap the Empress on all three occasions, delegating the actual job of handling the monster animal to a succession of underlings while speculating in fine art and generally making an ill-mannered, demanding and unpleasant nuisance of himself.

And yet, for all his faults – which are legion – compared to Bickersdyke et al he is *fun*, particularly his free-associating verbal delivery which even silences that inveterate stage-hogger Gally Threepwood. In this extract, Dunstable is discussing (or rather soliloquizing) his world view with Gally, beginning with the sanity or otherwise of his hosts:

> "[Clarence is] as potty as Connie. Pottier. Fact of the matter is, the whole world's potty these days. Look at Connie, going off to live in America with a man with a head like a Spanish onion. Look at those two nephews of mine, both married to girls I wouldn't have let them so much as whistle at if I'd been able to stop them. And look at my niece . . . "

And so on. Dunstable's definition of "potty" (his favourite adjective) is a broad one, embracing anyone who doesn't think or behave like him. Which is, thankfully, most people.

Running him a close second in the unpleasantness handicap is Sir Raymond "Beefy" Bastable, 52, from 1958's *Cocktail Time*. Another stout, florid gentleman, he earns a considerable crust as a Queen's

Counsel specializing in marital breakdown, and is considered by the roguish Uncle Fred to be "pompous, arrogant and far too pleased with himself", an assessment with which the narrator heartily concurs:

> There may have been men in London who thought more highly of Sir Raymond Bastable than did Sir Raymond Bastable, but they would have been hard to find, and the sense of being someone set apart from and superior to the rest of the world inevitably breeds arrogance. Sir Raymond's attitude toward those about him . . . was always that of an irritable tribal god who intends to stand no nonsense from his worshippers and is prepared, should the smoked offering fall in any way short of the highest standard, to say it with thunderbolts.

And that's the common denominator that really seems to irritate Wodehouse in this particular Establishment tribe – that air of entitlement. Everyone exists simply to dance attendance on them. Even standing on the pavement awaiting a cab, Bastable gives off "a sort of haughty impatience, as though he had thought that, when he wanted a taxi-cab, ten thousand must have sprung from their ranks to serve him". Not only does he treat everyone like dirt, but he also reduces his sister (and house-keeper) Phoebe Wisdom "to a blob of tearful jelly almost daily" – a rare instance of disquieting emotional cruelty slipping past the gatekeeper of Wodehouse World.

A brilliant cameo of this kind of titled arrogance arrives in 1933's *Heavy Weather* in the person of Lady Julia Fish, Connie and Clarence's wonderfully overbearing sister. Lacking the bluster of Plum's male grumps, she instead patronizes the hell out of anyone she comes across. In one of several cases in Wodehouse where the f. of the s. is deadlier than the m., she even lords it over the seasoned blowhard Tilbury, reducing him to a spot of grease on his office's expensive carpet. Another character who possesses "a supreme confidence in her ability to get anything she wanted out of anyone", she cordially greets the press baron "not actually patting [him] on the head but conveying the impression that she might see fit to do so at any moment". Cutting him down to size still further by describing his appearance as "bonny" (an adjective usually associated with babies in Wodehouse), she proceeds to belittle his entire business empire:

"So this is where you get out all those jolly little papers of yours, is it? I must say I'm impressed".

Which of course she isn't. Tilbury, only just able to keep a civil tongue in his mouth, responds with "the geniality of a trapped wolf" as her ladyship politely but insistently demands that he give her son Ronnie a job ("Surely you could let him mess about at *something*?). In this battle of the giants, Tilbury holds all the cards and for once, Lady Julia doesn't get her way, but not before disparaging everyone and everything she comes across.

In effect, Lady Julia lives on the borders of pantomime villain and Premier League "Fusser", the designation for Plum's legion of meddlers and tinkerers I explored in Volume 2. Bertie's Aunt Agatha belongs there too, expecting automatic complicity with everything she demands, whether it's forcing vegetarianism on her husband or dictating Bertie's choice of marriage partner. She's simply . . . imperious, one among several Wodehousean ladies of a certain age and class whose only function is to boss others around. But whereas Lady Julia is a good example of mid-season Wodehouse sublimating social themes *inside* a character, those same themes would occasionally leak out again later in Plum's career, harking back to the days half a century earlier when he was writing his pantos. For *Cocktail Time*, with Beefy at the heart of its plot, is nothing less than a return to writing a full-blown metropolitan satire, but a satire now (for the most part) leavened by Wodehousean lightness.

It's fascinating to see what has changed - and what hasn't − in the intervening 50-odd years. On the whole, England remains as potty as it ever was, but the quality of Wodehouse's rebelliousness has most definitely evolved; not exactly blunted, but very definitely softened, perhaps made sentimental by his years in exile (Plum hadn't set foot in his home country for almost 20 years by this point). Or maybe he was mellowing, for Beefy, if we gloss over his unpardonable meanness to his sister, is presented as not entirely unlikeable. Uncle Fred informs us he's actually quite "fond" of him (they are, after all, half brothers-in-law). He's not *so* bad, simply needing to be brought down a peg or two occasionally. So, Plum not only provides Beefy with the almost compulsory demeaning nickname just about every Wodehouse male of a certain social rank is branded with, he arranges for his dignity to be further compromised by having his top-hat pinged off in public with a catapult and a well-aimed Brazil nut. This minor assault proves to be the germinal incident of the novel: Beefy plausibly imagines the perp or perps to be youthful hell-raisers from the nearby Drones Club, and decides to rid the world of this infernal nuisance . . . but how?

Like many's the tick before him in Wodehouse, Beefy already has the money and is now seeking the power that would make him a true beacon of the Establishment by getting himself elected as a Member of Parliament – in this case for the cheerily violent constituency of Bottleton East. At this early stage in the story, his political party – by contrast with the earlier aspirants we've looked at – is not named; but we can make an informed guess by the tenor of Beefy's thoughts about his prospective constituents:

> Bottleton East, down Limehouse way, was one of those primitive communities where the native sons, largely recruited from the costermongering and leaning-up-against-the-walls-of-public-houses industries, have a primitive sense of humour and think things funny which are not funny at all.

Not flattering portraiture from one who is seeking the honour of representing them in a democratic forum. But what, Beefy also ponders, should he do about his titfer removal? Could he make political capital from it, decrying 'the youth of today' and demanding a return to civilized behaviour? The usual vehicle for protest would be an indignant letter for publication in the *Times*. But that would butter no parsnips with the good burghers of Bottleton should they get wind of the story. Far from sympathizing with him, they would most likely laugh like drains, or even worse for his election prospects, judge him a coward for not fighting back. Wise as ever, Uncle Fred offers the following psephological insight:

> "You know what the British voter is like. Let him learn that you have won the Derby or saved a golden-haired child from a burning building, and yours is the name he puts a cross against on his ballot paper, but tell him that somebody has knocked your topper off with a Brazil nut and his confidence in you is shaken . . . I don't defend this attitude, I merely say it exists".

Satire meets lightness in that last comment, for Uncle Fred, the wily old fox, claims to stand aloof on the issue – while actually being the Dead-eye Dick with the catapult. For rebellion in Wodehouse is a many-splen-doured thing: remember Lord Emsworth, Connie and Beach's exploits with the air rifle in 'The Crime Wave at Blandings'? Or the one about the headmaster and the bishop who painted a statue pink? Sometimes the armchair rebel rises from his comfy seat and acts on impulse, Plum hinting that we all have an anarchist inside us somewhere, no matter how successfully we try to disguise him or her with wealth, title and privilege.

Ever the spreader of sweetness and light, Uncle Fred makes the somewhat unorthodox suggestion that Beefy should air his grievances in a witheringly satirical novel:

> "You could have got those views of yours on the younger generation off your chest in a novel. Something on the lines of Evelyn Waugh's *Vile Bodies* – witty, bitter, satirical and calculated to make the younger generation see itself as in a mirror and wish that Brazil nuts had never been invented".

Great idea, thinks Beefy, and as we follow the novel's road to market, so the repercussions from the hat incident start to spread out like the ripples of a stone thrown into a still pond, to touch further aspects of so-ciety ripe and ready for Wodehouse's brand of gentle, satirical mockery.

Notice how once again literature lies at the heart of a Wodehouse plot. Having already compared Beefy's putative novel to Evelyn Waugh's "satirical" work (a generous plug for his friend and support-er), the narrator compares the finished manuscript – also called *Cocktail Time* – to Kathleen Winsor's 1944 bestselling Restoration sex-romp *Forever Amber* - a copy of which graced the shelves of Plum's personal library (see Volume 2). In that book (according to the attorney-gener-al of Massachusetts who was trying to ban it) can be found 70 acts of sexual intercourse, 39 illegitimate pregnancies, 7 abortions, and "10 descriptions of women undressing in front of men". Not the kind of thing a prospective Parliamentary representative could put his name to, so Beefy wisely adopts the pseudonym "Richard Blunt" in case "[a] prudish Conservative Committee would reject him with a shudder and seek their candidate elsewhere". And there we finally have it; un-equivocal proof of Beefy's party political affiliations casually slipped in. Would its gatekeepers believe all that filth had been gathered from cases Sir Raymond Bastable Q.C. had fought in the divorce courts? No, of course they wouldn't. The man was obviously a sex maniac.

Having tinkered in political satire, Wodehouse then beats the retreat to his home turf. He rarely passed up an opportunity to bite the hand that fed him, and once again sinks his teeth into publishers, their inconsiderate treatment of authors, strange editorial policies and bizarre marketing strategies. Beefy's manuscript is given the run-around by a succession of imprints before ending up at Alfred Tomkins Ltd (a name reminiscent of Plum's own longstanding publisher Herbert Jenkins), who issue it "in a jacket featuring a young man with a monocle in his right eye doing the rock'n'roll with a young woman in her step-ins". As Plum was writing *Cocktail Time*, rock'n'roll had only just become a 'thing' in the general consciousness, and our 77-year-old front-line news reporter was yet again ahead of the pack in referencing it in his fiction, using this joyously incongruous image.

And so, trendily jacketed, Beefy's bonkbuster hits the bookstores to a disappointing wave of indifference:

> It has been well said that an author who expects results from a first novel is in a position similar to a man who drops a rose petal down the Grand Canyon of Arizona and listens for the echo.

Several parodies of lukewarm literary reviews follow – but still no sales. Until, that is, the Bishop of Stortford happens to read the odd paragraph over his daughter's shoulder, gets himself hooked, and ends up wrenching the book from her grasp in his attempt to find out what happens next. Having made trebly sure that he has not been mistaken, he is inspired to preach a fiery sermon on the degeneracy of modern literature, labelling the novel "obscene, immoral, shocking, impure, corrupt, shameless, graceless and depraved" from the pulpit of St. Jude the Resilient in London's über-posh Eaton Square. Immediately, many outwardly respectable (male) parishioners start "jotting the name down on their shirt-cuffs, scarcely able to wait to add it to their library list", and the sales floodgates are opened. I don't know whether this was true in 1958 or not, but the narrator helpfully projects that a good fire-and-brimstone denunciation from a senior cleric would usually translate into "10-15,000" additional hardback sales – and so it is that Beefy becomes an overnight sensation.

Wodehouse is now on a satirical roll, working his way through polite society institution by institution. Leaving the hypocrisy of the bishop and his posh metropolitan congregation behind, Plum now turns his fire on another of his regular employers, the press, and its perennial tendency to humbug:

> In these days when practically anything from Guildford undertaker bitten in leg by Pekinese to Ronald Plumtree (11) falling off his bicycle in Walthamstow High Street can make the front page of the popular press as a big feature story with headlines of a size formerly reserved for announcing the opening of a world war, it was not to be expected that such an event would pass unnoticed.

Remember our earlier headline "SURREY DOING BADLY"? Well, here we are again in the topsy turvy world of the Fourth Estate, whose sense of what's *actually* significant never ceases to surprise. Those mid-market dailies the *Mail* and the *Express* reliably get on Beefy's case and turn the sanctimony up to 11; just as they did when Plum was writing for them 50 years earlier, and still do in our own time.

And so it goes. *Cocktail Time* becomes a publishing phenomenon, perfectly reflecting the pattern and rhythm of what happens to this day. We need only reference E.L. James's 2011 erotic romance *50 Shades of Grey* for corroboration of how nothing seems to change; the various tribes of British (and American) society dutifully fall into predictable patterns of behaviour as they had with many another raunchy title. *Forever Amber* would soon be joined in 1960 by D.H. Lawrence's *Lady Chatterley's Lover* – and although it's familiar, I can't resist quoting the prosecuting council from that last legal fracas, the distinctly Wodehousean Mervyn Griffith-Jones Q.C. (a real-life equivalent of Beefy), who gained immortality when he instructed the jury to

> Ask yourselves the question: would you approve of your young sons, young daughters – because girls can read as well as boys – reading this book? Is it a book that you would have lying around the house? Is it a book you would wish your wife or servants to read?

Once again, I'll refer you to the title of this volume's second chapter. And of course, *Lady Chatterley* went on to sell 2 million copies in its first year as a paperback, its notoriety guaranteed by Plum's masterful 1961 rewrite of the lyrics to 'Anything Goes':

When the courts decide, as they did latterly,
We could read Lady Chatterley
If we chose,
Anything goes.

Plum the satirist was truly back on the case.

As for Beefy, his creator's warm-heartedness allows him to get off comparatively lightly: not only does he sell the book's movie rights to a Hollywood studio for $150,000, but he also ends up engaged to Barbara Crowe, an attractive and dynamic old flame who plans to whisk him off to the country where he can write the sequel. The only flies in his ointment are: (a) lacking sufficient stamina to write another sex-fest, he reluctantly ponies up £500 to Uncle Fred's impecunious godson Jonathan to ghost it, and (b) his long-suffering sister Phoebe is set to marry Peasemarch, a distinctly low-caste butler who hails from the (then) scaly London suburb of East Dulwich. So, although Beefy's parsimony and snobbery have both been assaulted, he's left with only minor flesh wounds. And we hear no more of his political ambitions.

Resident or not, Plum could always find rich pickings for satire in his native land. But even as he cast a wry eye over its enduring eccentricities, he must have been aware that in the course of his long life – he was 77 when *Cocktail Time* was published – he had been round this particular block several times. Although the tone of the novel's narration remained that of the amused, occasionally exasperated spectator he had been using for nigh on 60 years, there is a distinct undertow in this and much of his later fiction of 'been there, seen it' that comes with long exposure to that ebb and flow of time, those rhythms and cycles of relevance and redundancy. Human folly of every kind and from whatever source always amused him, and his satirical antennae would continue to register it as reliably as they ever had. What's more, his targets hadn't really changed much, from figures like Sir Alfred Venner in his debut novel right the way through to an old curmudgeon like Mr. Cook in his last, a short, red-faced elderly gentleman with the disposition of a dyspeptic rattlesnake who sunders his daughter's relationship with Orlo Porter on account of the latter's far-left politics.

At the root of this chapter on polite rebellion, however, I can't help feeling that Plum could never get his head around those who, finding themselves in authority over others – or simply assuming it – try to prevent them doing what they want to do. 'Live and let live' would be a plausible motto for the Wodehouse coat of arms, and those who forced their opinions, values or codes of behaviour on others quite simply needed *their* behaviour altering using any means necessary.

You'll have noticed the contradiction at the heart of that sentence; one that can be traced back to 1900, when, in his early journalism, Plum had shown himself impatient with the editors of the *Malvernian* school magazine who had failed to use their privileged literary platform to "rend to pieces" those of their "Contemporaries" that deserved it. But don't we just love it when justice, however effected, is seen to be done and things turn out right for those characters we care about? When the Beefys and Connies and Dunstables of this world are thwarted, as of course, they always are? For the quietly subversive armchair rebel doesn't need to go around assaulting policemen to salve his grievances. Like Horace, he doesn't get mad – he gets even.

CHANGING
TIMES

Chapter 4:
Changing Times

"Those haughty English aristocrats are like that. Tough babies.
Comes of treading the peasantry underfoot with an iron heel"
Summer Moonshine

"We Earls step high," Lord Ickenham assured her.
"It must be great being an Oil".
"It's terrific. I often lie awake at night, aching with pity
for all the poor devils who aren't".
"Though I suppose you know you're an anachronistic
parasite on the body of the State.?
Uncle Dynamite

These times in which we live are not good times for Earls. Theirs
was a great racket while it lasted, but the boom days are over.
Spring Fever

His lordship was like a fallen country
with a glorious history.
A Gentleman of Leisure

In January 1919, Plum and Ethel sailed back to England for their first visit after an absence of four and a half years, during which time the First World War had come and gone, leaving a set of indelible scars on their home country. The death toll of over 700,000 troops from the British Isles was compounded by 1,675,000 wounded, 17,000 civilian casualties, and a further 228,000 fatalities from the 1918 influenza pandemic.

Much of the ethos that informed the early years of Plum's writing had also been ruthlessly swept away: that long, sunny (and somewhat fanciful) afternoon garden party beloved of later historians was well and truly over, and as peacetime beckoned and the era of post-war reconstruction began, so a titanic struggle kicked off between the conflicting forces of old and new, change and stasis, tradition and innovation. But where would Plum and his nascent world fit into this process, being so deeply immersed in an age that was by now distinctly old hat?

The received wisdom goes that as Plum approached 40 and Wodehouse World teetered on the threshold of mid-season glory, its

Edwardian origins meant it would always be swimming against time's tide – indeed, I suggested this myself in the opening sentences of Volume 1. It's a perfectly respectable argument, and scholars with a biographical or historical bias will almost inevitably arrive at this conclusion; Plum himself adapted it in the 1950s to help him ward off those who considered his work hopelessly outdated. However, once we start poking about in his writing, things aren't quite so cut and dried, and we can now finesse that earlier argument by proposing a less orthodox, more ambivalent relationship between his imaginative world, time and change. For Wodehouse World was starting to embrace Progress.

In Plum's more mature work, marching to the rhythm of precedent is rarely presented as healthy; and although a significant majority of his plots are more or less circular in shape, they rarely end up at the exact same point they started out. Something has usually changed – and for the better – by their close: a problem has been solved, a fusser thwarted, lessons learned, perspectives altered, new alliances proposed and forged. The trajectory is always onwards and upwards; so, when history *does* repeat itself as, say, when Bertie refuses to profit from experience and dives back into the bouillon with one of his snooterers, Plum presents this as atypical, wilfully perverse behaviour ripe for ridicule (more of which in Chapter 7). And it's the same with Lord Emsworth's militant passivity; his uncanny knack of staying rooted to the spot is a rare talent not granted to many, but it's hardly normal, even though it seems to suit him to a tee and can even be viewed from certain angles as slightly heroic. Already, it's possible to see how things are getting more complicated, as Clarence is happily marooned on his Shropshire sandbank while the tide of human affairs flows on around him.

Now contrast these two stationary gentlemen with Archie Moffam, who doesn't let the grass grow under *his* feet. In the 1920 post-war short story 'The Man Who Married a Hotel', he finds himself demobbed from the army, and being a younger son who will play no part in running the family estate, has to find something to do with his life. Armed only with his Knut-ish brand of goofy charm and a can-do attitude, he packs himself off to America, where in little more than a fortnight he finds himself happily married to Lucille Brewster, the daughter of a wealthy New York hotel owner. Not a typical story, perhaps, but a charmed existence that almost mirrored Plum's own American sojourn. While Archie had fallen on his feet in double-quick time, Plum had been grafting from the moment he disembarked; but there can be no doubt that by contrast with the majority of their fellow Brits, both men were sitting pretty as the world re-adjusted itself to peacetime operations, precisely because they *hadn't* stayed still.

Indeed, so successful was Plum, that during that immediate post-war period he might as well have been living in Archie's world of fiction, one where everything was positive and moving in a satisfying forward trajectory. He was making his first significant inroads into London's West End with his musical comedies *Oh, Joy!* and *Kissing Time*, both of which had already been hits on Broadway, where he and Bolton and Kern had been the talk of the town from 1916 onwards. Since the opening of hostilities, he had published three novels and a collection of short stories, started to build a cast of regular characters with the introduction of Blandings, Bertie and Jeeves, and had got happily married immediately prior to starting out on the road to fame and serious wealth. He was also working on his novel *A Damsel in Distress*, which Plum's biographer Robert McCrum describes as "a kind of lunatic elegy for a lost world". That lost, Edwardian pre-war world, presumably.

But . . . is it? For if you read that novel's opening page, the narrator categorically states that "[o]n the glorious past of the Marshmoretons I will not even touch". And he doesn't, despite the fact that the family's lineage stretches back more than 500 years. For the past, in this story, is presented right up front as something that stifles progress, a weighty inheritance England will need to throw off if it is to thrive in the future. Lord Marshmoreton actively wants to escape the rat-race of titled privilege rather than buy into it, a state of affairs that chimes with Plum's predictions in the scripted 'interview' he gave the *New York Times* in 1915 entitled 'War Will Restore England's Sense of Humor'. In it, he had expressed the hope that once the war was over, humour in his homeland would become more 'democratic'; and now that time had come, here he was, true to his claim, writing a novel that embodied the theme of moving on.

Here's some snapshots of dear old Blighty from Plum's 1915 perspective:

> No English humorist writes for a paper which is to be read, for example, by a prosperous business man *and* his chauffeur [italics mine]; to reach these two men it is necessary for him to write two different sorts of jokes for two separate publications.

> The English humorist . . . leads a sheltered life. Generally

he is born in the private income class; he goes to a public school, then a university, and then he probably is called to the bar. He writes for people with similar experience and traditions, and he is careful to write nothing that might offend them.

The English humorist has had ten years' training in repression . . . he would like to be funny, but he is haunted by the fear of being vulgar.

The typical British joke of the best sort has to do with motor cars or butlers or Bishops or week ends [sic].

Which, of course, is what Wodehouse's own stories would 'ha[ve] to do with' for the rest of his life, for our armchair revolutionary would, characteristically, always play the hand he'd been dealt. But it's quite clear from those extracts that even before the Great War, Plum had thought that British humour (and by implication, the society of which it was a reflection) needed a mighty kick up the backside, being fenced in on all sides by considerations of class, taste, suitability of subject, and the fact that its practitioners, who were drawn from a shallow gene pool, always seemed to stick with what they knew for fear they might violate the unwritten rules of good taste.

Once again, it's possible to accuse Plum of exactly the same conservatism. Fortunately, however, his continuing rapidly developing sense of lightness was starting to come into play in the post-war period, one of whose key ingredients would be *possibility*, which would help his writing wriggle free from beneath the cold, dead hands of history, tradition and, above all, snobbery. For what *was* humour, if not iconoclastic? It didn't have to go out of its way to offend people; indeed, for commercial reasons, it was better if it didn't. But it did have to have some life about it, alerting its audiences to fresh, alternative perspectives, even if the subject matter was familiar. Wodehouse had already witnessed first-hand how this "New" type of humour was the general currency in America, originating, he tells us, with the recently deceased Mark Twain. Now Plum would bring this knowledge back home, and *A Damsel in Distress* was to prove a modest but significant staging post in the evolution of his humour.

Others quickly grasped its possibilities. In the year of the book's publication, it was turned into a silent film, then a stage play that enjoyed a successful run in London, and later a movie musical with music and lyrics by George and Ira Gershwin and starring Fred Astaire, George Burns and Gracie Allen. As Plum put it in his "New Preface" to the 1975 reprint, "[a]lmost everything happened to it that can happen to a book, short of being done on ice". But not quite; for almost exactly 100 years after its first appearance, a team of Bollywood filmmakers re-worked the novel into the 2019 movie (*Ek Ladki Ko Dekha Toh Aisa Laga*) about the struggles of a closeted lesbian who is trying to come out from her conservative and traditional family and (spoiler alert) eventually succeeds. Which, on the surface, represents quite a stretch of imagination. But then again, no; for the writers successfully identified two of the novel's underlying themes – those of change, and the freedom to think outside the envelope – then picked them up and successfully ran with them. One mainstream reviewer described the film as "a whiff of fresh air . . . [that] goads the audience to think differently without trying to deviate from its primary purpose, which is to deliver entertainment". And I reckon Plum would have been more than happy with that, however unfamiliar the setting. For once again, as I noted at the close of the previous chapter, a pair of loved-up characters refusing to conform to social precedent is a perennial Wodehouse plotline.

And so, to argue that he was in the business of writing elegies to lost worlds is well wide of the mark; he certainly wouldn't have been *intending* to, since elegies are more about misty-eyed nostalgia, and Plum's vision was rather more dynamic and forward-looking than that. His prolonged American sojourn had granted him fresh perspectives on his native soil, and from the very first time he had set foot there on 25 April 1904 for a month's break, it had struck him as new, exciting, fresh, open to possibilities – and perhaps most importantly to a young-ish tyro who was watching his pennies – more egalitarian and meritocratic than what he'd been used to back home. In 'Leave it to Jeeves', Bertie describes how he has been welcomed into the Big Apple's social set with open arms:

> I'm bound to say that New York's a topping place to be exiled in. Everybody was awfully good to me, and there seemed to be plenty of things going on, and I'm a wealthy bird, so everything was fine. Chappies introduced me to other chappies, and so on and so forth, and it wasn't long before I knew squads of the right sort, some who rolled in dollars and houses up by the Park, and others who lived with the gas turned down mostly around Washington

Square – artists and writers and so forth.

By the time he wrote those words in early 1916, Wodehouse himself had fallen in with a good, mixed crowd, and was on his way to being a wealthy New Yorker, freed from the additional worry of justifying who he was and whether his family featured in *Burke's Landed Gentry*.

The irony is that it actually did, even though it had seen better days. Plum's father Henry, a colonial magistrate, liked to describe his branch of the family as "downstarts", existing amid what McCrum calls a "riot of ancestry" stretching back through a line of Norfolk knights to the Middle Ages. His mother's lineage pre-dated even that, traceable to a Norman noble at the court of Edward the Confessor, whose kingship ended in the fateful year of 1066. But all that was as naught: by the early 20th century, any social prestige the family enjoyed was confined to a distant branch of the clan, one of whom, John Wodehouse, 2nd Earl of Kimberley, would become the first member of the British Labour Party to take a seat in the House of Lords. According to the *Daily Telegraph*'s obituaries column, Plum became the 4th Earl's god-father in 1924, proudly encouraging his charge's career as a member of the British bobsled team, toasting his vice presidency of the World Council on Alcoholism, and questioning his keen interest in U.F.Os. On the downside, however, he was "notorious for his bad luck at gambling, business and marriage", being wed six times and having to sell off much of the family estate to pay his considerable debts.

Anyhow, while Plum repeatedly demonstrates that he is only too aware of issues of class and status in his plots, his transatlantic sojourn seems to have enhanced his natural inclination to take people as he found them. A letter to Bill Townend in 1929 describes a fascinating en-counter with the celebrated author H.G. Wells, his near neighbour and dining companion in the south of France, and shows what can happen when a writer starts worrying about his social status:

> [Wells's] first remark, apropos of nothing, was 'my father was a professional cricketer'. A conversation stopper if ever there was one. What a weird country England is, with its class distinctions and that ingrained snobbery you can't seem to escape from. I suppose I notice it more because I've spent so much of my time in America. Can you imagine an American who had achieved the position Wells has, worrying because he started out in life on the wrong

side of the tracks? But nothing will ever make Wells forget that his father was a professional cricketer and his mother the housekeeper at Up Park.

Even that great Fabian dignitary George Bernard Shaw seemed to take great delight in rubbing Wells's nose in his humble ancestry, a bone he wouldn't stop gnawing even as he wrote the latter's obituary, remarking that "HG was not a gentleman" and labelling him "petit bourgeois". Plum's inclination, by contrast, is to defend his fellow writer and his undoubted achievements from those who would use his family tree as a stick to beat him with. Neither he nor Wells had been fast-tracked to literary success by useful family connections (nor had Shaw, for that matter), and while the raw material of Plum's mid-season stories inclines to the higher end of society, this does not imply that he was in any way captivated by those who had been born into it.

And that, it seems to me, is the main reason why Plum liked America, which, although it had elites of its own, wasn't in the same league as Britain when it came to snobbery. As far as it's possible to tell, Plum was happy simply being rich and successful, which seemed to open just as many doors to him as a title. Indeed, by the time he wrote that letter sympathizing with Wells, he himself was already effectively a tax exile. A quick glance at the index of McCrum's biography gives a good indication of the rarefied strata Plum was accustomed to moving in after he became well-off; and had he been inclined to work at his social life, he would undoubtedly have been even better connected. It's just that schmoozing and wasn't really his dish, for writing would always trump networking on his to-do list.

The absence of definitive authorial statements on the subject has prompted a good deal of debate about Wodehouse's views on the aristocracy and its stranglehold on British society. George Orwell contributed the following well-known paragraph in 1945:

> [I]n creating such characters as Hildebrand Spencer Poyns de Burgh John Hanneyside Coombe-Crombie, 12th Earl of Dreever, Wodehouse is not really attacking the social hierarchy. Indeed, no one who genuinely despised titles would write of them so much. Wodehouse's attitude towards the English social system is the same as his attitude towards the public-school moral code – a mild facetiousness covering an unthinking acceptance. The Earl of Emsworth is funny

because an earl ought to have more dignity, and Bertie Wooster's helpless dependence on Jeeves is funny partly because the servant ought not to be superior to the master. An American reader can mistake these two, and others like them, for hostile caricatures because he is inclined to be anglophobe [sic] already and they correspond to his preconceived ideas about a decadent aristocracy. Bertie Wooster, with his spats and his cane, is the traditional stage Englishman. But, as any English reader would see, Wodehouse intends him as a sympathetic figure, and Wodehouse's real sin has been to present the English upper classes as much nicer people than they are.

There are some palpable hits in that paragraph, particularly the first half, although trying to explain *why* something is funny is, more often than not, a fool's errand. But really, could anyone hate Lord Emsworth simply because he was 'born' a toff? That's only possible if (a) we were insisting that Clarence is an authentic representation of a real earl, (b) we were ideologically opposed to the existence of an aristocracy, (c) we weren't entirely comfortable reading fiction and most importantly (d), our sense of humour wasn't working properly. Orwell seems to satisfy all four criteria on this occasion, concluding that "Wodehouse is not anti-British, and not anti-upper-class either. On the contrary, a harmless old-fashioned snobbishness is perceptible all through his work". Which is just plain wrong: but as we'll see in Chapter 6, Orwell's motive in writing his essay was to defend Wodehouse from those baying for his scalp following the Berlin Broadcasts Business, and by painting the writer as an upholder of the status quo, he was hoping to head off the witch hunt that had branded Plum a traitor to his country. But while Orwell's refutation remains well-argued and hugely persuasive, it did not prove to be the last word on the broader question of Plum's social allegiances, and the debate continues to this day.

In 2014, there was a nice little canter in the centre-left *Guardian* newspaper's online book club, prompted by one reader's remark that:

Some say that the first world war precipitated the gradual decline of the English privileged class system. If it did, it had considerable help from PG himself, whose books were a hall of mirrors far too funny to be anything but subversive.

By making his earls certifiably dotty rather than a bunch of noble and upstanding Squire Allworthys, Plum was undermining the received order of things. But then a second correspondent came up with this, referring to *Leave it to Psmith*:

> This is gentle mocking, nothing hurtful or cynical, the reader is invited to push aside any prejudices against the casual degeneracy of the idle rich characters presented in the book.

Which makes the valid point that it's perfectly possible to mock the things you love just as readily as those you despise, and that for all his satirical mischief, Plum never posed any kind of threat or challenge to those at the top of the tree. And so, it was left up to the club's moderator, Sam Jordison, to diplomatically wrap things up by stating that Plum seems to have been "empty of snobbery and full of sympathy for those repressed by the English class system".

Having rehearsed the central tenets of the argument, the absence of any decisive conclusion once more alerts us to the fact that not enough cold, hard thought has been given to how Wodehouse's World and our own seem to know each other rather better than we've been led to believe. And yet in *A Damsel in Distress*, written as Plum stood on the verge of his mid-season form, we begin to witness them starting to rub along rather nicely, particularly if we examine the book from the perspective of the class struggle. Debuting as a serial in May 1919, the novel was conceived during the early stages of the Russian Revolution, even as Tsar Nicholas II and his family were executed by the Bolsheviks. But although Plum occasionally has his more left-wing characters longing for the day when the gutters of Park Lane run with blue blood and aristocrats swing from its lampposts, he proposes an altogether less dramatic solution to the problem of what will happen to the upper crust in the brave new world - one that involves rather less mopping up. For in Wodehouse World, high position can confer soul-sapping burdens as well as privilege on its recipients; and once they've experienced the new post-war reality of being lords, those lords might not actually *want* to be lords. For this reason alone, the novel is worth taking some time over, since it serves to illustrate the broader historical tensions at play in contemporary English society through the eyes of a single character. And more than that, it's a blueprint for future Blandings outings, which would hijack its setting, *dramatis personae* and plot trajectory almost wholesale, only with the addition of greater lightness and an enormous pig. And so it is our gaze returns to the fortunes of John Belpher, Lord Marshmoreton, a conflicted blue blood who straddles past and present, torn in either direction by the demands of tradition and his personal happiness, pre- and post-war worlds colliding head on within the confines of a deceptively frothy romantic comedy.

The first thing to notice, which is addressed on the novel's opening page, is what the narrator tells us about its contemporary setting. These, he says, are days of "rush and hurry", so he's going to have to get the preliminaries of the scenario out of the way fast, "leap[ing] into the middle of his tale with as little delay as he would employ in boarding a moving tramcar". Failure to do so would result in "people throw[ing] him aside and go[ing] out to picture palaces". 89 words later, the *mis-en-scène* is done and dusted, with all the characters crisply introduced. History, he tells us, is bunk; there simply isn't time for it. But then he straightway whisks us off to rural Hampshire and Belpher Castle, which has history to spare.

When we first meet him, its castellan Lord Marshmoreton is to be found pottering among his roses in his worn gardening corduroys. Already, he doesn't look or behave like an earl. Shouldn't he be dressed in his finery, and have a team of flunkies doing the dead-heading for him? Despite these shortcomings the ancestral pile appears to be free of the financial hardships and problems with staff recruitment that many of Plum's future stately homes would experience, and the weekly open day on Thursday (entry fee, one shilling) seems more a feudal obligation than a necessary money-making enterprise. We're told the Earl can scrub up well when he wants to; it's just that he *doesn't* want to, disliking all manifestations of pomp and circumstance. Unlike his sister, the tyrannical Lady Caroline Byng (essentially a nasty version of Connie Threepwood), who is obsessed with correctness and status, he just wants to be left alone to do what he wants. Not the traditional backwoods peer, then; an image Plum reinforces almost immediately:

> The hatred which some of his order feel for Socialists and Demagogues Lord Marshmoreton kept for rose-slugs . . . [a] simple soul . . . mild and pleasant.

It's just that he's nothing of the kind. Imagine the equanimity and contentedness of Lord Emsworth, then picture its opposite – that's Lord Marshmoreton. The Earl seethes with contradictions convincingly concealed behind his stiff upper lip – which, as we'll see in a moment, is prone to quiver. One of the major sources of his discontent is his ongoing authorship of a "History of the Family", a task he symbolically loathes but Lady Caroline, also symbolically, is extremely excited by, nagging him to complete the task at every available opportunity. To his secretary, Alice Faraday, the family's aristocratic past "had glamour"; to her employer, it's a burden from which he longs to free himself. Not just the boring old writing, but the mental prison represented by history itself.

Change is in the air, however, and it comes to seek him out in the person of his daughter, the highly-eligible Lady Maud, who is beautiful, headstrong and endowed with a sense of humour – like all Wodehouse's mid-season Eligible Women, those WEWs we met in Volume 2. Anticipating several other happy father/daughter combos in Plum's stories, she and the Earl are on the same wavelength, while her petulant older brother tends to side with his aunt. And so the battle lines are drawn: open-hearted change will take on ill-natured snobbery.

For all his lofty status, Lord Marshmoreton is something of a rebel. Unlike the grumpy old right-wingers of the previous chapter, many of whom have scrambled up the greasy pole to achieve their high status, the Earl, who was born atop it and has nothing to prove, is as far removed from these self-seeking upstarts as it's possible to get, showing himself happy to slide down it, caring little for rank or title. When his son Percy kicks a policeman in the stomach and is jailed overnight, "he privately held the opinion that nothing so became him as this assault on the Force". He too "had committed all the follies of youth" and seems aching to do something similarly reckless in his straitened adult life – it's just that the worm has not yet turned. In conversation with Maud's American suitor George Bevan, he manages to unburden himself of at least some of his pent-up mental anguish, telling George he doesn't want him as a son-in-law – but that it's nothing personal:

> "I know what you'll be saying to yourself the moment my back is turned. You'll be calling me a stage heavy father and an old snob and a number of other things . . . and you'll be wrong . . . If I were the only person concerned, I wouldn't stand in Maud's way, whoever she wanted to marry, provided he was a good fellow and likely to make her happy. But I'm not. There's my sister Caroline. There's a whole crowd of silly, cackling fools – my sisters – my sons-in-law – all the whole pack of them! If I didn't oppose

Maud in this damned infatuation she's got for you . . .
what do you think would happen to me? I'd never have
a moment's peace! The whole gabbling pack of them
would be at me, saying I was to blame. There would be
arguments, discussions, family councils! I hate arguments!
I loathe discussions! Family councils make me sick! I'm a
peaceable man, and I like a quiet life! And damme, I'm
going to have it".

There's a lot going on below the line of what is, in Wodehouse, a rare
emotional rant. George is a successful theatre composer and is rich –
though his wealth confers no advantage in Caroline's world view, she
being a 24-carat snob ("Mr Bevan is nobody. He comes from nowhere.
He has no social standing whatsoever"). Lord M, being a passionate
theatre fan himself (a good thing in Wodehouse World), has instantly
taken to George, a partiality that is reciprocated.

So, reproducing this exchange live on stage (*A Damsel in Distress* was
turned into a play), an actor speaking these lines would have the difficult
job of making it clear that his character means what he is saying – but
at the same time doesn't. There is already an understanding between
the two men beneath their words, as the friendly and almost flippant
tone of George's responses make clear. It's just that Lord M is not *quite*
ready to make his break with his past, so yes, he *is* playing the role of the
"stage heavy father" that he actually, in his heart, isn't. In the middle of
that explosion (and hidden inside my second ellipsis), the theme of the
rant is not so subtly revealed:

> "*I* don't think the Marshmoretons are fenced off from the
> rest of the world by some sort of divinity. My sister does.
> Percy does. But Percy's an ass!"

As, by implication, is Caroline. Kind hearts *are* worth more than coronets in Lord M's view, and his outburst seems to have acted as a pressure
valve that that has released a dangerous head of steam.

At its next escape later in the novel, his audience comprises George
and Billie Dore, yet another of Plum's big-hearted chorus girls we encountered in the previous volume. Being American, she loves the kind
of English heritage Lord M is so exercised about:

> "Quit knocking your ancestors! You're very lucky to have

ancestors. I wish I had . . . Gee! I'd like to feel that my great-great-great-grandmother had helped Queen Elizabeth with the rent. I'm strong for the fine old stately families of England".

Ironically for the citizens of a republic, Americans appear to adore the English aristocracy; a theme Plum had recently explored in 1917's 'Jeeves and the Hard-Boiled Egg', in which Francis ("Bicky") Bickersteth, domiciled in New York, needs money to free himself from the controlling caprice of his miserly uncle, the Duke of Chiswick, who pays him an allowance. And it is Jeeves who comes up with the cunning plan that will solve the problem, informing Bertie that:

> The inhabitants of this country, as no doubt you are aware, sir, are peculiarly addicted to shaking hands with prominent personages. It occurred to me that Mr Bickersteth or yourself might know of persons who would be willing to pay a small fee – let us say two dollars or three – for the privilege of an introduction, including handshake, to His Grace.

Improbable as it may seem to Bertie and Bicky who have acquired rank, status and titles with their mothers' milk, people would "part with solid cash" for just such an introduction, since it gives them "social standing among the neighbours". So, the Duke, over from England for a visit, is unwittingly turned into a tourist attraction; and until he discovers the plot, simply thinks that Americans are uncommonly friendly.

Back in *A Damsel in Distress*, Billie is revealed as one such aristo-groupie: "[E]very time you cut yourself with your safety-razor, you bleed blue", she teases Lord M, unable to imagine how an earl can actively loathe his heritage. An argument he proceeds to rehearse once again in a rant that's so long I'm going to drastically précis it:

> "Stately old fiddlesticks!! A silly lot of old nonsense! This foolery of titles and aristocracy. Silly fetish-worship! One man's as good as another . . . When I was a boy, I wanted to be an engine-driver. When I was a young man, I was a Socialist and hadn't any idea except to work for my living and make a name for myself. I was going to the colonies. Canada. The fruit farm was actually bought. Bought and paid for! . . . "

Quick paraphrasis to save time . . . Lord M's father being a second son wouldn't have inherited *his* father's earldom. But his elder brother and his elder brother's only son both die, and then he does, conferring the title on our Lord M – a line of succession that was never meant to happen:

> ". . . [a]nd there I was, saddled with the title, and all my plans gone up in smoke . . . Silly nonsense! . . . And you can't stand up against it . . . It saps you. It's like some damned drug. I fought against it as long as I could, but it was no use. I'm as big a snob as any of them now. I'm afraid to do what I want to do. Always thinking of the family dignity. I haven't taken a free step for twenty-five years".

Which, at 48 years old, is over half his life. So here we have a peer on the verge of a nervous breakdown; and of course Billie, being the emotionally generous type, sympathizes with him. Indeed, we are told that "[t]he glimpse she had been given of his inner self had somehow made him come alive for her".

With inevitable consequences. Almost immediately, the fire within him having burned itself out, Lord M quietly explains his dilemma one-on-one to Billie. He's not a snob, he re-iterates, nor even "the Earl of Marshmoreton"; rather he's "a poor spineless fool who's afraid to do the right thing because he daren't go in the teeth of the family". Forty pages later, he's screwed his courage to the sticking place and married her – informing his sister and son in nine short words and bolting from the room "like a diving duck" before they have time to react. The worm may still be a worm, but he locates his spine just long enough to secure his future and make good his escape. The Old World has forged links with the New World, U has embraced non-U, and the English gene pool stands a chance of being replenished. Unless you're Lady Caroline or Percy, what's not to like?

Now I'm not 100% sure of the facts, but there can't be many Socialist peers in British fiction of that era, and it remains an interesting question as to why Plum gave Lord Marshmoreton, a character of whom he seems rather fond, a complex and not wholly necessary back story involving left-of-centre politics, train driving, Canada and fruit farms. Could it be there was something in the air which Wodehouse could sense from 3,000 miles away? Even as the First World War was drawing to its close, a more democratic Britain had been ushered in by the Representation of the People Act of February 1918, which almost tripled the electorate at a stroke from 7.7 million in 1912 to 21.4 million and gave most women over 30 the chance to vote for the first time. This was a massively significant development, even though it stopped short of true equality (men only had to be 21). And while a single piece of legislation didn't on its own translate into a more egalitarian society, considered in tandem with other legal reforms from the previous ten years, Britain was heading, albeit slowly, incrementally and sometimes quite grudgingly, into an era where societal inequality was at least being addressed. Lord M is quite the progressive thinker in this respect, and his rushed exit leaves us with a number of related questions that may trouble us beyond the novel's end. Having gained his freedom from vassalage, will he continue writing the family history? Will he and his new wife live on at Belpher? Can Lady Caroline remain under the same roof as the newlyweds? And when Lady Maud marries George Bevan, how will that work with *two* American "nobodies" in the family? Plum's later romantic comedies wouldn't normally end in such a ragged fashion, but the forward momentum arising from *A Damsel in Distress* makes for interesting speculation.

None of those lines of inquiry can be conclusively answered, nor can the intriguing possibility that Wodehouse was not altogether – how can we put it? – *unsympathetic* to the spin on Socialism (the initial capital is Plum's) exemplified by (a) Lord M's disinclination to snobbery; (b) his wholehearted embrace of social mobility; and (c) his enthusiasm for earning a living. If we insist on posing the question, Plum isn't going to make it easy for us to answer it, just as his evident warmth for the radical Mr Waller while scorning the similarly radical Comrade Prebble has already served to muddy the pool. But that (a), (b) and (c) of the brave new post-war world Lord M seems to embrace and even to a point represent are closely related themes Wodehouse would return to time and again for the rest of his career. And, indeed, almost immediately. In 'Jeeves in the Springtime' from 1921, Mortimer Little comes out with this:

> "Let me tell you, Mr Wooster, that I appreciate your splendid defiance of a purblind social system. I appreciate it! *You* are big enough to see that rank is but the guinea stamp and that, in the magnificent words of Lord Bletchmore in *Only a Factory Girl*, "Be her origin ne-er so humble, a good woman is the equal of the finest lady on earth!"

Bertie is at this point pretending to be Rosie M. Banks, whose syrupy brand of romantic fiction has persuaded Mr Little to bless the marriage of his nephew Bingo to a humble waitress. Indeed, he himself is proposing to marry his cook, being no longer "a slave to the idiotic convention which we call Class Distinction".   And there's plenty more examples of social levelling where this comes from, so it might not be a bad thing if we try and lure Plum out of his hidey-hole on this issue before we proceed much further. Once again, I've tried to tease all the different lines of argument out into neat, separate strands – only it hasn't worked, so tightly are they interwoven in Plum's imagination. So, I'm afraid that that follows might flit about somewhat.

In that *New York Times* article, Wodehouse had informed his American readers that Britain was a divided nation – and not in a good way. *Everything* was separated into upper- and lower-class. Railway carriages had *three* classes. In his own field of publishing, there were posh humorous magazines like *Punch* (cover price 3d [threepence]) and their more numerous downmarket competitors which cost 1d or even ½d. As early as 1903's *A Prefect's Uncle*, Plum had taken a swipe at "those halfpenny weeklies which – with a nerve which is the only creditable thing about them – call themselves comic" and even invents one called *Comic Blatherings.* Here he is clearly referring to magazines (once more) from the Harmsworth stable like *Chips* and *Comic Cuts* which had both been founded in 1890, and which spearheaded a massive, lucrative sub-culture both in reading and associated commerce that the wealthier classes would scarcely have known about – and if they had would have dismissed as trash, as Plum well knew. In a short piece he wrote (ironically for *Punch*) at about the same time, a character named Pettifer admits to his friend Smith that he regularly reads "one of our great halfpenny journals" but whispers its name just in case anyone hears him. He then adds, somewhat gratuitously, that "[i]t has a circulation five times as large as any penny morning paper".

Benjamin Disraeli's concept of "Two Nations" – a phrase the former Prime Minister had used as a subtitle for his influential 1845 novel *Sibyl* – was evidently alive and well seventy years on. Neither the working classes nor the professional/leisured classes had any experience of 'how the other half lives' (or as the mathematically challenged Bertie puts it, "half the world doesn't know how the other three-quarters lives"). But while he was never going to write a crusading 'Condition of England' novel as Disraeli had done, nor even a full-on *roman à these*,

Plum would regularly drop in a social observation or several. In 1912's 'The Goalkeeper and the Plutocrat', he had clumsily satirized the aristocracy's obliviousness to these parallel cultures when the Honourable Clarence Tresillian is forced to scour the deepest recesses of his memory to see if he knows anyone who actually has a job:

> "Work? Well, of course, mind you, fellows *do* work," he went on, thoughtfully. "I was lunching with a man at the Bachelor's only yesterday who swore he knew a fellow who had met a man whose cousin worked . . .

> His father raised himself on the sofa.

> "Haven't I given you the education of an English gentleman?"

> "That's the difficulty," said Clarence.

Then as now, spending those formative years from 8 to 21 at Eton and Oxbridge won't exactly broaden your social horizons. You'll just meet more people like you. It's a problem faced by the penniless Lord Dreever in *A Gentleman of Leisure*, who claims not to be against the *idea* of work, it's simply that he does not quite know what he could actually *do*, lacking the necessary "specialized education" now required. And in 1916's 'The Aunt and the Sluggard', in a moment of blinding insight, Bertie – at his most Knutish – wakes up to the fact that not everyone has a gentleman's personal gentleman like Jeeves to bring him tea in the morning and press his trousers. This, to his credit, saddens him:

> It was rather a solemn thought, don't you know. I mean to say, ever since then I've been able to appreciate the frightful privations the poor have to stick.

Not to the extent of doing anything *about* that regrettable situation, of course, and he quickly drops the subject. But it's Freddie Rooke in *Jill the Reckless* who most perfectly combines his ignorance with a redeeming conscience. On meeting the American chorus girl Nelly Bryant, he suddenly becomes aware that

> Life had treated him so kindly that he had almost forgotten

that there existed a class which had not as much money as himself . . . The thought hurt Freddie like a blow. He hated the idea of anyone being hard up . . . Except for the beggars in the streets, to whom he gave shillings, he had not met anyone for years who had not plenty of money. He had friends at his clubs who frequently claimed to be unable to lay their hands on a bally penny, but the bally penny they wanted to lay their hands on generally turned out to be a couple of thousand pounds for a new car.

In Plum's stories, class, and its attendant snobbery, is not simply a function of heredity; it's just as often – if not more so – to do with money, the gulf between the haves and the have-nots. This made the disease not just genetic, but acquirable and even contagious. In *Piccadilly Jim*, Eugenia Crocker, despite being American, has been "sedulous" in her study of the English aristocracy such that she can "conceal beneath a mask of well-bred indifference any emotion she might chance to feel". And not only that; she has acquired the transatlantic habit of judging everyone by looks rather than personality. So, when she is first introduced to brother-in-law Peter Pett, the spectacularly rich but easy-going New York financier, she is distinctly unimpressed by what she sees:

> She was thinking how hopelessly American Mr Pett was; how baggy his clothes looked; what absurdly shaped shoes he wore; how appalling his hat was; how little hair he had; and how deplorably he lacked all those graces of repose, culture, physical beauty, refinement, dignity and mental alertness which raise men above the level of the common cockroach.

Nice-guy Peter may be rich, but Eugenia's cultivated brand of buttoned-up snobbery considers him way beyond the pale, Plum seeming to imply that the judger rather than the judged is the sadder of the two case studies on display here. Mrs Crocker has actively *taught* herself to be repressed, isolating herself from anyone who is not like her. Unfamiliarity breeds contempt, and social conformity is everything. The English class system has taken another prisoner, even at a distance of three thousand miles.

So far in this argument, it's looking like I'm going to conclude that Wodehouse wasn't remotely a snob, and yet – you're probably getting fed up with me saying this by now – things aren't as simple as all that, and we would not be entirely justified in drawing that conclusion without a few provisos, both biographical and literary. For a start, he seems to have preferred individuals to groups or crowds, having a handful of good, loyal friends which was all he seemed to require. The very opposite of sociable, he was nevertheless typically gracious, agreeable and sensitive to the thoughts and feelings of others. So, I think it's fair to say that while he liked the *idea* of a common humanity, actually going out and mingling with it wasn't his cup of tea. And he was just as likely to be repelled by his own class *en masse* as any other: in a letter to Bill Townend from 1927, he pops into the Garrick Club (q.v.) for something to eat, "took one glance of loathing at the mob" then legged it a mile down the road for a solitary pub lunch at the Cheshire Cheese in Fleet Street (and very good they are too, nearly one century on). Individuals he could cope with; large groups made him less comfortable; large groups of a different class – well, we have no record of Plum's reaction to those.

As we'll start to see in a moment, his portrayal of the working class was comically clichéd, so to stipulate that a more universal humour would evolve from "[t]he classes . . . getting to know each other" would never make it past the theory stage in his own work – and perhaps his life too. Although he had praised fellow English humourist Jerome K. Jerome for not "patronizingly and unsympathetically" chronicling the lower-class and branding them "queer people", he was perhaps tacitly recognizing a tendency in his own writing to do just that. An extreme example can be found in 1935's 'The Come-Back of Battling Billson', in which Ukridge describes the mighty boxer as nothing but a "bone-headed proletarian", a denizen of Wapping whose idea of "the highest thing in the social scale" is a Silver Ring bookie. But even though they aren't his direct words, Plum does tend to use members of the working class – like most humourists back through time - as comedy acts. That's when he notices them at all, for they aren't terribly numerous. For every sympathetic portrait like that of Gladys and Ern, the poor 'fresh-air' London urchins in 'Lord Emsworth and the Girl Friend', there are several drunken, uncouth, feckless, stupid or dodgy rude mechanicals who collectively form something of a stereotype, like that feckless multitude from Panto 4 we met earlier.

Wodehouse employed 11 staff at his 16-room Mayfair gaff ("the gol-darnedest house you ever saw") which he inhabited on-and-off from 1927 to 1934: a butler, a cook, parlourmaids, uniformed footmen, two secretaries and a chauffeur for the Roller. And although he most likely approached them with the same courtesy and friendliness he typically demonstrated to everyone else, Ethel would have had rather more to do with the hiring and firing as the house's châtelaine. Indeed, according to Robert McCrum, this opulent lifestyle was almost entirely Ethel's creation, although Plum "rather enjoyed it" on the quiet. Yes, he was conspicuously rich – even a millionaire (and at 1927 prices); but as he had noted in 1920's *Jill the Reckless*, directly engaging with those lower down the social ladder could be awkward.

Once again, we can use Freddie Rooke as our social litmus, who playfully chastises Jill Mariner for pitching in to help "a lot of fellows shove along a cart that had got stuck" in Bond Street, evidently before it had been tarmacked over. While he's not "blaming" her, Freddie is evidently displaying some discomfort at her "[v]ery decent" offer of assistance to the labouring classes. Jill is one of Plum's golden women; happy, caring, spontaneous and sympathetic, so by the standards set by the novel she's quite clearly in the right, and Freddie is even a tad envious of her social adaptability ("You're so dashed chummy with the lower orders"). Naturally, Jill is indignant, prompting the following exchange:

> "Don't be a snob, Freddie".

> "I'm not a snob," protested Freddie, wounded. "When I'm alone with Barker [his valet] – for instance – I'm chatty as dammit. But I don't ask waiters in public restaurants how their lumbago is".

> "Have you ever had lumbago?"

> "No".

> "Well, it's a very painful thing, and waiters get it just as badly as dukes".

Much to Freddie's exasperation, Jill then goes off to inquire after his valet's chilblains, for which she had earlier prescribed a proprietary ointment. Checkmate.

Freddie, as he later demonstrates, isn't remotely a snob either; it's just that being so well-bred, his spontaneity has been surgically removed and replaced with a priggish good manner which he will have to un-learn before he can re-join humanity. In fact, this conversation takes place while he and Jill await the arrival of a proper 24-carat solid gold snob, Lady Underhill, so frigid she might well have been one of Eugenia Crocker's English mentors. She is due to meet Jill for the first time to assess the latter's suitability as the bride of her son Derek; with such a dyed-in-the-wool aristo, it was an encounter never destined to go well.

Prior to her ladyship's appearance, Jill suffers considerable anxiety: to one of her emotional generosity, this one-way, meat-market approval process is all so "vulgar", something that "only happened in the comic papers and in music-hall songs". And is if to prove her point, she sings one on that very theme, a 1906 smash hit called 'Poor John':

John took me round to see his Mother
His Mother, his Mother
And while he introduced us to each other
She weighed up everything I had on
She put me through a cross examination
I fairly boiled with aggravation
Then she shook her head, looked at me and said
'Poor John, Poor John.'

As far as Jill is concerned, it's quite clear that to one of Lady U's loftiness, just about everyone is lower class, her son's prospective bride being just as vulgar and insignificant as the blokes who dig the street up.

Interestingly, Plum opts to report the meeting offstage through the eyes of Freddie's valet Barker and his wife Ellen, the cook. It's like a mirror image of Freddie's perspective, this time from the bottom up instead of the top down, and although it's his habit to be deferential, Barker takes strong exception to "the old fossil's" haughtiness, which he considers unjust and uncalled for. When he ventures that "Miss Mariner's a long sight too good for her precious son", Ellen's instinctive reaction is that this can't be true, for Sir Derek is a Baronet. Rank cuts no ice with Barker, however, for which he is accused of "talking Socialism". No, he retorts, he's talking "sense" – and, as things turn out, he's proved right: Wodehouse makes sure that Jill ends up with a much more suitable match – which is very possibly *his* comment on the situation he has engineered. Sir Derek may be a sir, but he's a chip off the old block, calling off his marriage to Jill the moment he discovers she's a chorus girl. You wouldn't, Plum implies, want to get hitched to a "blighter" like that.

Fifteen years later, his lightness now firing on all cylinders, Wodehouse was still mulling over the practicalities of the class divide in the superlative 'Archibald and the Masses', in which the narrator (the rascally Mr. Mulliner) pertinently observes that "it's not much good a chap loving the Masses if he never goes near them". His nephew Archibald, a Drone of considerable boneheadedness (whose main claim to fame is his uncanny impersonation of a hen laying an egg), one day encounters "a man of seedy aspects" who, realizing there's one born every minute, reels off a catalogue of afflictions which concludes with the rhetorical flourish, "I wish, sir, you could hear my children crying for bread". At which point Archibald utters the immortal request, "But tell me about bread", as if it's the first time he's heard of such a thing. The panhandler replies:

> "Well, sir, it's this way. If you buy it by the bottle, that's expensive. What I always say is, best to get in a cask. But then again, that needs capital".

Which tired old music-hall joke secures him a fiver – a sum that in 1935 would have bought him well over 100 pints of beer.

Archibald, who appears to know very little about any aspect of day-to-day life, is completely unaware that he has been well and truly soaked, which of course doesn't matter, since there are plenty more fivers where that came from. But the encounter leaves him with "a curious gravity, an odd sense that life was stern and life was earnest" (a slight misquote from the American poet Longfellow), and he asks his valet Meadowes about the non-availability of bread. As it turns out, Meadowes is a member of a far-left group, the League for the Dawn of Freedom, whose ambition is to "hasten the coming revolution", and he lends Archibald a few pamphlets relating to "the martyred proletariat" that excite him strangely. Archibald's fiancée Aurelia rightly points out that he "wouldn't know a martyred proletariat if they brought it to you on a skewer", even as he wrestles with the basics of wealth redistribution:

> "What it all boils down to, if you follow me, is that certain blokes – me, for example – have got too much of the ready, while certain other blokes – the martyred proletariat, for instance, haven't got enough. This makes it fairly foul for the m.p., if you see what I mean".

Unfortunately, Aurelia fails to follow him, at which point Archibald utters another immortal zinger, à propos his hen impersonations:

> "But it seems so shallow. Sir Stafford Cripps doesn't imitate hens".

Cripps was a recently elected Labour Party M.P. who by 1935 had made a name for himself by calling for the abolition of the House of Lords, and urging any future Labour administration to rule by decree, by-passing Parliament in order to enact emergency Socialist-inspired legislation. This ambitious political program would have left him little leisure for hen-imitating. At which point, Archibald decides to undertake a fact-finding trip to (where else?) Bottleton East to mix and mingle with "the m.p." up close and personally. Meadowes clearly has an inkling how things will turn out, noting "There must always be martyrs to the cause, Comrade Mulliner", pouring Archibald a stiff drink before sending him on his way.

The expedition doesn't begin too badly; Archibald had clearly imagined working class life to be conducted in some sort of "grey inferno", only to discover that Bottleton East appears to be "a perfect maelstrom of gaiety". Plum now treats us to a slice of working class life that is straight off a movie set (think of the bustling tavern scene in *Oliver!*) full of chirpy Cockernee types, many of whom appear the worse for drink:

> On every side, merry matrons sat calling each other names on doorsteps. Cheery cats fought among the garbage pails. From the busy public-houses came the sound of mouth-organ and song. While, as for the children, who were present in enormous quantities, so far from crying for bread, as he had been led to expect, they were playing hop-scotch all over the pavements.

And just in case we feel he's singling out the poor for mockery, Plum then includes this telling and slightly subversive comment:

> The whole atmosphere, in a word, was, he tells me, more like that of Guest Night at the National Liberal Club than anything he had ever encountered.

For as we know, if we've been paying attention to Plum's stories, bad behaviour fuelled by alcohol (or indeed Buck-U-Uppo) is not confined to the lower orders – one of the few things that unites the highest and lowest in the land. *In vino unitas*.

With all the grinding poverty Archibald has been led to expect, he is "just a bit disappointed" that things appear otherwise: in fact, everything seems rather "[t]oo bright . . . too bally jovial". Lurking among the humour, there's actually some quite involved psychology in that brief observation: Archibald, whose aim is to show solidarity with the working classes, is slightly crestfallen and even a bit miffed to discover that they seem to be doing alright without his help – and, of course, his condescension. And this might set us to thinking how the impulse to charitable giving can be hijacked by selfish considerations. And yes, it is a comic short story doing this, not some worthy sociology thesis.

Back in the 1880s, *Punch* had cause to pillory the fashion for clergymen (known as "Mashers") who solicited money from the well-to-do in return for escorting them round their deprived parishes, so that those privileged types could exercise their pity and feel all the more virtuous for engaging in charitable activity. Well, fifty years on, Archibald is indulging in the same kind of 'poverty tourism', only – ill advisedly – without a guide. He has fallen into the trap of sentimentalizing the socially disadvantaged and has ended up aiming to do the right thing for precisely the wrong reason. Hence his disappointment that the urban poor aren't behaving in the way they should in order to solicit his sympathy. To a certain class of philanthropist, the proper role of the poor is to be gratefully patronized, and to demonstrate contrition for being poor in the first place. In this way they can make themselves worthy of charity, for which they should be properly demonstrate "tearful gratitude" as Plum puts it here. And then there's the attendant issue of the poor being used to help grind political axes on both the Right and Left: Meadowes's pamphlets come with a political agenda which the well-meaning but dim-witted Archibald (a man "incapable of subterfuge") couldn't possibly begin to fathom – and further disillusion inevitably follows.

Nothing abashed, Archibald, armed with a hefty quartern loaf, goes off in search of a starving child in need of sustenance. Unfortunately, the child he selects would have preferred a gift of sweets and lobs the bread back at his benefactor, hitting him square on the nape of his neck. Here is yet another theme that is regularly played out in newspaper reports to this day – the-poor-who-will-not-be-helped-but-live-off-fags-booze-scratchcards-and-Haribos. Archibald, the spurned philanthropist, instantly sees red and gives chase to his retreating malefactor:

> The thing seemed to him a straight issue. This child needed bread, and he was jolly well going to get it – even if it meant holding him with one hand and shoving the stuff down his throat with the other. In all the history of social work in London's East End there can seldom have been an instance of one of the philanthropic rich more firmly bent on doing good and giving of his abundance.

The ungrateful child quickly gives him the slip. But Archibald, determined to pursue his mission, next finds himself in a pub buying drinks all round, and "his favourable opinion of the Masses", somewhat punctured by the young bread-flinger, returns as he finds himself the centre of attention, his audience hanging on his every word as if he is the "Master Mind". Fellowship with the working classes *is* possible, Archibald now believes; you only have to take the trouble to meet them on their own ground. And, as Mr Mulliner speculates, that "first half-hour in the tap-room of the Goose and Gherkin was . . . the happiest of my nephew Archibald's life," for no-one it seems has ever listened to him before, let alone taken him seriously. For the merest hint of time, Archibald, like Lord Marshmoreton before him, becomes a fellow human being we can sympathize with, even if his audience is a bunch of drunks whose temporary attention he has bought. It's more than a little poignant.

But then, somewhat inevitably, Plum pricks this fantasy when Archibald discovers his wallet is missing, presumed stolen. Credit being hard to come by in Bottleton East, it is assumed he's trying to bilk the barman big-time and he is vigorously assaulted by that formerly jolly publican before being pursued hither and yon by a selection of his erstwhile compadres. Once again, Archibald's opinion of the Masses swings to the darker side such that, we're told, both Sir Stafford Cripps and Stalin would have heartily disapproved, for he wishes that "the martyred proletariat would choke". It's all a far cry from where the story started out.

But are there any lessons we can take away from this excellent satire? No, of course not – or at least not ones that will stick. Plum's mid-season lightness has seen to that, despite the topical references and spot-on social observation. For the way he metabolizes politics and social issues, juxtaposing the real with the fantastical, doesn't quite allow us to do so with any genuine conviction. It somehow feels wrong-headed and even pretentious to read anything serious into something so wonderfully light-hearted. Yet that kernel of reality is still very much there, the satire all present and correct. What's actually happening is that satire, which is itself a subversive genre, is routinely being subverted by comedy, making any 'message' we might take from the story lighter than light and not to be taken seriously. The well-meaning but ignorant Archibald tries to convince himself that those he is trying to help are worth the effort, while routinely being disabused of that idealism, creating a pendulum effect reflected in his mood swings. By the end, however, he decides these "tortured bounders" aren't worth his sympathy, and he returns to his natural home in Mayfair, chastened by his failed experiment in social mobility – but not before he has confirmed his patrician status by landing the customary blow to a policeman's abdomen, for which he'll likely get fourteen days without the option.

'Archibald and the Masses' turns out to be a highly ambivalent story. The two nations are quite clearly still divided; but where does the blame lie for this mutual lack of understanding? It's difficult, if not impossible to tell, for what Plum presents us with is blank incomprehension on both sides: each is equally exotic to the other, which doesn't bode well for any bridge-building and certainly not upward mobility. It's a problem that seems ripe but not necessarily ready for solving. Similarly inconclusive is a telling incident from 1931's *Big Money*, in which the class conflict erupts into violence even in a district as peaceful and idyllic as Valley Fields – in real life, Plum's beloved Dulwich.

Once more, as in the case of Beefy Bastable, the catalyst is a top hat – grey, this time. Lost and in need of orientation, Lord Hoddesdon, the wearer of the headgear in question, addresses a red-eyed man in a cloth cap leaning against the wall of a pub. Given that his lordship is perpetually broke, he is in no position to exercise any patrician privilege, or as the narrator grandiloquently puts it:

> Impecuniosity and the exigencies of a democratic age had combined to cause his lordship to be sparing of the *hauteur* which so often goes with blue blood.

But even the simple act of democratically asking for directions occasions the following tirade from one clearly on the opposite side of the class divide:

> "[S]' enough to make a man sick. They wouldn't 'ave none
> of that in Moscow. No, *nor* in Leningrad. The Burjoisy,
> that's what you are, for all your top-'ats. Do you know what
> would happen to you in Moscow? Somebody – as it might
> be Stayling – would come along and 'e'd look at that 'at
> and 'e'd say "What are you doing, you Burjoise, swanking
> around in a 'at like that?"

Once again, Plum makes his representative from the working class
somewhat the worse for drink. Note also his difficulty in pronouncing
names and words from overseas, and as if to further emphasize the difference between the classes, the narrator positively erupts into French:

> In Bond Street, or Piccadilly, a grey top-hat is *chic, de rigueur*,
> and *le dernier cri*. In Valley Fields, less than seven miles
> distant, it is *outré* and, one might almost say, *farouche*.

Unfortunately, the offence the topper causes the red-eyed man extends
beyond posh words; indeed, he feels as though "his manhood and self-respect had been outraged" by Lord Hoddesdon's toffee-nosed choice
of headgear. This "imperfect sympathy" between the pair doesn't improve, and after a random urchin gets involved – who turns out to be the
drunk's son – a chase ensues with the Earl as the prey. Finally giving his
pursuers the slip, Lord Hoddesdon gains his release "from the society of
one on whom he could never look as a friend", and another opportunity
to bridge the class divide is lost to eternity.

It seems meaningful reform of the social order won't be effected by
breaking down social divisions, which are just too deeply ingrained. But
what about the re-distribution of wealth? That might work. And not
just Archibald's brand of charity either, but a root and branch restruc-
turing of society. As Archibald's distant cousin Mervyn Mulliner walks
along Piccadilly – the spine and central nervous system of Wodehouse
World – in 'The Knightly Quest of Mervyn', he reflects on the issue of
why the rich are getting richer and the poor remain poor:

> As he surveyed the passing populace, he suddenly realized
> . . .what these Bolshevist blokes were driving at. They had
> spotted – as he had spotted now – that what was wrong with
> the world was that all the cash seemed to be centred in the
> wrong hands and needed a lot of broad-minded distribution.

Where money was concerned, he perceived, merit counted for nothing. Money was too apt to be collared by some rotten bounder or bounders, while the good and deserving man was left standing on the outside, looking in. The sight of all those expensive cars rolling along, crammed to the bulwarks with overfed males and females with fur coats and double chins, made him feel . . . that he wanted to buy a red tie and a couple of bombs and start the Social Revolution. If Stalin had come along at that moment, Mervyn would have shaken him by the hand.

As you stroll down Piccadilly in the 21st century, deafened by £900K supercars roaring past, you might also give some house room to his frustrations. But it turns out that Mervyn is only feeling sorry for himself, the source of his revolutionary fervour being Oofy Prosser, the pimpled Drones Club millionaire who has failed to pony up a much-needed loan of 20 quid. Oofy is often the lightning rod for such socialistic feelings, given that he would rather walk 500 miles in tight shoes (and then 500 more) than dig into his wallet to help a friend in need. From his debut in 1931 right the way through to 1974, his name is a by-word for tight-fistedness, dodgy dealings and chancy schemes – as well it might be, 'oof' being slang for money and a 'prosser' being one who borrows or is mean with it. Unfortunately, however, Mervyn is long on theory and short on solutions, so instead of plotting the overthrow of the Burjoisy, he retires to his club and downs three Martini cocktails to rid himself of his social angst. Alcohol – that cause of, and solution to – many of the world's problems, triumphs again.

Back in *Big Money*, we have another socialist theoretician, this time Godfrey Edward Winstanley Brent, otherwise known as Lord Biskerton, or "Biscuit", son of the fugitive Lord Hoddesdon of the offensive top hat. Having judged that all society's ills stem from the inequitable ownership of wealth, he proposes a scheme that would, if adopted, "scatter sweetness and light and . . . scatter them good", as well as "increase the sum of human happiness a hundredfold". Twice a year, the rich (or as Biscuit describes them "these old crumbs with their hoarded wealth") would be arraigned before an "Examiner" and quizzed as to whether they had put their money to good use. If they'd simply hoarded it, they would be subject to a massive penalty that would be given to the deserving poor – such as Biscuit and his friend Berry Conway. And then having "conjured up" this self-serving financial "Utopia", Biscuit's inspiration dries up. Once again, it looks like the Great Society is going to have to be put on hold while someone comes up with a better idea.

But even if social mobility and genuine equality could somehow be brought to pass, would anyone be happier? This is one of the issues Plum jokily addresses throughout 1931's *If I Were You*, in which Anthony Claude Wilbraham Bryce, 5th Earl of Droitwich ("Tony"), appears to be the victim of some raw work in the nursery. His nanny – yet another of Plum's working-class tipplers – has a son, Syd, of a similar age, and while in her cups might have got the babies mixed up. Syd now runs a barber's shop in upscale Knightsbridge, home then as now to Harrod's department store. And so, the scene is set for a *Prince and the Pauper*-type plot in which the two men swap lives while the case of who-is-who is settled, and Plum can rehearse some of his favourite themes pertaining to the social divide – only in rather greater depth than is customary in his stories.

First, we are introduced to the 'new money' characters: Tony – at this stage still a toff – is engaged to the stunning Violet Waddington, heiress to the Waddington's Ninety-Seven Soups empire, who has travelled over from America with the specific aim of bagging an English aristo. As far as she is concerned, the relationship is purely transactional, as she tells her father:

> "[Y]ou know and I know that it's simply a business deal. I provide the money. Tony supplies the title. Do let's be honest. You brought me down here to land Tony. And I've landed him".

Tony's money-conscious family has helped stage-manage the betrothal, so much so that Violet feels that "the whole thing was like shooting a sitting bird . . . All that annoys me is that it was so darned *easy*". Violet clearly isn't one of Plum's many open-hearted, sympathetic American women of the kind we met in the previous volume. But Polly Brown, the humble manicurist whom Tony meets at Syd's salon most definitely is, and he naturally ends up falling for her guileless charm and evident intelligence. This isn't the problem it might be; as soon as there's any doubt about Tony's parentage, his "market value" is compromised and Violet helpfully dumps him, proving that once more in Wodehouse World, wealth pursued for its own sake has a corrosive effect on those who chase after it – Violet being a particularly unpleasant example of cold calculation. More of her in a moment.

Next, we have the 'old money' characters – the aristocrats themselves. Lady Lydia and her husband Sir Herbert Bassinger (a refugee
from *Big Money* who has made his fortune from cloves, of all things)
are the comic turn whose interests dovetail perfectly with those of the
American adventurers. But Tony is a different proposition altogether.
When we first meet him, he is soiled and dishevelled from tinkering
with his car, branding him one of Plum's 'modern' characters – an earl,
like the Lords Marshmoreton and Emsworth, who isn't afraid to get
his hands dirty. His instincts are on the egalitarian side both in outlook
and behaviour, at least compared with his Knut-ish brother Freddie,
who dismisses Syd as a "highly septic little bounder". Tony, by contrast,
displays a natural ease when chatting with the hairdresser, seemingly
unconcerned by the social gulf that separates them. Indeed, when he
learns that Syd is imperilling his (Tony's) social standing, he seems remarkably sanguine about the whole affair. Even when the switcheroo
has been completed and he's reduced to working as a barber, Tony takes
a dim view of Lydia and Sir Herbert's conniving to return him to his
'rightful' position, even though up to this point he's allowed himself to
be carried along by their scheme:

> "I should have thought that the only excuse for people like
> us is that we're sportsmen. Every time, in the old days, that
> I got a twinge of conscience at the thought that I was living
> off the fat of the land and doing nothing to deserve it, I
> used to console myself by reflecting: "Well, at least, I'm a
> sportsman!" And here I am, lending myself to a conspira-
> cy to cheat this poor little blighter out of his rights".

Once again, there's some interesting psychology going on here. Whoever's who, there's absolutely no question that Tony and Syd can ever
be considered as equals. Look at Tony's description of Syd as a "poor
little blighter", with the emphasis on "little" – a word that his brother
Freddie has already used to label the pretender. He doesn't necessarily
mean to be, but Tony's being intensely patronizing here, his casually
assumed superiority shining through for all his talk of sportsmanship.
Then again, we might argue that this small but telling faux pas isn't terribly significant; what we should take away from this is that Tony feels
everyone should be *treated* the same, not that they *are* the same.

If after this we're still in doubt as to which baby was which (which
the plot requires we do in order to work properly), the ambiguity poses

a further question: if Tony is the genuine toff, this would indicate his superiority is innate; if he isn't, it has had to be learned. Nature versus Nurture isn't a theme that's often examined in any depth in Wodehouse World, but here it is, being just one of the threads in this satirical and quite nuanced dissection of good old-fashioned English snobbery. On balance, Tony *does* appear to feel sorry for Syd, and consequently the argument he enters into with his relatives (with Violet back in tow) grows quite heated. Perhaps he's fighting his own casual assumptions just as much as everyone else's.

In the beginning, Uncle Herbert suggests – utterly hypocritically – that in doing Syd down, he and his wife are selflessly acting in Tony's best interests and not their own, reasoning Tony instantly dismisses. Sensing his lack of appreciation, Violet tosses in an apposite Shakespeare quote from *As You Like It* directed at Tony ("Blow, blow, thou winter wind/ Thou art not so unkind/ As man's ingratitude"). Tony snaps back, "Oh, for God's sake . . . don't be funny!", wondering "[m]ore than ever before . . . how he had ever come to make a fool of himself with this loathsome girl". As Tony gets more aerated, we can see that fairness is a principle he feels passionately about, having broken what the narrator mysteriously refers to as "the Code", which seems to be based on the rules of cricket – not the game itself, but the public-school principle of playing a straight bat in our relations with others, whoever they might be and wherever they're from. Tony does not want to be seen to be "playing a dirty game", a suggestion Sir Herbert dismisses out of hand:

> Don't you realize . . . that if this fellow wins his case it will
> be a menace to the whole peerage?"

The social order, the status quo, the way things *should* be – will collapse if any old Tom, Dick or Harry can get into the House of Lords. To which Tony correctly responds that there have been "common men in the peerage before". And it's at this point the argument grows even more complex and ridiculous at one and the same time.

By Sir Herbert's lights, those plebeians who were made into peers essentially lucked out. They were one-offs and didn't "represent a tradition". But Syd *might* have been born a lord; yet despite enjoying that "sacred heritage of birth" and having "the blood of God knows how many earls in his veins", he can only act like a "costermonger" because he knows nothing different. Which introduces the possibility that in reality, being accepted as an aristocrat is wholly dependent on Nurture and not Nature. Syd may have blue blood but doesn't *behave* like an aristocrat should: the Nature is there but the Nurture is absent, and in a world where looks are everything, this effectively means he *isn't* one. Dolly back one level of perspective as Lady Lydia now does, and the issue becomes even more involved: the whole edifice that is the English "aristocracy" isn't real, but one big act:

> "[T]he whole British social system . . . rests on the princi-
> ple that a man with [Syd's] ancestry can't be a vulgarian".

Poor old Syd can't win: if he wasn't born a lord, he plainly isn't Lord Droitwich; but even if he were proved to be Lord Droitwich, he still isn't *because no-one will believe he is.* If he could walk the walk and talk the talk, he might just pass muster – which is the entire theme of George Bernard Shaw's *Pygmalion*, a play with which *If I Were You* has much in common. But in this case, it's clear that no amount of grooming and instruction will work. Syd is not necessarily *who* he is but *what* he is – which, if he is a lord, threatens the mystique of the aristocracy, making it more of a catwalk parade than a "sacred heritage of birth". Who said Plum wasn't a Radical?

Tony is unmoved by all these complicated arguments, at which point his interlocutors brand him "insane", switching their strategy back to their self-interest rather than all that spurious concern for the future of the aristocracy. Tony admits that Syd is a difficult person to like, but that is no reason to deprive him of his birthright. For which Sir Herbert accuses him of being "like one of those men on soap-boxes in the park" – for which read "Socialist". At which point, the *Pygmalion* theme clicks in good and proper, as we compare the two men in their new unaccustomed roles – a sort of double-symmetry *Pygmalion* in fact, with both characters having to un-learn who they were and learn who they're now supposed to be, one going down in the world, the other going up.

Tony, aided and abetted by having fallen in love with Polly, is really rather enjoying being a barber. It's all a question, she says rather gnomically, of being "comfortable" with who you are:

> "Nobody's going to be happy in this world if they're not
> comfortable. A king wouldn't be happy if his shoes pinched
> him".

Which sounds like something out of Aesop's *Fables* or *Forrest Gump* – take your pick. Only it does ring true here: at least for the brief time he wears them, Tony's new shoes seem to fit quite well; like Lord Marshmoreton unburdening himself of the family history, "[he] had never been happier in his life". On being rid of Violet and the future straitjacket she represents, he feels "free at last".

Syd's enslavement, by contrast, is only just starting. He is being cynically groomed by Sir Herbert and Lady Lydia, whose motives are every bit as conflicted as Henry Higgins with his pupil Eliza Doolittle. Syd wants to renounce his title when he discovers that being an aristocrat involves doing everything this "Cockney to the marrow" can't stand: going to art exhibitions, lectures and concerts, and above all else riding in Rotten Row. Unfortunately for the conspirators, Tony continues to play his straight bat by helpfully separating out some of the desirables from the essentials in the aristocrat's job description. "What", he asks Syd, "is your mental picture of an earl?" To which Syd answers with what he's been told:

> "Oo . . . Well, I don't know . . . 'Igh-class sort of feller . . . [w]ith a taste for concerts and lectures, and at the same time a crack shot, a splendid horseman, a good dancer, a brilliant conversationalist and an amusing after-dinner speaker".

To which Tony replies:

> "If you can find one earl who fills the bill, I'll eat my hat . . . Nine earls out of ten . . . wouldn't be able to tell Brahms from Irving Berlin, and wouldn't want to. Seventy per cent of them never attended a lecture in their lives. Eighty-five couldn't make a speech if you paid them. And, to cap it all, there are at least one or two who can't ride".

Syd is gobsmacked that aristocrats can be so conniving, particularly since Sir Herbert and Lady Lydia are his 'relatives'. But then Tony disabuses him of another illusion, one which was encapsulated in that tortuous argument a few paragraphs back: "they don't feel they *are* your relations", he explains, adding somewhat ambiguously, "You can't blame them really". Although Plum has dangled the possibility that a barber might one day become an earl, there is never any real danger that it might *actually* happen. Even the narrator, at times, allies himself with the anti-Syd camp, indicating that by the end, the social structure will remain unthreatened and the mystique of the aristocracy preserved.

And then comes the denouement: whoever turns out to own the barber's shop will inherit the formula for a patent hair restorer that Freddie has successfully sold to a rich American investor. So faced with the choice of being an aristocrat or simply rich, Syd renounces his claim to the Droitwich earldom quick as a flash, leaving Tony with his title and free to marry Polly. Although some more eligible débutante from a good family is destined to be disappointed, Lady Lydia throws in the towel and gives the couple her blessing. Thus, while there may be a touch of social mobility in the plot, it's not of the headline-grabbing variety there would have been had Syd won his case in court. Money, and once again American money, has helped put everything right, and although Polly has scruples about being a countess, Tony jokily assures her that "They're just as good as you are" – and not, you'll notice "You're just as good as they are".

Plum has things both ways, as Tony's closing speech makes clear. If he was always an earl, nothing has changed. But there is that second possibility, as he tells Polly:

> "When you accepted me, I was a barber. By industry and enterprise I have worked my way up to being an earl. You can't let me down now. It would be a blow to all ambition. Think of the young men, trying to get on in the world, whom it would discourage. What's the use of sweating to make good, they would say, if your girl's going to chuck you in the hour of triumph?"

Social mobility is possible . . . possibly. But Plum isn't going to burden his readers with a clearly stated message of any kind, preferring to raise questions rather than provide neat solutions. Tony proves himself a cricketer whether he has a title or not; and the good – who are not necessarily the great – will end up finding one another whichever end of society they come from. And so, as regards the subject of this chapter, Plum is dangling the *prospect* of change in front of us, while not holding out too much hope that it's going to happen in any systemic way. For the will to change seems to come more from the individual within than society without, and for people like Lord Marshmoreton and Tony, theirs are personal struggles for happiness that don't necessarily reflect a more general longing – or the possibility – for a more egalitarian social order. What never changes in Wodehouse World is the principle that love conquers all. Love sets Tony free, whoever he is, whereas a union with Violet would have had the opposite effect, whoever he was.

Fortunately, the estate of Langley End, the family seat of the Droitwiches, appears to be in good financial shape. We are not told of any life-sapping difficulties the earl will have to tackle, so all is set fair for the couple's future happiness. But this is not the case with many another of Plum's stately homes. With the Burjoisy in the ascendant, real wealth is being created and hoarded by that middle-aged, dyspeptic gang of businessmen and Napoleonic entrepreneurs from Chapter 3, with practically everyone else having to scavenge a living on the margins of their activities, including a goodly number of those who were formerly rich but aren't any longer. Once more it's a cue for Plum to turn on the satire, creating storylines documenting how society changes when money gets too tight to mention.

THE STATELY HOMES

OF ENGLAND

Chapter 5:
The Stately Homes of England

"The stately homes of England / How beautiful they
stand! / Amidst their tall ancestral trees / O'er all the
pleasant land".
Felicia Hemans, 1827

"The stately homes of England / We proudly represent /
We only keep them up for / Americans to rent".
Noël Coward, 1938

"[Y]ou can get an American to buy any old bit of black
timber, just by telling him it comes from the Forest of
Arden, or was sneezed on by Shakespeare, or something".
Sarah Waters, The Little Stranger, 2009

Nothing in Wodehouse World epitomizes the pace of change in the
20th century so piquantly as the decline and fall of the English country house. As Plum helpfully informs us in his 1959 essay 'My World',
armed with half a crown, you can go and visit over 300 such institutions
which, as he puts it, are "now in the side-show business":

> Drop in, for instance, on the Duke of Bedford at Woburn Ab-
> bey . . . and you will not only be greeted by His Grace in person,
> and shown the house and all its artistic treasures but will get a
> snack lunch and be able to listen to the latest hits on the juke-
> box. The same conditions prevail at Chatsworth, the Duke of
> Devonshire's little place up Derbyshire way . . .

Plum, by this stage permanently domiciled across the Atlantic, had no
doubt gleaned this information from his newspaper, and there is a distinctly ambivalent tone in those lines. Is this the way things should be, or
some dreadful modern imposition born of guilt or a shortage of funds?

His Grace's dilemma reminds us of the scenario of 'Lord Emsworth
and the Girl Friend', in which, as Lord of the Manor, Clarence is forced
to endure the annual invasion from the great unwashed on the August
Bank Holiday. Unlike his modern equivalents, however, Clarence isn't
throwing wide his gates to boost his income, but as a nod to those feudal
days when the manor was the biggest building for miles around, and

the hub of the entire local community. Back when these ancestral piles were built and their grounds laid, money was often no object, with everything conceived on the grand scale – perhaps not *quite* as OTT as Welbeck Abbey which we visited earlier in this book, but grand nonetheless. In *Company for Henry*, the narrator's eye dwells for a short time on the Regency splendour of Ashby Hall's artificial lake:

> It was a lake of considerable size. One of the many things Beau Paradene, when building the hall in the eighteen-twenties, had resolved not to economize on had been the sheet of ornamental water which the custom of those days held indispensable to the country seat of a man of property. Its construction had called for the services of a small army of diggers and paving the floor with stone had not been cheap, but he had a soul above all sordid consideration of expense. The result was in every way satisfactory to him, especially after he had caused a few statues to be scattered around and had added the marble temple without which no gentleman's ornamental water was thought complete.

Scroll forward a century and a half, and that pleasing prospect has become something of a millstone. This is certainly the case at Mellingham Hall from 1970's *The Girl in Blue*, in which Crispin Scropes, the beleaguered head of the household, is forced to take in paying guests while still owing a longstanding debt over £200 which a broker has been sent to collect. In this, the last of his stately piles, Plum definitively itemizes its numerous liabilities, and the personal anguish finding that money entails. Crispin, in sheer exasperation, almost spits out the following paragraph:

> "Who wants a house nowadays that's miles from anywhere and the size of Buckingham Palace? And look at the way it eats up money. Repairs, repairs, everlasting repairs – the roof, the stairs, the ceilings, the plumbing, there's no end to it. And that's just inside. Outside, trees needing pruning, hedges needing clipping, acres of grass that doesn't cut itself, and the lake smelling to heaven if the weeds aren't cleaned out every second Thursday. And the tenants. Those farmers sit up at night trying to think of new ways

for you to spend money on them. It's enough to drive a man dotty. I remember, when I was a boy, Father used to take me round the park at Mellingham and say "some day, Crispin, all this will be yours". He ought to have added, "And may the Lord have mercy on your soul"."

This is the modern reality of running a stately home. And in *Pearls, Girls and Monty Bodkin* from 1972, we discover that the Hall has been finally rented out– to Grayce Llewellyn, the wife of movie mogul Ivor – and you can't see Crispin for dust. He's long gone, having rid himself of the family burden, of which he considers himself well shot.

Since 1909's *A Gentleman of Leisure*, Plum had been chronicling this decline in the fortunes of the aristocracy, the English country house often being the decaying symbol of its fall from prominence. In that novel, as we've already seen, the family fortune has been steadily frittered away in fruitless speculation and gambling by Regency bucks: by the early 20th century, there's "about eighteenpence [left] in the old oak chest". Enter Sir Thomas Blunt, the Napoleonic chairman of Blunt's Stores Ltd., somewhat inevitably an M.P., and "one of the finest and most complete specimens of the came-over-Waterloo-Bridge-with-half-a-crown-in-my-pocket-and-now-look-at-me class of millionaire in existence", an unlikely white knight who marries into the family, assumes control of the purse strings and treats the castle much as he would a branch of his retail empire. This includes strongly encouraging the hereditary owner, Lord Dreever, to marry into serious money when in fact, like Lord Marshmoreton, he fancies someone further down the social pecking order (Katie, the daughter of a mere general).

These old country piles may ooze history and tradition (in *The Prince and Betty*, Norworth Court is possessed of an "atmosphere of permanence" that is "frightening" to its overseas visitors), but in reality, they are well past their sell-by date. In 1915's *Something Fresh*, we are already being told that the estate adjacent to Blandings has been vacated and rented out to a dyspeptic American multi-millionaire in an early example of 'new' money displacing inherited wealth ("Damme, they all seem millionaires in America", comments Lord Emsworth, "Wish I knew how they managed it"). English earls may dine out on the sanctity of the family traditions, but to a seasoned fraudster like Soapy Molloy in *Money for Nothing*, they're nothing but "glorified farmers" up for any get-rich-quick deal that'll get them out of a financial hole.

And the biggest hole was tax owing to the Chancellor of the

Exchequer. The problem is succinctly expressed by the Biscuit early on in *Big Money*:

> "What with the Land Tax and the Income Tax and the Super Tax and all the rest of the little Taxes, there's not much in the family sock these days, old boy. It all comes down to this . . . If England wants a happy, well-fed aristocracy, she mustn't have wars. She can't have it both ways".

Wars have to be paid for, and by 1931 when this story was written, the U.K. was only just starting to address the debt from the 1914-18 conflict – a series of loans that wasn't fully paid off until March 9, 2015. And no, that's not a typo. But as we saw back in Chapter 1, prior to the war baby steps had already been taken as regards the more equitable distribution of wealth, and one of the first revenue raisers to help pay for this was the land tax reform proposed in 1909's so-called People's Budget. If an aristo wanted to raise some ready cash by selling off land, a 20% capital gains tax was now payable, which would be put towards the creation of a rudimentary welfare state. To many of those affected, this was the thin end of a Socialist wedge, but justifying the move, the Liberal politician David Lloyd George fired back that "a fully-equipped duke costs as much to keep up as two Dreadnoughts [large battleships]; and dukes are just as great a terror and they last longer". He was to win the argument.

After the war, further pain arrived with the 1919 Finance Act, which ramped up inheritance tax to a maximum of 40% on estates valued at over £2 million. Which meant that the custodians of Highclere Castle (where *Downton Abbey* is filmed) had to shell out £500,000 when the fifth Earl of Carnarvon died in 1923 – a sum equivalent to over £30 million at today's values. And if land and inheritance taxes weren't enough trouble, there was a further tax issue that crops up in several Wodehouse plots, where an aristo with immediate cashflow issues isn't allowed to sell off family assets such as art, antiques or jewels, since they form part of his estate on which taxes will be payable at his death. No wonder many of Plum's belted earls – and even some of his landed gentry – are portrayed as hard up, because in real life they actually would have been.

Take Mr Smith, father of Psmith, as an example. Although not titled, he proves to be the financial deus ex machina at the close of *Psmith in the City*, paying for Mike Jackson's place at Cambridge and subsequently employing him as land agent on his estate. By 1923's *Leave it to Psmith*, however, it's all gone horribly wrong, as Mike's wife Phyllis informs us:

> "We had hardly got married, when poor Mr. Smith died and the whole place was broken up. He must have been speculating or something, I suppose, because he hardly left any money, and the estate had to be sold. And the people who bought it - they were coal people from Wolverhampton - had a nephew for whom they wanted the agent job, so Mike had to go".

Once again, we see the Bourjoisy – the industrial Bourjoisy this time – hoovering up assets that had previously belonged to those with wealth and privilege. As David L. Leal correctly notes in the Spring 2020 edition of *Plum Lines*, "The words 'coal' and 'Wolverhampton' were undoubtedly chosen to convey the horror of a world turning upside down".

And of course, Plum had his own issues with money – not so much its availability, but the difficulty of hanging on to it. By 1921, he had tried to limit his payments to the taxman by living outside England for six months in the year, continually commuting across the Atlantic throughout that decade, and later holing up in France. It's no coincidence that four of his novels have 'Money' in their titles, and in chapter 13 of Robert McCrum's biography, the history of Plum's finances is crisply and conveniently rehearsed, so no need for duplication here. Suffice to say that references to tax in his stories begin as early as 1924's *Bill the Conqueror*, his personal problems reaching a crescendo in 1933 as the revenue authorities in both Britain and America pursued him for unpaid money. The U.K. Inland Revenue alone were chasing him for £40,000 (nearly £3 million today – and no, that isn't a misprint either, for these values come direct from the U.K. Government's Consumer Prices Index comparator). Not surprisingly, Plum embarked on an appeal – which he won, dedicating 1934's *Right Ho, Jeeves* to Raymond Needham Q.C. – the silk who had got him off – "with affection and admiration". But that was not the end of things: ping-ponging between Britain and America, his income was always likely to fall between the two stools, tax officials from each (or sometimes both) countries gleefully eyeing it up at least until 1948, when he took up full-time residence in the U.S., before finally becoming a citizen in 1955.

It's against this background of debt and taxation – personal, institutional and even national – that many of Wodehouse's plots play themselves out. Britain is poor, and even its aristocracy, the very class everyone imagines has all the money, is often revealed as having moths in its wallet. Remember that well-to-do gentleman from Panto 4 back in 1907? Same principle. And so, in 1928's *Money for Nothing*, Lester Carmody, trustee of Rudge Hall, explains to Soapy Molloy about the impossibility of flogging its many heirlooms, and how all this "potential wealth" is "allowed to lie idle" when it could be put to better use. "Everything that comes in goes out again as expenses", he explains; and he needs to keep a decent war chest going in case of trouble from his tenant farmers, whose habit is to "sit up at night trying to think of new claims they can make against a landlord". In Lester's case, however, he is pleading poverty while still well off. The second son of a second son (cf. Lord Marshmoreton) he was sent to work in the City, where he made a sizeable packet which he means to hang on to and even grow where feasible. Hence his plan to have the heirlooms stolen so he can trouser the insurance, for he seems to view his life as "one long series of disbursements". So it proves, for as with many another greedy individual in Plum's stories, his account ends up in debit by the plot's end, having literally paid the price to put everything right in the final act.

Some of Lester's fellow country house custodians are not as financially fortunate as he. In *Big Money*, our top-hatted friend Lord Hoddesdon, having made the mistake of marrying a chorus girl rather than seeking out an American millionairess, is on his uppers thanks to the continuous drain on his finances that is "his old ancestral seat" Edgeling Hall, which "costs a fortune to keep up", is "too big to let" and "a white elephant generally". In *Thank You, Jeeves* from 1934, Bertie's mate Chuffy of Chuffnell Hall is

> . . . dashed hard up, poor bloke, like most fellows who own land, and only lives at Chuffnell Hall because he's stuck with it and can't afford to live anywhere else. If somebody came to him and offered to buy the place, he would kiss him on both cheeks. But who wants to buy a house like that in these times? He can't even let it.

And that's not all:

> Chuffy also owns the village of Chuffnell Regis – not that that does him much good, either. I mean to say, the taxes on the estate and all the expenses on repairs and what not come to pretty nearly as much as he gets out of the rents,

making the thing more or less of a washout.

In these extracts, Plum is chronicling the precipitous decline of a way of life that had continued unbroken for pretty much a thousand years. The great hall, with its service village just outside its gates, was – and is – a fixture of the British landscape that now, in the modern age, was more of an albatross round its owner's neck than a treasured family asset. By the 1930s, the gentry's financial plight had been further worsened by the global fallout from the financial crash of 1929 (in which Plum estimated that he and Ethel had dropped £150K – a staggering £10 million at today's prices). So, all was not well with the toffage as the 1930s wore on – quite apart from the gathering political storm clouds in Europe.

Plum's troupe of custodians have numerous ingenious ways of addressing their lack of even the smallest of small change. Perhaps the most drastic can be witnessed in 1934's 'The Fiery Wooing of Mordred', in which Annabelle Sprockett-Sprockett of Smattering Hall, Lower Smattering-on-the-Wissel, invites Mordred Mulliner to stay at her grand homestead, which the family wish to burn to the ground so they can collect on the insurance. And Mordred, being a negligent smoker who has already torched two rented apartments seems the ideal house guest with such a project in the offing.

On his arrival, Mordred discovers Smattering to be

> one of those vast edifices, so common throughout the countryside of England, whose original founders seem to have budgeted for families of twenty-five or so and a domestic staff of not less than a hundred . . . Romantic persons, confronted with it, thought of knights in armour riding forth to the Crusades. More earthy individuals felt that it must cost a packet to keep up.

Mordred tries his best to incinerate it with a carelessly discarded cigarette, but his fellow house guests manage to douse the flames, leaving Sir Murgatroyd and Lady Sprockett-Sprockett to lament their bad luck, stuck in "this infernal family vault". All they wanted was a decent conflagration, a cheque for £100K from the insurers and a "nice little flat" in London that would be handy for his club, the shops and the theatre. But being apprised of their plan, Mordred steps up to the plate and, praising the qualities of paraffin as an accelerant, sets off for the cellar to do the job properly.

Not all Plum's hereditary landowners are so radical, sometimes despite extreme provocation. In 1938's *Summer Moonshine*, Sir Buckstone Abbott loses no time in venting his spleen about the vast "eyesore" that is his family inheritance: Walsingford Hall, a winning combination of classic Elizabethan architecture and the worst kind of Victorian embellishment, comes complete with salmon pink glazed bricks, minarets and a large conservatory which disfigures one elevation "like some unpleasant growth". No doubt he wishes he could set fire to it, but in recent times Sir Buckstone has managed to keep the wolf from the door by reducing this mongrel blot on the landscape to the status of a "rural doss house" taking in paying guests who he describes as "squatters". His daughter Jane considers this nothing to be ashamed of since "[h]alf the landed nibs in England take in paying guests nowadays", but her father isn't happy with the way his life has panned out, never imagining he'd end up as a hotelier with a bunch of perpetually whingeing lodgers. When a boy, Buck entertained the idea – just like Lord Marshmoreton – of being an engine driver; but here he was, saddled with a hideous inheritance that no-one will buy off him. And once again, his mistake was to marry an utterly lovely but impecunious chorus girl, the union of "[t]he great English lord and the little American Cinderella", as his brother-in-law Sam Bulpitt puts it.

Eventually, this transatlantic connection comes good when it's revealed that Sam is fabulously wealthy. Not only does he buy the Hall, he also gives Jane a $500K dowry; indeed, as the Wodehouse scholar Richard Usborne so aptly puts it, "pecunia vincit omnia" – money conquers everything. But note once again that it's American money, which will be invested in transforming the Hall into a country club. In Sam's view, it's "[j]ust the right distance from London. Plenty of Room. Spacious grounds. Picturesque outlook. The boys and girls would come out in their cars in thousands". Where Buck sees ugliness, Sam sees a business opportunity; and it's this broader perspective, coupled with seemingly boundless energy and the availability of seed money that habitually separates the English from the American attitude to business in Wodehouse World, can't-do being trumped by can-do, old-fashioned entropy by forward-thinking drive.

Plum seems perfectly at ease with this, showing himself happy that the characters he cares for end up happy, whoever they are and wherever they're from. And if that means the English are selling their history and traditions by the pound then so be it, for unburdening themselves of their past seems, as often as not, an escape from bondage rather than a surrender to the demands of modernity. Plum's lightness again; and the point is rubbed in two years later on the opening page of *Quick Service*, when it is revealed that Claines Hall, a moated Tudor mansion in Sussex, has been acquired by a Mrs Howard Steptoe of Los Angeles, who is buying her way into the class system rather than going through the tedious necessity of being born into it.

Yet another desperate aristocrat awaits us in *Money in the Bank*. In the previous chapter, I proposed addressing a number of themes related to change simultaneously, and here they all are conveniently assembled in one place in the person of George, 6th Viscount Uffenham, who is arguably Wodehouse's third favourite toff after Lord Emsworth and Uncle Fred. The chatelain of Shipley Hall, he has leased out the ancestral house and grounds lock, stock and barrel to Clarissa Cork who runs it as a health farm. In what is Plum's boldest piece of social mobility to date – and unbeknownst to Mrs Cork – his lordship has stayed on at the Hall in the guise of Cakebread the butler, who spends many of his spare moments searching the old homestead for some diamonds he put in a safe place, the location of which he can no longer remember. Not remotely bothered about his straitened status, Lord U is more than a reasonable facsimile of a salaried employee such that most of the interns have no cause to doubt his identity; aside, that is, from his regularly being caught in the guestrooms searching high and low for the missing diamonds, which he intends to give to his niece Anne as a dowry. He has no airs and graces whatever and is perhaps the least peer-like peer you could wish to meet. Utterly grounded, with a sense of mischief and a sharp tongue, he is set to return to the fray in 1957's *Something Fishy*, by which time he's reduced to renting a house off his former butler (Keggs) in Valley Fields, having let Shipley Hall to a "frightful young man", the American millionaire Roscoe Bunyan.

The triumph of money over class is now complete in Wodehouse World, the aristocracy downgraded to a quaint but impotent relic in the social order. In 1948's *Spring Fever*, when Augustus Robb drunkenly complains that Earls "make me sick" and spend their time "[s]wanking about and taking the bread out of the mouths of the widow and the orphan", what had sounded reasonable in 'Archibald and the Masses' 20 years earlier now comes over as somewhat old-fashioned; and in any case, we are informed by the book's narrator, this "drift to Moscow" is ill-founded:

These times in which we live are not good times for Earls.

> Theirs was a great racket while it lasted, but the boom days are over.

At which point Plum weighs in with a litany of burdensome taxes and super-taxes similar to the one he regaled us with in *Big Money*.

The put-upon peer in this book is Lord Shortlands (hereafter 'Shorty'), who is cut from similar cloth to Lord Uffenham, only not quite as hard up. He still retains the services of a butler (Spink) at the family pile Beevor Castle, only it's difficult to tell who is who, since Plum presents us with "an Earl who looked like a butler and a butler who looked like an Earl". Perhaps in his creative imagination, Plum's 1915 prediction that the classes would come together after the First World War was now a reality; it had just taken rather longer (and a second global conflict) to bring this about. Shorty is "square and stout and plebeian" while Spink is "tall and aristocratic and elegant". As different as chalk and cheese, they are united in their desire to marry the cook, Mrs Alice Punter – only Shorty lacks the £200 it would take to install them in a London pub, where he would serve as landlord. Another peer in search of meaningful employment, he's instead stuck at home, "a bird in a bally mausoleum".

Shorty's lack of room to manoeuvre arises from the fact that he's asset rich but cash poor; and in any case it appears that what money the family now possesses has arrived courtesy of his stuck-up daughter Adela's wealthy husband, Desborough Topping, who is on the Bradstreet rich list. Even so, the family has symbolically moved from the "disused wing" of Beevor which had been built in 1259 to the "modernized section" ("stuffy in summer and cold in winter") which is periodically leased out to, yes, rich Americans to help swell the coffers. Moreover, Shorty has handed over the castle's financial management to Adela, who pays him a monthly allowance, the remains of which, when we meet him, consists of the princely sum of 2/8d (13 pence). As a result, "[a] sullen dislike for the home of his ancestors and everything connected with it had been part of his spiritual make-up for some years now", and, to cap it all, as it were, his favourite hat "with the broken rim and the grease stains" has gone missing. On all sides, the old is being trumped by the new, the familiar by the unfamiliar and it's a toss-up as to which Shorty finds the more annoying, for he doesn't seem to fit anywhere. As his favoured daughter Terry comments, "You don't like Ye Olde much, do you?" And nor does he. But what can the future hold for a penniless peer?

By the close of the novel, however, a solution presents itself – as it always does. Terry, who has served her time as a chorus girl, is due to marry Mike Cardinal, a Hollywood agent, who proposes the trio move to "Dottyville-on-the-Pacific" where Shorty can make some cash playing English butlers in the movies. Plum was well aware that the land of his birth had already become a film set in the American imagination, something he had been quietly and consistently exploiting since his first lengthy sojourn there from 1914 to 1919. Now it seems the metamorphosis of Plum's homeland from the real into the filmic had reached its apogee, with a real aristocrat, not an actor, joining the talent pool in the role of a menial. "All sorts of English oddities turn up in Hollywood", we're told; and just in case we're worried that actual butlers are being done out of acting jobs, Plum arranges for the glacially suave James Phipps to be plucked from servitude by Medulla-Oblongata Glutz Pictures and placed in front of the camera three years later in *The Old Reliable*.

As we'll see in the next chapter, the changed reality in his two main bookselling markets unsettled Plum, and for several years he had trouble understanding where he and his created world belonged. In his immediate post-war novels, even an aristocratic title no longer seems to have the allure it once enjoyed. Bill Shannon – the "Old Reliable" herself – tells her sister Adela that if she insists on marrying the "quarter-witted ornament of the British peerage" Lord Topham, "you'll have half a dozen imbecile children saying "Absolutely, what?" all the time in an Oxford accent". And it's true; "Toppy" is a particularly dense example of a Wodehousean Knut separated from where he truly belongs in time and space by 30-odd years and 6,000 miles. By now, the work ethic has comprehensively trounced breeding in the great scheme of things, and it's most definitely the mercantile rich who are running the show, although this isn't presented as an ideal state of affairs either. Harking back to those fussy, overbearing *nouveaux riches* we encountered earlier in this volume, Plum occasionally lets slip a distaste for the clientele who can afford to flash the cash at Barribault's grill room:

> [B]eing a favourite haunt of the wealthy, and the wealthy being almost uniformly repulsive, its lobby . . . is always full of human eyesores. (*Spring Fever*)

Although in this example the narrator is drawing attention to physical ugliness, there is the strong undertone in Plum's writing that the outward appearance of these wealthy people also serves as a window on their souls. In the same novel, and in only the second paragraph, G. Ellery Cobbold is unflatteringly described as "a stout economic royalist" whose stated purpose is to "prise another wad of currency out of the common people", a role he is clearly fitted for temperamentally and even physically, resembling "a cartoon of Capital in a labour paper". In this ambition he is joined by R.P. Crumbles the sardine magnate from the 1948 story 'Excelsior', who shares that description word for word. Then there's the aforementioned Roscoe Bunyan, this time described as "a cartoon of Capital in the *Daily Worker*" [a British Communist newspaper] – the sort of person an old aristo like Gally Threepwood simply can't get his head around, despite being a man of slender means himself:

> "I can't see what these fellows see in money to make them sweat themselves to get it". (*A Pelican at Blandings*)

Spoken like a true aristocrat who's never had to earn his keep. Gally isn't quite fed by the ravens, being a second son on a regular allowance from the Blandings Estate, which seems not to suffer the same financial buffets as many of the other stately homes we've come across in this chapter. But sweating themselves for their money is what's put the financiers on top, so the last laugh is on the high-ups who failed to adapt to a changing world and are forced to live on incomes that don't always match their needs and wants – in Gally's case, the desire to spread sweetness and light as widely as possible. Sometimes that ambition needs bankrolling, at which point he has to call on his elder brother's chequebook.

On balance, however, Plum's social allegiances don't seem to have changed, at least within his fiction: his later novels and stories reveal that he'd rather have a penniless aristo than an arrogant plutocrat any day, and nowhere more so than in *Ring for Jeeves* (1953), the only Jeeves and Wooster novel not to feature Bertie. But before we examine this fascinating also-ran from the Wodehouse catalogue at some length, it's worth beginning with a short parish notice. *Ring for Jeeves* began life as a play (*Come on, Jeeves*) that Plum co-wrote with his regular theatre collaborator Guy Bolton, and both properties bear evidence of the latter's slightly coarser, jokier, broader-brush brand of satire, which is not as seamlessly integrated into the storyline as if Wodehouse was working alone. Occasionally Bolton's heavier hand suggests itself, as in the reason given for Bertie's non-appearance, which Jeeves explains to an uncomprehending William Egerton Bamfylde Ossingham Belfry, 9th Earl of Rowcester ('Bill' for short):

"Mr Wooster is attending a school which does not permit its student body to employ gentlemen's personal gentlemen".

"A school?"

"An institution designed to teach the aristocracy to fend for itself, m'lord. Mr Wooster, though his finances are still quite sound, feels that it is prudent to build for the future, in case the social revolution should set in with even greater severity. Mr Wooster . . . is actually learning to darn his own socks. The course he is taking includes boot-cleaning, sock-darning, bed-making and primary-grade cooking".

"Golly! Well, that's certainly a novel experience for Bertie".

"Yes, m'lord. Mr Wooster doth suffer a sea change into something rich and strange".

The closing quote from *The Tempest* is likely to be Plum's, but that ingenious excuse, amusing though it be, is a tad too unsubtle to be confidently credited to him. Whoever devised it, however, Bertie's nightmare of not having someone to wake him with a cup of the healing oolong (from 'The Aunt and the Sluggard') has now all but come true: sundered from Jeeves, albeit voluntarily, he is having to learn to fend for himself. And what is the "social revolution" that has brought this about and is name-checked at least three times in the course of the novel? It's the legacy of the Labour Government under that ex-Haileybury rebel Clement Attlee, which unceremoniously booted Winston Churchill out of 10 Downing Street by a massive landslide in the 1945 General Election and introduced a raft of ambitious social reforms that ushered in a cradle-to-the-grave welfare state.

With Plum effectively exiled from his homeland, neither he nor Bolton seems to have had a complete picture of what was going on in the new socially democratic Britain. But what did ring true in the novel was the renewed urgency for large estates to find novel ways of generating income. Of the stately homes that weren't sold off, most reluctantly threw open their doors to the public (Chatsworth), built safari parks in the grounds (Longleat) and car museums in the stables (Beaulieu), converted their land to organic farms (Canon Frome Court) or rented it out for film sets (Castle Howard) or concert venues (Knebworth – a legacy of commercial innovation that's still growing and developing even now. When *Ring for Jeeves* was published, this new era of money-making activity was only just beginning, yet from the perspective of ex-pat Captain Brabazon-Biggar who is visiting from out East, the whole of England itself is a different place; it's "[a]mazing the way things have changed since I was here last", he says. For a start, there's "[n]o idle rich . . . Everybody [has] got a job of some kind". And as if to prove it, we're about to meet Sir Roderick Carmoyle, who has become a floorwalker at Harrige's (!) department store despite being "a tenth baronet or something". When Rory first enters, he is discussing Bill's troubled finances with his wife Monica, who remarks that her brother can't "run a castle on a cottage income". At which point Rory asks:

> "Why doesn't he get a job like the rest of us? . . . everybody's doing it. Nowadays the House of Lords is practically empty on evenings and bank holidays".

To which Monica can only reply that "[t]he Rowcester men have all been lilies of the field" who toil not neither spin. Yes, her brother agrees, those idle aristocratic genes account for Bill's lack of drive:

> "[T]he sort of drive you see so much of at Harrige's. The will to win, I suppose you might call it. Napoleon had it. I have it. Bill hasn't".

This is not altogether true, as we'll see in a moment. But it can't be denied that Rowcester Abbey, which has 147 rooms and is leaking like a sieve, is desperately in need of emergency repairs, since, as Rory puts it, "[t]his bally place looks mouldier every time I see it". As the novel progresses, the scale of the immediate problems faced by the Bills of this world are gradually revealed:

- The pages of *Country Life* (a real-life British magazine that concerns itself with . . . life in the country) are awash with stately homes up for sale – or at least those the National Trust has turned down as bequests;

- Those landowners still in residence are taxed to the hilt to pay for the social revolution, or as Jeeves puts it, "Socialistic legislation has sadly depleted the resources of England's hereditary aristocracy. We are living in the Welfare State, which means – broadly – that everybody is completely destitute";

- Even if that hereditary aristocracy could afford staff, there are none to be had. Not good ones, anyway. "In England today", the narrator informs us, "the householder in the country has to take what he can get in the way of domestic help". All that Colonel Wyvern of Wyvern Abbey has managed to get hold of is a butler and cook who are respectively 16 and 15 years of age, drawn from "the scourings of the local parish school".

And so on. The result is that in "the degenerate world of the 1950s" it appears that "Civilization is in the melting pot". By which Bill means that the way of life enjoyed by his ancestors has finally and irrecoverably hit the buffers.

And it's not just the Abbey either. Britain, at least to judge from the Goose and Gherkin public house in Rowcester village, is tired, worn out, threadbare and, well, *old* – and not in a quaint, chintzy chocolate-box way. Like many other English wayside inns,

> [It had the usual dim religious light, the customary pictures of *The Stag at Bay* and *The Huguenot's Farewell* over the mantelpiece, the same cruets and bottles of sauce, and the traditional ozone-like smell of mixed pickles, gravy soup, boiled potatoes, waiters and old cheese.

Now that *is* Plum's writing – you can actually smell that smell even now at certain change-resistant out-of-the-way English pubs, so particularly is it described. Anyhow, by comparison with the beautiful, wealthy, well-preserved, elegant and fashionably attired American Rosalinda Spottsworth who is sitting in its coffee room, the whole place appears irredeemably shabby and down-at-heel, having seen better days.

In short, it's the difference between England and America. Although both were on the winning side in the war, the contrast could not be more evident: one is exhausted, bombed out and saddled with mountainous debts; the other is in better economic shape than any other nation on the planet and all set for the consumer boom of the late 1940s and 50s. In fact, Mrs. S is so rich, even those "blood-sucking leeches of the Internal Revenue Department" (the U.S. taxmen) have to raise their "filthy hats" to her (Plum probably wrote that line too). She has crossed the Pond to buy Rowcester Abbey because she's keen to commune with the spirits from the past that are said to inhabit it. Roddy, on the other hand, thinks it's only fit to be nuked by one of those new-fangled atom bombs, or at least doused in paraffin and torched in the manner of Smattering Hall. Once again, we witness the difference between wanting to preserve the past and be free from it in the respective attitudes of the two nationalities.

But where is Bill while all this background stuff is going on? Rather than sourcing lions, monkeys and giraffes for his new safari park, he's dressing up as a silver ring bookie complete with hideous checked suit and false moustache, trading as "Honest Patch Perkins" and is accompanied to various racecourses by a shifty looking sidekick who turns out to be none other than Jeeves, also heavily disguised. Desperate remedies indeed, which, when they all go a. over t., generate what little plot there is. The solution to everything, is, as per usual, money, with Mrs Spottsworth being persuaded to open her cheque book and buy Rowcester Abbey, demolish it and rebuild it Stateside in a spot with a more pleasant climate. In the play version, Captain Biggar, who is to marry Rosalinda, will become "the new Hopalong Cassidy" on TV, "liv[ing] in the hearts of twenty million children"; and Jeeves is to be mercifully reunited with Bertie, who has been expelled from his reformatory for cheating in the sock-darning exam.

While not exactly a state-of-the-nation portrait like Plum's pantos 50 years earlier, there's much about *Ring for Jeeves* that rang true at the time it was written. And the theme of an impoverished gentry – landed with enormous rural properties they either love and try to hold on to or loathe and end up selling – would serve Wodehouse well until pretty much the end of his career. In the 1952 story 'Big Business', Sir Jasper Todd, a former financier, has purchased Wissel Hall, immediately regretting his decision when he discovers how much it costs to run. His plan to burn it to cinders and collect on the insurance is foiled, and like most of Plum's dastardly money men, he ends up out of pocket, on this occasion to the tune of £50K. Fifteen years later, *Company for Henry* opens at Ashby Hall, an enormous millstone that in its heyday required 50 staff to run but is now reduced to a single employee, the wife of a neighbouring farmer who doesn't pitch up until noon.

And yet . . . although the English country house can be a grand façade behind which lurks penury, frustration and not a little anguish, when Lord Uffenham returns to Shipley Hall having leased it out in 1957's *Something Fishy*, it's quite the sentimental reunion:

> Some poignant stuff was written by the poet Thomas Moore in the nineteenth century descriptive of the emotions of the Peri who was excluded from Paradise, and those of the British landowner who is revisiting the old home which poverty has compelled him to let furnished to a rich American are virtually identical.

In that extremely obscure poem, 'Paradise and the Peri' (which Plum would return to in *Company for Henry* to illustrate a similar theme) the Peri, a fairy, is eventually re-admitted to her Paradise; and yes, it really is "poignant stuff", particularly if you're a fan of gloopy sentiment:

> *"Farewell, ye odours of Earth, that die*
> *Passing away like a lover's sigh –*
> *My feast is now of the Tooba tree,*
> *Whose scent is the breath of Eternity . . . "*
>
> *"Joy, joy for ever! My task is done –*
> *The Gates are pass'd, and Heav'n is won!"*

Maybe Plum was getting nostalgic in his old age, for by the end of the novel Lord Uffenham – his third favourite peer, let's not forget – appears to have acquired sufficient money to buy his way back into his "Paradise" should he choose. And so, in this almost unique example of the clocks being turned back, the English country house *could* be a kind of timeless, regainable Paradise Lost, a symbol of – well, we'll decide that in the next chapter but one when we return to that good old reliable, Blandings Castle.

As things would turn out, this was a brief moment of transcendence, for by the following year in *Cocktail Time* reality has returned with a vengeance. The stark social and economic realities of the modern age have stranded Hammer Hall on a bank and shoal of time from which there are few means of escape, being "one of those betwixt-and-between stately homes of England" large enough to cost "the dickens of a lot to keep up" but not sufficiently grand to "lure the populace into packing sandwiches and hard-boiled eggs and coming in charabancs to inspect it at half-a-crown a head". In breach of the taxman's regulations, its artworks, tapestries and furniture are gradually being sold off to generate some much-needed cash, and in keeping with the 'country house as theatre' motif I first explored at the beginning of Volume 2, Plum describes the decaying Hall's slowly diminishing collection of heirlooms in the manner of a stage set being struck, the props disappearing one by one until eventually nothing will remain. Perhaps the same could be said of England too, the land from which Wodehouse had become a *de facto* exile, and which he was destined never to see again, following a brief stint in front of a microphone in Berlin.

THE BEST OF TIMES...
THE WORST OF TIMES

Chapter 6:
The Best of Times . . . The Worst of Times

The workings of the political and bureaucratic machine perpetrated,
and for 35 years perpetuated, a grave injustice upon Wodehouse,
which he took to his grave . . . The normal inclination of Govern-
ment departments, when in doubt, to maintain the status quo, had
triumphed over the requirements of natural justice.
Iain Sproat, *Wodehouse at War*

He was reviewing the recent scene and wishing that he had come
better out of it. He was a vague man, but not so vague as to be
unaware that he might have shown up in a more heroic light.
'The Crime Wave at Blandings'

It has been well said of Bertram Wooster that though he may sink
onto rustic benches and for a while give the impression of being licked
to a custard, the old spirit will come surging back sooner or later.
The Mating Season

By this stage, you'll have noticed that this book's main thesis requires
that Wodehouse World and contemporary reality aren't the sworn enemies they're sometimes made out to be. In fact, they rub along perfectly
well when they aren't being prised apart. Now though, we've reached
a point in our sort-of chronological canter through Plum's aesthetics
where outside events conspired to wreck that healthily symbiotic relationship: for our next topic is that persistent gorilla in the room of P.G.
Wodehouse studies, the BBB (or 'Berlin Broadcasts Business').

There's no getting round it, unfortunately. But you might be pleased
to know that I have no intention of raking over the coals one more
time in the hope they might give off some last therms of heat. Instead,
I'm going to approach the subject from the perspective of Wodehouse's
writing; how the fallout from history invaded his fictional world; what
steps he took to address those altered circumstances; and how events
conspired to get his career back on track. For those five radio talks (plus
one interview), originally transmitted between 28 June and 6 August
1941, threatened Wodehouse World with oblivion, blasting the alternative reality it represented to smithereens and its author along with it.
Actual reality had finally caught up with him, and for an extended period
following the end of the Second World War Plum seemed to lose his

creative mojo, his self-confidence sputtering into life only intermittently as he struggled against the forces of history that had, for the second time in less than half a century, changed the real world beyond recognition. Even as he sought to maintain the impression of business as usual, he was all too aware that everything he had striven for was facing an existential threat, and this, might, finally be the end of all things.

In effect, the 1950s were Plum's lost years. It was only once he'd exhausted his wartime stockpile of manuscripts with 1949's *The Mating Season* that his creative problems became apparent, and he had to endure what for him was a worryingly fallow interlude before re-emerging into a more settled groove that eventually saw him out. That troubled period, which arguably stretched until around 1957, will be the subject of the latter half of this chapter, as Plum slowly tried to find where exactly Wodehouse World fitted – if it fitted at all – into the new post-war reality, effecting a workable reconciliation between the two both in his own mind and the outside world's.

During those years, only novels featuring the Blandings crew (1952's *Pigs Have Wings*) and Jeeves and Bertie (*Jeeves and the Feudal Spirit*, 1954) catch him writing at anything like full power. A series of below-par efforts, stretching from *The Old Reliable* via *Barmy in Wonderland* arguably as far as *Something Fishy*, witness Plum struggling to muster much belief in what he was doing. Stuck in the doldrums with little wind in his sails, he cashed in his chips and wrote three volumes of unreliable memoirs, which would buy him some time. But on the eve of his 80s, he wasn't about to change horses in midstream, and while you could teach an old dog the occasional new trick, a whole new act was clearly out of the question. Fortunately, by that time, there were encouraging signs that the real world was slowly catching up with *him*, rather than the other way round – but that's for Chapters 7 to 9. Now though, we're off back to 1941, where the seeds of this chapter were busy germinating.

Without a doubt, the fullest and most accurate account of Plum's vertiginous fall from grace remains Iain Sproat's excellent *Wodehouse at War* published in 1981, a work of dogged sleuthing that finally shed light on the facts of the matter – but only after an interval of 40 years, and, shamefully, the death of the author. Only the awarding of a knighthood weeks before Wodehouse died in 1975 would hint that the British Establishment had consigned his case to history, and even then, quite *why* Sproat had to spend eight years extracting the relevant information from the British Home Office is a question that remains imperfectly answered. Nevertheless, his book remains a godsend to Wodehouse fans, exonerating the author of much of the guilt that has been regularly heaped on his reputation – and occasionally still is – by those who have a spurious axe to grind or, having failed to do their homework, imagine they're on to a scoop.

Back at the start of the war in September 1939, Wodehouse was not only writing in mid-season form, but widely regarded as the doyen of prose humourists. Even the mighty brains of Oxford University had celebrated his "whole crowd of witty, humorous, charming, amusing, uproarious creations" by awarding him an honorary Doctor of Letters. He was regularly feted by his fellow writers as literary royalty; one, Hilaire Belloc, had even called him the head of his profession. Things continued this way into the conflict, with Plum surfing a wave of popularity and general acclaim. As the gravity of renewed hostilities with Germany gradually sunk in during the so-called "phoney war" (which lasted from September 1939 to around April 1940), the appropriateness of humour as a response to national trauma began to be seriously questioned. The BBC sparked a debate in its house listings magazine, the *Radio Times*, posing the question "Radio in Wartime: Should it be Grave or Gay?". Fortunately for its listeners (and the war effort), the latter view prevailed. Radio comedy would prove one of the Corporation's greatest morale boosters, offering a heartening alternative to the steady diet of doom and gloom emanating from its news bulletins.

Wodehouse's work more than played its part in those early days – sometimes in unexpected ways. In September 1939, the *Daily Express*'s radio critic Jonah Barrington had already noticed that German shortwave propagandists, beaming what is now called "fake news" over to Britain, were adopting what they imagined to be the spoken mannerisms of an English aristocrat. From listening to one such broadcaster, probably Wolf Mittler (who may or may not have been wearing spats), he formed the following mental image:

> [F]rom his accent and personality I imagine him with a receding chin, a questing nose, thin, yellow hair brushed back, a monocle, a vacant eye, a gardenia in his button hole. Rather like P.G. Wodehouse's Bertie Wooster.

Barrington described that accent as being of "the haw-haw, damit [sic]-get-out-of-my-way variety", and when William Joyce arrived on air some days later using the same style of delivery, the nickname stuck and "Lord Haw-Haw" was born. Thus did Plum, domiciled near Le Touquet, help to name one of the most notorious traitors of World War Two, probably without knowing it.

So threatening a figure did Joyce become, it was seriously mooted in government that "a humourist" like Wodehouse could "caricature his Lordship" in print and at least go some way towards countering his malign influence on the country's self-confidence. Nothing came of the suggestion, but in any case Wodehouse was already all over the radio schedules like a rash, with productions of 'Meet the Prince' (a musical based on Plum's umpteenth rewrite of *The Prince and Betty*), *Uncle Fred in the Springtime*, 'Uncle Fred Flits By', four Ukridge stories, 'Lord Emsworth Acts for the Best', 'The Crime Wave at Blandings' and 'Pig Hoo-o-o-o-ey!' all broadcast on the BBC Home Service between September 1939 and New Year's Eve 1940. Of that last title, the billing ran as follows:

> There is nothing like a P. G. Wodehouse story to make one forget the war, and the inhabitants of Blandings Castle are among the author's most humorous creations. Few of the highly-born occupants can be said to have a mind at all. It is just because of their lack of intellect that the characters are so funny. There is no moral in 'Pig-hoo-o-o-o-ey', but that in itself is a holiday in these strenuous times.

That closing line almost reads like an apology, either to those who disapproved of levity during wartime or those who were suffering privation of one kind or another; but at least to the BBC schedulers, the plays and readings were doing their intended job of cheering people up. A repeat broadcast of 'The Crime Wave at Blandings' attracted the following pre-publicity:

> Here is a hilarious addition to this big week of radio drama, a play that was specifically asked for by a great number of listeners who revelled in the first broadcast of the play in July.

And it wasn't just on the radio that Plum was helping the war effort. On 13 December 1939 and Valentine's Day 1940, he published two anti-German pieces in *Punch*, respectively 'The Big Push' and 'Shock Dogs' that, as far as I can tell, are both uncollected – and most definitely overlooked. In the former, reverting to the surreal satire of *The Swoop!*,

Plum has Hitler proposing to invade Britain with oompah bands that will play day and night, depriving the citizens of their sleep to the point they will pay them any amount of money to go away. The economy will tank, and thus will Britain be subjugated. "Heil Hitler!" shouts Goering, "Against this secret weapon of our Leaders the British have no defence". 'Shock Dogs' is even more preposterous, a vehicle for one of Mr. Mulliner's most credulity-taxing yarns involving a crack squad of Nazi dachshunds undermining the foundations of the Maginot Line, a huge 280-mile-long concrete fortification built by the French to protect their country from German attack (as things turned out in real life, the invaders adopted the simple expedient of marching around it). As a bonus, Plum also casts light on the difficulties faced by Russia (then an Axis power) in its attempts to annexe Finland: the bulk of Russian troop movements taking place by rail, all the dastardly Finns had to do was destroy the third-class tickets, forcing Stalin to put his invading force in first class and bankrupting his war chest in the process. It was all going so well . . .

Ironically, it was the medium of radio, and the desire not to appear "grave" during his captivity that got Plum into such hot water over the BBB. On the strength of those five Berlin scripts (not forgetting the one interview) his work was banned from the BBC, and it was radio that first alerted many of the British public to Wodehouse's blunder when William Connor (writer of the 'Cassandra' column in the *Daily Mirror*) read out an editorial at 9.20p.m. on Tuesday 15 July 1941 which concluded that Wodehouse had ended "forty years of money-making fun with the worst joke he ever made in his life". Put up to the stunt by Home Secretary Alfred Duff Cooper, Connor excelled at his brief and Wodehouse's name was now, officially, mud. One fact about the broadcast I haven't see mentioned before is that it was a rush job, shoe-horned into the schedules at the last minute. The *Radio Times* listing for that day had promised a 15-minute talk by the Right Honourable Ernest Brown, M.P., the Minister for Health. What listeners got instead was, as McCrum rightly has it, a "breathtakingly intemperate [script], a polemic unique in the annals of the BBC" – whose Board of Governors was dead against broadcasting it but were overruled by the 'emergency' measures Duff Cooper had at his disposal. As things turned out, the BBC's postbag registered a score of 31 in favour of Cassandra, 133 against. But it was too late – the mud had already stuck.

Reading Plum's Berlin scripts now, we may find it remarkable that they caused such a fuss: indeed, it's difficult to know quite how extensive that fuss *actually* was, for it doesn't rate a mention in Asa Briggs's comprehensive, scrupulously evidenced, 800-page official history of British wartime broadcasting. Those evening talks regularly pulled in audiences of over 10 million – television had gone dark for the duration of the war – so the 31 listeners who took the time to write in to the BBC supporting Connor were, essentially, a storm in a thimble. Wodehouse's conversational, Horatian tone is almost identical to the one he had employed virtually from the start of his career, their style the sort of sideways take on reality familiar from his non-fiction articles. Here's a quick sample for corroboration:

> There is a good deal to be said for internment. It keeps you out of the saloons and gives you time to catch up with your reading. You also get a lot of sleep. The chief drawback is that it means your being away from home a good deal. It is not pleasant to think that by the time I see my Pekinese again, she will have completely forgotten me and will bite me to the bone – her invariable practice with strangers. And I feel that when I rejoin my wife, I had better take along a letter of introduction, just to be on the safe side. Young men, starting out in life, have often asked me 'How can I become an Internee?' Well, there are several methods. My own was to buy a villa in Le Touquet on the coast of France and stay there till the Germans came along. This is probably the best and simplest system. You buy the villa and the Germans do the rest.

Harmless enough, we might think. But then as now, there is no measuring the sanctimony of the British Press when it finds a convenient hobbyhorse it can ride. And this virulent outbreak of humbug most definitely did alter the context in which Plum's words found themselves. Indeed, it couldn't be denied that Wodehouse World, so long a fixture on the literary scene, was suddenly fighting not just for its continued relevance, but its right to exist. At a stroke, as the *Daily Mirror* (Cassandra's employer) baldly stated at the time of the broadcasts, "Wodehouse [is] funny no longer".

The lightness that had allowed Wodehouse World to soar above the everyday cares of life had nosedived into reality, and for the next decade would be, along with its author, 'on trial'. Almost literally – in 1941 the lifelong blowhard Quintin Hogg, a Conservative M.P. who habitually spoke uncannily like the Duke of Dunstable, demanded that Wodehouse should be punished as a traitor and shot. Over three years later on 6 December 1944 in the House of Commons, he still wouldn't let things lie, harassing Foreign Secretary Anthony Eden as to whether he would further investigate Wodehouse's "trading with the enemy". Eden demurred on the basis that there were no legal grounds on which to proceed, and fellow Tory Godfrey Nicholson thought it might be "better if this gentleman [PGW, not Hogg] was relegated to obscurity", a view echoed by Plum's old mate Winston Churchill, who wished he would simply "go to hell as soon as there is a vacant passage". Opinions, as they say, differed. But then Plum wasn't exactly Churchill's best buddy either, as we've already seen.

Given that treason still carried the death penalty, the topmost priority among Plum's sympathizers was to clear his name, and this process necessarily involved teasing out his world view. Had he, like many in the upper echelons of British society he ostensibly wrote about, ever entertained Nazi sympathies? Was he really a Quisling? Had the broadcasts been his ticket out of prison? Had the Nazis paid him money?

Gathering evidence was always going to be problematic. As the war ended, Wodehouse was living in Paris; he had given no public testimony; the contents of his post-war interrogations by British and French Intelligence had not been released; and he was by nature a private man, who, when asked anything of a serious or personal nature, tended to feint. So, anyone seeking answers to questions about his motivations or his subsequent life in Berlin had virtually nothing to go on and would be forced to glean whatever they could from his writing. All he had ever published about the Nazis in addition to those satirical *Punch* pieces was Bertie's put down of Roderick Spode, and this less well-known opening from the 1936 Mulliner story 'Buried Treasure':

> The situation in Germany had come up for discussion in the bar parlour of the Angler's Rest, and it was generally agrees that Hitler was standing at the crossroads and would soon be compelled to do something definite. His present policy, said a Whisky and Splash, was mere shilly-shallying.

> "He'll have to let it grow or shave it off".

Unfortunately, a frank exchange of views on the dead Führer's facial hair wasn't going to be much help to British officialdom in deciding what to do with Plum now the outcome of the war had been decided.

But the fact that Wodehouse World was fictional didn't stop George Orwell using it as a central plank in his spirited vindication of the author, having lunched with Plum in Paris in 1944. His subsequent article 'In Defence of P.G. Wodehouse', published in *The Windmill* magazine in its July 1945 number (but written three months earlier) has been regularly anthologized ever since, and is at the same time brilliantly disputed yet studiedly disingenuous.

Orwell, who had been a Wodehouse fan since the age of eight and shared a public school background, argued Plum's innocence on the grounds that his global perspective was essentially "historical". From this position he could assert that Plum had demonstrated a "complete lack — so far as one can judge from his printed works — of political awareness" and claimed that a man who spent most of his waking hours writing about a long-dead made-up world probably lived in one too, and was unlikely to have a firm grasp of the realities of contemporary wartime politics. His only offence was to have been ideologically illiterate, which was not a crime but merely an unfortunate blind spot in his intellectual make-up. Moreover, Plum was simply too fond of his aristocratic subjects to be actively satirizing them: he was simply bringing out their "comic possibilities" rather than offering a searching critique of a decadent society. Which meant he wasn't being unpatriotic, and ergo could not be a traitor to his country. The English aristocracy could breathe again, knowing that Plum wasn't its sworn enemy.

Although – being just out of nappies at the time – Orwell was likely unfamiliar with Plum's 'Parrot' poems and the pantos for the *Daily Express*, he was nevertheless a canny man who probably realized his subject simply couldn't have been as politically unaware as he had painted him. But the article was an exercise in urgently winning over hearts and minds by whatever means necessary, so rather than engage in an involved ontological debate on the relationship between fantasy and reality, it was far easier to assert that Plum was "his own Bertie Wooster" – which of course he wasn't, and never had been, as we'll investigate in the following chapter. Wodehouse's *actual* issues with reality were rather trickier to explain and might even have been amusing had they not led to such bitter consequences.

First was his unerring inability to see what was obvious to everyone else, and to draw the wrong conclusions from what he actually *did* know; second, much of his thinking was shot through the prism of writing and publishing to the point of monomania. Both these limitations conjoin in a letter to Mollie Cazalet (Leonora's mother-in-law) written on 10 July 1939, describing a visit to London. Talk of war was on everyone's lips, but what Plum "noticed chiefly" was that "plays were doing badly and books not selling . . . Thank goodness, my last book has had a record sale". He signed off with the cheery opinion that "I don't think Germany will risk a war". Seven weeks later, on 3 September, war with Germany was duly declared; and in a little over three months Plum was describing himself as running a "doss house" for French officers in the "staff wing" at his house in Le Touquet. Still, he looked on the bright side: "They all say that there is going to be a big boom in books . . . so maybe we shall be all right". Indeed, until the arrival of the invading German army his only serious qualm appeared to be the irregular availability of type-writer ribbons. This kind of evidence, if he'd had it, would have been materially useful to Orwell, although it wasn't so much indicative of Plum living in the past as not being equipped to live anywhere, except in a place that allowed him to write his books undisturbed.

Quite how many people actually read Orwell's 'Defence' essay at the time, and hence how useful it was in arguing Wodehouse's case is difficult to judge. It first appeared in the second-ever edition of a low circulation literary journal, which nevertheless punched far above its weight if the quality of its contributors is anything to go by; in the same issue as the Wodehouse essay, articles could be found by Stevie Smith, C.P. Snow and Olivia Manning, probably making it something of a hit among the chattering classes of the metropolis, but not much further afield. However, a more important question for the present discussion is the legacy Orwell's ingenuity left on Plum's own understanding of his created world. The following lines from the essay are perhaps the ones that registered most forcefully (Note: Harry Flannery was the Berlin correspondent of the American CBS network, who in 1944 had published a memoir, *Assignment to Berlin*, about his tour of duty):

In his [1941] radio interview with Flannery, Wodehouse wondered whether "the kind of people and the kind of England I write about will live after the war", not realizing that they were ghosts already. "He was still living in the period about which he wrote," says Flannery, meaning, probably, the nineteen-twenties. But the period was really the Edwardian age, and Bertie Wooster, if he ever existed, was killed round about 1915.

This means that Bertie and Lord Emsworth, who had respectively made their debuts in the story 'Extricating Young Gussie' and the novel *Something Fresh* – both published *in* 1915 – had arrived stillborn in history, even as they had helped usher in Wodehouse's golden age as a humorous writer. Whether that proved a revelation to him or not, Plum wrote to Orwell on 1 August 1945 praising his "masterly bit of work" and adding "I agree with every word of it".

Or did he? Before we take this concurrence at face value, it must be noted that Wodehouse was punctiliously polite and tended to like anyone who liked him or did him a good turn; and Orwell was generously throwing out a wonderfully contingent argument Plum himself would begin using shortly afterwards to pour oil on the waters he had so consummately troubled. But even if Orwell got him off the hook, did Wodehouse World really *matter* anymore? Having, in Orwell's view, lived on borrowed time for three decades, was it really – finally – on the wrong side of history?

On 16 April 1945, after completing the manuscript of *Uncle Dynamite*, Wodehouse confessed to fellow novelist Dennis Mackail that his batteries were nearly flat, and that he was now "relying on technique instead of exuberance". By June, he was writing to Frances Donaldson (later his biographer):

> It seems a waste of time to write about butlers and country houses if both are obsolete, as I suppose they will be. I can't see what future there is for Blandings Castle, and I doubt if Bertie Wooster will be able to afford a personal attendant with the income tax at ten shillings in the pound.

The existential threat was all too real: not only did there appear to be nothing to write *for*, but it also seemed there was no longer anything to write *about*. Indeed, the market for butlers appears to have been his benchmark for deciding the viability of Wodehouse World, and as their number plummeted in the immediate post-war era, the only one of his characters with any chance of post-war survival would be that peerless human cockroach Stanley Featherstonehaugh Ukridge – though even he would have to up his game if those ten-bob touches were to keep rolling in now that no-one had any money.

But it wasn't all doom and gloom. Even as Plum doubted his future prospects, some of his pep and vim may well have been restored when his U.K. literary agency informed him that from 1941 to mid-1944, he had managed to sell close to half a million books ("in all the cheap editions") in Britain alone (see Sophie Ratcliffe's *A Life in Letters* p363). And that, despite his supposed pariah status. So, it made sound business sense for his publishers on both sides of the Atlantic to gamble on his rehabilitation – which they did. All through his various confinements, Plum had somehow managed to build a stockpile equivalent to several years' worth of releases, from which *Money in the Bank* was the first to see the light of day in the U.K. in May 1946, having appeared in the U.S. four years earlier. As he awaited its publication in his home country, Plum may have been parroting Orwell's argument that "my books [are] early Edwardian", but there seems something slightly jauntier, more self-confident in a letter he wrote to Denis Mackail immediately before Christmas 1945. After all, he protests, Dickens "was writing gaily about stage coaches etc long after the railways had come in. I don't believe it matters and I intend to go on hewing to the butler line, let the chips fall where they may".

And so he did. Once he'd crossed that mental Rubicon, his correspondence reveals a sense of the worth of his work slowly returning, and he started having thoughts as to how it could be re-branded to suit the new realities. Making a virtue out of necessity, he comments in March 1946 that his novels could indeed be marketed as historical literature – but in a good way. Although *Money in the Bank* "assumes a state of affairs that is as out of date as *Three Men in a Boat*" [Jerome K. Jerome's comedy classic from 1889], he hopes that "people will jump at something that takes them away from modern conditions", before adding that "my stuff has been out of date since 1914, and nobody has seemed to mind". The following month, writing to fellow novelist Compton Mackenzie, he says much the same thing:

> I'm hoping that people, in America at any rate, will overlook the fact that they are completely out of date and will accept them for their entertainment value. I think they're all pretty funny, but, my gosh, how obsolete!

As things turned out, he needn't have worried. On 17 June 1946, Plum gleefully informed Mackail that U.K. hardback sales of *Money in the Bank* had reached a respectable 21,000 within two months of publication (at the height of his popularity in 1939 he had remarked that 20,000 was a solid achievement). Five days earlier, it had been favourably reviewed on BBC radio by the novelist V.S. Pritchett, who had delivered "a perfect eulogy", for which Plum thanked him profusely by letter. In it, he recalled how he had been forced to flesh out the story during his incarceration, in a room where "a hundred men were playing darts and ping-pong", before adding this heartfelt codicil:

> You can probably imagine how I felt when I heard of your talk, for it was not without diffidence that I agreed to the publication of the book. I saw myself rather in the position of a red-nosed comedian who has got the bird in the first house on Monday and is having the temerity to go one and do his stuff at the second house, outwardly breezy and cheerful but feeling inside as if he had swallowed a heaving tablespoon of butterflies and with a wary eye out for demonstrations from the gallery. And now comes this applause from the stalls, thank God! Bless you!

The relief is touchingly palpable.

By this time, he must have already written the Preface to his next stockpile release, *Joy in the Morning*, which includes the candid, devil-may-care admission (aided and abetted by a quotation from Rudyard Kipling's poem 'Recessional') that his world had "gone with the wind and is one with Nineveh and Tyre. In a word, it has had it". Not in America it hadn't: within eight weeks of publication, it too had hit the 20,000 mark (it wouldn't surface in the U.K. until the following year); and he still had *Full Moon*, *Spring Fever*, *Uncle Dynamite* and *The Mating Season* waiting in the wings.

But even if his work *was* being re-contextualised as history, its future wasn't quite what it had been: Plum wasn't out of the woods yet and wouldn't be for quite a while. In fact, things would get worse before they got better as members of the arts Establishment on both sides of the Atlantic struggled to adapt to the new realities. An immediate worry was his agent's inability to place short stories in the weekly and monthly magazines that until the war had been one of Plum's main sources of income. Many of the magazines themselves had gone out of business, but those that remained weren't exactly falling over themselves to give him work. From 1945 to 1975, he managed to sell only a tiny fraction of the stories (around 30) he had been able to publish pre-war, and the editor of the *Saturday Evening Post*, long his American mainstay, confided to Plum's lawyer in 1950 that he found his client's stories "dated and out of place". Plum himself considered it "extraordinary how the public taste [in America] has changed": "English dudes" were out, displaced by "stodgy grey stuff about life in the swamps of the Deep South", with the result that he had "more or less given up hope of making any money with short stories".

Indeed, from 1945 to around 1960 those who had professional dealings with Plum's world didn't truly understand where it fitted into their own activities, and his personal travails on this account appear a model of consistency when set against the confusion that seems to have reigned in the wider worlds of theatre and publishing. In 1946, he complained to Bill Townend that editors "do think up the damnedest objections to an author's work":

> In Joy in the Morning Bertie speaks of himself as eating a steak and Boko is described as having fried eggs for breakfast, and [Derek] Grimsdick of Jenkins [Plum's U.K. publisher] is very agitated about this, because he says the English public is so touchy about food nowadays that stuff like this will probably cause an uproar. I have changed the fried egg to a sardine and cut out the steak, so I hope all will now be well.

In the straitened post-war world, rationing would be a feature of British everyday life until 1954 – but the possibility that his public would be exercised by a fictional character tucking into a fictional luxury food-stuff at this *particular* point in history was unfortunately all too real and risked the eruption of more anti-Wodehouse sentiment just as things were starting to settle down.

Here, once more, we have real life poking its nose into where we might think it had no business. But Plum's work was being consumed in "real time", his publisher acknowledging that even this unremark-able imaginary incident might all too easily cross some kind of notional boundary between one world and another. Of course, Plum was in a unique situation among writers and was still very much on probation, but even so, he grumbled that Agatha Christie didn't have to mind her Ps and Qs to this exaggerated degree: in fact, he was really rather heart-ened that in her brand new 1946 Hercule Poirot mystery *The Hollow*, set in a country house, "people in it simply gorge duck and soufflés and caramel cream and so on". The blurring of the line between fact and fiction was further emphasized when Plum somehow discovered, perhaps from his friend Malcolm Muggeridge who repeats the claim in his essay 'Wodehouse in Distress', that what he called "the War Department" of the U.S. government had been using the texts of his Berlin broadcasts "as samples of anti-Nazi propaganda throughout the war" [underlining Plum's], which must have galled and amused him in equal measure. What was once potentially treasonous was now, somehow, patriotic. Or something.

You can forgive Plum for being confused about what was real and what wasn't – and where other peoples' confusion on that score left *him*. One of his biggest stage successes during these years, *Don't Listen, Ladies!*, a play by Frenchman Sacha Guitry that Plum had adapted, ran for 219 performances in London without its audiences having any clue that he was involved, for even by 1948, someone connected to the production, possibly Plum himself, wasn't sure whether knowledge of his participation would be viewed as a help or hindrance. Ironically, when the show transferred to Broadway (again minus the Wodehouse name), the influential critic Walter Winchell shot it down in flames when he revealed that Guitry had been accused of collaboration with the Nazis, charges which never stuck, but which doomed the show nonetheless. There was some compensation when a revival of another Wodehouse adaptation *with* his name attached, *The Play's the Thing*, hit paydirt on Broadway from April to December 1948, helping Plum consolidate his finances and no doubt boosting his self-confidence. But then the subsequent tour unexpectedly bombed, "[just] as I had got accustomed to my weekly cheque". Plum had always experienced ups and downs in the theatre, but his continuing anxiety whether or not he was *persona non grata* must have given the flops an added, troubling significance they hadn't once had.

Moreover, Wodehouse World was coming under attack from a second front – this time from an enemy within. Quite simply, midway into his 60s, Plum was finding it difficult to summon the creative energy necessary to take his work forward. Was he losing his touch? From day one, he had believed he was good; now it seemed he wasn't so convinced. This uncertainty is perhaps best typified by an absurd note he wrote in December 1946 to George Shively, an editor at Nelson Doubleday (one of his American publishers) in which he ponders whether to kill off Jeeves on the strength of a single bum review in the *New Yorker*, which opined that the character had "frankly . . . become a bore". He hadn't, of course; but certainly from 1947 to 1954, it's difficult to argue that Plum's muse was firing on all cylinders. As Sophie Ratcliffe politely and correctly puts it, this was a period of "consolidation rather than intense creativity" during which his muse was *actually* all over the place, his problems with self-confidence reducing the flow of his creative juices to a trickle – though you'd never guess it by looking at his publishing schedule.

By the time that amazingly business-as-usual wartime stockpile had finally been exhausted with *The Mating Season* in 1949, he was already being forced to scrabble around for fresh material, "always with the prospect that the bottom will drop out of everything". If aspects of *The Old Reliable* (1951) seem to closely resemble *Spring Fever* (1948), that's because the former was re-worked from an unproduced stage version of the latter. And if you're already confused, just read chapter 5 of Tony Ring's revelatory *Nothing is Simple in Wodehouse* and follow the evolution of this fated project through its 14 different versions and four titles. Nobody seemed to have confidence in it, and by 1954 Plum ended up *giving* the script of rewrite number six to an amdram company in Devon, where it was performed by a cast including a sanitary inspector, a builder, an oil salesman and two farmers, one of whom was so shy he had to be coached in the love scenes. Yes, it *had* come to this. Another of his stage adaptations (this time of a thriller by E.P. Conkle, variously known as *Keep Your Head* and *Don't Lose Your Head*) crawled onto the stage in Nottingham in May 1950, but then it was tinkered with by other hands, flopped in London and after further Wodehouse tinkering opened in Bermuda, of all places. After more rewriting, it disappeared from Plum's radar, never reaching its intended Broadway destination. Reading his own summary of the original plot, it's amazing he involved himself at all; "Burmese headhunters coming to an English inn and trying to secure the landlady's head" should have perhaps alerted him that this was always going to be a hard sell.

And there's more. The dated theatre satire *Barmy in Wonderland* (1952) saw Plum actually *buying* a substantial amount of dialogue from *The Butter and Egg Man*, a play originally written by his friend George S. Kaufman in 1925; *Nothing Serious* is an uneven collection of the six short stories Plum *did* manage to sell during the period 1947-51, together with one ('Bramley Is So Bracing') dating back to 1939, and three his agent hadn't succeeded in placing. In 1953, he agreed to re-write and update his lengthy 1909 school novel, *Mike*, which was to be re-issued in the U.K. as two volumes, *Mike at Wrykyn* and *Mike and Psmith*. Apart from the bifurcation, this updating most notably involved changing the names of Edwardian cricketers to members of the post-war England squad, and while Plum would do virtually anything to turn an honest nickel, he very soon afterwards realized this hadn't been such a great idea, as he confessed to Richard Usborne:

> I think myself it was a mistake. Not quite as bad as trying to modernize Tom Brown but definitely wrong. The whole tone of the story is 1900-odd, and I don't believe anyone could mistake it for a modern school story, however much you change [Wilfred] 'Rhodes' to [Jim] 'Laker'.

It was that "tone" that gave things away – all the more reason to stick with what he knew best and had always done.

Except he didn't: in 1953, he went out even further on a limb when he novelized his stage play *Come On, Jeeves* as *Ring for Jeeves*, both versions omitting Bertie's character altogether. It was an experiment too far; Plum had had an idea kicking around that would feature Jeeves, then dropped him in favour of a butler named Ponsonby, then at some point re-instated Jeeves to make it more bankable – then almost immediately realized he'd "made a bloomer" of the highest magnitude. This dithering notwithstanding, Jeeves without Bertie, either on the stage or the page was, quite simply, unthinkable – and a token of how desperate he was to push out almost anything that would keep him in the public eye. If Wodehouse wasn't actually blocked during this period, the creative poverty of some of these offerings (at least by his own standards) might well have frightened him, and while in later years he would complain that he was no longer as productive as he had been, these lash-ups did serve to indicate that all was not well with his muse.

This is not to say that even amidst these flounderings, positive things weren't happening in Plum's world, or he was incapable of producing good, high octane work. The brilliant short story 'Rodney Has a Relapse' came out of these years, a cruel satire on his erstwhile friend A.A. Milne's 'Christopher Robin' poems fuelled by not a little Juvenalian vitriol (Milne had sided with the anti-Wodehouseans during the war). Then the old reliable itself, Blandings Castle, helped nudge things forward, both artistically and sales-wise: 1952's *Pigs Have Wings* marked a partial return to form, selling a healthy 25,000 copies in England. Penguin Books printed a million copies of five back-list titles, attracting, according to biographer Robert McCrum, "a huge new readership of paperback buyers". Even the BBC had come back on stream, lifting their ten-year radio ban in 1951 with a serialization of *A Damsel in Distress* in their popular 'Book at Bedtime' slot on the Home

Service. Over in the States, Plum had a new editor (Peter Schwed) and publisher (Simon & Schuster) who clearly understood him. He'd finally put down his roots in a quiet corner of Long Island where he would live for the rest of his life, and he took out American citizenship in 1955. By the mid-1950s, Plum must finally have been feeling more settled as he slowly rebuilt his world piece by piece.

But it was with his unreliable memoir, 1953's *Performing Flea*, that he at last started to draw a line in the sand, putting the past behind him and looking forward to the future. Ending years of false starts and further ditherings, he decided to close the sort-of-autobiography with 40-odd pages from what he called "my Camp book", a diary he had written chronicling his wartime incarceration at Huy and Tost. Funny, moving and completely lacking in self-pity, it was the perfect answer to his critics, its tone beautifully judged and in its own way, a small masterpiece. Taken in conjunction with a selection of Wodehouse's letters to Bill Townend from 1920 to 1952 (which as we'll see in a moment were heavily revised) McCrum judges that *Performing Flea* represented "the closing of a terribly painful period" in Plum's creative and personal life, Townend confirming that it "had helped him", not least when it received a slew of positive reviews. It was also one in the eye for Irish playwright Sean O' Casey, who had sought to demean both Wodehouse's talent and literary standing by applying that entomological description to him at the time of the BBB. Together with his demolition of A.A. Milne, that made two scores quietly settled: a third was ticked off in *The Mating Season*, when a drunken Gussie Fink-Nottle gives his name as "Duff Cooper" when arrested for swimming in the fountains in Trafalgar Square.

But more significantly than any of this, *Performing Flea* also marked the watershed moment when Plum finally managed to take back control of his own history *from* history by the simple expedient of selectively rewriting it as a sort of 'improved' reality. From 1941 to 1953, his world had been eclipsed by what had happened *outside* it. That would now change, and for the rest of his life the two would re-acquaint themselves, each tolerant of, but not always comprehending the other. From this point on, Plum slowly ceased to be history's victim and started to ignore, exploit and even shamelessly play with it. While the past was undeniably another country, that didn't mean it was 'past' in the sense of 'over and done with' if it could be made newly attractive. Plum was now back doing what he did best, confidently reshaping reality – real reality – into his own image, a process that had come to define his mid-season period.

The green shoots of recovery in his fiction were evident in 1954's *Jeeves and the Feudal Spirit*, and the intermittently charming *French Leave* from the following year.

With this gradual recalibration came a somewhat more bullish approach to his created world, as if he were defending it from attack. As early as 1951, he seemed to have performed a handbrake turn in his view of Orwell's article, writing to Mackail that it was "practically one long roast of your correspondent". Now back in America and out of immediate threat of prosecution, Plum accuses his benefactor of having "falsif[ied] facts in order to make a point". Unfortunately, Orwell was no longer alive to debate that point, having died of tuberculosis in 1950 at the age of 46 ("poor chap"). But while Wodehouse still reckoned that it had been "perfectly all right for him – or any other critic – to say that my stuff is Edwardian and out of date", a certain asperity had crept into his tone:

> [W]hy try to drive it home by saying that my out-of-touchness with English life is due to the fact that I did not set foot in England for sixteen years before 1939?

He belligerently continued:

> If only these blighters would realize that I started writing about Bertie Wooster and comic Earls because I was in America and couldn't write American stories and the only English characters the American public would read about were exaggerated dudes. It's as simple as that.

Finally, he fulminated:

> Another thing I object to in these analyses of one's work is that the writer picks out something one wrote in 1907 to illustrate some tendency. Good Lord! I was barely articulate in 1907.

The first of many things we could flag in these three quotations – all taken from the same letter – is the utter confusion between what is historically accurate and what isn't; which parts of his biography mattered and which didn't; and whether those distinctions are ultimately important. In the first he's berating Orwell for saying that he (Plum) wasn't historically accurate while being historically inaccurate himself, as we'll see in a moment; in the second, he's maintaining that he was deliberately exaggerating the historical truth to suit his American readership; and in the third he's claiming that the school stories he was writing in 1907 had no bearing on anything, because they weren't up to much and time marches on. I'm not completely sure what this proves; but what's more interesting is what he did with the letter two years later.

The three above quotations are taken from Sophie Ratcliffe's scholarly edition of Plum's original, private correspondence: but read the version Plum doctored for publication in *Performing Flea* and you get a somewhat different picture. For a start, he fillets the 1951 version, embroiders it, then conflates it with a second letter dated August 27, 1946 written to Bill Townend. That middle quotation about exaggerated dudes has gone, and the first now reads:

> George Orwell calls my stuff Edwardian (which God knows it is. No argument about that, George) and says the reason for it being Edwardian is that I did not set foot in England for sixteen years and so lost touch with conditions there. Sixteen years, mark you, during most of which I was living in London and was known as Beau Wodehouse of Norfolk Street.

The argument now flows rather better: Orwell *was* correct in his assessment of Plum as a historical novelist, but that history was real, not fondly imagined from the perspective of 3,000 miles. When he wasn't living in Hollywood or France, "Beau Wodehouse" actually *was* in London and on the case, not writing in a vacuum; and by back-dating the letter to 1946 he is implying that he never entertained the slightest doubt about the integrity – both historical *and* imaginary – of his world. And notice how careful he is in that matey interjection in the 1953 rewrite ("No argument about that, George") to give the impression that Orwell is still alive, even as he's fabricating history to make his fictional 'history' seem genuinely historical. I *think* that's right.

Under the surface, though, he of course knew that things had been rather different: writing to co-conspirator Bill Townend while the contents of *Performing Flea* were still being re-engineered, he deemed it imperative that the book avoided "the slightest hint that I was ever anxious or alarmed or wondering if I should have lost my public", hammering the point home just a few lines later ("I don't want the public to know that I ever had a doubt about my future"). The confusion and disillusionment he so clearly felt in 1944-46 (and probably beyond) was to be replaced by "a rather amused aloofness", and an altogether more robust attitude to the new, modern world. Now, he had *never* for a moment doubted the loyalty of his readers or the validity of his work: those "portentous conclusions" of Orwell's were altogether too serious and anyway were themselves out of date. In Plum's revised chronology, his late friend's "masterly" criticism was something to be quickly swatted away, not dwelt on for nearly seven whole years as it probably had been. Continuity was to be everything, as if Wodehouse World, like an elegant swan, had always been gliding over the surface of the troubled pool of history – while it was actually pedalling like fury beneath the surface of the water trying to save itself from drowning. Once the interruption of the war was over, Plum's new history asserts, it had been back to business as usual. Which of course it hadn't been, and still wasn't, even in 1953.

Knowing what we do now, some of the correspondence pertaining to both *Performing Flea* and his theatrical memoir of the following year, *Bring on the Girls* is wonderfully entertaining, with Plum playing fast and loose with the truth as his creative instincts dictated. During the former's gestation in August 1952, he wrote to Derek Grimsdick:

> What I feel about the book is that it is hopeless to stick too closely to what I actually wrote. What I must do is to write a lot of entirely new stuff and to hell with whether it is not word for word what I wrote to Townend on June 6. 1931! That is to say, those letters are simply a vehicle.

Which, we might add, is exactly what reality had *always* been to Wodehouse – a peg to hang a story on, but a real peg nonetheless. He continued à propos *Bring on the Girls*:

> [W]e simply can't stick to the actual text. One thing I want to do is to think up a lot of funny stories and jam them in. Our slogan must be Entertainment.

And there we have another shaft of daylight let in on the magic of Plum's augmented reality. As he wrote to Guy Bolton about their joint project later the same year:

> I think we shall have to let truth go to the wall if it in-
> terferes with entertainment. And we must sternly suppress
> any story that hasn't a snapper at the finish . . . Even if
> we have to invent every line of the thing, we must have
> entertainment.

A number of these 'true' stories, he added, could safely be attributed to the third member of their musical comedy triumvirate, the compos-er Jerome Kern, who had conveniently died in 1945 and so couldn't register his disapproval or libel anyone. All he and Bolton required, he concluded, is "a couple of days together, plotting the thing out as if it were a play or a novel".

In these letters, in addition to revealing a somewhat Machiavellian side to his personality that isn't often evident, Wodehouse appears gen-uinely excited about the twin projects. When reading the autobiogra-phies of ageing artists, there's often the accompanying suspicion that the story of their lives is all they have left to sell, and they know they're effectively signalling the end of their careers. But Plum's twin volumes are genuinely amusing works of fictive non-fiction (or non-fictive fiction if you like) that give the impression he's still in the game – "WE MUST BE FUNNY!!!!!!" he tells Bolton, complete with an evangelist's upper case and exclamation marks. And if the 'luvvieness' of *Bring on the Girls* doesn't prove annoying, and you aren't repulsed by the whiff of old ham, the two books form interesting companion pieces that came along just at the right time in Plum's career, drawing that line under the past, consolidating his reputation, and giving him a platform from which to launch himself into the future – which simply involved doing what he'd always done.

Given the carelessness with historical accuracy on display in both volumes, it's interesting and even significant that the words 'history' and 'chronicle' enter Plum's fiction far more regularly in the post-war period. In 1960's *Jeeves in the Offing* and 1963's *Stiff Upper Lip, Jeeves* Bertie even refers to his "archives", as if Plum is toying with the idea that his creation is writing an alternative vision of the 20th century that *will* have value as history. Fast forward to 1959, and Plum has got this pose of his-torian off pat, reworking that somewhat joyless 1946 *Joy in the Morning* preface into the somewhat perkier 'My World and what happened to it' that has already made several appearances in this volume.

But even though half a century had passed since the Edwardian era Plum celebrates in the essay, the world of the late 1950s seemed rather more in tune with Plum's creative vision than it had been at the end of the Second World War. Standing tiptoe on the edge of John F. Kennedy's New Frontier and with the 'Swinging 60s' only a year away, culture on both sides of the Atlantic was more upbeat and ready to play. Literature was changing too, and although Plum may have railed at the seriousness of theatrical trends (as documented in Volume 1), overall, the picture was one of expanding sympathies that could seemingly embrace almost anything, however old and fantastical. Lightness was returning to the world and things *could* 'be otherwise', as the 1960 Lady Chatterley trial *inter multa alia* had demonstrated. Plum cheekily predicted that his world might soon be newly relevant in all its good-natured happiness, at which point he would be able to square up to his critics, look them in the eye and declare: "Where do you get that Edwardian stuff? I write of life as it is lived today".

Actually, he already could – if we ruthlessly tight-frame our argument. In Britain, the notorious gangs of 1950s 'Teddy Boys' were so-called because of their adapted Edwardian tailoring that favoured long frock coats, tapered trousers and colourful waistcoats. Ten years later, the Beatles, the Kinks, Jimi Hendrix and many others were sporting psychedelicized versions of Edwardian dandy attire; in music, the Temperance Seven unearthed original vaudeville and dance band standards, introduced them to brand new audiences, and had two top ten hits produced by George Martin; the New Vaudeville Band reached the top of the American, Canadian, Australian and South African charts in 1966 and won a Grammy award (ironically for Best Contemporary Song) with an ersatz 1920s music-hall number 'Winchester Cathedral'; Paul McCartney wrote several Beatles tunes in a vaudeville style, as did the Bonzo Dog Band. Plum even had a Top 40 hit on both sides of the Atlantic when the title song of *Anything Goes* (minus his lyrical revisions, however) was covered by San Francisco pop band Harper's Bizarre. And so on. The ethos of Plum's world was so aesthetically on-message and wildly fashionable during this period of wonderfully skewed reality, his stories started to appear in *Playboy* (seven are collected in the 1966's *Plum Pie*, and the magazine itself is namechecked in *Pearls, Girls and Monty Bodkin*). Plum was rather tickled to find his work wrapped around "photographs of Jayne Mansfield in the nude" and pondered that "[i]t would be great if I found myself listed among the dirty writers".

Occasionally, he would peer out from his Remsenburg retreat to meet the modern world halfway: the Twist, Sputniks, canned TV laughter, Aldermaston marches, Roger Bannister's 4-minute mile, student riots, turtle-neck pullovers, air hostesses, electric guitars and hippies make sporadic guest appearances in his late-period stories, while in 'Jeeves and the Greasy Bird' the world's best-known factotum no longer looks forward to shrimping in Herne Bay but catching tarpon in Florida. Plum's books were given slightly saucy titles like *No Nudes is Good Nudes* (*A Pelican at Blandings* in the U.K.) and *Ice in the Bedroom* (tellingly re-titled *The Ice in the Bedroom* in the U.S.). Although Robert McCrum isn't much amused by what he views as these somewhat desperate attempts to stay 'with-it', I think they're rather fun – given that they too are now hopelessly of their time. As Plum approached his 90th birthday, it must have all seemed rather puzzling, but at the same time oddly gratifying that the wheel of popular culture – and history – had, if only for a brief time, come full circle. For the same author to be published in *The Sunday Magazine* (an improving journal aimed mainly at Christian women) in 1903, and in *Playboy* in 1959 without any material alteration in his style or point of view, must say *something* about the different ways his work has been perceived – although for the life of me I can't really think what that might be.

INNOCENCE,
GUILE AND
STORYTELLING

Chapter 7:
Innocence, Guile and Storytelling

Little boy kneels at the foot of the bed,
Droops on the little hands little gold head,
Hush! Hush! Whisper who dares!
Christopher Robin is saying his prayers.
A.A. Milne, 'Vespers'

Timothy Bobbin has ten little toes.
He takes them out walking wherever he goes.
And if Timothy gets a cold in the head,
His ten little toes stay with him in bed.
'Rodney Has a Relapse'

Hush! Hush! Nobody cares!
Christopher Robin has fallen downstairs.
Dorothy Parker (Wodehouse fan)

In his public defence of Wodehouse in 1945, George Orwell referred to the prevailing "mental atmosphere" of Plum's stories, by which he seems to mean the nature of the mind that could have created them – or, put another way, what sort of man Plum was in order to have written the books that were published under his name. Until that point, very little of pith and moment had been written either about Wodehouse or the nature of his achievement beyond reviews and brief commentaries (Orwell cites an article by literary scholar John Hayward from the 1942 *The Saturday Book* anthology, which is all he'd managed to unearth). But two ideas Orwell himself helped make respectable, still common currency to this day, are a hopeless confusion between Wodehouse World and the living, breathing writer who created it, and the primal innocence of both. Although Orwell only uses the idea on a single occasion (to describe Wodehouse as "a political innocent"), it has proved something of a crowd-puller for scholars who assume that because our world isn't innocent, an innocent world like Wodehouse's isn't ours. Which means it must be situated somewhere or other, but definitely not *here*.

So, was Plum an innocent man? And did that have a bearing on the sort of world he created? Nothing was particularly sacred to this equal-opportunities satirist, but one thing that rarely gets a glowing press in his stories is, ironically, innocence itself. Just look at the way he writes about those traditional symbols of simplicity, children: Jesus may have been fooled by the young, but Plum wasn't, for in his fiction most are portrayed as trainee fiends in human shape, insufferable brats or just plain ugly. From his earliest journalism onwards, innocence as a metaphor for 'goodness' seemed to get right up Wodehouse's nose. Far from being a primal state, it's more usually a smokescreen for hiding a devious nature, or a means of deceiving credulous, sentimental adults.

It's a sentiment borne out in *French Leave*, in which Old Nick thinks of his new-born son and heir as a "revolting poached-egg-like little object"; or in 'The Rough Stuff', where a young infant is said to resemble "a skinned poached egg" – except, of course, in the eye of its adoring mother, who insists on addressing it in an unappealing form of jibberish ("Chicketty wicketty wicketty wipsey pop"). Even the usually soft-hearted Bingo Little's own recently born flesh and blood has "the aspect of a mass murderer suffering from an ingrowing toenail" ('Leave it to Algy'). Major "Barmy" Plank from *Stiff Upper Lip, Jeeves* offers to show Sir Watkyn Bassett the scar on his leg, "the direct result of being ass enough to judge one of these [bonny babies] competitions", adding that "the little beasts" are "bad enough themselves, dribbling out of the side of their mouths at you and all that sort of thing" without having to deal with their mothers, who seem to turn feral at the slightest pretext. Next on the stand we have Tootles from 'Helping Freddie', whose behaviour, in Reggie Pepper's view, is less than optimal:

> The kid had started to bellow by this time, and poor old Freddie seemed to find it rather trying.
>
> "Stop it!" he said. "Do you think nobody's got any troubles except you?"
>
> The kid came back at him with a yell that made the window rattle. I raced to the kitchen and fetched a jar of honey. It was the right stuff. The kid stopped bellowing and began to smear his face with the stuff . . .
>
> Just then the kid upset the milk over Freddie's trousers, and when he had come back after changing his clothes he began to talk about what a much-maligned man King Herod was.

Babies (should they survive such Herodian attentions) turn into toddlers, and in *Uneasy Money*, the soft-hearted Lord Weatherby insists on painting a study of a small, waif-like child he proposes to call 'Innocence'"; his wife Lady Pauline Wetherby has other ideas, suggesting "The Black Hand's Newest Recruit" as a better title, namechecking the ruthless Serbian gang whose murder of Archduke Franz Ferdinand (q.v.) had kicked off the First World War. In the same novel, when Claire Fenwick describes her adorable little brother back home, Dudley Pickering cruelly pictures him as "a small, delicate, wistful child pining away for his absent sister. Consumptive probably. Or curvature of the spine". Similar opprobrium is showered on young Timothy Spelvin in 'Rodney Has a Relapse', an "unfortunate little rat" and "wretched little moppet" who comes out with things like "Daddee . . . are daisies little bits of the stars that have been chipped off by the angels?" and "Daddee, I've made friends with such a nice beetle".

Things get even worse when these young delinquents start to grow up and develop attitude. Exhibit A is the "plug-ugly" Braid Bates, who may just be "the rudest child this side of the Atlantic Ocean" despite being a mere nine summers old. He is

> . . . in appearance a miniature edition of William [Richmal Crompton's fictional schoolboy] and in soul and temperament a combination of Dead End Kid and army mule; a freckled, hard-boiled character with a sardonic eye and a mouth which, when not occupied in eating, had a cynical twist to it. He spoke little as a general thing, but when he did speak seldom failed to find a chink in the armour.

A thug in the guise of a child; but in a death match between Braid and Timothy, there's absolutely no question which one Plum would be rooting for. Then there's Ogden Ford of *The Little Nugget* and *Piccadilly Jim*, a surly "little brute" who smokes, talks back, and in the opinion of his stepfather "ought to be sent to Sing Sing". And talking of young thugs, an entire thesis could be written about adults vs. children from a reading of *Laughing Gas* in which, Reggie, Third Earl of Havershot and Hollywood child star Joey Cooley exchange bodies on account of some raw work in "the Fourth Dimension". An adult becomes imprisoned in a child's body and a child in an adult's, yet before the swap takes place, their personalities are already the reverse of what we might expect. Reggie the 27-year-old adult is the child-like innocent, whereas Joey, aged

12, is the hard-bitten graduate of University of Life, already plotting dire revenge on those in the studio system who have done him wrong. Post-switch, in the body of an adult (and a particularly "gorilla"-like adult, being 6'1" and 14 stone with a boxing blue from Cambridge), he has both the motive *and* the means to mete it out. Reggie, by contrast, is even more the Peter Pan than he already was.

Scratch an adult in Wodehouse's stories, and you often find a hideous child lurking beneath the thin veneer of civilization conferred by education and good parenting. When grown-ups recall their youth, they don't often think of a time when they were more innocent and angelic, but a period when they got up to all kinds of mischief. In *Bill the Conqueror*, Bill West and Flick Sheridan channel their inner brats when, after trampling all over Montague Grayson's herbaceous borders, they hide in some convenient shrubbery while Sir George "Stinker" Pyke gets the blame:

> There is something about the mere act of treading on somebody else's flower-beds that automatically puts back the clock and makes us children again; and Bill and Flick, as they slunk away, were feeling about ten years old. It was just such behaviour as theirs that led to no jam for tea[.]

And are they sorry for their misdemeanour? No sir, absolutely not. Bill, now on a roll, bribes a small boy to throw stones at a posh limousine. And does the boy – being a Wodehouse child – refuse? Once again, the answer is no:

> [H]is head seemed suddenly to split in the middle. A vast grin gleamed like a gash beneath his snub nose. Stunned for a moment by the tremendous reflection that he was going to be paid a huge sun for indulging in his favourite sport, he recovered quickly . . .

. . . and performs the job brilliantly, causing the driver to leave the vehicle unattended while Bill steals it, his youthful mischievous streak still very much upon him. Or how about Charlotte Mulliner and Aubrey Bassinger taking pot-shots at Colonel Sir Francis Pashley-Drake with an air gun from a vantage point high up in a tree in 'Unpleasantness at Bludleigh Court'? The wayward child is often the father (or mother) to the man (or woman) in Plum's writing, and there's full scale regression in the story 'Portrait of a Disciplinarian' when Frederick Mulliner, as an adult, meets his former nanny Nurse Wilks.

Much is made of Wodehouse's childlessness, with all kinds of theories bandied about as to why he didn't get round to procreating. Every theory, in fact, except the simplest one: the possibility that he may not have *liked* children that much. Or perhaps he resembled Uncle Chris in *Jill the Reckless* who, although "fond" of young children was also "bored" by them, for "they made the deuce of a noise and regarded jam as an external ornament". Moreover, to one with Plum's almost pathological work ethic, they would inevitably prove a distraction. The well-known dedication of 1926's *The Heart of a Goof* hints as much:

> To my daughter Leonora without whose never-failing sympathy and encouragement this book would have been finished in half the time.

Yes, it's a joke, and an affectionate one aimed at a young woman he loved dearly. But there might just be a grain of impatience in there somewhere – and in any case it's a better theory than childhood mumps. I'll close this little canter with my particular favourite put-down, courtesy of Bertie and Jeeves, in re: Harold, the loathsome, practically spherical pageboy at Twing Hall:

> "What are the chances of a cobra biting Harold, Jeeves?"

> "Slight, I should imagine, sir. And in such an event, knowing the boy as intimately as I do, my anxiety would be entirely for the snake".

If we're trying to pin innocence on Wodehouse, he's not going to give in without a struggle. Malcolm Muggeridge has a good go, writing of his friend that although he was "not a religious man, goodness shines out of him, and it is a goodness based on innocence," elsewhere remarking that he was not so much "other-worldly, or unworldly, so much as that he is a-worldly; a born neutral". Fanning through these three possibilities, Muggeridge convincingly conveys Wodehouse's status as a sort of inactive combatant, *of* but not always *in* the world, whose glass was usually half-full, who would make the best out of any situation and avoid direct confrontation wherever possible. Unfortunately, by choosing the word "innocence" to encapsulate these character traits, he also paints

Plum as a dreamer (unworldly), a divine (other-worldly) or just plain disengaged (a-worldly); and he really can have been none of these, for the simple reason that neither idealists, visionaries or ascetics tend to write great comedy. And yet scholars and commentators still try to fit Wodehouse up as one of life's innocents who was born with a significant part of his brain missing – a vacancy reflected in the make-up, as they see it, of Wodehouse World.

Pico Iyer shrewdly notes in the March 2013 issue of *Harper's* that Plum didn't help himself in this regard by insistently showing us the world "on its best days", conveniently side-lining the rest. But this bias has also prompted Richard Lamey, writing in the *Church Times* in 2015, to conclude that "Wodehouse is delighting in an innocent world, and inviting us to share his pleasure"; Jay Ruud telling subscribers to the learned journal *Connotations* that reading Wodehouse allows us to "escape into a more innocent world wherein the dangers are produced by folly rather than malice"; and William Vesterman in his 2014 essay 'Plum Time in Nevereverland: The Divine Comedy of P.G. Wodehouse' stating that "there is little or any difference between Bertie's happy and innocent world and certain visions of Christian heaven". Which is quite a burden for a bunch of frothy romantic comedies to have to shoulder.

These three last writers discuss Wodehouse World in the context of otherness, or at the very least, parallelism to somewhere *apart* from where we, his readers, live. Ruud confidently asserts that it is a place we "escape *into*", while Vesterman (accompanied by a host of internet bloggers) goes the whole nine yards, projecting that there is something *beyond* the stories that we can access, a spiritual, even religious dimension that lends them added resonance. Perfectly properly, these writers are seeking to put flesh on the bones of that "something understood" I've been touting since Volume 1; and as we'll see in the following chapter, this approach to Wodehouse can be traced back to the 1950s when the perceived innocence of Plum's world saw it likened to the pre-lapsarian Garden of Eden by some pretty serious literary brains. Unfortunately, many of these attempts are, at base, the 'Plum as fantasy writer' idea dressed in borrowed robes in a bid for intellectual respectability; a miss which, as we'll see in a moment, is as bad as a mile, despite being well-intentioned. While it was a heartening development that Plum was starting to be taken seriously, comedy doesn't always welcome such earnest ministrations; so, before I have my turn at the coconut shy, it'll be worth taking considered aim before pitching the ball.

INNOCENCE, GUILE AND STORYTELLING

Having confidently stated for the last six chapters that Wodehouse World has a complex root system in both reality and history, it's now time to leave this argument behind to look at how it needs to transcend both so as to become the sort of writing that is eventually honoured by a memorial in Westminster Abbey. This will involve examining what it is *within* Plum's writing that resists ageing, or how, to use David Damrosch's terminology, it's possible to read Wodehouse "along two registers, the ethnographic and the universal" *at the same time*, which, in his view, is "a key element in [his]success as a writer of world literature" (Damrosch, *What is World Literature?*, pp. 217-8). Rendered less technically, all that means is trying to explain how Bertie, despite being an Edwardian Knut – a highly time-and-place-specific, real-life social substratum which died out around 1914 – can still resonate in the world's collective imagination over a century later, in an age when most readers won't be familiar with what a Knut even is. So, we have both the time-bound "ethnographic" Bertie (Bertie the Knut) and a time-less, "universal" Bertie co-existing within a single character. Simple as that. All standout characters in great literature conform to this model, and their creators usually have very little control over, or knowledge of, how this happens. They simply write the best story they can and leave external circumstances, including the ministrations of scholars and critics, to do the rest. And here we are with Wodehouse.

On one level, it's simple to write about what keeps Wodehouse World afloat: it's the humour and the language. Of course it is, and a good deal of heavy-duty attention has already been paid to both, which is all perfectly proper. But if we propose to examine *what* it is about the humour and the language that keeps them vibrant, and *how* they echo through the precincts of time and history, things aren't so straightforward. So I'm going to return to that idea of innocence, even though it's not quite right, simply because it crops up in Wodehouse studies so often that there must be *something* to it, as Stephen Fry implies when he writes in his introduction to the 2011 anthology *What Ho! The Best of Wodehouse* that Plum was "a *kind* of innocent" [italics mine], while sagely warning us that "true adult innocence, is a characteristic so rare we often call it blessed and ascribe it only to saints". Plum, while generally a kind, benign and thoughtful man, was never a candidate for beatification, as is sometimes inadvertently hinted. Therefore, let's make our base-camp there and venture out from it.

On January 4, 1944, before Orwell had published his essay but going on for three years after the BBB, the journalist and politician

PELHAM GRENVILLE WODEHOUSE

Harold Nicolson had written in his diary:

> I do not want to see Wodehouse shot on Tower Hill. But I
> resent the theory that "poor old Wodehouse is so innocent
> that he is not responsible". A man who has shown such
> ingenuity and resource in evading British and American
> income tax cannot be classed as impractical.

Nicolson was completely wrapped up in the BBB, both as a BBC governor around the time of the 'Cassandra' broadcast in 1941, as well as serving under its instigator Duff Cooper at the Ministry of Information. So, he would have known far more about the situation than most. But whether we agree with his assessment or not, it gives the lie to the abiding image of Plum as completely other-worldly. Even if we hadn't trawled through the political satire in the front of this volume, it would still be difficult to justify using that particular adjective if we stop to think for a moment, for Plum didn't simply charm himself into his great wealth. As early as 1921, he had written to Bill Townend:

> I find that if I spend more than six months in this country
> I'm liable to pay income tax on everything I make in
> America as well as in England, in addition to paying
> American income tax. This is no good to Pelham, so I'm
> skipping.

And skip he did, for one reason or another, for the next 25 years or so until he settled permanently in America. As we've seen on several occasions in this trilogy, and particularly in the previous chapter, that third person "Pelham" could be focused and calculating, not necessarily in his one-to-one dealings with people, but where his livelihood was concerned. While showing little interest in 'political' politics, he was completely saturated in the politics of writing, reading and publishing – everything, in fact, to do with his career. His regular correspondent Denis Mackail, remarked in his autobiographical *Life with Topsy* that whenever they met, Wodehouse was "determined to talk about nothing but ink." Threaten *that*, and you might see a very different, distinctly non-innocent side of his personality. Could a literary eremite have written this utterly patronizing, sexist broadside, addressed to Nancy Spain of the *Daily Express* in 1953?

My poor old girl. You certainly made a pretty bloody fool of yourself over Performing Flea, didn't you? You should have waited to see what the other fellows were going to say. I'll give you a tip which will be useful to you. Always read at least some of the book before you review it. It makes a tremendous difference, and you can always find someone to help you with the difficult words. What the devil was all that bilge about me being 'bewildered'? There is certainly no suggestion of it in the book. You really must read it some time.

In what was more of a diary piece than full-on review, Spain had re-marked, rightly but with a charmless degree of snark, how *Performing Flea* sought to "whitewash the Wodehouse sepulchre" by recycling old letters to his "school chum". At which point the red mist clearly descended on our hero; for as we saw a few pages back, re-writing history in his favour actually *was* one of Plum's ambitions for the book, as he disclosed to that very same school chum Bill Townend in the correspondence leading up to its publication. In other words, he had been found out – ironically by a writer on his former paper. He probably wasn't enamoured of Spain's choice of that "sepulchre" metaphor either, which implied his career was already dead and buried.

Particularly in old age, Plum could be contrary, grouchy and even occasionally exploded into private anger, usually with critics: "One yip out of any of the bastards and they get a beautifully phrased page of vitriol which will haunt them for the rest of their lives", he once boasted, no doubt wishfully rather than accurately. But the thought was there. He called these letters "stinkers", and although outbursts like this appear to have been comparatively rare, they do serve as a timely reminder not to identify Plum *too* completely with his fictional world. After all, it's easy to argue that many novels, from *The Wind in the Willows* to *The Diary of a Nobody* create innocent worlds that are pretty much malice, death and guilt-free without anyone rushing to claim that Kenneth Grahame or George Grossmith were in any way innocents. For the double perspective essential to the writing of both satire and humour is simply not compatible with innocence, which can only see things from a single, incomplete viewpoint. As Tim Andrew, Chairman of The P G Wodehouse Society (UK) has it, "you can't write humour that hits the bulls-eye as often and unerringly as Wodehouse's unless you have real insight into the foibles of mankind" (*Plum Lines*, Vol. 24 no.1,

2003). Which innocence, by its very nature, doesn't have.

What is rarely acknowledged in the use of "innocent" in a Wodehousean context is the tension that exists at the heart of its dictionary definition: which is, quite simply, (a) a sense of true innocence as contrasted with (b) a dangerous ignorance. But while Wodehouse was absolutely brilliant at writing *about* innocence of the kind that propels Bertie through his accident-strewn life, to suggest (as Orwell did) that Plum *is* Bertie or even somehow *like* Bertie is to overlook the fact that true innocence cannot recognize its own innocence until that innocence is lost. *Ergo*, lacking this necessary perspective, Plum couldn't have created Bertie, whose particular brand of innocence is governed, regulated and perpetuated by having the under-developed intelligence of a peahen married to an over-developed sense of *noblesse oblige*. We lose count of the number of times his innocence gets him into hot water, but we mustn't forget that it's Plum who intentionally *gets* him into that hot water; and that it was Plum who created Jeeves, the means by which he gets out of it. For Wodehouse had an outsider's angle on innocence that the true innocent doesn't (and indeed can't) have. In fact, we could claim that Bertie's fictional life is an extended meditation on the *dangers* of innocence – for on those occasions when Bertie takes matters into his own hands, his innocence inevitably ends up making matters worse. I would argue, therefore, that rather than look at innocence from the point of view of Plum's biography or personality, it is – once again – more profitable to look at how he uses it in his writing, as a function and a theme of his plotting; for to a writer who needs to generate plots, innocence can be a wonderfully catalytic resource.

Writing in *Newsweek* in 2007, David Gates pondered the evergreen relationship between Jeeves and Bertie:

> Wodehouse's most popular creation, the team of foppish, feeble-brained Bertie Wooster and his quietly omniscient valet Jeeves, is a common literary archetype: Don Quixote/Sancho Panza, Mr. Pickwick/Sam Weller, Lear/the Fool, Frodo [Baggins]/Sam. But Wodehouse adds a folktale element: Bertie is a descendent of those witlings and third sons who complete their quests because of their innocence.

Notice – in passing – how Gates uses the word "archetype" in the sense of a recurring motif, which drives Jeeves and Bertie in the direction of

Damrosch's idea of "world literature". The brilliantly realized chemistry in their relationship makes them another of those timeless two-person partnerships that litter great writing down the ages, representing 'something' beyond themselves. That 'something' is a moveable feast, a constellation of ideas that has one-to-one friendship at its centre, with one character the social inferior of the other.

As with Bertie, the innocence that governs the thinking and behaviour of all the 'masters' in that list is a cocktail of ignorance, inexperience, immaturity, soft nature, stupidity and delusion. And yet each of those negatives helps initiate or at least progress the stories in which their respective creators place them. Innocence is a great plot enhancer precisely because it is a vacuum in the character's knowledge, experience or personality that exists to be filled (good) or exploited (bad); and how that happens is often the crux of the plot. Fools can be made to rush in where wise men would never tread, getting them into all kinds of scrapes 'normal' folks like us (!) avoid, because our life experience and native cunning wouldn't permit it. Mostly, we don't repeat the mistakes of our innocent childhoods because we've learned, or been taught, that it's not a good idea. But it's not the same for these guys, who, whether comic or tragic, are all doing some belated growing up in front of two audiences – one inside and one outside the work in which they feature.

By the end of their stories, each has learned something which, to a greater or lesser degree, has modified their original innocence, and this progress has allowed them to advance their understanding of the world – even if it only means they can die happier. Fortunately, they're all blessed with a foil who knows more than they do, that foil being a mix of servant, teacher and lifesaver. And although Sancho *et al* may have been born into a lower stratum of society, they can help navigate their master's way through the vagaries of the journey. Those who *shouldn't* know more actually *do* know more; and in all four cases this front-loads the comedy – yes, even in *King Lear*.

Now let's stir Bertram Wilberforce Wooster into that mix. Bertie differs from each of those other 'masters' by dint of the fact that he *never* seems to learn from his experience, his innocence remaining intact and exultant throughout the 59 years of his existence. Once Jeeves has solved each of his serial problems, his errant master breathes a sigh of relief before promptly diving into the mulligatawny one more time. If Bertie *had* learned anything, Plum would have needed to develop his personality in a way not usually open to a comic character: a chastened, more knowledgeable Bertie quite simply wouldn't *be* Bertie, and in the interests of protecting and preserving his mid-season formula, Plum denies him the chance to learn from his mistakes. Nor does he have to since Jeeves is always on hand to fix them and clear up any collateral damage.

Try to imagine Bertie as a case-hardened veteran who eschews the company of his snootering exes, or who tells his aunts Agatha and Dahlia to take a hike every time they demand that he jump. He may make token attempts to wriggle out of the plots that stretch ahead of him, but his good, innocent nature always makes him set forth on his "quest". Which of course it has to or he would remain permanently holed up in 3A Berkeley Mansions waiting for Plum to find him something to do. One only has to read Ben Schott's ingenious reboots of Jeeves and Wooster (2018's *Jeeves and the King of Clubs* and *Jeeves and the Leap of Faith* from 2020) to see what happens when you mess with the goods. In making Bertie more intelligent (and therefore less innocent), Schott takes him outside the established formula and his fanbase beyond its comfort zone – at least to judge by many of the reviews. In denying him his innocence, he has to *be* something – in this case a spy – rather than simply existing beautifully, unemployed and up for anything.

And it's not just Bertie: elsewhere in Wodehouse, innocence offers almost limitless potential for things to happen, again and again. Even the double-dealing Ukridge is a kind of innocent who never tires of thinking his get-rich-quick schemes have the slightest chance of working, which makes him all the more determined to find one that will eventually deliver the goods. Which of course he never does, despite being the veteran of one novel and 19 short stories, and Plum's longest-serving character. Or take Blandings, the innocence of which consists – among other things – of its utter porosity as regards imposters. You'd think, after the castle had been infiltrated by one or two, that the powers that be would have learned to pre-vet their invitees more thoroughly. But no, this rarely happens until it's too late and the imposter has safely passed beneath the transom, as Gally exasperatedly points out in *A Pelican at Blandings* on discovering Vanessa Polk is a member of this none-too-exclusive club – and more importantly, one who he himself hasn't introduced:

> "It's an odd thing about Blandings Castle, it seems to attract imposters as catnip does cats. They make a bee line for the place. When two or three impostors are gathered together, it's only a question of time before they're saying

"Let's all go round to Blandings", and along they come. It shakes one. I've sometimes asked myself if Connie is really Connie. How can we be certain that she's not an international spy cunningly made up as Connie? The only one of the local fauna I feel really sure about is Beach. He seems to be genuine".

"It shakes one"? Well, it really shouldn't, so often does it occur. As readers, we are aware of this Wodehousean innocence, which allows all kinds of improbable things to happen that normally wouldn't. It's all too easy to meander through a typical Plum plot asking ourselves, "Why didn't so-and-so do such-and-such, then this or that wouldn't have happened". But the answer to that question is embedded in its last four words: those improbable things *need* to happen – and keep happening – to allow Plum's comic lightness to stay afloat. In *King Lear*, the consequences of Lear's innocence lead inexorably to death; but in a romantic comedy, the worst Bertie can suffer is some temporary personal discomfort or minor reputational damage that generates even further laughter.

And so, at the beginning of every story, we're almost back where we started: Bertie is reassuringly ready to get himself into further scrapes; Ukridge has hatched a new can't-fail venture; and Blandings throws its doors open to a fresh set of imposters. The long-running sagas within Wodehouse World do not move in a linear, chronological progression like, say, Anthony Powell's *A Dance to the Music of Time* or C.P. Snow's *Strangers and Brothers* sequence; rather they are a series of repeated rituals whose rhythms we quickly get used to.

So, whether we realize it or not, the familiarity and lightness engendered by Plum's take on "innocence" is what keeps us returning to his books. At the close of a Wodehouse story, circumstances may have altered slightly from those at its opening, and a great deal will have happened; but nothing of importance will have been learned. Jeeves doesn't learn because he seems to know everything already; Lord Emsworth can't learn because he would forget whatever it was almost instantly; George Tupper goes on giving Ukridge fivers because he seems to have more good nature than sense; Connie can't help but interfere in the love lives of the younger set because she is a prisoner of her snobbish ways, set as if in concrete; Alaric Dunstable keeps trying to steal the Empress because, as *per* Einstein's definition of insanity, he keeps repeating the same action expecting an outcome other than failure – and there are plenty more examples where those came from, all of them oiling the wheels of Plum's plotting.

But it wasn't simply Plum's use of innocence as an eternally gen-
erative principle in his work that lets us know he knew *exactly* what innocence was and how best to exploit it in his storytelling. As regular
readers of fiction, our habitual and necessary suspension of disbelief is,
in effect, a type of willed innocence ripe for exploitation – something
Plum routinely demands as we enter Wodehouse World. In *Pigs Have
Wings*, the narrator informs us that

> The world may be roughly divided into two classes – men
> who, when you tell them a story difficult to credit, will not
> believe you, and men who will.

Lord Emsworth's pigman, George Cyril Wellbeloved, belongs in the latter category, especially after he's had a few; "his whole aspect", we are
told, "was that of one who believed everything he read in the Sunday
papers". We are all – potentially – George Cyril Wellbeloveds when we
enter fictional worlds, more so in Plum's than elsewhere, for there is so
much storytelling going on *within* his stories. Take Mr Mulliner and his
shaggy dog yarns, which almost without exception tax the credulity of
his listeners – and us, his readers. In the very first of the collected stories – 'The Truth About George' (the version in *Meet Mr Mulliner*) – the
theme of gullibility is addressed not just in the title, but right up front
on the opening page. Fishermen, with their tales of 'the one that got
away' are "traditionally careless of the truth", claims the story's opening
narrator, only for Mr Mulliner to politely but firmly jump on him from
a great height:

> "[Y]ou must not fall into the popular error about fish-
> ermen. Tradition has maligned them. I am a fisherman
> myself, and I have never told a lie in my life".

But as we get to know Mr Mulliner in more than 40 further episodes -
during which I can't remember him ever picking up a fishing rod - we
recognize that he rarely strays into the remotely plausible while all the
time insisting he's simply a conduit for the truth. With "the extraordinarily childlike candour of his eyes" which are "large and round and
honest", his first ever audience (of one) "would have bought oil stock
from him without a tremor". Or sell you Christmas cards in January,
for Mr Mulliner plays the innocent while playing *on* the innocence of

his listeners, never shifting from the position that he's a reporter rather than a congenital fantasist. And in that respect, he perfectly mirrors the ambitions of his creator. So much so, that I am prepared to amicably challenge Robert McCrum's assertion that of all Plum's characters, Lord Emsworth bears the closest resemblance to the author himself by substituting Mr Mulliner in his place.

It is the thesis of this chapter that Plum's much-vaunted innocence shouldn't encourage us to address his world by its correspondence with our own, *but through the quality of belief he demands of us as readers*. It's not Wodehouse World that's innocent, or even Wodehouse himself. It's *us*. And in any case, it's not innocence we're dealing with here, or even credulity, but a kind of trust, what the poet Samuel Taylor Coleridge labelled "the suspension of disbelief" back in 1817. Yes, it's nothing new in literary criticism, but it's a commonplace and widely understood concept that is for some reason ignored time and time again by Wodehouse scholars, while being the perfect answer to all those who consider him a fantasist. Every storyteller without exception exploits this trust, whether he or she knows it or not. Realists, for example, try to convince us that their created worlds are, well, as real as the real one. Which, after what we learned in Chapter 2, can't always be taken for granted. But for writers like Wodehouse who trade in a richer blend of reality and invention, what literary critics call "truth" or "meaning" is a much more ineffable thing, still requiring us to 'buy into' it, only with much less evidence to guide our instincts. Wodehouse World, as I've already hinted in this book but never explicitly stated, needs to ring true to us – and it does, or else he wouldn't still be read. At the close of that first story, Mr Mulliner invites his auditor to "believe me or believe me not", as he claims the stuttering wreck that was his nephew George "is now the chosen orator at all political rallies for miles around". But does his listener believe him? And for that matter, do we? Is the story good enough for us to 'buy into' its obvious fictionality? And does it make us 'innocents' if we've enjoyed it? No, of course it doesn't, any more than it makes Wodehouse an innocent for having written it.

From the very earliest times, writers have played wonderfully entertaining cat-and-mouse games with their readers' credulity, seeing how far they can stretch it before it snaps. It's a sort of 'trial by innocence' – some readers take to it, others don't. Mr Mulliner is a past master at it; rather more so than the Oldest Member, the narrator of Plum's golf stories, who at least skirts the shores of plausibility, often involving himself in his tales to give them a kind of eyewitness authenticity.

From the very first of *his* collected stories ('The Clicking of Cuthbert', originally published in 1921), Plum makes him more of a historian, the voice of experience who "as the poet says, has seen Golf steadily and seen it whole". He is the "Sage", who occasionally rounds off his story with a lesson to be learned, even if it's something as vague and sententious as "golf can be of the greatest practical assistance to man in Life's struggle". Mr Mulliner tends not to do this; his stories seem to arrive second-hand and on trust from one or other of his extended family, which allows him greater latitude in straining our gullibility, for we know he wasn't actually there when the events took place. Both men are, however, master storytellers who, each in his own way, trades in *imaginative* truth, a currency which has less to do with whether a story is true or real, and more with how compellingly it buttonholes its audience. And here it is I'm going to take the first of several punts at defining just what it is that makes Wodehouse continue to be read in the 21st century; not the upfront things like the fun, the language, and the characters, but that elusive "something understood".

I sometimes wonder whether Plum had ever read Oscar Wilde's short dialogue piece *The Decay of Lying*, which brilliantly lets the light in on this kind of ludic storytelling. Published in 1891, with a title adapted from a Mark Twain essay of 1880, it talks more sense about literary theory in a short space than just about any book of lit crit I've ever come across. And what's more, it's funny, which is why I'm going to quote from it below. Its chief protagonist Vivian has much to say on the changing relationship between writer and reader, which is why, in his view, the quality of contemporary fiction is declining:

> One of the chief causes that can be assigned for the curiously commonplace character of most of the literature of our age is undoubtedly the decay of Lying as an art, a science, and a social pleasure. The ancient historians gave us delightful fiction in the form of fact; the modern novelist presents us with dull facts under the guise of fiction . . . The loss that results to literature in general from this false ideal of our time can hardly be overestimated . . . Many a young man starts in life with a natural gift for exaggeration which, if nurtured in congenial and sympathetic surroundings, or by the imitation of the best models, might grow into something really great and wonderful. But, as a rule, he comes to nothing. He either falls into careless habits of

accuracy, or takes to frequenting the society of the aged and the well informed. Both things are equally fatal to his imagination, as indeed they would be fatal to the imagination of anybody, and in a short time he develops a morbid and unhealthy faculty of truthtelling . . . and often ends by writing novels which are so like life that no one can possibly believe in their probability. This is no isolated instance that we are giving. It is simply one example out of many; and if something cannot be done to check, or at least to modify, our monstrous worship of facts, Art will become sterile and Beauty will pass away from the land.

For all his exaggeration, Wilde was right on the money. At the close of the 19th century and on into the 20th when Plum was just starting out, the shibboleth of truth to life grew ever more imperative in some literary circles, as reality was seen to be growing grimmer. Literature had to reproduce life as it was lived, or risk irrelevance. Some writers, objecting to the tyranny of fact, went off at 180-degrees in the opposite direction, and the satire in Plum's beloved *Patience* skirted this very theme. But the very opposite has since proved to be the case: although Wilde and Wodehouse are still widely read, 'realistic' novels like George Gissing's *New Grub Street* and Walter Greenwood's *Love on the Dole* aren't anywhere near so well known. And while Plum awkwardly flirted and then wrestled with this more realistic approach to writing in his early career – as this study proposed in Volume 1 – he never wholly bought into it. Hence Mr Mulliner, who is Wildean through and through, teases us that his outlandish stories might *actually* be true, while we are fully and joyously aware that they aren't.

Without exception, his tales don't simply try their listeners' innocence, they actively test it to destruction and beyond. The second story collected in *Meet Mr Mulliner*, mischievously titled 'A Slice of Life', opens with the prospect of Vera Dalrymple being turned into a lobster by a mad professor in a "film-serial". Preposterous? No, says Mr Mulliner. It is typical of the modern age for a "sceptical attitude of mind" to automatically dismiss things that are "a little out of the ordinary run of the average man's experience". It would be better, he implies, if we were to be even more open to our world in all its variety and strangeness. And so, claiming to "speak nothing but the bare truth", he launches into the unlikely tale of quack chemist (sorry, holistic therapist) Wilfred Mulliner and his battery of patent remedies. In stories three and four ('Mulliner's

Buck-U-Uppo' and 'The Bishop's Move') his fantasies meet with no resistance among his audience, but by the fifth, 'Came the Dawn', rebellion is starting to stir in the bar-parlour. As the opening narrator tells us, "we have been trained to believe almost anything of Mr Mulliner's relatives, but this, we felt, was a little too much", which the reverend gentleman counters with all the indignation of the falsely accused innocent: "I have never deviated from the truth in my life".

Mr Mulliner's masterful and entertaining formula was to be repeated for another four decades. His audience at the Angler's Rest may occasionally bridle, but it cannot be denied that in its chief storyteller's absence, "the tide of intellectual conversation" tends to "run very low". For although Mr Mulliner's listeners are at perfect liberty to dismiss his stories as the ravings of a diseased mind or believe in them as gospel, there is also the sense that one of the reasons they give him house room is that they enjoy having their credulity challenged. How far will he go this time? Does he really expect us to believe him? And in that sense, Plum is challenging *our* credulity too. In Mr Mulliner's masterpiece, 'Honeysuckle Cottage' from 1925, he demands of the initial narrator whether he believes in ghosts, which elicits hesitation and the reply "Well no – and yes". At which Mr Mulliner sighs as if exasperated. The narrator, sensing this impatience, tries to clarify his position by citing Henry James's evergreen ghost story *The Turn of the Screw*, at which point he is cut short: "I am not talking about fiction" insists Mr Mulliner. And as the narrator tries the opposite tack which opens with "Well, in real life – " his interlocutor again intervenes, this time substituting a story of his own whose theme, as I explored at some length in Volume 2, is neither fact nor fiction but the polyvalence of truth – especially the kind of 'truth' found in fiction which keeps a foot in both camps; just enough fact to be credible, just enough fiction to be entertaining.

Unlike his listener, Mr Mulliner doesn't allow himself the luxury of disbelief – or rather he professes not to. For his stories to work, he 'knows', like his creator, that he has to hold his audience's attention, to involve and immerse them in this strange world he's busy creating for our entertainment, or as Mr Mulliner would see it, our education. He is our guide: and our innocence, as embodied in both our openness to possibility and a trust in our narrator allows us to collaborate by the simple act of withholding our judgement, thereby giving the storyteller more elbow room to work within. Every great writer, even those who profess to 'realism', knows how to work this; and in James's *The Turn of the Screw*, the story itself, and the masses of critical attention it has attracted over the last 120 years or so, has focused on whether the haunting at the centre of the plot is real or imagined. James wanted to keep things as ambiguous as possible; and as things have turned out he was absolutely right to court this uncertainty, for the novella remains one of his perennially intriguing – and most enduring – titles. Plum, by contrast, being a comic writer, did not have to be so scrupulous in keeping his narratives balanced on this knife edge between fact and fiction. He can tempt and taunt us all he likes.

The difference between the Henry James approach and Mr Mulliner's technique can be illustrated by another of Plum's storytellers, Thomas G. "Soapy" Molloy. Mr Mulliner *could*, we've already been told, sell oil stock without a scintilla of doubt crossing the buyer's mind; but Soapy actually makes a living doing precisely that. So, whereas it's of no great consequence whether or no Mr Mulliner's audience of Ninepennyworths of Sherries or Small Ports in the bar parlour believe him, Soapy's solvency – his whole career -- hinges on the quality of his persuasive talents, allowing Plum to further explore the truth behind the fiction writer's calling.

Soapy plies his trade in four novels dating between 1925 and 1972, and in *Ice in the Bedroom* manages to offload shares "in non-existent oil wells" to Freddie Widgeon (to the tune of £1,000), Lord Blicester (£1,000) and Oofy Prosser (£2,000). Those gentlemen are Soapy's rubes, and their innocence is primed not by curiosity or the desire to be entertained, but need or greed, pure and simple. They actively *want* to believe in something that's too good to be true, which does half of Soapy's job for him. But in order to make the scam work, he first has to look trustworthy, which fortunately he does, resembling "an American senator of the better sort". Next, he has to spin a good yarn, which he believes he does; by his own admission, "[i]t was his modest boast that if he were allowed to wave his arms and really get going on the sales talk, he could unload Silver River oil shares on prospects hailing from even Aberdeen or New England" – two places which, Plum implies, have more than their fair share of sceptics and/or tightwads. In *Ice in the Bedroom* his ambitions seem to have grown, as has his professional pride, when he claims he could sell the Brooklyn Bridge to "a nice smooth-working sucker", never being one to give that sucker an even break.

And that's really all there is to Soapy's winning narrative formula; with good looks and a strong sales patter, he can sell anything to anybody. He has to make his pitch just plausible *enough* to hook his prey. Musing on his technique with his wife Dolly, Soapy seems to know his audience, a sort of "sixth" sense about who will take his bait and who won't. In *Pearls' Girls and Monty Bodkin*, Ivor Llewellyn's wife Grayce, unlike her husband, isn't sufficiently naïve to fall for his line, for she is not only risk averse, but suspicious. Which, in Soapy's view, is eminently reasonable, as he debates with Dolly:

> (Soapy) "It isn't as though there really was a Silver River oil well".
>
> "Perhaps there is. Somewhere".
>
> "Maybe. You never know".
>
> "Be quite a coincidence if there was".
>
> "It certainly would".

When is a lie not a lie? Soapy is under no illusions that he's a born liar; but Dolly introduces the idea that plausibility is just as valid as any truth. If you can persuade some innocent party that something *is* the truth, that's as good as reality. And in the case of some of Soapy's victims, particularly Oofy Prosser, we'd find ourselves on Soapy's side; the unattractively parsimonious Oofy won't miss a few quid from his vast fortune, although he would grieve over every pound swindled from him as if it were a deceased firstborn. But how do we feel about Soapy swindling the good-natured Freddie Widgeon, whose entire happiness is invested in that £1,000? Mr Mulliner's games with the truth have no serious consequences, but Soapy's do, or rather, *can*.

Playing on someone's innocence then becomes an equivocal activity that can muddy our sense of right and wrong. Soapy and Dolly are a great double act, which is why Plum kept bringing them back for more. But should we really *like* them? If we do, are we valuing ingenuity and resourcefulness over the innocence they're exploiting? This is further complicated when, in *Money for Nothing*, we finally get to witness Soapy's much-vaunted technique, and we quickly realize that he too is something of an innocent if he considers himself a sophisticated yarn-spinner, because – frankly – he's so transparent as to be a parody of a cartoon conman. Here he is in action with Hugo Carmody:

> "[T]he fact is I'm all fixed up in Oil. Oil's my dish. I began in Oil and I'll end in Oil. I wouldn't be happy outside of Oil . . . Yes, sir . . . I put my first thousand into Oil and I'll put my last thousand into Oil. Oil's been a good friend to me. There money in Oil . . . Oil", said Mr Molloy, with the air of one making an epigram, "is Oil".

And you can't argue with that. Or rather, you absolutely can, for Soapy and his ilk represent the dark side of storytelling, when what is essentially a playful activity is used to swindle people out of their hard-earned. Neither Soapy nor Dolly appear to have been gifted much of a conscience, but we can also argue that if you fall for patter this pathetic, it's almost criminal that you've got money in the first place. You almost *deserve* to lose it.

As Monty Bodkin would say, there are wheels within the wheels of Plum's innocence, particularly in a world where conmen and their victims appear to be as innocent as one another. So, although it is perfectly possible to claim Wodehouse World for innocence, it would be a bad mistake not to realize that an awful lot of calculation, cunning and guile went into creating it. Simply on the level of knowing how stories work, Plum demonstrates a massive amount of savvy – something that is regularly recognized by his fellow writers, although less so by reviewers and commentators. Had Plum paraded his nous before us in the manner of T.S. Eliot, it would probably have done him no good, for comic writers are rarely given credit for their knowledge of literary theory. But we must remember that those comedy sidekicks we met earlier in this chapter knew a thing or two when it comes to the way the world works, more so than their masters; and in Plum's case, there is a great deal of art in his seeming artlessness. Perhaps he is thought of as innocent because he makes storytelling look as natural as breathing, needing only the lubricant of a hot scotch and lemon to churn out peerless, entertaining fiction. But at his best Plum knew *exactly* what he was doing, as evidenced by yet another Mulliner ripper in which the central figure is thought to know everything while in fact being absolutely clueless – the very opposite of the writer creating his fictional world.

In 'The Smile That Wins' from 1931, Adrian Mulliner is cast as a private detective whose job it is to piece together stories and solve cases. And he's good at it, as long as things don't get too complicated. For instance, in "The Adventure of the Missing Sealyham", the solution is handed to him on a plate when he finds a stray dog, reads the name on its collar and promptly restores it to its owner. Mystery solved. Or finding a vanishing cake of soap, which was last seen as the bather in question hit the high note of "Sonny Boy", at which point his hand muscles involuntarily contracted around the slippery tablet, shooting it into the air. It is but the work of an instant to locate it where it fell on the bathroom floor. It's all in a day's work for our quick-witted Sherlock. But things get rather more complicated when, laid low by a bout of dyspepsia, Adrian's physician recommends that he smile more. Being a melancholy type, he is somewhat out of practice, and the resulting facial contortion, which appears both "sardonic and sinister" seems to convey a certain smugness, as if Adrian is familiar with the innermost secrets of whoever it's directed at. As the story progresses, a number of upper-crust ne'er-do-wells convince themselves he must have sussed out all their former felonies, and quickly mend their ways.

Plum wasn't one for creating idiot savants, usually confining himself to mere idiots like Bertie, but Adrian fits the bill admirably. Perhaps more accurately, we should call him an idiot thought-to-be savant, since for the life of him Adrian can't make out why people he's scarcely met are suddenly trying to grease round him. Rather than being a fatal weakness ripe for exploitation, innocence is now, improbably, on the front foot and even a means of righting wrongs. After feeling the full force of Adrian's leer, Sir Sutton Hartley-Wesping, Bart, guiltily replaces all the wedding gifts he has purloined and was planning to take down to the pawnbrokers, for, as he later confesses, Adrian has "one of those smiles that seem to go clean through you and light up all your inner being as if with a searchlight". Lord Brangbolton, Adrian's future father-in-law, can only agree, the erstwhile bath time warbler who Adrian later 'catches' cheating at cards: "[f]eller struck me as having some sort of sixth sense if you know what I mean, dash and curse him". Lastly, the financier Sir Jasper Addleton, who, Soapy-style, has some dodgy deal going on involving the Bramah-Yamah Gold Mines flotation, packs in his engagement to Lady Millicent Shipton-Bellinger, leaving the field free for Adrian to marry her, with a nice fat cheque as a dowry – or a bung that will guarantee Adrian's silence, if you prefer. All the way though the story, Adrian hasn't the first clue why Lady Luck is smiling on him in such a benevolent manner – and Plum never lets him find out, making him a total innocent right to the end. And then at the wedding that closes the story, Adrian smiles a smile of genuine happiness at the Very Reverend the Dean of Bittlesham, who, as the curtain comes down, requests a word with him in private.

Both Plum and his mouthpiece Mr Mulliner wisely avoid extracting a moral from this unlikely chain of events. And I will follow their example, except to say that we should never underestimate the positive power of innocence. It's not all ignorance and vacancy; but then again, nor is it to be held aloft as some kind of ideal for living. Plum's can be called a *knowing* innocence; the sort that Adrian Mulliner is thought to have but actually doesn't. It's an oxymoron, yes, but it's a perspective, or "atmosphere", that underpins much of Wodehouse World, contributing in great measure to its lightness.

HISTORY AND MYTH

Chapter 8:
History and Myth

[Wodehouse] is a writer who is going to last.
Philip Hensher, The Spectator, 2002

No one could have been the bumbling idiot of Wodehouse's own self-portrait and yet have written so much, so elegantly and with such a keen eye to his public. Clearly he developed a protective irony to guard his privacy, and this makes him a clever old stick.
Sebastian Faulks, The Independent, 25 October 1992

To Lord Emsworth the park and gardens of Blandings were the nearest earthly approach to Paradise.
Something Fresh

"Sad," [Psmith] sighed, "that these idyllic surroundings should have become oppressed with a cloud of sinister menace. One thinks one sees a faun popping about in the undergrowth, and on looking more closely perceives that it is in reality a detective with a notebook. What one fancies was the piping of Pan turns out to be a po-lice-whistle, summoning assistance. Still, we must bear these things without wincing. They are our cross".
Leave It to Psmith

On 15 July 1961 at 10.10pm, almost exactly 20 years to the minute since Cassandra had torn Wodehouse to pieces on the radio, the BBC's Home Service broadcast "an act of homage and reparation" delivered by Plum's friend Evelyn Waugh, whose solo script contained the following ubiquitous, almost inescapable quotation:

> For Mr. Wodehouse there has been no fall of Man; no "aboriginal calamity". His characters have never tasted the forbidden fruit. They are still in Eden. The gardens of Blandings Castle are that original garden from which we are all exiled . . . Mr. Wodehouse's world can never stale. He will continue to release future generations from captivity that may be more irksome than our own. He has made a world for us to live in and delight in.

This wasn't the first time Wodehouse World had been called an Eden, but it did end up being the most memorable use of that metaphor, for the simple reason that in slightly edited forms it has adorned just about every Penguin edition of Plum's work since Waugh first read it out. Sixty years later it shows no sign whatever of being retired; there it is again, dutifully reprinted on the inside flap of all 99 Everyman/ Overlook hardback re-issues published between 2000 and 2015. Not surprisingly, this wonderfully lyrical, wistful, utterly sincere tribute has stuck in readers' minds by dint of sheer repetition, serviceable short-hand for describing what Plum had created in his long literary career. We'll be returning to it in a few pages' time.

The same year that Waugh uttered these words, Plum turned 80, the attendant media ballyhoo generating, according to his English publisher, a good "500 inches of press stuff and more coming in all the time". Stateside, a notice of birthday greetings was published in the *New York Times*, which included good wishes from among others W.H. Auden, James Thurber, John Updike, Lionel Trilling and Nancy Mitford. Add to that the publication of the first full-length study of his work – Richard Usborne's *Wodehouse at Work* – and 1961 represent-ed something of a mini-revival in Plum's fortunes. Writing to Denis Mackail on October 16, the day after his birthday, he remarked that "I seem to have become the Grand Old Man of English Literature" – for so he had, and deservedly so. But this flurry of activity was also symbolic of a gradual change in the way Wodehouse's literary legacy was being thought about. Waugh's encomium and Usborne's book were early signs that his tireless work over the previous six decades was now, finally, being considered as a whole, or as literary scholars term it, 'rec-ognized as an oeuvre'. It was not before time.

As we've already seen, even after the BBB debacle, Plum's books continued to sell well, carrying him through his troubled post-war years to what we might call this 'point of retrospection'. By which I mean the following: whenever a figure in the arts, be they writer or rock star, reaches a certain arbitrary but advanced age and their work attains a certain critical mass, the retrospectives start to appear. Slowly swelling in number on each significant birthday or release of new material, critics and fans pick apart the secrets of their subject's continued success and how he or she has managed to make it this far. And it's from these modest beginnings that what a writer has created starts to be considered outside the steady progression of calendar time, taking its first faltering steps up the steep, narrow path to immortality. A major award such as the Nobel Prize for Literature can boost a writer's chances of survival, although never in its 120-year history has it once been conferred on a humourist. Quite the reverse: in 2015, to pick a year almost entirely at random, Plum would have had his literary prejudices confirmed when the Russian language writer Svetlana Alexievich bagged it for creating "a monument to suffering and courage in our time". But even lacking this exalted kind of gongage, Wodehouse World was taking baby steps in the right direction, and Plum's passage from time-bound to timeless, from history to what I'm calling myth, will be the subject of what follows in this chapter.

Wodehouse had probably long since reconciled himself to being an outsider, it being the fate of all comic writers not to be mentioned in the same breath as their gloomier, yet more fashionable peers. Indeed, he had started to satirize the Culture Industry long before his worldwide fame and fortune, and it proved a lifelong habit he could never kick. As early as 1903's *A Prefect's Uncle*, young Pringle discusses the set theme of Beckford College's annual poetry prize with Colonel Ashby:

> "Death of Dido this year. They are always jolly keen on deaths. Last year it was Cato, and the year before Julius Caesar. They seem to have very morbid minds. I think they might try something cheerful for a change".

To which one might respond, "Don't hold your breath": Cato famously ripped out his own giblets rather than live under Caesar's rule, and then Caesar got his comeuppance two years later, stabbed 23 times in the Senate house for wanting to be an Emperor. Colonel Ashby then tells the story of a friend who once bought a book under the impression its subject was steeplechasing:

> "I shall never forget his disappointment when he opened the parcel. It turned out to be a collection of poems. *The Dark Horse, and Other Studies in the Tragic*, was its full title . . . Great nonsense it was, too . . . I'm no judge of poetry, but it didn't strike me as being very good".

Even at this early stage in his career, Plum was challenging the widely held assumption that serious intent and/or lofty subject matter necessarily produced better quality writing than comedy. Even that book's author dismisses it as embarrassing juvenilia ("I used a pseudonym, I am thankful to say. As far as I could ascertain, the total sale amounted to eight copies. I have never felt the slightest inclination to repeat the performance"). But for all its failings *The Dark Horse* did contain a poem about the death of Dido, which Pringle decides to plagiarize, having been sub-contracted by fellow-pupil Lorimer to write his entry for the prize. This, we're told, would avoid "wast[ing] his brain-tissues in trying to evolve something original from his own inner consciousness", time which he could better spend playing cricket. He justifies his decision thus:

> Besides, the best poets borrowed. Virgil did it. Tennyson did it. Even Homer – we have it on the authority of Mr Kipling – when he smote his blooming lyre went and stole what he thought he might require. Why should Pringle of the School House refuse to follow in such illustrious footsteps?

Why indeed? At various points in his career, Plum reminds us that as well as being the undisputed King of Literature, Shakespeare was a common or garden plot thief. But this practical, down-to-earth view of the way great writing gets written wouldn't be shared by the poetry prize's judge, Mortimer Wells, a former pupil made good who has adopted the "superior" literary sheen of an Oscar Wilde – only without the latter's facility for humour. Fully expecting our agreement, the narrator describes Wells as "something of a prig" – the first of many such pretentious literary figures who would regularly appear in Plum's novels and stories.

As we saw in Volume 2, Wodehouse was no philistine, equally at home with High Culture and the pulpiest popular literature even as he regularly mocked them both. But he couldn't take arty posturing at any price, and one of his less familiar satirical targets was the literary salon of the kind he may well have attended as he furiously networked in and around west London's more salubrious suburbs in the early years of his career. These gatherings, which usually convened in the private houses of ambitious socialites, embodied everything Plum loathed about Culture, being a writer who actually wrote, rather than one who played at *being* a writer.

His first such fictional matinée is organized by society hostess Mrs Keith in the 1910 story 'The Good Angel' – a modest affair on Thursday afternoons which usually included "a poet, a novelist, or a painter", but which on this occasion has been stretched to a fortnight's literary retreat at her country estate. As usual, love is in the air, with the "big and outdoorsy" Martin Rossiter pitted against the aggressively indoorsy Aubrey Barstowe – author of *The Soul's Eclipse and Other Poems* – for the hand of Mrs Keith's daughter Elsa. No prizes for guessing who gets the girl, and as if to rub it in, Plum has Martin read Elsa the text of sardine advertisements as an antidote to all the Tennyson and Shelley she's had to endure from Aubrey:

> "'Langley and Fielding's sardines . . . for breakfast, lunch, or supper. Probably your grocer stocks them. Ask him. If he does not, write to us. Price fivepence per tin. The best sardines and the best oil!'"

> "Isn't it *lovely?*" she murmured.

> Her hand, as it swung, touched his. He held it. She opened her eyes.

> "Don't stop reading," she said. "I never heard anything so soothing".

Arch and clumsy satire, perhaps, and not the most conventional of seductions (in the American version of the same story, re-titled 'The Matrimonial Sweepstakes', sardines are replaced by baked beans). But it does serve as an index of just how aggressively grounded Plum could be when provoked by pretension.

A more ambitious set of salonistas can be found in *Piccadilly Jim*, in which Mrs Nesta Ford Pett of Riverside Drive, New York is described as being afflicted with "a strong literary virus" so infectious that she houses six scriveners of one kind or another beneath her roof, "mostly novelists who had not yet started and poets who were about to begin". In giving these "young and unrecognized geniuses" house room she is perhaps assuaging her guilt, for Nesta herself writes fabulously popular pulp thrillers with titles like *At Dead of Night*. Unfortunately, just about every salon in Wodehouse comes with a long-suffering cohabitee, usually male, who just wants some peace and quiet in which to smoke his pipe unmolested. Mrs Pett's husband – our old acquaintance Peter – is one such forlorn figure, "wandering like a lost spirit" through his own mansion trying to find sanctuary from all the literary small-talk.

Listening at the door of the morning room, he knows he will find no refuge there, hearing "a remark in a high tenor voice about the essential Christianity of the poet Shelley filtering through the oak" (which Plum knew was nonsense, since Shelley proclaimed his atheism on several occasions). In 'Jane Gets Off the Fairway', golfer William Bates suffers similar travails, though he's rather more pushed for space in the couple's attic apartment which is "handsomely furnished with cushions and samovars, where Jane gave parties to the intelligentzia" [sic]:

> His idea of a pleasant social evening was to have a couple of old friends in for a rubber of bridge, and the almost nightly incursion of a horde of extraordinary birds in floppy ties stunned him. He was unequal to the situation from the first.

Jane is not to be swayed, however, and the salons continue. But when William discovers that living in "the artistic zone" is starting to affect his golf, it's the final straw, and he walks out. Everything comes right again – naturally – when Jane grows tired of smoking Turkish cigarettes and talking pretentious twaddle. The salons are discontinued and she and William return, joyously reunited, to the links. Golf 1, Culture 0.

'The Golfers versus the Cultured' is once again the battleground in 'The Clicking of Cuthbert' from 1921, one of the Oldest Member's best yarns which features a brief cameo from Plum himself. Mrs Willoughby Smethurst, a hard-nosed and ambitious socialite, has engineered the schism and means to win the battle for the "Soul" of "the little settlement of Wood Hills" from the golfers by importing rising young novelists like Raymond Parsloe Devine to address its literary society. But then at some point during the opening skirmishes, a sort of *Romeo and Juliet* situation arises when Cuthbert Banks (golfer) falls head over heels with Adeline Smethurst (culture vulture). Adeline, however, doesn't immediately reciprocate, preferring the "more spiritual, more intellectual" Devine as her future soulmate. Cuthbert then joins the Wood Hills Literary Society so he can be near her, forcing himself to attend "eleven debates and fourteen lectures" on subjects including "*vers libre* poetry (one of Plum's particular bugbears), the Seventeenth-Century Essayists, the Neo-Scandinavian Movement in Portuguese Literature and other subjects of a similar nature". But when it's announced that the eminent but distinctly gloomy Russian novelist Vladimir Brusiloff has been persuaded to give a talk, the excitement within the little group can scarcely be contained since, according to Adeline, "[y]ou've got to be Russian or

Spanish or something to be a real success".

This plot wrinkle satirizes the real-life craze for all things Russian that had been a feature of British cultural life a few years previously, when Dostoyevsky, Chekhov, the Russian ballet and even balalaika ensembles were suddenly all the rage. Bertie Wooster, for one, isn't keen on this cultural invasion: Chekhov's *Seagull* [sic], he opines in *Jeeves in the Offing*, is over-full of "cock-eyed goings-on". But he would have been in a minority, for when Igor Stravinsky's *Petrouchka* premiered in London, one critic gushed that "the whole thing is refreshingly new and Russian, more Russian, in fact, than any ballet we have had", words echoed by Adeline when she describes Devine's poetry to an uncomprehending Cuthbert:

> "The critics say he is more Russian than any other young English writer".

> "And is that good?"

> "Of course it's good".

> "I should have thought the wheeze would be to be more English than any young English writer".

> "Nonsense! Who wants an English writer to be English?"

Critics and crazes, the more exotic the better, were the life blood of these coteries, and seemed to bring out Plum's inner conservative (small 'c') like almost nothing else.

But relief is at hand. A fellow sufferer turns out to be Brusiloff himself, who at Wood Hills is attending his "eighty-second suburban literary reception" and is both exhausted and profoundly bored. When he testily denounces the poet Sovietski, to whom Devine's work has been favourably compared, the latter's hitherto adoring acolytes "drew away from him slightly" sensing they may have to switch their literary allegiances in pretty short order. Floundering somewhat, Devine dismisses this allegiance as youthful folly; no, it's Nastikoff who is now his idol. To which Brusiloff replies:

> "Nastikoff no good . . . Nastikoff worse than Sovietski . . . I spit me of Nastikoff!"

Instantly, Devine's stock plummets even further, his reputation forever shot. It's then his erstwhile admirers, feeling themselves betrayed and taken for fools, turn on him in no uncertain manner:

> They had allowed him to play on their innocence and sell them a pup. They had taken him at his own valuation, and had been cheated into admiring him as a man who amounted to something.

Devine stands in the literary all-together, suddenly alone, stripped of his borrowed robes. And then the rowdy protests begin:

> Mrs Smethurst eyed him stonily through a raised lorgnette. One or two low hisses were heard, and over at the other end of the room somebody opened the window in a marked manner.

At which point Adeline makes a mental note to burn the three signed photographs Devine has sent her, and to gift the autographed presentation set of his books to the grocer's boy.

Brusiloff chooses this moment to play his ace. Throwing off his literary gloom, he declares himself a passionate golfer, recognizing Cuthbert (whom he insists on calling "Cootaboot") as a glorious winner of the French Open – a notable achievement Adeline had earlier poo-poohed. The scales fall from her eyes, and Cuthbert is suddenly a romantic prospect to be reckoned with. Golf 2, Culture 0. Moreover, having denounced all contemporary writers except himself, Brusiloff singles out two he can just about tolerate: Tolstoi [sic] and P.G. Wodehouse who are "not bad. Not good, but not bad". And so, the scene is set for Cuthbert and Adeline's union and Devine's exile to California, where as punishment for being a dilettante, he will be forced to write scenarios for the Flicker Film Company. As the Oldest Member concludes:

> It was hard, I consider, on Raymond Parsloe Devine, but that is how it goes in this world. You get a following as a celebrity, and then you run up against a bigger celebrity and your admirers desert you. One could moralize on this at considerable length, but better not, perhaps.

And nor, then, will we. Silly, yes, but a silliness with a serious satirical theme. For make no mistake, Plum was that long-suffering man who abhorred all the social rannygazoo that usually accompanies outbreaks of High Culture.

Down the years, Plum was something of an inverted snob on this issue; and while he greatly enjoyed airing his views on books and writers in his private correspondence, he actively pities the likes of Brusiloff and even Devine who have entered into a devil's pact to discuss their work in public. However, 40 years on from 'The Clicking of Cuthbert', his status as the "Grand Old Man of English Literature" and his own 'point of retrospection' being reached, the mailman's sack would now be swelled by requests from scholars and researchers – a needy bunch who would seriously eat their way into his writing time given half a chance. Can the addressee of Plum's 'autobiography' *Over Seventy*, the fictional J.P. Winkler, possibly be related to Usborne? For both men present Wodehouse with lengthy sets of questions requiring full, frank and time-consuming answers:

> Are you influenced by criticism of your books? Have you ever written poetry? Have you ever lectured? What do you think of television and the motion pictures? I see you are living in the country now. Do you prefer it to the city? Give us the overall picture of your home life and describe your methods of work. And any information concerning your experiences in the theatre and any observations of life in general, as seen from the angle of over seventy, will be welcome (*Over Seventy*, p. 15)

But Usborne's list of demands gave Plum an idea: soon after giving his blessing to the project some time in 1955, he cheekily began to compile his own "Autobiography with Digressions" in parallel with the proposed *Wodehouse at Work*. After all, if he was going to act as Usborne's unpaid gopher, he might as well take a slice of the pie, while efficiently recycling some of the articles he was writing for *Punch* during this period.

Having a much simpler brief than Usborne, Plum published the resulting *America, I Like You* just one year later in 1956 and its somewhat different U.K. equivalent *Over Seventy* in 1957. As with his two earlier volumes of memoirs, Plum's own books would only reveal what he wanted his readers to know, a principle he addresses right up front on page 2, claiming "it would be laughable for me to attempt a formal autobiography" since "I have not got the material". Or rather he had, but the personal bits were going to remain strictly off limits. The "innocent" Wodehouse knew exactly what he was doing and how he needed to do it, explaining to Bill Townend as early as May 1952 that he wanted the 'official' version of his life to tally as far as possible with the image his audience might have formed of him from reading his books, so that each would be consistent with the other:

> I want the reader to say "Dear old Wodehouse. What a charming nature he must have! Here are all the people writing nasty things about him, and he remains urbane and humorous. Bless my soul, what a delightful fellow he must be!"

In carefully nurturing a sympathetic idea of 'Wodehouse the Man' and 'Wodehouse the Writer' as one and the same, notice how he even borrows Lord Emsworth's favourite interjection in order to make his point. What he was actually in the process of creating was 'Wodehouse the Myth' – how he wanted to be seen by his readers, his critics, the publishing industry and perhaps even posterity.

This is a further example of Plum's lightness in action, for he no doubt reasoned that having made his name as a writer of airy, romantic comedies, it wouldn't be good for business if he were outed as a serial killer in his spare time – the mismatch between his created world and his extra-literary hobbies being something of a distraction. The BBB notwithstanding, Plum's closet wasn't overly packed with skeletons, but even so, one could never be too careful. And so as far as was plausible, he cast himself as a citizen of his own created world – hence the confusion that often surfaces in what's written about him.

Not every author is so careful or controlling; at the time of writing, for example, J.K. Rowling has been plunged into hot water for tweeting about trans-sexuality, which is not, as far as I'm aware, a major theme in her *Harry Potter* universe. Plum would never have been tempted to create such a violent disjunction between what Sebastian Faulks calls his "bumbling idiot" routine, and what that bumbling idiot wrote. Of course, there's a lot of Wodehouse *in* Wodehouse World, but a failure to acknowledge that he kept some – oh, alright a lot – of himself reserved and apart from his public image can lead us into erroneous judgements not just about who he was but the nature of his achievement – as we'll see in this volume's conclusion.

This modest subterfuge is hinted at on the jacket of the recent

Everyman/Overlook edition of *Over Seventy*, the publisher's blurb justi-
fiably posing the question, "When is an autobiography not an autobiography?" "When the author is P.G. Wodehouse" comes the immediate
answer, and what follows is so utterly on point, it's worth quoting at
length:

> *Over Seventy* purports to be a series of answers to stray ques-
> tions . . . given by a rambling old gentleman full of irrele-
> vant anecdote and wise saws, but when the rambling old
> gentleman happens to be P.G. Wodehouse we know that
> this persona is a shrewd literary strategy . . . Presenting
> himself as a traditional Englishman who deplores the
> baring of souls – and doubts if he has a soul of his own to
> bear – Wodehouse neatly sidesteps difficult biographical
> questions in favour of self-deprecating humour and comic
> vignette. But if *Over Seventy* is deliberately evasive, its very
> discretion tells us a lot about one of the most celebrated
> twentieth-century writers.

Spot on; what Plum leaves out is just as significant as what he includes,
and even now *Over Seventy* must represent a profound disappointment to
those who long for something a little more meaty and revealing. But his
not-too-revelatory forays into self-revelation were how *he* chose to write
about his life and work; by contrast, Usborne's scholarly book, when it
finally appeared, would be an altogether different kettle of fish (but not
can of worms).

As 1957 wore on, Usborne's research was only just hitting its
stride. Unfortunately, discussing his least favourite subject – himself
– and looking backwards through time as he did so were guaranteed
to provoke Plum's inner grouch. Perhaps he hadn't fully appreciated
what a slog writing about P.G. Wodehouse might be, since by this stage
he'd already published nearly 80 books that would all have to be picked
over with a fine-tooth comb. Early replies to Usborne's enquiries were
politely co-operative, even enthusiastic ("Let's have some more questions. We must make this book a world-beater!") and he returned some
interesting, fresh material. But after only a few weeks, his letters start to
be more wary, business-like, impatient and occasionally grumpy. It took
him six weeks to reply to Usborne's missive of April 25, 1955, which
had included 16 questions, some open, some specific; and while he was
still erring on the side of politeness, it's clear that being forced to look

back at his earliest work was beginning to irritate him. Leafing through his accounts book, in which he kept a record of everything he'd sold until 1908, he found it "slightly depressing as it shows the depths I used to descend to in order to get an occasional ten-and-six". And there was much more where that came from: "What a curse one's early work is. It keeps popping up"; "Gosh, what a lot of slush I wrote" and "Who wants three or four pages giving the plot of a thing I wrote for *Chums* in 1905?" are just three of the complaints he lobbed back at Usborne as they discussed his less than fondly remembered juvenilia.

It was the intrusion such a study represented that really seems to have got Plum's goat – that and harping on about the past. He started glossing over Usborne's questions several at a time, and with a level of terseness that betrays both impatience ("No. I have never sung at a village concert") and exasperation ("Heaven knows where I got "blinding and stiffing". Isn't it a fairly well-known phrase?") – and no, it wasn't, either then or now. In his 1958 novel *Cocktail Time*, written as this Q&A process was well under way, he slipped in the following comment:

> The question of how authors come to write their books is generally one not easily answered . . . Milton, for instance, asked how he got the idea for Paradise Lost, would probably have replied with a vague 'Oh, I don't know, you know. These things sort of pop into your head, don't you know,' leaving the researcher very much where he was before.

For "Milton" read "Wodehouse" in unco-operative mode. Finally in 1960 a draft manuscript arrived, to which Plum was granted access and which elicited the following verdict: "[Q]uite good, but there is so much rambling off-the-ball stuff that the good parts are smothered". Particularly irritating was the section on the BBB, about which he was "absolutely furious" when he first read it, soliciting this *ad hominem* remark in a letter to his editor at Barrie & Jenkins, Derek Grimsdick:

> [Usborne] is an extraordinary ass, though. Fancy not realizing – as I suppose he didn't – what the effect of digging up all that old stuff would be. Just as everybody or nearly everybody has forgotten about it.

What Plum never truly appreciated was that unlike him, Usborne didn't have the luxury of leaving bits out. In the interests of completeness and accuracy, literary biographies, even one as light-hearted and sympathetic as *Wodehouse at Work*, couldn't pretend things simply didn't happen, particularly when those things were a matter of public record. In one letter to Grimsdick, Plum speaks in terms of a personal betrayal: he had offered Usborne his full and friendly co-operation, and he comes out with *this*! But as publication day approached, and he managed to excise the worst of Usborne's 'faults' ("I am also cutting . . . all the stuff about fights at school. He seems to have an obsession about fights") he appears mollified and even reconciled ("I think that what is left will make a very good book").

As things turned out, Plum was lucky to have had such a sympathetic and well-informed fan as his first serious literary biographer; and he was doubly fortunate that Usborne and his publisher seem to have allowed him to veto passages he didn't like. The same month the book was published (January 1961), Plum also learned of Waugh's planned broadcast that would air in six months' time, and one likes to think that he might actually have allowed himself a few moments of self-satisfaction as it became clear that while his head had been buried in work since he left school, he had created a considerable literary legacy without being fully aware of what he'd achieved.

And here it is we reach a watershed in this book's argument. As with any writer whose work reaches a point of critical acceptance, those keen to get under the bonnet and find out how things work politely ask him or her to vacate the driver's seat and step away from the vehicle. From now until this book's end, I'll be focusing on stuff that Plum could not possibly have known or consciously intended concerning his literary reputation and the means by which it has stood the test of time. For with one small step, we're passing out of the solidly founded house of history and into the airier, insubstantial purlieus of myth.

Before we begin, however, I'd better quickly explain what 'myth' means in its slightly more specialized sense, which doesn't confine itself to the usual definition of stories, like those of Mr. Mulliner, that strain our credulity or are demonstrably false. Myths can also be stories that chime with their readers not only in one place, but in many places, not just at one time, but at many times. Myths are that part of the human genome that pertains to storytelling – part of our birthright, if you will. Waugh's borrowing of the Eden myth to help explain the ethos of Plum's created world is easily the best-known example of this critical approach in Wodehouse studies, but he was by no means the first to think that Plum's writing belonged among the select body of literature that is able to transcend the time and place in which it was originally conceived.

As early as 1941, in George Sampson's preface to *The Concise Cambridge History of English Literature*, we find this:

> His almost uncountable volumes have enriched the national mythology with the universally-known figures of Bertie Wooster, the vacuous, amiable idiot of aristocratic connections and his butler, Jeeves, the grave, orotund and infallible retainer.

Not every writer is privileged to create a fictional world that does its bit for "the national mythology"; but according to Sampson, that's precisely what Wodehouse had achieved with his "universally-known figures". A mere quarter-century on from their first appearance in print, Jeeves and Bertie had become so familiar, so perfectly in tune with their place of origin that they had gained entry to what is called "the stuff of England", that ragbag of materials from which the time-*less* idea of 'Englishness' is patched together. And although Sampson was writing almost 80 years ago, commentators are making similar observations into the 21st century. In 2002, Philip Howard wrote in the *Times* that:

> [Bertie Wooster] and Jeeves, Lord Emsworth and Mulliner belong to the pantheon of English characters, along with Falstaff and Pickwick, Sherlock Holmes and Billy Bunter.

Notice already how reality and fiction are being subtly blurred: fictional characters are opening a vista onto something real – what it's like to experience a particular place. This confusion between actual experience and imaginative projection makes myth, when it is objectified as art, a transformational phenomenon. For example, Sampson's use of the adjective "orotund" in connection with Jeeves is further evidence that he was mentally picturing what an archetypal – ahem – "butler" *should* look like, for nowhere does Wodehouse describe Jeeves as being overweight or even remotely podgy. So, we can claim that another strength of myth is that it's possible to personalize it in whichever way we want; the reader *internalizes* it, bringing its significance *into* him or herself as the "imaginative truth" I mentioned earlier. This collaborative act renders it not just personalized, but memorable – even when it's not entirely correct. Sampson's Jeeves works for him yet is different from my Jeeves and (no doubt) your Jeeves – and almost certainly the Russian oligarch's view of Jeeves we'll be investigating in the following chapter. Cumulatively, all these different versions of Jeeves form a composite or mythical Jeeves, distilling the essence or "Jeeves-ness" of Jeeves, if you like.

Further evidence of this imaginative truth is provided by those commercial artists who have been hired to illustrate Jeeves and Bertie stories. With virtually nothing to go on from Wodehouse, they have been forced to fall back on how Jeeves appears in their mind's eye, sometimes, it seems, without the benefit of having read the relevant books. Some simply assumed Jeeves to be a butler and drew him as such. Indeed, the most regular image of the great man that pops up on internet searches comes from the 1920 Newnes printing of *My Man Jeeves*, which pictures him as stocky and middle-aged, with tired, hooded eyes, a straight, disdainful mouth indicating slightly constipation, and – worst of all – sporting what looks like a dyed, jet-black combover.

Now in *my* conception of Jeeves that last detail is, I'm afraid, sacrilege; a man of such consummate taste and discernment would never, ever countenance such an ill-advised contrivance. And yet the artist concerned wasn't alone: Andrzej Klimowski's 2003 image from the jacket of *Carry On, Jeeves* sports similar tonsorial engineering and, what's more, appears to be puckering up while pointing to something we can't see over his shoulder. Ionicus (for many years the Penguin cover artist) comes closest (IMHO) to getting it right; a high forehead denoting intelligence, but with hair swept backwards rather than horizontally. But that's just my opinion, myth allowing me (and you and everyone) the prerogative of forming our own mental picture of Jeeves's coiffure. As I noted in Volume 2, Plum isn't one for providing us with detailed descriptions of anything in Wodehouse World, allowing us to picture it pretty much how we like, with only a few telling steers to help us on our way. Was Stephen Fry well-cast as Jeeves in the TV adaptation? Opinions differ: was his age, physical presence, his voice and delivery how you imagined they would be? There's a *very* long digression to be written on this theme, only unfortunately now isn't the time.

Perhaps surprisingly, this process of personalization can be a two-way street: by which I mean that as Plum's created world floated free from history and causality, it seemed to carry reality off with it, subliminally influencing its actual source. As we've seen before, Life begins imitating Art rather than the other way round. Which is not, in the view of some, the way things are supposed to happen. In 2002, documents released by the Public Records Office in the U.K. revealed that when Plum was put forward for a knighthood in 1967, a vehement objection was raised by Sir Patrick Deane, then British ambassador to Washington and possibly – ironically – a distant relative of Plum's mother. Wodehouse, he claimed, had done nothing for British interests overseas that would qualify him for such an award, in fact, a knighthood "would . . . give currency to a Bertie Wooster image of the British character which we are doing our best to eradicate". Completely at odds with Prime Minister Harold Wilson's preferred trope of a modern, thrusting Britain forged in the "white heat [of] the scientific revolution", dear old Bertie had travelled beyond his historical Knut-ishness and even beyond satire into something that made the land of his 'birth' appear rather silly and backward looking.

If, as some have speculated, this was the real reason for denying Plum a gong, Deane's explanation is actually more ridiculous than anything Wodehouse could have dreamed up. Then again, lurking somewhere in amongst the unintended irony of an actual English toff surreally censuring a fictional English toff for making his job more difficult, is an acknowledgement of the power of myth. In fact, Deane was perfectly correct in his belief that once a myth lodges itself in the collective unconscious, it's nigh on impossible to sweep it under the carpet. As time and truth fall away, the *essence* of the story – that "imaginative truth" again – takes on a life of its own, freeing it to appear in further iterations over time. As 18th century artist and poet William Blake has it when speaking of *The Canterbury Tales*:

> Chaucer's Pilgrims are the characters which compose all ages and nations: as one age falls, another rises, different to mortal sight, but to immortals only the same . . . Accident ever varies, Substance can never suffer change or decay (Quoted in Peter Ackroyd, *Albion: The Origins of the English Imagination*, 2002, pp. 309-10)

In literature and art down the ages, myth channels time-resistant, but often difficult to define qualities (what Blake capitalizes as "Substance") into avatars that materialize at certain specific points *in time*. And so when journalists claim that a particular fat-headed English politician (no names, no pack drill) "*is* Bertie Wooster" and not "*like* Bertie Wooster", they're helping the process along. The Bertie Wooster-ness of Bertie Wooster has found another real-life avatar, leaving little doubt there'll be further fat-headed English politicians in a continuing line of fat-headed English politicians stretching into the future and even eternity. Which has proved depressingly true. Scarily prescient, Rajeev Balasubramanyam noted in a 2016 edition of the *New Statesman* that:

> A nation led by Bertie Wooster would be a disaster, but one led by an unfeeling mastermind hiding his megalomania behind a Wooster-shaped mask would be far, far worse.

Indeed.

Once it's reached this level of general application, the myth has grown more powerful than any of its individual manifestations. Which is why its survival isn't always dependent on having a physical analogue. It simply *is*, having an existence all on its own somewhere in our collective cultural imagination. It can wait, floating somewhere out in the ether, biding its time, waiting for the next suitable avatar to come along.

And it doesn't just work with characters either. Remember back in Volume 2 Sue Brown's induction into the inner Blandings circle because she 'gets' the atmosphere, the 'Blandings-ness' of Blandings? Here's a reminder:

> From the flush on her face and the sparkle in her eyes, she seemed to be taking her first entry into Blandings Castle in quite the proper spirit of reverential excitement. To be at Blandings plainly meant something to her, was an event in her life. (*Summer Lightning*)

That's myth in action right there: *something* about Blandings clicks into place within Sue's imagination, though neither she nor the narrator can articulate precisely what it is. It's a bit like déjà-vu: she has never visited Blandings before, yet she somehow understands it *feelingly* – and fortunately it's a good feeling. And we can feel it too when we read a story about Blandings. We're happy to be there.

Collectively, what we might call these '-nesses' – Jeeves-ness, Bertie-ness, Blandings-ness and so on almost *ad infinitum* – permeate one another to form what is 'Wodehousean' about Wodehouse's writing, and *that's* the Wodehouse myth that is being carried forward through time by us, his readers, who are lucky enough to 'get' him. "Wodehouse-ness" is traditionally imagined as something not beyond the realms of plausibility, but most definitely at the more eccentric end of reality, and it remains a currency which, if anything, appears to be growing stronger and more valuable over time. Although not quite up there with 'Orwellian' or 'Kafka-esque' in frequency of use, 'Wodehousean' (or 'Wodehousian') is nonetheless a recognizable 'thing'.

Ancient Greek philosophy had a word for this (of course it did – it always gets there first): ἕξις ('hexis') is a concept that isn't particularly easy to define – you just know it when you see it. In a Wodehousean context, it's a sort of unconscious familiarity with the tone and timbre of his work we carry around with us not just when we read him, but at other times when our day-to-day experience chimes with it. Certain situations, people, perspectives and behaviour trigger this sixth sense of 'Wodehouse-ness': indeed, if you read *Wooster Sauce*, the quarterly journal of the P G Wodehouse Society (UK) and turn to its regular column 'Recent Press Comment', you'll find a minimum of 30 or so references to Plum and his work in every issue, some of which demonstrate this principle in action.

One recent favourite was the 2018 obituary of the internationally respected scientist Fred Hamblin (who had died aged 103) headlined "Wodehousian chemist who was a key figure in the development of plastics at I.C.I. [who] once stole a steamroller and almost blew up his school". Among many quotable paragraphs is this:

> Hamblin's first job after completing his doctorate was also like something penned by P.G. Wodehouse. In 1937 he applied for a job with the plastics division of I.C.I. The interview small talk over, he was asked about his hobbies. When he said "keeping fish", the man interviewing him, a retired colonel called Sampson, beamed and said that he was constructing a pond in the garden. For the rest of the interview, all 45 minutes of it, they discussed how it should be stocked and what plants would be required. The door of the office then opened and the research director, a man who rejoiced in the name of Dr. Caress, came in. When Dr. Caress asked Sampson how the interview was going, he replied: "He's a splendid fellow, knows all the right things — we should take him on!"

And a glorious career similarly rich in absurdity was to follow. Even now, it is quite remarkable how often Plum's work is roped in to help illustrate an aspect of contemporary life or human behaviour. Which brings us back to Evelyn Waugh's use of that Eden metaphor to try to explain what – for him – was Wodehousean about Wodehouse World.

Those millions of us all over the globe familiar with the biblical origins of the Garden of Eden will each have our own version of what it means to us, as did our forebears and as will our descendants. Generally, though, these various meanings coalesce around an ideal, paradisiacal state or place that can only exist in our imaginations. Waugh's use of it to help explain the significance of Wodehouse World to his radio audience chimed perfectly with his personality and outlook, both of which were prey to the nostalgic melancholia that defines his most serious novel, 1945's *Brideshead Revisited*. To one so disposed, the prelapsarian Eden, "that original garden" from which mankind has been banished, was a perfect mythical fit, an idyllic retreat from the vale of tears we are all destined to inhabit in our daily lives. Nor was he the only wisebrow to borrow it for this purpose: at around the same time, W.H. Auden, who from 1955 to 1961 was Professor of Poetry at Oxford, had begun thinking about Wodehouse in a mythical context in lectures that would reappear in his 1962 publication *The Dyer's Hand*. In one of them, 'Dingley Dell and the Fleet', Auden confidently proposes that the four great "experts on Eden" are Dickens, Oscar Wilde, Ronald Firbank and P.G. Wodehouse". A motley crew, one might think; but the essay is a masterpiece of rhetoric that compellingly links each of these writers' work with Christianity's foundation myth.

Auden's complex, erudite essays are not exactly bedtime reading outside academia; yet whatever we might think of his argument's rele-vance to Wodehouse World, here was an established poet, three times a Nobel nominee and a figure of considerable standing and influence in the Art establishment taking the work of a comic writer seriously and, moreover, linking his output not just to literary giants like Wilde and Dickens, but to one of the cornerstones of Western civilization. It was a typically bold and playful intellectual move on Auden's part, and while it is something of a labour of love to follow the ten "axioms" of his argument (which I'm not proposing to do here), the essay represents a significant leap forward not just in Wodehouse's post-war rehabilitation, but in the status of his work. Auden was emphasizing that Eden, when considered as a scholar's myth (and not a believer's history) was a broad and not unattractive collection of ideas from which to fashion a fictional world. And Wodehouse, whether he knew it or not, had done just that.

Though they shared an impish disposition, both Waugh and Auden were committed Christians (Waugh Catholic, Auden Anglican) and would not have undertaken this identification lightly, or as an academic *jeu d'esprit*. And while neither went so far as to claim Plum for their respective faiths, there is the clear implication in both men's assessments that there is more to Wodehouse World than 'mere' comedy, something either anthropological (Auden) or spiritual (Waugh). These public endorsements would have been one in the eye for those naysayers like Queenie Leavis and Cyril Connolly who, as we saw in Volume 1, had hoped Plum would be forgotten for the greater good of 'serious' literature. Yet Waugh was already anticipating the "future generations" that Wodehouse World would free "from captivity that may be more irksome than our own", while asserting that for the present, his listeners could celebrate the fact that "he has made a world for us to live in and delight in". With big-hitting friends like that, any salonista who had previously dismissed Plum's artistry might be forced to think twice before going public with such heresy again, and in his thank-you letter to Waugh, Plum proclaims that his radio address had "pulverized the opposition". Whether we fully understand what on earth they were going on about or not, it can't be denied that Plum had some friends in high places.

The thing is, though, that like Jeeves's hairstyle, Auden and Waugh's conception of Wodehouse World as Edenic needn't necessarily be yours or mine. As I've already noted, myth doesn't deal in unitary interpretations, and for my part, I would argue that Eden isn't a viable metaphor at all, being booby-trapped with associations that aren't just inappropriate but plain wrong:

- The prior knowledge we have of Eden from our exposure to religion and art – that it is a paradise lost through sin and only truly regained in death – is surely a cause for regret, and that's most definitely *not* what we should be thinking about – even in the deepest recesses of our subconscious – when caught up in Wodehouse's creation. Even in man's brief period of pre-lapsarian happiness, God had deviously sabotaged His own paradise with exotic varieties of apple and talking snakes, reminding us that in this set-up, Man was born to lose. Contrary to all Wodehouse's plot trajectories, everything is destined to end in tears, exclusion and perpetual guilt.

- Then there's Eden's door policy. Wodehouse World is always open; all you need is access to a text. By complete contrast, entry to Eden is a whole new world of pain – God even places Cherubim armed with "a flaming sword flashing back and forth" at the turnstile so we can't be re-admitted having once lost our innocence.

This set-up has no parallel in Wodehouse, especially at Blandings, which is his closest approximation to Paradise. In *Full Moon*, Gally likens Lady Hermione Wedge to one of those Cherubinic bouncers when she boots Bill Lister, disguised as the portraitist Messmore Breamworthy, out of Blandings. But rather than the banished Bill exiting the Garden weeping and wailing never to return, he girds his loins, borrows a false beard and immediately starts looking for a way back in, and not only succeeds – twice – but gets the girl. To be permanently exiled from Eden is the root of mankind's eternal tragedy, but in Wodehouse, it's merely a temporary setback that can be overcome with just a little grit and ingenuity. Security isn't exactly tight: both goodies and baddies seem to have free and equal access. But notice how it's only the goodies like Bill who emerge from Blandings with exactly what they came for, which perhaps, dare I say it, represents an improvement on the biblical model, since everyone ends up happy.

Unfortunately, then, Waugh and Auden's annexation of the Eden myth doesn't allow us to bask in the full splendour of Wodehouse World's sweetness and light. Moreover, it subliminally imports anti-comedic notions of sin and guilt into an ethos that doesn't welcome them, or even recognize their existence. Wodehouse World is something to be celebrated, not mourned; not confined to the past, but ever-present; not somewhere else, but here. In short, not Paradise Lost, but Paradise Found. So, while I would concede that myth is exactly the right *mechanism* for shedding light on how Wodehouse World works its magic on us being time- and place-less, it would help if we chose the right myth. And Eden, I'm afraid, with all due deference to Evelyn and Wystan, isn't quite it. Not only do its systems of loss, redemption and salvation represent baggage not wanted on the voyage, there is the additional hazard that as with those writers we looked at in Chapter 7, we might be tempted to think that Plum is sneaking coded messages of great spiritual pith and moment in through the back door. Which he really and truly isn't. So sorry, lads: close, but no cigar.

We can salvage something from the blazing wreckage of their argument by simply remarking that Plum's Eden need be nothing more than a function of mood – and one he enjoyed experiencing, since he uses the Biblical phrase "earthly paradise" in 32 of his books. Early in *Something Fresh*, even as we're told that Lord Emsworth considers the parks and gardens of Blandings "the nearest earthly approach to Paradise", son Freddie is to be found slouching around them "with an air of crushed gloom which would have caused comment in Siberia". Over 30 years later he's doing much the same thing in *Full Moon*, "mooning about looking like a bored and despairing sheep". To Uncle Fred, in *Service with a Smile*, Connie's reign over Blandings makes "the whole set-up sound extraordinarily like Devil's Island". And then there's the Duke of Dunstable, who in *Uncle Fred in the Springtime* likens the Castle to a "private asylum". Different strokes for different folks; Blandings is only Eden when a featured character is feeling good, and although the dominant aura of the place is one of wellbeing, the default setting to which it always returns at a story's end, there's never any serious suggestion that we should think of it as *the* Eden. It's simply a state of mind in which everything is, however temporarily, 'right' – as in those meteorologically-perfect novel openers I quoted at the start of Volume 2.

And this principle extends to Plum's other picturesque country seats: in *Quick Service* Joss Wetherby describes Claines Hall as "[a]n earthly Paradise" – but only when Sally Fairmile's around; "A gas works in Jersey City would be all right with me", he tells her "so long as you were there". In *Jeeves in the Offing*, Brinkley Court can only be Bertie's earthly Paradise when Aubrey Upjohn isn't in residence. Heaven, it would seem, is some*thing* we carry around with us, not necessarily some*where*; and that feeling of heaven can ebb and flow. Although, having said that, when we're fully immersed in the Wodehouse myth as readers, it truly *feels* like an idyllic place to while away our time in – a statement as true in the 21st century as when Wodehouse started creating it a hundred-odd years ago, and as it will no doubt prove for those living in future epochs that may be more irksome than our own.

AGED YET
AGELESS

Chapter 9:
Aged Yet Ageless

The best-known fictional manservant, and the archetype of the quintessential British butler, is himself not a butler at all.
Wikipedia entry, 'Butler'

If I have a fault as a writer, which is very doubtful, I should say that it was a tendency to devote myself a little too closely to the subject of butlers. Critics have noticed this complex of mine.

. . . .

Some are born to butlers, others achieve butlers, and others have butlers thrust upon them.
'Butlers and the Buttled'

You feel cared for, comfortable and at ease, like returning to a cosy home after a stressful journey.
Robert Pimm

Just how old *is* Bertie Wooster? And when did he take Jeeves into his employment?

On one level, those are simple questions to answer, the 1916 story 'Jeeves Takes Charge' providing all the necessary information. In its opening paragraph, we are told that the partnership has existed for "about" six years – so 1910-ish; and when, later on, Bertie regales us with the story of how as a 15 year-old he had been chased by Lord Worplesdon with a riding crop after being caught smoking a cigar, and that this incident happened "nine years before", we can do the math and confidently assert that he is now 24, which makes his date of birth 1892 or thereabouts. After this helpful precision, Bertie's age isn't directly mentioned again – ever. So, in the absence of any further help, we could assume that 59 years later, in his final appearance in 1975's *Aunts Aren't Gentlemen*, Bertie is 82 or 83.

This, of course, would be utterly preposterous. Time doesn't work that way in fiction, and fictional characters don't age like we do – or perhaps we should say *needn't*. It suits some writers to mature their characters in real time, as it were, whereas Wodehouse chose not to – which, as things turned out, was a wise move. In 1916, he couldn't possibly have known how Jeeves and Bertie (or, for that matter, he himself) would enjoy such astonishing longevity, nor that they would be the torchbearers for his cavalcade of comic characters as it marched into the future. Moreover, if Bertie were to end up in his mid-80s, Jeeves, being approximately ten years older, would be a mid-nonagenarian, long past retirement age. Would he still be able to shimmer and glide? Or would arthritis have put paid to his legendary deportment? The answer doesn't really bear thinking about.

Our evidence for Jeeves's age comes in a letter Plum wrote in 1961 to the American scholar Robert A. Hall Jr., in which he notes that "I always ignore real time". And, we might add, continuity:

> Keggs in *A Damsel in Distress* is supposed to be the same man who appears in *The Butler Did It* [*Something Fishy*], but does it pan out all right? It doesn't if you go by when the books were written. The *Damsel* was published in 1919 and the *Butler* in 1957.

So, no it doesn't pan out. At all. And Plum doesn't seem to really care that much – after all, it was fiction he was writing. He also fails to mention, perhaps because he'd lost all track of them, that there may have been no fewer than six separate Keggses employed on two continents, dating between 1903 (in the fourth of the series 'Mister Punch's Spectral Analyses') through to 1961's *Ice in the Bedroom*, by which time he has made his fortune and invested in three modest properties in Valley Fields, one of which he rents out to his employer of thirty years before, Lord Uffenham, who also appears in *Money in the Bank*. But Keggs's interwovenness within Wodehouse World doesn't end there: his sister Flossie is married to Wilberforce "Battling" Billson, a regular from the Ukridge saga; and in 1910's 'The Matrimonial Sweepstakes' he or his namesake is employed by Lord Emsworth. But not Clarence, 9th Earl of Emsworth; another, separate Lord Emsworth who pops up in that story never to be heard of again. Then in 'Jeeves Takes Charge', Bertie claims to know the more familiar Lord Emsworth, creating a sort of worm hole between the two mighty Wodehousean sagas of a kind Plum highlights in his Preface to 1929's *Summer Lightning*:

> This story is a sort of Old Home Week for my – if I may coin a phrase – puppets. Hugo Carmody and Ronnie Fish appeared in *Money for Nothing*. Pilbeam was in *Bill the Conqueror*. And the rest of them, Lord Emsworth, the Efficient Baxter, Butler Beach and the others have all done

their bit before in *Something Fresh* and *Leave it to Psmith*.

Several more worm holes there, which have the effect of pulling the drawstrings of Wodehouse World more tightly together into a pleasing artistic whole – as long as we don't stress too much over the continuity issues.

Once again, Lord Emsworth can serve as an illustration of how things sort of hang together. If we do the arithmetic from the hints we are given in 1923's *Leave it to Psmith*, he was born in 1859, which would make him aged 56 on his debut in 1915's *Something Fresh*. Yet in 1962's *Service with a Smile*, he tells us that he used to sing the music-hall staple 'Bill Bailey, Won't You Please . . . Come Home?' when a pupil at Eton College. Which wouldn't have been easy, as 'Bill Bailey' wasn't published until 1902, when he would have been 43, a somewhat advanced age for a schoolboy. For most of the time, however, Clarence hovers around the age of 60. His brother Gally is even more remarkable, being something of a time traveller. In 1933's *Heavy Weather* and *Full Moon* from 1947, he is 57 precisely. Then in *Galahad at Blandings* which appeared in 1965, he has regressed to his early 50s. Confused? Absolutely!

Whether unforced errors or not, these inconsistencies further add to the sense of temporal dislocation at work in Plum's novels, giving the impression they exist in a time-less dimension, but without the author necessarily intending that effect. We can simply claim that he enjoyed the sound of that pleasing monosyllable 'Keggs' – perhaps its association with beer – and park our argument there, accepting that Plum wasn't one of those authors who could be bothered to maintain a card index with all his characters' names, birthdays, favourite colours and shoe sizes, unlike some of his more fastidious colleagues. And so, there are dozens of examples of Plum stuffing up on the continuity front, among the best known being the name of Lord Emsworth's favourite author. In 1936's 'The Crime Wave at Blandings', he is Augustus Whiffle, genius of animal husbandry and author of *The Care of the Pig*. Thirty years later, in *Galahad at Blandings*, the great man has changed his name to Whipple. And in the manuscript of 1977's *Sunset at Blandings*, Plum has crossed out 'Whipple' and replaced it with 'Whiffle'. It's all very puzzling, particularly since in every other aspect of his craft, Plum was a stickler for getting things absolutely right.

The net result of this joyful confusion, if we even notice it, has a similar effect to coming across mistakes and inconsistencies in that other literary titan, Homer, who, as the satirist Horace informs us, was occasionally guilty of "nodding" ("dormitat Homerus"). If anything, this merely serves to emphasize the 'otherness' of Wodehouse World, which doesn't always sync up with our own and is all the more intriguing for it. The action in 1971's *Much Obliged Jeeves*, for example, follows on almost immediately from that in *Stiff Upper Lip, Jeeves*, despite there being eight years of actual time separating the two books' publications. And so on. All of which serves to illustrate that Wodehouse World was for the most part a mammoth improvisation held together inside a sort-of chronology that marches to its own time signature. It's not so much a sequence of stories as a constellation. And while we might glimpse a discernible pattern or shape in there *somewhere*, it's difficult to see it steadily or see it whole.

By the time his mid-season form arrived in the early 1920s, Wodehouse wasn't making many concessions to changing circumstances, keeping on doing what he did with only minor adjustments to the bitter end. He had hit on a successful formula that worked for him and his readers and, as we'll see, even survived his death; for what "Wodehousean" signifies has evolved into something of a universal 'brand' (dread word). Throughout this progression, Reginald Jeeves has stood at his creator's shoulder, emerging from his historical roots in the Victorian service industry, through global popularity as a fictional character and on to being a proper noun that has entered the lexicon, with no fewer than three variants ('Jeeves', 'Jeevesian' and 'Jeeves-like') in the *Historical Thesaurus of the Oxford English Dictionary*, where he will remain, in all probability, for eternity as a symbol of . . . well, whatever it is Jeeves has grown to be a symbol of – which will be the subject of the rest of this chapter. Along the way, I will be attempting to write a biography of this remarkable figure as he rose in status from plot furniture to brand ambassador; the character who, arguably more than any other, has carried Plum's timeless humour *through* time and continues to meet and greet successive generations, inviting them into the Wodehouse legendarium. Indeed, it's one character's journey from (a) history to (c) myth via (b) imagination, a process I'm now going to condense into a few pages, making it easier to witness not just how Jeeves became the best-known manservant who ever lived, but how Wodehouse World as a whole has cheated time without ever meaning to.

So, let's start at the very beginning (a very good place to start, apparently) with:

AGED YET AGELESS

History

Wodehouse, not yet ten years old, was first conscious of meeting and mingling with the servant classes in the late 1880s, on the regular occasions he was shipped to his widowed grandmother Louisa's house for extended visits with his spinster aunts. Cheney Court, situated in the Wiltshire village of Box, is a Jacobean pile that was sufficiently large to have above and below stairs domestic staff, allowing the young Plum to appreciate the strict social demarcations that governed late Victorian society, not just between master and servant, but the various strata within the servant communities themselves.

Then there were family outings to the neighbouring manors, in which there were effectively two worlds running in parallel: one that was formal and dull upstairs; the other informal and fun downstairs, and he would long for the times, he confesses, when "my hostess, smiling one of those painful smiles, suggested that it would be nice [for me] to go and have tea in the servants' hall". It's on these visits that I suspect the seeds of his lifelong distaste for seriousness, fuss and formality were sown, serving to sharpen an instinctive dislike of assumed airs and graces. Away from the starchy formality of the drawing room, he could be more himself, or was at least allowed to act his age: "I loved it", he recalled in *Over Seventy* (in a passage that rings truer than much of that book), "I forgot to be shy and kidded back and forth with the best of them".

Unlike those upstairs, the lower-ranked underlings granted him the rare privilege of being both seen *and* heard – at least for the brief period until he was frogmarched back to the bosom of his family. At that point, "the quips would die on our lips" and "the young gentleman would shamble out, feeling like 30 cents". The fun might have been over, but the memory lingered: "My mind today is fragrant with memories of kindly footmen and vivacious parlour-maids", he rhapsodizes – for Plum rarely seems to have forgotten acts of generosity, particularly those directed at himself. And while some children of his social status might have instinctively scorned those below stairs or simply ignored them, Plum not only seems to have engaged with his social inferiors, but came to associate them with happiness and even freedom.

The roots of Jeeves, however, can be found in the starchier upstairs domain of the English butler, the stern figure who would have been called upon to supervise the frogmarching of young Master Wodehouse away from his new friends in that informal creche. And while Jeeves – as any fule kno – isn't a butler, there's absolutely no mistaking where many aspects of his outlook, speech, behaviour and demeanour originate. "Butlers have always fascinated me", Plum wrote in *Louder and Funnier* – a somewhat redundant confession when we learn that he created no fewer than 82 of them (and 36 valets) down the years, starting almost immediately with Parker, the Headmaster of St Austin's servant, from 1902's *The Pothunters*. Plum later summed up their attraction thus:

> Mystery hangs about them like a nimbus. How do they get that way? What do they really think about? Where do they go on their evenings off?

Clearly the young master's imagination was piqued, and would remain so, for what is Jeeves but the ultimate Wodehousean enigma? Perhaps it was the anomalous position the butler occupied within the household that made him such an intriguing proposition – and, as we'll see in what follows, almost perfect myth-making material. Having regular and significant interactions with the nobs, his liminal status issued him with a passport to both upper and lower worlds while allowing him full citizenship of neither. Always at the centre of things, he nevertheless stands aloof and apart, sometimes even cutting a lonely figure. This, and the burden of overall responsibility for the house and its occupants made considerable demands on the individual man's character, influencing his personality in different ways.

This makes Plum's fictional butlers something of a mixed bag, the head servant's bearing usually falling somewhere between the two extremes of 'sniffy, silent and superior' and 'roguish, familiar and jovial' – though with a heavy bias towards the former. Plum rehearses the origin of this distinction in 1915's *Something Fresh*:

> Butlers as a class seem to grow less and less like anything human in proportion to the magnificence of their surroundings. There is a type of butler, employed in the comparatively modest homes of small country gentlemen, who is practically a man and a brother; who hob-nob with the local tradesmen, sing a good comic song at the village inn, and in times of crisis will even turn to and work the pump when the water supply suddenly fails. The greater the house, the more does the butler diverge from this type.

Until this point in his work, up to and including the first appearances of

Beach and Jeeves in 1915, Plum's manservants were usually one-dimensional characters. Parker, that very first butler, is relegated to the odd monosyllable (usually "Yessir"), and at all other times "[tries] to look as like a piece of furniture as possible". In *The Head of Kay's* from 1905, Watson, the headmaster's manservant escorts Fenn unto the presence with three simple words, "This way, sir". Yet even this efficient expressiveness comes as something of a shock, as the narrator informs us:

> Those were his actual words. Fenn had not known for certain until now that he *could* talk. On previous occasions their conversations had been limited to an 'Is the headmaster in?' from Fenn, and a stately inclination of the head from Watson. The man was getting a positive babbler.

In 1909's 'The Gem Collector', the redoubtable Keggs (#2 of 6) is relegated to banging gongs and bringing soup, giving us few clues as to the titan he would become as early as the following year – although we're given a slight clue when Bowery Boy Spike Mullins notes that he's "de best ever at handing out long woids". Then there's Beach's debut:

> Blandings Castle was one of the more important of England's show-places, and Beach, accordingly, had acquired a dignified inertia which almost qualified him for inclusion in the vegetable kingdom. He moved, when he moved at all, slowly. He distilled speech with the air of one measuring out drops of some precious drug. His heavy-lidded eyes had the fixed impression of a statue.

On this first showing, Beach is most decidedly a Watson, fully conversant with "the language of the eyebrow".

But what earthly use to a storyteller is a butler who doesn't move or talk, and is almost a "vegetable"? Plum was missing a trick here, and it took him quite a while to realize it. The Beach of *Something Fresh* rarely travels beyond this Trappist cipher, almost unrecognizable in the above description from the avuncular, even loveable figure into which he later develops. Here, he is a snobby, largely taciturn hypochondriac who is wheeled out to deliver a portentous comic monologue on his various ailments. Could anyone guess that he was soon to become a much more useful pig-stealing, dart-playing, port and brandy-dispensing confidant and all-round good guy beloved of all, the heart and soul of Blandings, his pantry the communications hub of the books' plots? Definitely not – but then, this was before Plum had fully formulated his comic lightness.

Even Jeeves gets this perfunctory treatment on his debut in 'Extricating Young Gussie', the future star of Plum's entire *oeuvre* getting only two token lines to speak ("Mrs. Gregson to see you, sir" and "Very good, sir. Which suit will you wear?") and takes next to no part in the mechanics of the plot. His very existence merely serves to indicate that Bertie wasn't short of the readies: a man of his station living in town would have to have a gentleman's personal gentleman for the sake of verisimilitude. It would have seemed odd if he wasn't there. This modest entrance later puzzled Plum himself: in his introduction to *The World of Jeeves* anthology from 1967, he confessed to finding it "curious, now that I have written so much about him, to recall how softly and undramatically Jeeves first entered my little world. Characteristically, he did not thrust himself forward". From which we can deduce that in the early stages of their evolution, Plum's butlers and their subordinates existed to *do* stuff, not *be* anyone in particular; and in writing about them in this documentary manner, their creator was trying to keep things real.

But even if the young Wodehouse *had* managed to figure out what makes these gentlemen tick, we never hear it from the mouth of the sphinx-like Jeeves. For such a compelling presence, he is motivationally a black hole, making him a method actor's nightmare. To the bitter end, we're only supplied with the occasional, tantalizing nugget from his back story, few of which shed any real light on why he does what he does. And yet, knowing so little, we never think of him as insubstantial. He is a shadow who himself casts a shadow – which is quite a trick for a writer to pull off successfully. But if we are ever so misguided as to think that we *know* Jeeves, we must remember that Bertie only learns his employee's first name – and then by accident – in 1971's *Much Obliged, Jeeves*, 56 years after his debut. Quite what to call him professionally is almost impossible to determine, for the 'essentials' and 'desirables' on his job description are so specifically tailored to the needs of his employer. So while he is definitely not a butler (despite being able to buttle with the best of them, as we're told in *Stiff Upper Lip, Jeeves*), he's variously called a valet, a gentleman's personal gentleman, a "Nannie", "father", "guide, philosopher and friend" (by Bertie himself), and a "keeper" (by Aunt Agatha, no doubt in the sense of animal husbandry). For he is all these things, and necessarily so. But what he shares with many of Plum's statelier butlers is gravitas; he's a deep one, and not to be messed with.

The essential seriousness of Plum's butlers would lead them out of their vegetable taciturnity and start them off down the road to becoming the mythical archetype so ably and amply embodied by mid-season Beach. As we'll see shortly, The Wodehouse Butler would eventually come to be thought of as *The* English Butler, at the expense of the garrulous "man and a brother type" which, with the exception of certain iterations of Keggs, Plum doesn't truly care for. Bertie's temporary valet Bingley (or Brinkley as he was previously known in yet another continuity error) falls into this latter category, a "Gawd-help-us fellow" who is "unduly intimate, too free, forward, lacking in proper reserve, deficient in due respect, impudent, bold and intrusive" (*Much Obliged, Jeeves*). Formality trumps familiarity from quite early on, and in 1910's 'The Matrimonial Sweepstakes' we're informed that "[a]ny man under thirty years of age who tells you he is not afraid of an English butler lies". And it's then we're introduced to Keggs (#3 of 6), who now – contrasting with his previous appearance in *The Gem Collector* – cuts quite a formidable figure:

> The effect that Keggs, the butler at the Keiths', had on Marvin Rossiter was to make him feel as if he had been caught laughing in a cathedral. He fought against the feeling. He asked himself who Keggs was, anyway; and replied defiantly that Keggs was a menial, and an overfed menial. But all the while he knew that logic was useless.

Plum reuses the ecclesiastical metaphor (or perhaps myth) when he notes that arguing with Keggs "is like quarrelling with Westminster Abbey" – he's now a lapidary presence with an air of mystery, sanctity and even a hint of menace. Marvin has something of a problem with this "bland dignity", such that "his self-respect left him and his back-bone became a mere streak of jelly". Similarly, Ashe Marson in *Something Fresh* remembers how the butler at a friend's house "terrified" him such that he "used to grovel to the man". Nearly 40 years later in *Pigs Have* Wings, the same feeling is experienced by Jerry Vale when he encounters Beach at Blandings:

> [T]hroughout this sojourn beneath Lord Emsworth's roof, Beach had been an aloof, supercilious figure who had paralysed him with his majesty. It is a very intrepid young man who can see an English butler steadily and see him whole without feeling a worm-like humility, and all Jerry's

previous encounters with Beach had left him with the impression that his feet were too large, his ears too red and his social status something in between that of a Dead End kid and a badly dressed leper.

This air of absolute, even divine authority is, Plum tells us in a later essay 'Butlers and the Buttled', a uniquely English phenomenon. Comparing the home-grown model with the American, Japanese and Filipino butlers he encounters in Hollywood, he finds the latter nationalities wanting, being either over-familiar, too demonstrative or temperamental. By contrast, the archetypal English servant is always the same, in any situation, which consistency and air of rock-like eternality already gives him the aura of a myth-in-waiting.

This is perhaps why Plum was so taken aback when, for the first and only time, he heard a butler laugh while on duty. The anecdote, reported in *Over Seventy*, takes us back to his youth when, sporting the generously cut castoffs of his Uncle Hugh, he visits a country house and takes his place at the dinner table. It's only during the fish course he realizes that the waistline of his trousers is steadily riding up in the direction of his sternum, and when it reaches the level of his white tie (as he leans forward to help himself to potatoes), the butler, no doubt picturing the diner drowning in his lower garmenture, "uttered a sound like a bursting paper bag and hurried from the room with his hand over his mouth". This momentary aberration only served to highlight what Plum calls "the universal gloom of butlers" – or, at least, the comportment of the sniffier kind – and he occasionally uses lapses from the stern stereotype to good effect in his fiction.

In *Pigs Have Wings*, as Beach peruses a humorous postcard in the company of Lord Emsworth and Gally, he almost unpardonably allows his lips to move a "fraction of an inch . . . [looking] like a butler who, for two pins, had he not been restrained by the rigid rules of the Butler's Guild, might have smiled". Behind closed doors, however, it's a different matter: Beach has a fantastic laugh on the odd occasion we're allowed to hear it, most notably in *Heavy Weather* when he's reading Gally's reminiscences in the privacy of his pantry. Reaching the story of Sir Gregory Parsloe-Parsloe and the prawns (an *histoire-célèbre* Plum never quite manages to share with us) we hear an intermittent "HA . . . HOR . . . HOO!" – the sound of Beach "casting dignity to the winds . . . apparently without a thought for his high blood-pressure and the stability of his waistcoat buttons". Percy Pilbeam, who happens to be earwigging outside Beach's pantry is shocked, for "he could not recall ever before hearing a butler laugh – let alone laugh in this extraordinary fashion".

Jeeves is similarly expression-free – most of the time. When at rest, he sports a look of "quiet intelligence combined with a feudal desire to oblige" (*Thank You, Jeeves*); when uncomfortable, or hiding something, he pulls an expressionless face which Bertie describes as resembling a "stuffed moose" (*Right Ho, Jeeves*) or "stuffed frog" (*Jeeves and the Feudal Spirit*). When very surprised, he will allow his eyebrow to elevate by a tell-tale small fraction of an inch (passim); and if he finds something amusing, the corner of his mouth twitches slightly (*Aunts Aren't Gentlemen*). Only Bertie would notice these facial tics, but he shares them with us as proof that Jeeves *is* actually human; to anyone else, his manservant's face is a window on his soul that is kept permanently and deliberately fastened shut. That said, Jeeves does *almost* laugh once when Bertie relates the misunderstanding that has led Sir Watkyn Bassett to label him a kleptomaniac in *The Code of the Woosters*: at which point Jeeves's "distinct simper" that threatens further development has to be hastily "re-assembled" after Bertie makes it clear this is no cause for amusement.

By this stage, Plum's lightness had started to put his manservants' gravitas – both in demeanour and avoirdupois – to better use, and once again his youthful experiences seem to be the real-life prompt. The adolescent Wodehouse, now dressed in a different set of ill-fitting hand-me-downs (courtesy of his older brother Armine) would pay house calls in the swankier districts of Edwardian London to be greeted at the door by:

> an august figure, weighing seventeen stone or so on the hoof, with mauve cheeks, three chins, supercilious lips and bulging gooseberry eyes that raked you with a forbidding stare as if you were something the carrion crow had deposited on the doorstep. (*Over Seventy*)

This is the archetype described almost identically in 1953's *Ring for Jeeves* (although the butler in question seems to have gained nearly a stone):

> [B]utlers who weighed two hundred and fifty pounds on the hoof, butlers with three chins and bulging abdomens, butlers with large, gooseberry eyes and that austere, supercilious butlerine manner.

This is also the generous cloth from which Beach is cut, being a portly man of a comparatively svelte 16 stone, yet whose waistcoat swells like the sails of a racing yacht and whose party piece is to imitate a hippopotamus. And although Jeeves may overlap with the traditional butler in several aspects of his attitude and behaviour, it's in his physical appearance that he deviates most markedly from what we might call Plum's 'classic' butler. But then, if we believe our guide and mentor, butlers themselves had undergone something of a makeover after the First World War. In 1932's *Louder and Funnier*, we are treated to a comparison between the old and new models, even as Plum updates and upcycles material from an article he wrote in 1916 for *Vanity Fair* ('All About Butlers', February edition):

> [T]hose were the days when butlers were butlers. You never met one under sixteen stone, and they all had pale, bulging eyes and tight-lipped mouths. They had never done anything but be butlers, if we except the years when they were training on as second footmen. Since then there has been a war, and it has changed the whole situation. The door is now opened to you by a lissom man in the early thirties. He has sparkling, friendly eyes and an athlete's waist, and when not opening doors he is off playing tennis somewhere. The old majesty which we used to find so oppressive between 1900 and 1910 has given place to a sort of cheery briskness. Formality has disappeared . . . [I]t takes away all that chill and discomfort which one used to feel in one's early twenties when, in a frock-coat which had not been properly pressed, one encountered the Spinks and the Merglesons.

Note how Plum appears to be writing a sociological thesis which nevertheless crosses over almost intact into his so-called fantasy world.

By these lights Jeeves would seem to be a composite of the two archetypes: he has the serious demeanour and authority of a pre-war Spink/Mergleson but the body of the post-war model who takes care of himself and is quite possibly an ex-soldier (it is revealed in *Ring for Jeeves* that our man "dabbled" in the war). Nor is he that old: once again, Plum wheels out holy imagery when describing Jeeves as "a youngish High Priest of a refined and dignified religion" (*Ring for Jeeves*). Nor is he fat or round of face, with exophthalmic rheumy eyes that resemble soft fruit: while sharing the necessary "grave" demeanour, this is communicated by his "finely-chiselled features" and an "eye [that] gleams with the light of pure intelligence" ('Leave it to Jeeves'). Perhaps the best-known thumbnail sketch of the great man comes from *The Mating Season*, courtesy of his employer. He is

> A godlike man in a bowler hat with grave, finely chiselled features and a head that stuck out at the back, indicating great brain power.

Both Jeeves and his brothers in service are considerable *presences*, while commanding attention in diametrically opposite ways. A Wodehousean butler is just *there*.

But how he *gets* there is often all too evident, for such a massy presence as the old-school model isn't always terribly light on its feet, particularly if, like poor old Beach, it is a martyr to corns, an ingrowing toenail and swollen joints. A course of 'Slimmo' has had little impact (*Pigs Have Wings*), but nonetheless, Beach makes the best of a bad job, and once again notice the religious overtones as, in *Leave it to Psmith*, he enters Lord Emsworth's library in "a dignified procession of one". Wodehouse's third-ever fictional butler Watson, who we met earlier, had this pontifical air nearly two decades before, conducting a visitor to the headmaster's office "with the air of a high priest leading a devotee to a shrine of which he was the sole managing director".

By contrast, there's something less than physical in the way Jeeves moves, a talent he may have inherited from Mr Teal, a butler who made his one and only appearance in 1914's 'The Hired Past', the year before Jeeves's debut. This gentleman, complete with his "priestly cast of countenance", has "the cat-like facility of entering a room perfectly noiselessly". As it is with Jeeves – by the time you've noticed him he's already got where he's going. Unlike his predecessor Meadowes who "had flat feet and used to clump", thereby announcing his entrance some distance away, Jeeves, on first introducing himself to Bertie "floated noiselessly through the doorway like a healing zephyr". This "impressed" his future employer, who was at that point wrestling with the mother of all hangovers: "This fellow didn't seem to have any feet at all. He just streamed in" – just the ticket when jarring noises need to be kept to an absolute minimum. And when he takes his leave, "he seemed to flicker, and wasn't there any longer". Jeeves's ability to move about in a wraith-like manner is most famously described as "shimmering"; in *The Code of the Woosters*, he also noiselessly "floats . . . stream[ing] silently from spot A to spot B, like some gas". His corporeality is once again called into question in 'The Artistic Career of Corky', when "he kind of manifest[s] himself" . . .

> . . . like one of those weird birds in India who dissolve themselves into thin air and nip through space in a sort of disembodied way and assemble the parts again just where they want them.

Once again, Jeeves is portrayed as something more than merely mortal, whereas the typical Wodehousean butler is, by contrast, all too physically human, but all the same a formidable example of nature's final word.

Next on our shopping list of archetypal butlerian traits is speech and language – what in *Something Fishy* Plum calls "butlerese". This manner of address is of course formal but involves a good deal of grandiloquence such that Lord Uffenham has to "unravel" and "translate" what Keggs (#6 of 6) is saying about some purloined correspondence (sorry, stolen letters – it's catching) before he can fully take it on board. Here's what Keggs actually means, post-translation:

> . . . some low blister, bought with Bunyan's gold, had sneaked into the girl's flat and pinched the bally things.

Now compare that with the way the butler expresses that thought:

> "Obviously an emissary of Mr Bunyan had obtained clandestine access to her apartment in her absence and purloined the communications in question".

"Long woids" indeed. Keggs's convolutedness dials down the emotion and never uses words of a single syllable when a polysyllable will suffice. This becomes the basis of a double act, as both registers alternate one with the other:

> "Didn't yer tell me once that that brother-in-law of yours used to be a professional scrapper?"

> "Yes, m'lord. He fought under the sobriquet of Battling Billson".

This formality can be somewhat intimidating, as Mortimer Bayliss, no mean circumlocutor himself, discovers. When Keggs passes judgement on the future marriage of Stanhope Twine and Jane Benedick, he pulls out all the linguistic stops:

> "I would not say that I consider Mr Twine an ideal mate for Miss Benedick, but she appears to be in favour of the union, so I am only too happy to be instrumental in bringing it to fruition".

To which Mortimer can only respond with "Golly!" Dazzled by this performance, which for Keggs is nothing remarkable, he asks "Has anyone ever called you the Boy Orator of Valley Fields?"

And so it continues in a bravura performance of linguistic whizzbangery – a far cry from Keggs's earlier incarnation nearly 40 years before in *A Damsel in Distress*, when he was made to speak in the manner of a Cockernee geezer who needlessly aspirated every word that began with a vowel while at the same time dropping his aitches when they *were* present. Now though, when he reveals he has put a private eye onto Bill Hollister, he claims it is "the simplest method of keeping . . . *au courant* with his affairs".

So here we have a neat reversal of what we might expect, with the employee speaking a more formal language than that emerging from the earl. And so "I could look up the number in the phone book" becomes "I could ascertain by consulting the classified telephone directory". It's easy once you get the hang of it, and of course we need look no further than Jeeves as the ultimate practitioner of this peculiar, formulaic way of talking:

- First and foremost, there is **understatement** – what grammarians call litotes, or sometimes meiosis. Everything, even the most cataclysmic, mind-blowing subjects are drained of all sensationalism and impact, such that a global conflict is reduced to "[s]ome slight friction threatening in the Balkans" (friction in the Balkans was what erupted into the First World War). This has everything to do with not making a fuss, a cloak of English anti-emotionalism that renders the wearer unflappable and on top of things – useful when trouble-magnet Bertie Wooster is the man paying your wages. It's a habit that cements Jeeves's reputation of being the go-to guy for solutions, his use of dispassionate language indicating that he is seeing things clearly, seeing them whole and yet still remaining totally unfazed;

- Second, **periphrasis**: the Keggsian butlerese that takes a perfectly innocent set of words and grandiloquizes them. Translating what Bertie has just said into his own idiom is something of a Jeevesian trademark, almost a reflex; in the opening paragraph of *Joy in the Morning*, Bertie tells us of his recent close shave at Steeple Bumpleigh, which Jeeves, by way of agreement, re-phrases as "Unquestionably affairs had developed a certain. menacing trend, sir". This elegant alternative to simply saying "Yes, sir" the whole time allows us to marvel at Jeeves's verbal dexterity and ingenuity – although sometimes he is apt to leave the young master behind. When in 'The Inferiority Complex of Old Sippy' Bertie buys a vase that Jeeves doesn't like, the latter notes that it "is not in harmony with the appointments of the room", prompting Bertie to add "whatever that means, if anything". On this occasion Jeeves uses formality to disguise hostility; in fact, it's an example of what we now call passive-aggression. But nothing is seriously amiss; unlike moustaches and banjoleles, vases can be easily dealt with by the judicious use of sudden-onset clumsiness (ta-da!), and we know from the very start what fate is likely to befall Bertie's ill-advised purchase by the end of the story;

- Third, we have **verbal punctuation**. As I noted in Volume 1, Plum's ear for the rhythms of conversation was incredibly finely tuned – something he passed on to Jeeves, who knows just the right moment to interject a timely "Indeed so, sir" to lubricate the flow of Bertie's speech, urging him on, steering him back on track or changing the subject as appropriate. As he is a paid servant, Jeeves's professional inclination defaults to consensus ("Yes, sir"; "Very true, sir"; "Precisely, sir") or a near approximation ("Very possibly, sir"). Sometimes, he politely solicits further information, encouraging Bertie to expand on what he's just said (Indeed, sir?" or even simpler, an upwardly-inflected "Sir?"). Occasionally, he appears at a loss, or is loath to comment ("I could not say, sir"). And finally, there's the wrap-up, in which an understanding has been reached and the subject may be closed, at least for the time being ("Very good, sir"). Only when Jeeves is far from gruntled does he resort to unadorned business-like phraseology and sentence construction, which brusqueness has the effect of shutting down the conversation;

- Finally, there is what we might call **anticipation and completion**. On many occasions, Bertie knows what he wants to say, but can't quite get the words out, so he provides Jeeves with prompts and clues which the latter instantly assembles into sense. Back in *Joy in the Morning*, Bertie is groping for the phrase that will become the novel's title:

"There's an expression on the tip of my tongue which seems to me to sum the whole thing up. Or, rather, when I say an expression, I mean a saying. A wheeze. A gag. What, I believe, is called a saw. Something about Joy doing something".

"Joy cometh in the morning, sir?"

"That's the baby".

As, indeed, it usually is. Being the perfect manservant doesn't simply involve looking after the master's wants and needs; Jeeves, as far as humanly possible, is on Bertie's wavelength the whole time. Just as he advises him on his choice of socks, suits and ties, so he helps him choose his words and formulate his ideas. Here, Bertie's "gag" actually turns out to be a quotation from Psalm 30, but Jeeves isn't distracted by the false scent, and gets the reference immediately.

Did butlers and valets *really* talk like that? Five will get you ten they didn't. Given the fetish for formality that characterized much of Victorian and Edwardian life in England, Jeeves would almost certainly be thought horribly bumptious and impertinent. More of which momentarily.

It took a second global conflict to render the butler/valet almost extinct, a fact Plum draws our attention to in *Over Seventy*. In chapter 5, he points up a review in the Communist *Daily Worker* that described Jeeves as a "dim museum-piece" and "a fusty reminder of what once amused the bourgeoisie", a comment echoing one made many years earlier in the 1922 short story 'Comrade Bingo', in which Old Rowbotham, who we met some while back, calls Jeeves "an obsolete relic of an exploded feudal system". Once more, Plum had got in first; it's just that by the mid-1950s when *Over Seventy* was published, it was pretty much the truth: as he puts it in the chapter 'Good-bye to Butlers', the butler "has joined the Great Auk, Mah Jong and the snows of yesterday in limbo".

And so it was. According to the U.K. national census of 1901, when Wodehouse was busy launching himself on an unsuspecting world, there had been around 1.5 million men and women employed as domestic servants in Britain. But that total had declined precipitately as those who had inherited their wealth had been forced to make drastic economies. No doubt, he writes . . .

> . . . in many English homes there is still buttling of a sort going on, but it is done by ex-batmen, promoted odd-job boys and the like, callow youngsters not to be ranked as butlers by one who, like myself, was around and about in the London of 1903, and saw the real thing. Butlers? A pack of crude young amateurs without a double chin among them? Faugh, if you will permit me the expression.

Now well over 75, Plum doesn't appear too enamoured of the present situation; the tone may still be jocular but there's a definite hint of nostalgia lurking in his commentary. In 1957's *Something Fishy* even Keggs (#6 of 6) has retired, yet still resembles "something out of an Edwardian drawing-room comedy . . . look[ing] almost precisely as he had looked a quarter of a century ago . . . a Roman emperor who had been doing himself too well on the starchy foods". For which read 'half a century ago', for as we've seen, Keggs had been around in one form or another since 1903. Back in *Over Seventy*, Plum informs us that "[t]he real crusted, vintage butler passed away with Edward the Seventh", and despite the author's best efforts to keep him alive in his fiction had finally died the death. Plum even imagines Beach in heaven offering Lord Emsworth

"Nectar or ambrosia" instead of sherry or hock – which somehow makes their partnership eternal.

By contrast with the real-life, all-too-mortal butler, Wodehouse might never have dared to hope that his literary butlers would not "grow old as we grow old" (*Something Fishy*). But even as butlers and buttling passed through their darkest days from approximately the close of the Second World War until the dawn of the 21st century, that moribund profession, complete with its quirky characters, ideals and rituals, was kept alive on the stage and page, and in the movies. And with Jeeves up there in the vanguard, it wouldn't always be clear where fact ended and Plum's fiction started. So it is that we come to the role of . . .

Imagination

Plum's portrayal of the archetypal English manservant that I've been cutting and pasting over the last few pages is another example of what is becoming a running theme in this volume – how Life ends up imitating Art. The myth of the English butler, which Wodehouse did so much to create and propagate, survived and even thrived as the 20th century drew to a close. We only have to watch a few minutes of Sir John Gielgud playing the English butler Hobson in the 1981 movie *Arthur*, Michael Gough's portrayal of Bruce Wayne's butler Alfred Pennyworth in the 1989-97 *Batman* cycle or even Robert Guillaume's *Benson* (1979-86) to realize the debt their performances owe to Wodehouse, and how his stories helped keep the butler myth alive during the profession's lean years.

To some degree, as we've seen, Wodehouse could draw on his life experience when constructing his butler figures; but even by the 1950s, he was anticipating the difficulties his successors might face. Quite simply, they wouldn't have first-hand experience of what a butler was, what he did or how he did it; anyone creating a fictional butler would only have secondary source material to go on – and even that was in short supply. When in *Over Seventy* Plum noted that his happy childhood cavortings with below stairs staff would have had him down as "[t]he life and soul of the party . . . if they ever wrote their reminiscences" he was already flagging that much of the history and folklore of domestic service was likely to be lost. And as things turned out, he was absolutely right. Those in service sadly didn't see the value of their life stories, and career historians were far too busy celebrating the deeds of the great and the good to address or even notice this deficiency.

That is a generalization of course, but one that, for the most part, holds true; there is very little first-person testimony of what went on below stairs. Although Margaret Powell's reminiscences became best-sellers in the late 1960s, bringing another handful of inter-wars maids' and cooks' memoirs out of the shadows, there's still precious little to go on. Even in this niche sub-genre, butlers are considerably under-rep-resented, no doubt because the indiscretion necessary to write such memoirs would be frowned on (as it was in the case of Princess Diana's butler, Paul Burrell when he went public with his reminiscences). Plum tried to fill this void with his creation (in 1938's *The Code of the Woosters*) of the Junior Ganymede Club and its infamous but strictly confidential 12-volume book which carries details of every member's employer. Had it existed in real life, those ledgers would have been a fabulous resource for later historians; without it, writers have had to fall back on their imagination or else borrow from one another. Indeed, Wodehouse, for all his first-hand knowledge, may have also resorted to a bit of cutting and pasting himself.

Plum once told Richard Usborne that the character of Ruggles in Harry Leon Wilson's 1915 novel *Ruggles of Red Gap* was a significant inspiration for his manservants, and yes, the novel's serialization in the *Saturday Evening Post* did coincide almost exactly with Jeeves's debut (there's a copy in Plum's personal library, and he included a passage from the book in his *A Century of Humour* anthology). Ruggles, a valet, is forced to relocate from a down-at-heel British to a *nouveau riche* American family after his original employer, "the Honourable George" loses him in a bet, and the style and tone of his narration does mark him down as a kind of low-octane Jeeves. But as George's more senior brother – the Earl of Brinstead – notes, Ruggles has "[g]ot a brain [but] can't use it", quite simply because he isn't encouraged to, while lacking the initiative to employ it for himself. When George gets involved with unsuitable women ("typing-girl, milliner, dancing person, what, what!"), Ruggles doesn't get involved, simply informing the earl who takes the necessary action himself. So far so not Jeeves; but Ruggles *is* strong on matters of dress and deportment, and "of a studious habit and anxious to improve myself in the fine arts". Here he is, having gone to great lengths to make his master fit for public consumption:

> At 6:30 in our Paris apartment I had finished the Honourable George, performing those final touches that make the difference between a man well turned out and a man merely dressed. In the main I was not dissatisfied.

His dress waistcoats, it is true, no longer permit the inhala-
tion of anything like a full breath, and his collars clasp too
closely. (I have always held that a collar may provide quite
ample room for the throat without sacrifice of smartness if
the depth be at least two and one quarter inches.) And it is
no secret to either the Honourable George or our intimates
that I have never approved his fashion of beard, a reddish,
enveloping, brushlike affair never nicely enough trimmed.
I prefer, indeed, no beard at all, but he stubbornly refuses
to shave, possessing a difficult chin. Still, I repeat, he was
not nearly impossible as he now left my hands.

Jeeves only ever narrated one story, 'Bertie Changes His Mind' from
1922, and, it has to be said that his narrative tone is almost identical,
if rather more self-assured, than Ruggles'. Both men's dislike of facial
hair is also evident. But while Jeeves seems to know everything, Ruggles
is an innocent abroad who has to learn – and fast – how to behave like
a toff when, in America, he's mistaken for a member of the English
aristocracy. He is sufficiently quick-witted to pass this off, but is cut from
an altogether coarser, thinner cloth than his successor, and one could
never be wholly confident of his ability to pull off the complex coups
that Jeeves manages.

One other fictional butler a theatre fan like Plum would surely
have known is the eponymous house-servant in J.M. Barrie's smash-
hit drama of 1902, *The Admirable Crichton*. Crichton, like Ruggles, is
thrust to the forefront of the plot when his employer and his family
are shipwrecked on a desert island, and only this "perfect butler" has
the remotest inkling of the skills necessary to ensure their survival. The
social order is temporarily reversed as the butler takes charge, but on the
family's rescue and return to London and the *status quo ante* resumed, it is
clear things can never be quite as they were. Jeeves resembles Crichton
in his conservatism (small 'c') and his range of abilities, but once again
the differences between the two characters only prove that the former
is wholly *sui generis*, and that Wodehouse was developing a true original,
one who would stand out from the crowd of stage butlers who seemed
to be dominating Broadway during his tenure as *Vanity Fair*'s drama
critic, which began in 1915.

The trouble was that fictional butlers of that era – in Plum's opinion
– were neither realistic, nor terribly interesting. "You cannot rely on the
drama as a guide when dealing with butlers", he states in his February

1916 article 'All About Butlers', since it nearly always consigns them to menial roles:

> A butler is indispensable to nine plays out of ten. Cut him out, and who is to enter rooms at critical moments when, if another word were spoken, the play would end immediately? Who is to fill in the gaps by coming on with a tray? Who is to explain to the audience at the opening of a farce that the Maarster is not on good terms with his wife and was out late last night? Ridiculous!

Plum clearly felt playwrights were missing a trick if that's all they could find for butlers to do. Unfortunately, as he wrote those words, it was a trick *he* had been missing too. But what could he do in order to bring out what he called the "poetry and romance" of the butler in his fiction? Barrie had faced a similar problem while contemplating Crichton, as he tells us in the introduction to the play:

> [H]e would not be a hero in these clothes of servitude; and he loves his clothes. How to get him out of them? It would require a cataclysm. To be an indoor servant at all is to Crichton a badge of honour; to be a butler at thirty is the realisation of his proudest ambitions.

Both Wilson and Barrie had found solutions, but only by transplanting their butler/valet into utterly alien environments, allowing them to act as masters rather than servants for strictly finite periods. Plum, by contrast, would manage to avoid credibility-straining cataclysms *and* keep Jeeves in his work clothes by making him a gentleman's personal gentleman (hereafter 'GPG'), who wasn't tied to a particular property as a butler would be, and whose employer was prone to landing himself in farce-type situations on a regular basis in London, all over Southern England and even across the Atlantic. Stir in his mysterious biography, which would allow him to have done anything, been anywhere and know everything – and a legend was born. Cannily, Plum would engineer a great deal of narrative space for his GPG to work *inside*, while adopting the age-old literary trope of making the ostensible servant cleverer and more capable than the ostensible master, switching the roles not just on a single life-changing occasion as with Ruggles and Crichton, but permanently. The title of the second story in the sequence (but not in order of composition) 'Jeeves Takes Charge' says it all: Jeeves *does* take charge, and never really lets go, through all the minor dust-ups, stand-offs and flounce-outs with Bertie.

And so, in the development of his archetypal manservant, Plum had needed to use his creative imagination to make Jeeves interesting and adaptable, while not having to stray too far from real life.

Now let's fast forward 70 or so years and join the Nobel Prize-winning author Kazuo Ishiguro as he lays the keel for his new novel, set in an English stately home during the inter-war years and beyond – a period in 20th century English history synonymous, by then, with Wodehouse. It is to be narrated by a butler, Stevens, and the first thing Ishiguro discovers on beginning his research is

> . . . how little there was about servants written by servants, given that a sizeable proportion of people in this country were employed in service right up until the Second World War. It was amazing that so few of them had thought their lives worth recording. So most of the stuff in *The Remains of the Day* . . . was made up.

More made up, we might point out, than the source material used by that so-called fantasist P.G. Wodehouse who had actually experienced what he was writing about . . . Anyhow, as he plotted and planned, Ishiguro needed a model to draw from, given his ambitions for the novel. In a *Paris Review* article from 2008, he stated he was "very consciously trying to write for an international audience. One of the ways I thought I could do this was to take a myth of England that was known internationally – in this case, the English butler". And, somewhat inevitably, "Jeeves was a big influence" (particularly *Right Ho, Jeeves* apparently). As the novelist Salman Rushdie (another Wodehouse fan) has written of Ishiguro's appropriation:

> This is a necessary genuflection. No literary butler can ever quite escape the gravitational field of Wodehouse's shimmering Reginald, gentleman's gentleman par excellence, saviour, so often, of Bertie Wooster's imperilled bacon.

Rushdie describes the figure of the literary English butler as "multiple and contradictory . . . like all good myths", by which he means that yes, art is once more invading real life. How a butler is *imagined* to be has somehow become more real than how he *actually* was. Which brings us neatly to . . .

Myth

Ishiguro seems to agree with Rushdie that what a butler actually represents is difficult to pin down. So much so that he introduces a perspective on the butler myth early in *The Remains of the Day*, for it underpins his central character's hazy understanding of what he actually is:

> [W]hat is a 'great' butler? I can recall many hours of enjoyable discussion on this topic around the fire of the servants' hall at the end of the day. You will notice I say 'what' rather than 'who' is a great butler; for there was actually no serious dispute as to the identity of the men who set the standards among our generation. That is to say, I am talking of the likes of Mr Marshall of Charleville House, or Mr Lane of Bridewood. If you have ever had the privilege of meeting such men, you will no doubt know of the quality they possess to which I refer. But you will no doubt also understand what I mean when I say it is not at all easy to define just what this quality is.

And it never is articulated, only demonstrated through the action in the book. This elusiveness, while "multiple and contradictory", is also necessarily vague, which not only allows the subject to be kept open to interpretation and revaluation, but to manifest itself in a wide variety of ways.

For one who fetishizes exactness and conformity in everything else he does, Stevens seems content with this imprecise state of understanding, noting that "there have been very few attempts within the profession to formulate an official answer". Only once has it been tried – by a fictional, defunct trade body Ishiguro names the 'Hayes Society', which tried to "devise criteria for membership". This abjectly failed in the attempt, revealing its instigators to be inveterate snobs who favoured those butlers employed by "true ladies and gentlemen" rather than newly wealthy *arrivistes*. Perhaps, Stevens ventures in a rare moment of independent thought, trying to pin down the myth is like defining feminine beauty; "it [is] . . . pointless trying to analyse it". A butler's "dignity" is what he aims at, something he feels he can "meaningfully strive for". And so just what it is that makes Jeeves "inimitable" also seems a mystery to Stevens; but whereas the former clearly 'has' it – whatever *it* is – and in spades, the latter has to consciously (and constantly) measure himself against a shadowy standard of his own devising that doesn't conform to anything *actual*. In other words, like Ruggles and Crichton, he has to consciously work to make it work, whereas Jeeves doesn't.

Understandably, Ishiguro hasn't wanted to labour the Wodehouse connection, but the parallels between the two writers' visions really are quite striking, such that it appears that Ishiguro has been influenced not just by Plum's characters, but many of the broader themes I've been turning over in the course of these musings. For a start, these two paragons among manservants both enjoy reading romantic novels: Jeeves characteristically never explains and never apologizes for his dedication to Rosie M. Banks's *oeuvre*, while Stevens characteristically furnishes us with the excuse that "it was an extremely efficient way to maintain and develop one's command of the English language" – something his distinguished colleague never has to worry about. Moreover, Stevens, like Beach, has his pantry, the nerve centre of operations at Darlington Hall and "the one place in the house where privacy and solitude are guaranteed". Also, like Ruggles but most decidedly not Jeeves, Stevens allows himself to be treated as one of the Hall's fixtures and fittings, or as he puts it, "part of the package". So when his longstanding employer Lord Darlington dies and the house is sold to "[a]n American gentleman" (yet another Wodehouse theme), Stevens stays put. Jeeves, by comparison, is the master of his own destiny and will take his business elsewhere at the drop of a hat – or perhaps more accurately, the plucking of a banjo string (*Thank You, Jeeves*).

More serious, however, is the thought Ishiguro has clearly given to his character's motivations, letting the daylight in on magic in a way Wodehouse and Jeeves never would. Among the most significant parallels is the concept of being on and off duty:

> A butler of any quality must be seen to *inhabit* his role, utterly and fully; he cannot be seen casting it aside one moment simply to don it again the next as though it were nothing more than a pantomime costume.

Jeeves would agree, never allowing himself to be caught 'off duty' even to those of us granted backstage passes to his life courtesy of Bertie's narrative indiscretions. He is the consummate professional, and even

Bertie doesn't really understand what makes him tick. The more we learn about him, the less we seem to know; for every question answered, several more are raised. For example: why is he "seldom without a small supply" of Mickey Finns (*Much Obliged, Jeeves*)? Or how did he learn about stealing dogs by attracting them with a few drops of aniseed on the trouser leg ('Episode of the Dog McIntosh')? All we can ever conclude is that he is who he is, even though we are never destined to discover *quite* who that might be. More so than his fellow fictional manservants, this contributes to his mythical status, for myths are most powerful when at their heart lies an enigma. Unlike Stevens who, deep into his novel, has a life-changing epiphany about who he is, Jeeves is never in a state of transition or becoming. He first appeared, fully formed, very nearly from nowhere; and the scanty, scattered details we are given about his life don't really add up to anything significant. In just about every aspect of his being, to paraphrase Bertie, there is none like him, none; he "stands alone", immune to our curiosity.

But what does that 'make' Jeeves? A myth is very different from a stereotype, and while he may be described as Ishiguro's "essence" of service, he is so much more than that. This is presumably why Ishiguro was drawn to him; not just the way he carries himself, or what he looks like, but what he stands for in his readers' imaginations. Indeed, what more inscrutable image of "butler-ness" (sorry) is there in the whole of literature? From a 21st-century perspective, Jeeves has somehow managed to *grow* in relevance, to be more universal with the passage of time. Here's a brief resumé of how both he, along with his creator, have come to be celebrated in legend and song:

1. On his 1915 debut in 'Extricating Young Gussie', Jeeves is a humble functionary with, as we've already seen, just two lines to speak. He has no precise role as yet and is simply described by Bertie as "my man", typical of around 30,000 such manservants in employment in England at the time of his debut (statistic courtesy *The Times*, 22 May 2018). One year later, however, Plum had sussed his future direction, and he takes top billing in the stories that feature him, as the man who rearranges things in Bertie's life – and those of his friends and family – as they *ought* to be;

2. Two decades later, Jeeves has become rather better

known out in the real world, his creator writing at the top of his mid-season form. In among the warm reviews of 1934's *Thank You, Jeeves*, our man is lauded as "a great national figure" by the *Evening Standard* and "a national institution" in the pages of the *Glasgow Herald*. This mere "valet" and "salaried attendant" (as Bertie peevishly describes him following that banjolele-influenced resignation), is now being made to represent a set of uniquely English ("national") traits, moving *out of time* into being a symbol of these more time-less, enduring attributes. Notice how concepts of fact and fiction are already starting to blur: Jeeves, a fictional character, is starting to embody qualities that are considered to exist in real life;

3. Also reviewing *Thank You, Jeeves* was an unnamed scribe from the humorous magazine *Punch*, who considerably upped the historical ante by promoting Jeeves to the status of an "immortal", which epithet had already been used in the front cover strapline of the first American edition of 1930's *Very Good, Jeeves* ("A new book about the immortal butler by P.G. Wodehouse" – yes, I know, I know). In a fine piece of marketing hyperbole, Jeeves was now *completely* out of time, promoted to some literary equivalent of Mount Olympus. In his introduction to the anthology *Week-end Wodehouse* from 1939, Plum's fellow writer Hilaire Belloc went even further, noting that Jeeves was Wodehouse's prime contribution to that long gallery of living figures which makes up the glory of English fiction . . . In his creation of Jeeves he has done something which may respectfully be compared to the work of the Almighty in Michelangelo's painting . . . If in, say, fifty years Jeeves and any other of that great company . . . shall have faded, then what we have so long called England will no longer be.

Like the ravens in the Tower of London, if Wodehouse was going down, he was taking England with him. Which although somewhat exaggerated, has proved oddly prophetic, as we'll see in a moment. Also in 1939, over in Hollywood, the quintessentially English Jeeves was satirized as 'Jeepers' in the romantic comedy *Never Say Die*, starring Bob Hope;

4. From being English and immortal, Jeeves in the company of his creator was now set to go global and Establishment – two more significant milestones on the journey to canonization. In 1941 the eggheads who compiled *The Concise Cambridge History of English Literature* lauded Plum as a writer who had "enriched the national mythology with . . . universally-known figures". So now brainy coves had judged that Jeeves and company were sufficiently timeless to be myths, and that those myths were now the property of everyone, everywhere. Which ubiquity had been anticipated in 1936 when Plum was awarded the Mark Twain medal "[in] recognition of [his] outstanding and lasting contribution to the happiness of the world". The *world*.

And so things remained for a good while. Wodehouse World's fortunes ebbed and flowed through the BBB, the 'swinging' 60s and even the author's death. But still Jeeves survived. And then, the month after Wodehouse's achievement was marked by the commemorative stone in Westminster Abbey, this happened:

5. On 22 October 2019, the *Guardian* reported that an advertisement had been posted on the 'Jobs in Childcare' website by a wealthy family on the lookout for a "butler". The successful candidate would need: to live in London and speak at least two languages with, at minimum, a working level of Russian; know all the best restaurants in the capital and the south of France; "be a diplomat and be able to solve any issue at school, at a shop, at a salon for the benefit of the family"; and lastly, have to watch the TV adaptation of *Jeeves and Wooster* [the Stephen Fry and Hugh Laurie version from the 1990s] "to see what is expected from the butler".

That's a very different kind of literary and cultural immortality than that conferred by a carved stone in a historic building. But cumulatively, all these entries on the ledger of fame add up, even though it *is* slightly crazy that a writer of romantic comedies born in the English Home Counties in 1881 has managed to persuade a 21st-century family who come from half a world away in Russia that a fictional GPG should generate the CV for one of their future employees – the manager of their household, no less. They are presumably aware that *Jeeves and Wooster* isn't a documentary; yet the degree to which the character is based on real life seems unimportant to them. It's Jeeves they want. Which makes the unsubstantiated claims long-ago ventured by those reviewers and academics in paragraphs 2 to 4 absolutely spot-on: whatever Jeevesian qualities those wealthy Russians are searching for in their prospective employee are proving both universal, enduring – and highly prized. Even if that might involve rebranding the entire Jeeves and Wooster canon as non-fiction lifestyle guides.

The ad was no one-off occurrence, however. The number of personal servants has been steadily growing worldwide from an all-time low in the 1980s when it has been estimated that there were only around 100 full-time butlers left in England. As they are no longer able to learn the ropes by rising through the ranks in a country house, academies of buttling have been established – many of them in England – to teach the skills that had very nearly been lost to posterity. In 2004, the BBC News website carried a feature entitled 'School For Jeeves', which opened with the following paragraph:

> Who would imagine Jeeves could be a bona fide star in the celebrity-fuelled 21st Century? Surely the job is an anachronism – a character from a time when monogrammed slippers were the height of fashion and port was passed to the left?

But no! One student tried to define what his future employer might be looking for:

> "There's so many different stereotypes of what a butler is. I think the actual butler persona is a mixture of all of those. He's a fount of knowledge, he's always there to help, he's a picture of discretion – that's the ideal butler, that's what everyone would strive to be".

And there we have it: Jeeves to Stevens and on to . . . real life.

The butler myth is still very much a thing, one whose influence seems to be growing as the number of the world's plutocrats increases. Some butler schools claim to be able to teach the necessary skills in intensive five or ten day courses run from the U.K., America, the Netherlands, Australia and the Middle East; others offer longer, more gruelling instruction that embraces "household management, event planning, the shoot, the finer points of chauffeuring, etiquette and protocol, clothing care, butler skills, table setting and service, risk management, housekeeping, security, managing the cellar, wine and spirits, cigars, caviar, first aid and human resources to name but a few". And somewhere in the reams of press coverage these establishments seem to generate, there is usually at least one mention of Jeeves: "Becoming Jeeves: Inside a Butler Academy"; "First modern-day Jeeves graduates from Blenheim Palace's butler school"; "School to teach Jeeves a lesson"; "By Jove, Jeeves! Half of all new butlers are women"; "Inside the Edinburgh butler academy where real-life Jeeves' are training to serve celebrities, billionaires and royals". And so on. But what is perhaps surprising about all these articles, no matter how wrong-headed and inappropriate some of them are, and no matter where or in what title they're published, *they all, without exception, take for granted that their readers know who and what Jeeves is* – and what he represents. And there's more:

> 6. Jeeves has also branched out into the commercial world, lending his name (or having it appropriated by) among others: a chain of London dry cleaners, a suite of business software, a taxi-booking app, a concierge service, an e-credit card, an artisan teasmith, a medical robot, a liqueur cordial and perhaps best known of all, an internet search engine. This latter company, which has now dropped 'Jeeves' and is simply knows as "ask. com", commissioned a giant Jeeves-shaped balloon for the Macy's Thanksgiving Parade in New York City, where it featured from 2000-2002 and again in 2004. For the record, it was the first-ever 'internet character' balloon to feature in the procession.

Slowly and stealthily, Jeeves – at least on this evidence – has joined what the poet Philip Larkin once called the world's "myth-kitty".

So more than just the ultimate GPG, Jeeves has morphed into a global symbol of . . . what, exactly? Englishness? Loyalty? Reliability?

Service? Resourcefulness? Trust? The answer is any or all of these things, and many more, for as we've learned in previous chapters, we can tweak or customize a myth to suit the time or place or even our personal circumstances. Provided we remain true to its original significance, anything we come up with will be perfectly valid, for just as we all have a mental *picture* of Jeeves (with or without a combover), so myth allows us to finesse our own *conception* of what he means to us.

The various businesses in paragraph 6 have done just that, annexing specific aspects of Jeeves's broader significance to bolster not just what they do, but to bruit it abroad that they do it faultlessly. Some are more appropriate than others, but in every one of those cases, you can clearly see what they were aiming at. Arguably, 'Jeeves of Belgravia' dry cleaners comes closest to being the perfect match, having apparently sought approval for their venture from Wodehouse himself in 1969. Their first outlet was indeed in Belgravia, a hyper-posh part of London that is a stone's throw away from Bertie's flat in Mayfair; it is a clothes valeting service, one of Jeeves's major responsibilities, and it provides a specialist service for luxury garments. Not only does it hold a Royal Warrant, it has branches in 13 countries around the world. For a GPG, Jeeves doesn't half get around. Then there are the artisanal teasmiths; not quite such a tight fit, but perfectly in keeping; Jeeves regularly brings Bertie his morning cup of the healing oolong, so why not? Even Jeeves the medical robot, who used to carry blood samples and medical notes around Northwick Park hospital in north-west London (and "in more than 50 American hospitals" according to the NHS archives) was wont to make "a polite request for people to step aside" if obstructed in the corridor. It's this very imprecision and flexibility that has helped to bolster Jeeves's air of timelessness – even if people STILL get his job title wrong. For many Wodehouse readers all around the world, he has been the gateway into Wodehouse World, the yin of order and reliability to the yang of chaos and uncertainty represented by Bertie.

So, we arrive at the present day, in which Wodehouse World seems, on the available evidence, to be just as popular as it ever was. To have fashioned a mythical world – in the sense I've been using the term – and be recognized for having done so is a writer's dream, giving him or her the assurance that their fictional creations will at least stand a sporting chance of outliving them.

Say "Jeeves", and you're already smiling. Try when you next take a selfie.

THE TIE
THAT BINDS

Epilogue:
The Tie That Binds

Instead of dirt and poison we have rather chosen to fill our hives
with honey and wax; thus furnishing mankind with the two noblest
of things, which are sweetness and light.
Jonathan Swift, 'The Battle of the Books', 1704

The pursuit of perfection, then, is the pursuit of sweetness and light
... He who works for sweetness and light united, works to make
reason and the will of God prevail.
Matthew Arnold, Culture and Anarchy, 1869

"A dogged attempt to cover the universe with mud, an inverted
Victorianism, an attempt to make crassness and dirt succeed where
sweetness and light failed".
E.M. Forster, Aspects of the Novel,
re: James Joyce's Ulysses

"You can't be expected to dish out happy endings all round".
Bertie Wooster, The Code of the Woosters

It's 1971. As Wodehouse approaches yet another significant birthday
on October 15, his forthcoming novel – bearing the working title *Much
Obliged, Jeeves* – is scheduled to be published simultaneously in the U.K.
and America in a co-ordinated marketing push to honour this landmark
event. The celebratory cover art by Osbert Lancaster is already in place,
showing Jeeves lighting candles on a large cake which bears the dates
"1881-1971", atop the caption:

P.G. WODEHOUSE
A 90th Birthday Celebration

All seems oojah-cum-spiff; but in the view of Peter Schwed, Plum's
American editor, the book's title and original ending are all wrong and
need changing. As originally submitted, Jeeves has destroyed Bertie's
18-page biographical entry in the Junior Ganymede Club's hallowed
ledger; but on telling his employer the good news, he is simply met with
a perfunctory "Much obliged, Jeeves"– and that's it. The End. With this
most throwaway of thank-yous, it's all over.

Schwed felt somewhat crestfallen; this wasn't giving him (or his marketing department) much to work with. It's true that earlier in the novel, and after a wait of 56 years, we learn that Jeeves's first name is "Reginald", but this wasn't enough on its own, for the earth-shattering significance of Jeeves's act of vandalism wouldn't register with those who weren't already J&W aficionados. And so Schwed wrote to Plum on February 12, saying how he loved the novel, but that its ending struck him as going out on "more of a whimper than a bang". He continued:

> [N]or . . . is it consistent with Jeeves' exemplary character. He wouldn't do such a thing to a sacred object like the club book without a rational explanation. So I've tried to give him one and, at the same time, work in a justification for the new title for the book which I now propose: Jeeves and the Tie That Binds
>
> I like that title because it's warm, means something if you accept my new ending idea, and, perhaps most important, because it somehow ties/binds together the Osbert Lancaster drawing I told you about, with Jeeves lighting 90 candles on a birthday cake, with the novel itself. The ties could be interpreted as being Jeeves to Bertie, or as being Jeeves to Wodehouse.

Schwed then fabricated a 221-word alternative ending – what he called a "little basic Wodehouse imitation" – which Plum could then re-work as necessary. Would that be OK?

Now Plum had always been one to humour his somewhat hands-on American editor. After all, this was the man who had changed the perfectly serviceable title *Galahad at Blandings* to *The Brinkmanship of Galahad Threepwood* and commissioned a jacket that made Gally resemble, in Plum's view, "one of the Beatles". It was changes like this that prompted Wodehouse to write to his British editor, J.D. Grimsdick, that his American counterpart "ought to rent a padded cell in some not too choosy lunatic asylum". Whether he had to swallow hard on this occasion isn't known, but he did end up very slightly amending the U.K. edition to read thus, as Jeeves reveals his page-tearing handiwork on the ledger (Plum's additions are underlined):

"I have already done so, sir."

I leaped like a rising trout, to the annoyance of Gus [the resident black cat at Brinkley Court], who had gone to sleep on my solar plexus. Words failed me, but in due season I managed three.

"Much obliged, Jeeves."

"Not at all, sir."

It's amazing what a few extra words can do: Bertie has already told us how his world is 99% perfect, the only cloud on an otherwise sunny horizon being his personal entry in the ledger, which, while it still existed, could be used to blackmail him by unscrupulous operators like Bingley, a somewhat disreputable and cranky former employee. By revealing that he has already taken care of this, Jeeves renders Bertie both amazed and thankful, such that he's struck dumb. Life suddenly *is* perfect, thanks to Jeeves. Note also how the guff about Gus gives both Bertie and us a short interval for the significance of Jeeves's six-word revelation to sink in. Eventually ("in due season") he manages to squeeze out just three words, which in their economy and formality now speak volumes, summing up the understanding between the two men that has grown over the 56 years of their partnership. What they don't say becomes just as important as the words they speak, and for all its brevity and decorum, it's actually rather touching; for Jeeves, once again, has plucked Bertie from the bouillon.

Schwed, however, was insisting that the full significance of this wonderfully economical moment should be laid bare for all to see in words of one syllable and at much greater length. Perhaps, in addition to the marketing angle, he was pondering that given Plum's advanced age, this might turn out to be the final Jeeves and Bertie adventure, and that the conclusion as originally submitted was something of an anti-climax. Wodehouse had been working with Schwed since the early 1950s, and so, possibly to avoid any further fuss, he reworked the proffered 221 words for the American edition, retaining only about a quarter of them and adding quite a few of his own to produce the following passage. Here it is in full, for those who don't have the relevant edition (the few words Plum retained from Schwed's proposal are underlined):

"I have already done so, sir."

"What?"

"Yes, sir."

You wouldn't be far wrong in saying that I was visibly moved – so visibly, indeed that Gus the cat, who had gone to sleep on my solar plexus, shot some inches in the air and showed considerable annoyance.

"Jeeves," I started to vociferate, but he cut in first.

"In taking this step, sir, I do not feel that I have inflicted any disservice on the Junior Ganymede Club. The club book was never intended to be light and titillating reading for the members. Its function is solely to acquaint those who are contemplating changing taking new posts with the foibles and eccentricities of prospective employers. That being so, there is no need for the record contained in the eighteen pages in which you figure. For I may hope, may I not, sir, that you will allow me to remain permanently in your service?"

"You may indeed, Jeeves. It often beats me, though, why with your superlative gifts you should want to."

"There is a tie that binds, sir."

"A what that whats?"

"A tie that binds, sir."

"The heaven bless it, and may it continue to bind indefinitely. Fate's happenstance may oft win more than toil, as the fellow said."

"What fellow would that be, sir? Thoreau?"

"No, me."

"Sir?"

"A little thing of my own. I don't know what it means, but you can take it from me as coming straight from the heart."

"Very good, sir."

"Yes, I didn't think it was bad myself," I said, and after a bit more kidding back and forth he shimmered out, leaving me to grapple with the problem . . . of how to get up and have my bath without waking Gus, who had now transferred himself to my Adam's apple.

Of the words that aren't underlined, we still can't definitively know which were written by Plum, for the surviving correspondence may be incomplete. With eight months left until publication (Plum's reply was dated February 18), there could have been several more to-ings and fro-ings. But whether or not, Wodehouse would have presumably had the final word on any emendations, and the above represents the final form of any subsequent deliberation.

So – where do you start with that "permanently in your service"? Schwed certainly had his climactic ending, for in the new passage Plum practically marries off his two lead characters for all eternity: no more Jeeves flouncing out over moustaches and banjoleles, ever. You'll have your opinion of this emendation just as I have mine and Plum seems to have had his – for only certain American editions continue to carry these changes. But things that are less than perfect can end up being revelatory – and this is one such occasion, for it lays bare how Plum was gilding the myth of his poster boys, perhaps with posterity in mind, above and beyond what Schwed had asked for. In short, he picked up Schwed's ball and ran with it.

"The tie that binds" is, as Plum perhaps knew, the first line of a hymn by the 18th-century Baptist theologian, John Fawcett, who had been enticed down from his native Yorkshire parish to London by the promise of a better-remunerated pastoral position in the capital. Having accepted it, he suddenly got cold feet and declined at the last minute, writing the hymn by way of celebration at having made the right decision to stay put in God's Own County:

Blest be the tie that binds
our hearts in Christian love;

the fellowship of kindred minds
is like to that above.

This was a pretty nifty piece of research on his editor's part and is entirely in keeping with the way Plum regularly embedded quotations from other writers in his work. As Schwed suggested, the new title serves to bring together not just Jeeves and Bertie, but Jeeves and his creator. To which pairings he might have added 'Plum and his readers' – for why would we be left out of this outbreak of matiness? As I wrote in Volume 2, Plum is an immersive author, and "the fellowship of kindred minds" is one of the hallmarks of Wodehouse World, whichever characters he happens to be writing about. In the J&W saga, the titles of *The Code of the Woosters* and *Jeeves and the Feudal Spirit*, along with Bertie's ongoing ambitions to be a *preux chevalier* indicate just three examples of unwritten and largely unformulated protocols that govern not just Bertie's understanding of the world, but the way he behaves within it. To which Schwed, with Plum's agreement, had now added a fourth, "the Tie That Binds". It's the winning combination of the ideal (Bertie) and the practical (Jeeves) that makes them such an attractive pairing – a team whose members will be forever associated with one another, like the bacon and eggs that Jeeves prepares and Bertie regularly devours at breakfast. Even without Plum's slightly forced announcement of their permanent conjoining, we never thought they were otherwise, so perfectly are they suited to one another. When Jeeves leaves Bertie, for whatever reason, he always ends up coming back.

But there's more to it than this. For the relationship between Jeeves and Bertie is not just the jewel in the crown, but a synecdoche of their creator's relationship with us. This makes Wodehouse World not so much a location as a sort of frequency Plum's readers can tune into anytime, anyplace, anywhere, courtesy of his lightness. In the previous volume, I referred to him as our host; and in all honesty, I can think of no other writer who takes so much care to make sure we're enjoying ourselves while we're on his premises. His patented narrative tone is a good example, being chatty, approachable and welcoming rather than formal, weighty and authoritative. His plots don't over burden us with expectation or suspense; the elegant flow of his timeless language doesn't tax our patience or understanding; the humour keeps us engaged and entertained; and when we've finished one title there are plenty more to choose from. It's quite a package, and one that has helped Plum's work stand the test of time by always putting himself in his readers' place. He did, as he put it "take care" – of us.

Over 100 years on, we can still experience this cordiality, this friend-liness. But although it came as second nature to Wodehouse, it was as much a practical as a philanthropic strategy; for we must never forget that even as we bask in his warmth, Plum was possessed of a shrewd and calculating business sense that never left him, as we've witnessed at several points in this volume. Being someone who lived almost aggressively in the here and now, his attention dominated by his work, he would have been little inclined to think about any literary legacy he might bequeath to the world, or what his body of work might cumulatively 'represent' to future readers. Nevertheless, there is an overarching geniality at work when we think about Wodehouse World that overrides any or all of these more business-like considerations. And here it is we return for the final time to the idea of "something understood" that not only acts as the tie that binds us to him but maintains the timelessness of Plum's writing. A number of writers have had a stab at defining this elusive quality, all juggling similar sets of ideas even as they reach somewhat different conclusions – not so much about how we read Wodehouse's stories, but how, down the years, they keep on reading *us*.

Here are three such attempts, arranged in no particular order, beginning with Auberon Waugh's 1973 essay 'Father of the English Idea', in which he describes how an enthusiasm for Plum's work was proving inheritable, having already passed through four successive generations of his own family, including of course his father Evelyn. Bron's daughter Margaret had just been smitten at age 10, something for which her father appears profoundly grateful and even a little relieved, for in reading Wodehouse:

> something of [his] gentleness and benevolence is bound to communicate itself; almost certainly it will remain a profound influence for the rest of her life, helping to shape her attitudes to her culture . . . and to all life's vicissitudes.

In a tender and uncharacteristically sincere few sentences, Waugh claims that an appreciation of Plum's humour will "equip her with a new critical dimension by which to judge the things which other people hold important and not the things which other people think funny". In this light, Plum's Unique Selling Point is an unconventional *perspective*, a way of looking at the world that can see beyond appearances through to the essential absurdity of just about everything, including the "personal, religious [and] political". This "little subversive corner" of her heart will prove seriously useful not just for her psychological well-being, but in her day-to-day dealings with the world: a place where she can nurture her sense of the ridiculous "every moment of the day".

This is more or less the perspective of the satirist, only with an added dimension: while the real world may indeed be crazy, negativity need not be the corollary of that insight. Instead of holding our heads in our hands and bemoaning the pointlessness of it all, or seething with Juvenalian anger and frustration, Wodehouse helps us to laugh a laugh of genuine amusement. Not grim, ironic or guilty laughter but real, unselfconscious laughter. And this is not just useful as a pressure valve: routinely appreciating the inbuilt absurdity of human affairs helps prevent our thinking hardening into the desperate remedies of dogma or doctrine. Stephen Fry's candid assertion that Plum "taught me something about good nature . . . [that] it is enough to be benign, to be gentle, to be funny, to be kind" sums up this fuzzy instinct rather touchingly, and were I a writer of fiction, I'd be more than happy with that sort of tribute.

In our second example, we have a form of appreciation that heads 180-degrees away from Waugh's joyous iconoclasm and *towards* dogma and doctrine. This is an instinct explored by the writers we first met back in Chapter 7 who were insisting that Plum's primal innocence was proof he was batting for the Lord's team whether he was aware of it or not. William Vesterman can stand for them all in his assertion that Wodehouse World is an exemplary creation that represents "an idyllic image of eternal bliss" not entirely unadjacent to the qualities to be found in "the kingdom of heaven". When Evelyn Waugh or W.H. Auden described Plum's world as "Eden", they were inviting us to think much the same thing, as did C. Stephen Evans, who in a closely-argued piece for *Books & Culture* magazine, claimed that Plum was to all intents and purposes a Christian, but one who had never taken "religious convictions into the core of his . . . own existence", a man "who finds religious questions deeply interesting, but who cannot find his way to a settled faith":

> Wodehouse fits this description perfectly. He was brought up in a Christian environment; parish priests are as much a natural part of his fictional world as are earls and good-for-nothing aesthetes. He effortlessly absorbed what we might call the stored-up capital of Christianity, and drew

on those stores without drawing undue attention to the source. Wodehouse embodies what William James, in *The Varieties of Religious Experience*, calls the "once-born" type of religiousness, the religious person who confidently trusts in the basic goodness of the world and the self.

Or, in other words, Christianity in all but name. Reading Wodehouse, it seems, can leave a positive legacy in not just our memory but our souls, and Evans doggedly argues that this higher perspective might as well be called his religion, but for the fact he was a self-declared agnostic.

Third and finally, we have a slightly different wrinkle on the above. The book Evans was reviewing in his essay happened to be Robert McCrum's biography, which in its Epilogue momentarily flirts with the idea that Plum's work has a moral dimension rather than a religious message:

> [T]he theme that animates Wodehouse's work, and gives it a moral purpose, is the quest for sweetness and light in the daily transactions of humanity, and for something approximate to love.

It's a shame McCrum doesn't elaborate on this observation, because of all the three arguments above, it takes the fewest liberties with what little we can actually know about what went on in Wodehouse's head. Few other scholars have explored the possibility of a Wodehousean secular morality, except in glancing references to the generally benevolent ethos of his work, or how the goodies always seem to triumph over such baddies as there are. "Love" is another intriguing possibility as the motive force of Wodehouse World, which was one of W.H. Auden's theses in an essay entitled 'Balaam's Ass' in which Bertie is celebrated as the ultimate – and unlikely – literary avatar of 'Agape', or Divine Love, trumping Don Quixote (Cervantes), Don Juan (Byron) and Prospero (Shakespeare) by dint of the "humility" which makes him the most happy and "blessed" of all of them.

Whether any of this chimes with our own experiences or not, each of the above examples represents a thoughtful and sincere attempt to pin down our "something understood", to rationalize what shores up Wodehouse's creative vision once we're done with the proximate attractions of laughter and language. And not only that, to find a practical application – a *relevance* – for his humour in our everyday lives. But, if we're going to travel down this road, surely we must ask ourselves whether Plum had the faintest inkling of what he was doing. If he didn't, was this added dimension, whatever it might be, a happy by-product of his writing? Or are we looking for something that isn't actually there?

But if we set out on this journey, are we loving Wodehouse not wisely but too well, perhaps overcompensating for those who have branded his work as trivial? James Wood, reviewing McCrum's biography for the *New Republic* in 2005, is all for nipping this tendency to earnestness in the bud:

> [H]alf of his obsessed readers would wilt away if they suspected the Master of such sweaty seriousness. What makes Wodehouse "serious" in a literary sense is the singularity of his achievement; and this singularity was owed not to moral seriousness, the possession of a thousand earnest scriveners, but to the absolute absence of it. That the work can march so easily, morally speaking, on an empty stomach; that it can achieve so many traditionally literary things without ever daring the scandal of meaning. . . is completely fascinating.

Which throws everything up in the air again. From Wood's perspective, Wodehouse World turns on its axis courtesy of one of the greatest and most prolonged literary sleights of hand ever perpetrated: a higher, if unintended, purpose (what Wood calls its "meaning") is most definitely *there*, while never once defining itself – or threatening to intrude on the laughter. Quite what the tie that binds actually *is* will most likely remain elusive, and in its ongoing absence Wood can only quote Bertie's wonderfully circular musings on the subconscious from *Right Ho, Jeeves*:

> I don't know if it has happened to you to at all, but a thing I've noticed with myself is that, when I'm confronted by a problem which seems for the moment to stump and baffle, a good sleep will often bring the solution in the morning . . . The nibs who study these matters claim, I believe, that this has got something to do with the subconscious mind, and very possibly they may be right. I wouldn't have said off-hand that I had a subconscious mind, but I suppose I must without knowing it, and no doubt it was there, sweating away diligently at the old stand, all the while the

corporeal Wooster was getting his eight hours.

Just as Bertie isn't conscious of his subconscious mind, so, Wood postulates, Wodehouse's comedy works its magic in ways that we either can't, shouldn't or don't need to rationalize quite simply because Plum doesn't require us to.

To which I can only respond, *rem acu tetigisti* – except that ending almost 1,000 pages of musings with such a non-conclusory conclusion would be something of a cop-out. No doubt it's more sympathetic to Plum's self-effacing personality – and a good deal less "sweaty" – to enjoy his lightness on its own non-specific terms, and yet I don't feel I can simply leave this "something understood" as simply "something". For the sub-title of this closing volume is "The Happiness of the World", and when we look at Plum's global reach, further relevant musings suggest themselves. Just how is it that a writer so quintessentially English can have sizeable followings all over the globe? Clearly that "something" is communicating itself way beyond its point of origin both in place and time.

Plum's stories have (so far) been translated into over 30 languages. From 1904 (when a Dutch magazine published a translation of the school story 'An Afternoon Dip') to December 2018, more than thirty Wodehouse titles have appeared in each of the following languages: Bulgarian, Czech, Danish, Dutch, Finnish, French, German, Hungarian, Italian, Norwegian, Russian, Spanish and Swedish; other regular languages include Burmese, Catalan, [simplified] Chinese, Estonian, Hebrew, Icelandic, Japanese, Latvian, Polish, Portuguese, Romanian, Serbian, Slovenian, Telugu, Turkish and Ukrainian. And in the late 1980s came a fascinating – and very Wodehousean – experiment in which 'The Great Sermon Handicap' was translated into 59 languages, both ancient and modern, including Middle English, Frisian and Old Norse (all statistics courtesy of Tony Ring, to whom grateful thanks). In the internet age, social media is alive with Wodehouse 'fan' pages and blogs, and there are currently well-established Wodehouse Societies in the U.K., U.S., Russia, Sweden, the Netherlands and Belgium, as well as smaller groups in India, Pakistan, Australia, Finland, France and Italy.

But that's by no means a comprehensive list of countries where Plum remains rather more popular than we might expect a writer of his singularity and vintage to be, and the various stories that continue to emerge from Wodehouse's international fanbase are just as illuminating, if not more so, than any amount of literary criticism. So here are four all-too-brief – and very different – case studies from different parts of the globe:

Russia: Touching historical testimony comes from Russia, courtesy of the late Dr. Natalya Trauberg, who translated all the Blandings titles (with the exception of *Leave it to Psmith)* and Uncle Fred novels into her native language. She told how she was introduced to Wodehouse by her film-director father, who, among the "bohemian young people" in the early post-revolutionary days of the 1920s, hoovered up Wodehouse editions published for mass consumption by small, local imprints. Poorly translated and abridged, the books about those "young men in spats" nevertheless encapsulated "the very life that their unfortunate Soviet counterparts were dreaming about". Plum's star waned in the 1930s, when he was denounced as a symbol of everything communism was fighting against (such bourgeois writing was known as "dlya zhyrnykh" or "fat tummy" literature); but Natalya was to discover his writing for herself when she came across a copy of *A Damsel in Distress* in the university library in Leningrad, where she was by now a student:

> I cannot express what a comfort his books provided in those difficult times. For that alone, I'll always be grateful to him. More than anyone, more than Chaucer, Dickens and Chesterton, he opposed the horror of those days.

Some years later, Natalya's father wrote to Wodehouse personally, and received autographed books and two signed photos in return; but it was only around the time of the fall of the Berlin Wall in 1989 that she embarked on her own Wodehouse translations. In 2000, she reported that a Moscow publishing house, Ostozhje, had begun "a sizeable series of Wodehouse", whose success "exceeded everyone's expectations" with the result that even a "classic" publishing house (Khudozhestvennaja Literatura) that had specialized in 'official' literature during the Soviet era had decided to get in on the act. Natalya concluded that even in the Putin era, "Wodehouse is the surest medicine against the rubbish that our minds and hearts were fed for many decades".

Japan: In 2018, Empress Michiko of Japan revealed that following her husband's abdication, she planned to spend her retirement re-reading all the Jeeves and Wooster novels and stories, sales of which promptly rocketed. Certain Wodehouse titles have appeared as manga cartoon books, and one of their creators, Bun Katsuta, travelled to England with the renowned translator Tamaki Morimura to immerse herself in the remaining "minutiae of Bertie Wooster's London" so she could capture the look and feel of the stories as accurately as possible. Tamaki herself has made a significant and lasting contribution to Plum's ongoing familiarity, having translated 19 titles since 2004, including two anthologies of Wodehouse stories. And in 2020, the 107-year-old, hugely popular all-female Takarazuka Revue Company mounted 15 performances of the Wodehouse/Bolton/Gershwin & Gershwin musical *Oh, Kay!*

Hungary: In 2004, Poór Bálint revealed that over 40 different Wodehouse titles had so far been translated into Hungarian, of which he had been responsible for four, each of them with respectable print runs of between 5,000 and 8,000 copies. He concluded his report by commenting that "[t]here seems to be no reason why the present regular supply of new Hungarian translations should peter out in the foreseeable future" – a prediction confirmed in 2016 when a member of the U.K. Wodehouse Society spotted dozens of translated Wodehouse titles on prominent display in a central Budapest bookstore.

But it's **India** where Wodehouse seems most closely interwoven with the nation's consciousness, his popularity not just undimmed but seemingly growing. Reports tell of the availability of his work on station platforms and airport bookstalls alongside the latest bestsellers, and down the years a number of writers in the U.K., U.S. and India itself have been prompted to speculate as to why this should be. In the same issue of *Wooster Sauce* (#36, December 2005) in which it was announced that *Right Ho, Jeeves* had been translated into Hebrew, Sushmita Sen Gupta wrote a considered piece detailing how the internet, then a mere infant, had already helped bring India's scattered but sizeable Wodehouse community together. Numerous sites continue to thrive, and so I decided to commission my own survey from the 'Fans of P G Wodehouse' Facebook group, which at the time of writing has 15,000 or so members and is the largest of several to be found on that platform.

Many commenters seem to have been alerted to the existence of Wodehouse by their parents or word of mouth, and, as Vikas Sonak points out, this has ensured that a love of Wodehouse has already been passed down through several generations. Of his own three children, one has taken to the Wodehousean "slant on life" while the others "just don't get" him. Others have noted that because English is widely spoken and formally taught in India (figures vary wildly, but it's conservative-ly estimated that around 10% of the population – that's 125 million people – regularly speak it), Plum's work has "invariably" found its way on to exam papers as examples of some of the finest prose ever written. Moreover, Wodehouse titles can often be found in local libraries, or those run by the British Council or the local British Consulate. Many of my correspondents have carried over that love of Wodehouse from their formative years into adulthood, praising its restorative qualities and the way it chimes with the Indian sense of humour and love of wordplay. Vikas also points out that Indian professionals, rather than brushing up their Shakespeare, would brush up their Wodehouse so as to "polish" their English, "in order to secure success in education and career".

I apologize to those who responded to my request for not being able to name them all individually, but from the dozens of replies, Karan Kapoor's stood out for his thoughtful exploration of Plum's "strangely subversive appeal" that very much chimes with Auberon Waugh's icon-oclastic take from a few pages back. Plum is

> Not subversive in the sense that his characters or settings were from anything but a bygone era, but because of his use of language to paint vivid, hilarious, chaotic and indel-ible images in our minds.

> Subversive also in that the style of prose lent itself well to political satire pointing out the absurdity as one son after the other also rose as a national political dynasty took root . . .

> And subversive in the sense that the old India (if not Calcutta) finally gave way to a new ethos, louder, brasher, more confident and ultimately perhaps more authentically representative of India.

Even from this brief summary, it's clear that the Indian 'take' on Wode-house is complex, and is rather more than purely escapist or nostalgic, somehow chiming at a deeper – and perhaps more disruptive – level than we might credit.

As evidence, Karan namechecked *Great Indian Novel* from 1989, Shashi Tharoor's satirical impression of the Indian independence movement, as having been influenced by Wodehouse's style and absurdist perspective. Indeed, 'perspective' is a word Tharoor himself sometimes uses in relation to Wodehouse and the English language, allowing him to step back from his twin careers in international diplomacy and later in Indian politics and appreciate the world with new eyes. The following is an unapologetically lengthy extract from a speech Tharoor gave at the 2008 Wodehouse Society dinner in London, which for me brilliantly sums up how Wodehouse World can be of this world and yet not of this world at one and the same time – while none of us remain any the wiser as to why that might be:

> While no English writer can truly be said to have a "mass" following in India . . . Wodehouse has maintained a general rather than a "cult" audience; unlike others, he has never gone out of fashion. This bewilders those who think that nothing could be further removed from Indian life, with its poverty and political intensity, than the silly escapades of Wodehouse's decadent Edwardian Young Men in Spats.

> India's fascination with Wodehouse is one of those endearing mysteries. Many believe that Wodehouse's popularity reflects a nostalgia for the British Empire in India. Writing in 1988, the journalist Richard West thought India's Wodehouse devotees were those who "hanker after the England of 50 years ago. That was when the English treasured their own language, when schoolchildren learned Shakespeare, Wordsworth and even Rudyard Kipling . . . It was Malcolm Muggeridge who remarked that the Indians are now "the last Englishmen".

> Those lines are more fatuous than anything Wodehouse would have written. Wodehouse is loved by Indians who loathe Kipling and detest the Raj . . . If anything, Wodehouse is one British writer whom Indian nationalists could admire without fear of political incorrectness. My former mother-in-law, the daughter of a prominent Indian nationalist politician, remembers introducing Britain's last viceroy, Lord Mountbatten, to the works of Wodehouse in 1947; it was typical that the symbol of the British Empire had not read the "quintessentially English" Wodehouse but that the Indian freedom fighter had.

Interesting, indeed. As Karan Kapoor noted, the "new ethos" of India seems just as much in need of its Wodehouse fix as the old. Back in my Facebook survey, Shreehari Aney contributed this:

> The class about which Wodehouse wrote – the genteel, well-heeled, lilies of the field class – exists in India even today. As a stratified society, we are more likely to appreciate the humour that results from the rubbing of shoulders of our landed gentry, our aristocracy, our business tycoons with their retainers and servants and gardeners and policemen. Indians recognize the milieu and take delight in it . . . Add to this the theatre of the absurd, which provides the stage for Wodehouse's stories. Indians love this absurdity, perhaps because they find themselves living their lives in a similar improbable framework. It makes for preservation of their collective sanity.

This can speak not just for India, but for all of us wherever we are. As traditional ways of ordering our world are wantonly trashed by those whose job it is to protect them, establishing a *modus vivendi* with the absurd is not simply a desirable facility but a necessary life skill. And while Wodehouse World – at least on the surface – may not appear to have much to do with the way we live now, the planet's collective subconscious, "sweating away diligently at the old stand" finds it difficult to let go. And if, in Bollywood, *A Damsel in Distress* can be successfully re-worked into a parable about coming out exactly 100 years after the novel first appeared – and turn a tidy profit – even those who dismiss Plum as a wilfully regressive and/or fantastical irrelevance must, in all fairness, concede that their argument is not the only game in town, or the world. Dotty earls may have been superseded by the lords and ladies of the new global plutocracy, but what are the worldwide box office smashes *Crazy Rich Asians*, *My Big Fat Greek Wedding* or even *Bridesmaids* if not the unlikely heirs of Wodehouse and the traditions of romantic comedy *he* was working inside?

If you're reading this book somewhere deep in the future, these last references will have long since ceased to have any meaning, while, of course, Plum's work will. But one of the many things those blockbuster movies share is that none of them is as dumb as it looks. It takes brains and/or extraordinary luck to make comedy successful *and* universal, and if you can't see the unbroken thread that leads back to Bertie *et al*, you may not be looking hard enough. What I've been calling 'myth' has long since facilitated the connection, allowing those movies to be story-boarded in the first place. Moreover, it must also be acknowledged that the cultural world's sniffy (perhaps guilty?) attitude to this type of light, romantic comedy continues to be way out of step with global popular taste – making Plum continue to be as "subversive" as my Indian correspondents claim. We shouldn't like this sort of frothy stuff, only we do – in some cases despite ourselves.

Writer and producer Richard Curtis (*Love Actually, Notting Hill, Four Weddings and a Funeral*), while nowhere on record a declared Wodehouse fan (although I simply can't believe he isn't), absolutely smashes the argument that laughter, however popular, cannot be worthy of serious attention:

> If you make a film about a man kidnapping a woman and chaining her to a radiator for five years – something that has probably happened once in history – it's called [a] searingly realistic analysis of society. If I make a film like *Love Actually*, which is about people falling in love, and there are about a million people falling in love in Britain today, it's called a sentimental presentation of an unrealistic world.

Which argument brings us right back where we started in the Preface to Volume 1 of this book. Comedy, for Wodehouse, was a serious business, and the creation of his patented brand of lightness involved, as we've seen, a lot of heavy-duty sweat. But this paid considerable dividends, for it has made his work not just universally sympathetic but permanently entertaining. Adaptability has proved the key to its survival, an instinctive involvement with elements of the human psyche that don't simply come and go or are confined to a single time and place. So, what's not to like?

So, to conclude; it is a truth (almost) universally acknowledged that Plum's lightness frees the human soul – wherever on the planet it may reside – from life's everyday trammels. Call it an escape, a guilty pleasure, a subversive act, a regaining of perspective or even a religious insight – whatever floats your boat. But what can't be denied is that the release of oomph accompanying that feeling of freedom is probably the closest literature gets to replicating a shot of dopamine. Bertie describes this mood-enhancing effect when, on his debut in 1915, he detects

. . . something in the air, either the ozone or the phosphates or something, which makes you sit up and take notice. A kind of zip, as it were. A sort of bally freedom, if you know what I mean, that gets into your blood and bucks you up, and makes you feel that . . . you don't care if you've got odd socks on. ('Extricating Young Gussie')

Matching socks is the usual sartorial prejudice but . . . in the great scheme of things, does it really matter? It would to Jeeves, of course, but then again, he represents the corresponding – and necessary – impulse that prevents his employer's blithe instinct for freedom and gaiety having too many damaging consequences. But as feelings go, there's not much to be said against this springtime of the soul: summer's on its way, and in the aptly named story 'Jeeves in the Springtime', Bertie has another attack of vernal giddiness:

"In the spring, Jeeves, a livelier iris gleams upon the burnished dove".

"So I have been informed, sir".

"Right ho! Then bring me my whangee, my yellowest shoes, and the old green Homburg. I'm going into the Park to do pastoral dances".

And with that slight misquote from Tennyson, we can be there too, along with Uncle Fred, who is virtually Plum's patron saint of the season, and an embodiment of all it symbolizes in poetry and song if not reproductive biology. In *Service with a Smile*, he even invents a seasonal cocktail he dubs 'Queen of the May', made of "good dry champagne . . . liqueur brandy, kummel and green chartreuse". This bilious-sounding and possibly dangerous concoction neatly demonstrates how spring is a time when everyone and everything acts as if it's drunk on something, spirituous or otherwise, and isn't too mindful of the consequences. And yet, amid all the light-headedness, Plum sometimes, although rarely, chooses to strike a minor chord. Indeed, in *Uncle Dynamite* it's just about possible to detect a thread of life philosophy running through the plot – perhaps not surprising since the novel was begun as he languished in Paris waiting for the Allies to liberate the city from German occupation in spring 1944.

The Tie That Binds

Though Uncle Fred is described as having "the fresh, unspoiled outlook of a slightly inebriated undergraduate", we are also regaled with an insight into what his cheery outlook has to overcome in order to function:

> In these days in which we live, when existence has become a thing of infinite complexity and fate, if it slips us a bit of goose with one hand, is pretty sure to give us the sleeve across the windpipe with the other, it is rarely that we find a human being who is unmixedly happy. Always the bitter will be blended with the sweet, and in this *mélange* one can be reasonably certain that it is the former that will predominate.

This observation is qualified by the very next line, confined to its own paragraph, as if Plum's narrator realizes that he's either gone a bit far, or, conversely, wants to underscore his message:

> A severe indictment of our modern civilization, but it can't say it didn't ask for it.

A slight rift in the lute between Wodehouse and life? It certainly pulls one up short after all that stuff about springtime; and having now completed three volumes about him, I'm more convinced than ever of something I can never truly know: that for his lightness to function to maximum effect, Plum needed the same kind of discipline in his head as is evident in his best writing. Or, to put it another way, his characteristic equanimity must have been hard won, given that his life had its fair share of downs as well as ups. As Bertie reminds us in *Stiff Upper Lip, Jeeves*, although it is his policy to always look on the bright side of life, "you have to have a bright side to look on" – and at certain times life stubbornly refuses to oblige.

Wodehouse's generally eupeptic outlook wasn't simply the product of that "innocence" we debunked in Chapter 7; nor even Lord Emsworth's instinctive ability to filter out life's worries; and definitely not that he lived in a fantasy Eden he carried around with him in his head. Rather, it was a sustained and even heroic act of self-will. No fan of the disruption caused by fuss and bother, he was fortunate in being able to farm out many of his day-to-day annoyances to third parties: his agents and editors, and of course most particularly to Ethel.

But just how far he was prepared to go to purge his personal world of the nagging distractions caused by negativity in all its forms is, for me, demonstrated by the remarkable manner in which he settled his account with William Connor, the yellow journalist who had, in 1941, sought to destroy his honour, reputation and everything he had managed to achieve in that sneering, venomous and wilfully inaccurate radio talk that cast a poisonous shadow over the rest of his life.

Twelve years on from that broadcast, Wodehouse must have dug incredibly deep when he invited his nemesis to lunch in what Robert McCrum rightly describes as "a masterstroke of magnanimity". Further meetings followed, and in 1961, on its 20th anniversary, Connor finally acknowledged in his *Daily Mirror* column that the broadcast had not been his finest hour, and he wished "to bury the whole story and to forgive and, where necessary, to hope to be forgiven". How easy it would have been for Wodehouse to nurse a personal hatred that might even have poisoned the well of his comic inspiration. Yet somehow – thankfully – he didn't, and a form of redemption – for both men – resulted. As Plum noted during his enforced sojourn in Germany: "I'm quite unable to work up any kind of belligerent feeling. Just as I'm about to feel belligerent about some country I meet a decent sort of chap. We go out together and lose any fighting thoughts or feelings". And so it proved in practice, albeit with a fellow-countryman who, frankly, didn't deserve such generosity. Plum had written in *Summer Lightning* that "[a]n author can't work if people depress him", and now he could finally cross Connor off his to-do list, one less thing to trouble his hard-won equilibrium, his mental double-entry ledger back in the black at long last.

Wodehouse's steely, lifelong determination to live on the sunny side of the street is both strangely compelling and – as far as I'm aware – utterly *sui generis* among writers. And while in person he could be petulant, grumpy and self-centred to the point of utter frustration, the tenor of his books never fails to give the impression that they, and their author were cut from the same cheerful cloth. The sleight of hand practised in those 1950s autobiographies and elsewhere in his journalism continues to work like a dream, persuading us that Plum's brand of comedy was all he *could* have written, given his disposition to suspend contradictions, iron out the rough spots and manoeuvre around stones in life's road by somehow levitating above them, keeping calm and carrying on, trusting in the basic goodness of people, and convincing us that things have a habit of working themselves out in the end. In his created world, Plum always chose order and closure, neatly tying up the loose ends of his narrative, demonstrating complete mastery over his material and method even as his plots threatened to spiral out of control. Ending his very first tale, written aged five, he felt impelled to inform his readers that "Now my story is done", a polite but firm insistence that what we had read was absolutely everything he intended to say, leaving no opportunity for further speculation. Indeed, sometimes I get the impression, albeit fleeting, that Plum was so relentlessly driven, focused, consistent, dependable and self-reliant that he must have endured periods of what the rest of us might understand and experience as loneliness. While on the page his characters are brim-full of bonhomie, fellow feeling, vim and vigour, their creator was hardly what we now call a 'people person', his literary ambitions compelling him to spend inordinate amounts of time closeted with only his imagination for company – happily and from choice, I hasten to add. And yet the unique and complex composition of his personality, by turns monastically detached from the world and yet engaged by it, sort of worked out for him, his writing, and us too, for he ultimately won the battle to see the world on his terms. Hence, we can turn to Wodehouse in times of trouble as we can with virtually no other author.

At the time of writing, the world is passing through alarming waves of the Covid-19 pandemic, and Plum is one of only a handful of writers who consistently feature in articles with titles such as 'My Choice of Lockdown Reading' and such like, allowing him to be marketed as the perfect antidote to stress and worry. One British national newspaper even began running 95-year-old stories from *Carry On, Jeeves* to help distract its readers from the devastating news carried elsewhere in its pages. On its own, that is no mean achievement for writing of Wodehouse's vintage. But his stories perform far more than that simple, transactional function, and those ties that bind, are still, thankfully, binding his world to ours. Writing to Derek Grimsdick in 1953, Plum had already decided that "I had better spend my last days strewing sweetness and light wherever possible" just in case there *was* a heaven and St. Peter ticked him off for sleeping on the job.

So the strewing continued for another two decades, further polishing the image of what he and his Knutish characters had always been: "genial and good-tempered, friends of all the world" whose "normal outlook on life" was "sunny . . . humble and kindly" as they went about "warming the hearts of stone". And like Uncle Fred, whose "resilient nature" can easily be brought "to a fine pitch of buoyancy and optimism" by relatively accessible life events such as "a restful night" or "a good lunch", one at least hopes that Plum experienced, as far as humanly possible, the state of consciousness he cooked up for his fictional creation, and his readers, back in 1948:

> There is an expression in common use which might have been invented to describe the enterprising peer at moments such as this; the expression 'boomps-a-daisy'. You could look askance at his methods, you could shake your head at him in disapproval and click your tongue in reproof, but you could not deny that he was boomps-a-daisy.

What mood could be more conducive to the spreading of sweetness and light?

Thank you, Plum.

WHAT
NEXT?

Afterword:
What Next?

"What have you been reading lately?" . . .
"I am in the process of plugging away at a thing called The Mystery of the Pink Crayfish" . . .
"How can you fritter away your time like that, when you might be reading T.S. Eliot?"
Jeeves and the Feudal Spirit

Eliot's admiration of P. G. Wodehouse was only 'just this side of idolatry'. The great poet had an entire collection of Wodehouse publications, items from which he lent very rarely and then only to close friends and under severe conditions.
Christopher Sykes, Evelyn Waugh: A Biography

[T]heir son Cosmo [had] been detained at home by a rush order from the Booksy Weekly *for an article on Albert Camus and the Aesthetic Tradition.*
'Joy Bells for Walter'

Until he started on it, he had had no notion what blood, sweat and tears are demanded from the poor sap who takes a pop at the life literary.
'The Word in Season'

I first discovered Wodehouse thanks to the happiest of accidents, particularly for one who wasn't, until that point in my life, mad keen on fiction.

Aged about 12, I came across a schoolfriend reading a paperback with a rather attractive cover design signed 'Ionicus'. It was *Psmith in the City*, and when he'd read it, he passed it on to me. The shark bit immediately, and I finished my first Wodehouse that same day. Fortunately, the school library had a dog-eared and rather grubby paperback of *The Inimitable Jeeves*, and the local branch of W.H. Smith in my provincial town stocked a few other Penguin titles (a snip at 60 pence each). Trying to fill the enormous gaps in my collection introduced me to the joys of rummaging around in second-hand bookshops – a second habit that continues to take up rather more of my life than it should. I still remember the sheer joy and surprise that accompanied my biggest haul; I was around 14, on a family holiday to Stratford-on-Avon, and I bagged a record eight mint-condition Wodehouse titles in nearby Warwick. At least until I discovered alcohol and nightclubs, life didn't get any better than that (although I'm still four short of the − I think − 58 'Ionicus' Penguins, 46 years on).

The biggest snag in those early days of collecting was that prior to the internet, and before any reference works on Wodehouse had been published, there was no easy way to find out how many books he had actually written or what their titles were. 'Other P.G. Wodehouse Titles Available' teasers hidden among the back pages of printings were pretty much all there was to go on. Even worse, these were never complete lists, only the titles that publisher had recently licensed. Unfamiliar names like *Do Butlers Burgle Banks?* or *Doctor Sally* would loom out of the fog to be scribbled on the 'to get' list, which seemed to grow frustratingly longer the more Wodehouses I bagged. I even used to keep a small supply of 'doubles' (duplicate copies) for barter and exchange among like-minded fellow pupils.

Good-luck stories such as mine will always play their part in the survival of a writer's work, as will those other serendipitous factors, word of mouth and personal recommendation. And, of course, the availability of Wodehouse books has improved immeasurably since my own first encounter in the early 1970s. All that hard-to-come-by, painfully assembled intel can now be accessed with a few clicks of a mouse. No more driving hundreds of miles to medieval county towns in the Midlands on the off-chance of bagging a stray title, for Plum's complete 'offer' - as the marketing people have it - is now instantly downloadable. Even though the thrill of the chase has been considerably diminished, this instant gratification does have its upsides.

Even better, the Everyman/Overlook re-issue series of 99 volumes (published between 2000-2015) has made it easier to get our heads round the size and scope of Plum's lifetime achievement. From a great farrago of titles reissued in dribs and drabs by various different imprints, here at last was a single publishing house curating a uniform, considered, attractive edition of pretty much the whole of Wodehouse's prose legacy. This has blessed us with a stable, organized, well-edited body of material to refer to and work with − to comment on, to write about, to publicize and promote, alerting us that Wodehouse World is an actual, graspable *thing*. An enormous thing to be sure, and ruinously expensive to buy if you want the whole shebang, but for all that, his expansive legacy is in pretty good physical shape to face the future.

Of course, there's always more that can be done to help keep Wodehouse in the public eye − and this is the real subject of this brief

Afterword, to sow one or two ideas about how this might happen. Most of the project-based exploitation of Wodehouse World – publishing initiatives, TV serials, audiobooks, flashy websites and so forth – is the province of various branches of the media and outside the influence of most of us. But in four intensive years spent writing about Plum, I've become convinced that more back-end activity is needed to support these commercial endeavours, which will involve a strategic re-focusing of the way his work is generally regarded. In public relations-speak, this is called 'reputation management', and I reckon Wodehouse – and Wodehouse World – could do with some. It may prove a long game, but it's one we can all join in, simply by adjusting the way we think and talk about him.

As I argued at the very start of these ramblings, Wodehouse deserves to be considered not just a great comic writer, but a great writer *period*. Not a "minor stylist and humourist" as one critic would have it, and *definitely* not the creator of a world that is "frivolous, empty and perfectly delightful" in the words of another. For all his comic lightness, there is real weight and heft in what he achieved – it's just that Wodehouse scholarship is not as far down the road of actively demonstrating this excellence as it should be. In the years since Plum's death almost half a century ago, biography has taken pole position in Wodehouse studies, with critical investigations of his writing stuck at the back of the grid. Where it has been addressed at all, what he wrote and how he wrote it has been approached through the context of his life, not his literary awareness, which has led to some unhelpful and distracting misunderstandings it will take time to dislodge. Wodehouse is far from being the only victim of this critical approach, which has been the vogue in tertiary education both in the U.S. and Europe for almost two generations. During that time, imaginative invention has been cast in a supporting role to influence, possibility to proof – and that, with respect, is not the only way creativity works. Although, as this particular volume has demonstrated time and again, Plum's real-life experiences were regularly alchemized into his art, not everything needs to have come from somewhere, and there are more things in heaven and earth than are dreamed of in this transactional kind of approach. Isn't it rather easier to look for the necessary evidence of Wodehouse's greatness in what is literally under our very noses – his books?

The thing is, Plum knew his trade inside out and backwards. His prolific reading and catholic tastes fostered a deep understanding of exactly how literature 'worked', learning he chose to wear lightly as he plied his craftsman's trade. So lightly in fact, it has led to a general disinclination to get to grips with the nuts and bolts of his writing. To some, it's like the proverbial Swiss watch; it runs so efficiently, it's easy to forget there's a complex but unseen mechanism of cogs and gears that keeps things moving. Others are so caught up in the "perfectly delightful" aspects of his work, they doubt the validity of such intrusions. But we can't even begin to claim that Wodehouse's romantic comedy was just as much a slog to write as high tragedy unless we can conclusively *prove* that it was, and in order to carry things forward, we're going to have to keep breaking into Plum's toolbox and have a good old rummage around to see what's in there. There's simply no other way: for unless and until comic writers of his calibre are judged using exactly the same methods and criteria as those who write stories as "grey as a stevedore's undervest" (as Plum puts it in *Ice in the Bedroom*), we will not have created the level playing field necessary for Wodehouse to give of his best. It may take time until that body of critical work is forthcoming, but it will have been worth the effort if we can mention Wodehouse in the same breath as Ibsen without prompting sharp intakes of breath from our cultural gatekeepers.

The two main approaches Wodehouse scholars can pursue to aid this ambition have made regular appearances throughout this trilogy. The first is literary context and provenance: where do we position Plum in the ongoing historical narrative that is The Story of Literature? Although Wodehouse is very much a one-off, neither his patented romcom formulas nor his distinctive writing style arrived out of nowhere, so thinking of his output in terms of periods, schools, movements or genres can be helpful as long as we acknowledge that the whole is usually greater than the sum of the parts. In Volume 2, for example, I traced his writing's ancestry back through Classical and Romantic literary sensibilities; and earlier in this book, I looked at the roots of his art in satire. For reasons of space and the generalist parameters of my argument, this research is far from complete, and will repay many future visits as Plum's literary ancestry is further investigated. For the same reasons, I haven't had time to dwell on his addiction to popular literature, in particular school stories, crime thrillers and romance. There are also several papers to be written on his relationship with English Comic Drama from pre-Shakespearean times through to 20th century stage farce and even TV sitcoms. Wodehouse and vaudeville/music hall? Bring it on. Wodehouse and English Restoration Comedy? Some spin on the ball there, as Freddie Widgeon would say. There are so many ways Wodehouse is caught up in the warp and weft of comic writing down the ages that a lifetime of reading would scarcely be sufficient to unpick it all.

The second approach is getting down and dirty with the text itself, a process I began in the later chapters of Volume 1. Wodehouse's aesthetics are endlessly inventive and fascinating for all that he was working inside a tightly-controlled formula. As formal English clashes with the American vernacular, Wodehouse is the grammarian's, the linguist's and lexicographer's delight. How he *heard* language needs far more detailed attention paying to it, and his use of rhyme, rhythm, tone and register remains almost virgin territory. Then there are formal issues, such as how he opens his books, structures a scene, generates plot and dialogue - all basic themes whose surfaces have only just been scratched . . . and so on and so forth and all that sort of thing.

In short, much remains to be done, and only once that process is well under way can Wodehouse be meaningfully taught, as well as read and recommended. Aye, and there's the rub. For in order to sell Plum's comedy into the increasingly tick-box world of education, we have to convince its panjandrums of his comedy's seriousness as a subject for study. That he has sufficient clout to be considered alongside his sweatier colleagues on the curriculum. *That laughter is not incompatible with learning.* Any viable pitch isn't much helped by the fact that in academic criticism, too few resources have been devoted to comedy, leaving it bereft of a developed language that helps us speak about it. Things have a habit of turning mighty serious mighty quickly, something that even the most cursory internet searches for "theory of comedy" or "comedy studies" will quickly reveal. Plum recognized this tendency as far back as 1934 in his preface to his anthology *A Century of Humour*:

> [N]obody, I think, can deny that the swiftness with which I have become a force in English letters is rather remarkable. It is a bare thirty-four years since I started earning my living as a writer . . . a job which entitles me to wear pince-nez and talk about trends and Cycles and the Spirit of Comedy and What Is The Difference Between Humour and Wit.

Comedy is indeed a serious business, but that doesn't mean it has to be written about solemnly and in language brimming with jargon. What needs fostering is not just the urge to study Wodehouse, but an undertaking to engage with him *in an appropriate spirit*, one that will not do violence to his comedic intentions nor ride roughshod through his lightness, for that too will end up throwing the baby out with the bathwater. Plum's final word on the subject seems to be "[o]ne never quite forgets a story that has made one laugh" - and he's dead right, for they are all too rare.

A good place to start studying Wodehouse – aside from actually reading him in bulk – is the online provision of research materials. With this in mind, the P G Wodehouse Society (UK) has already produced a comprehensive series of "Information Sheets" on its website which address several fundamental questions about his writing (www.pgwodehousesociety.org.uk/sheets). More will undoubtedly follow. There is also a six-page list of helpful publications in the 'Practical Bibliography' at the end of my Volume 1, recommending further reading in the fields of criticism, biography and reference. Together with the Everyman/ Overlook texts, these represent about 90% of the materials I have used to put this trilogy together. Then there's:

- the ever-growing, utterly indispensable www.madameulalie.org, which hoovers up and meticulously curates all the Wodehouse novels, stories and journalism that annually fall out of American copyright. Supremely practical, you can even conduct word searches in it;

- critical and bibliographical articles published in *Wooster Sauce* and *Plum Lines*, respectively the journals of the British and American P.G. Wodehouse Societies (memberships required). Much of this material is already available online, or if it isn't, soon will be;

- the Wodehouse collection at the British Library in London, accessioned in 2016.

That's more than enough to get the ball rolling.

And that's almost it. Before we lower the curtain, however, I should mention three crucial works on Wodehouse that were published too late for inclusion in my Volume 1 bibliography:

- *Who's Who in Wodehouse* (Third Expanded Edition) by Daniel H. Garrison and Neil Midkiff (Published by the authors, 2020, ISBN 978-1-7343967-2-0). An exhaustive alphabetical guide to 4,400 Wodehouse characters that is both addictive and funny. An invaluable time saver too.

- *Nothing is Simple in Wodehouse* by Tony Ring (Harebrain Publishing, 2021, no ISBN, available direct from the author). 75 enervating cruxes in Wodehouse studies carefully demystified to stop people like me falling into obvious traps, written by The Man Who Knows.

- John Dawson's compendious *P.G. Wodehouse's Early Years: His Life and Work 1881-1908* is indispensable, not least because it robustly confronts the more fanciful theories of some of Plum's previous biographers with actual evidence. As a bonus, it also contains the full text of *Money Received For Literary Work* in which Plum detailed his earnings from 1900 to February 1908.

And with that we come to the end of this trilogy. I very much hope that as well as informing and entertaining, it may just set some wheels in motion of the kind I have described in this Afterword. We can all do our bit to spread Wodehousean sweetness and light, and I for one am not done yet. So, it's really only au revoir rather than adieu, for I've at least two more Wodehouse books planned for the future. The first of these will be *Wodehouse At the Theatre* (its working title), so please keep an eye open for it.

Thank you.

ENVOI

Whate'er he meant it matters not a pin.
Ye critics, who have columns ye must fill,
Look for some other target for the quill.

('Tell Me No More', November 1904)

THE P G WODEHOUSE SOCIETY (U.K.)

The P G Wodehouse Society (U.K.) is a friendly and active literary society that exists to promote the enjoyment of the greatest humorous writer in the history of the English language. We hold a number of meetings and events for our members throughout the year, which include lectures, quizzes and performance, and there's a biennial black tie dinner in London. We also publish a quarterly magazine, *Wooster Sauce*, which contains news, reviews and scholarship from correspondents around the world. For further information and details on how to apply for membership, visit *www.pgwodehousesociety.org.uk*

FORTHCOMING P. G. Wodehouse titles from Paul Kent

PLUM'S LITERARY HEROES

It's widely acknowledged that P. G. 'Plum' Wodehouse is the greatest humorous writer England produced in the 20th century. The creator of Jeeves and Bertie, the Blandings saga, Ukridge, Mr Mulliner, Psmith and Uncle Fred, his output totalled almost 100 volumes of peerless comic invention. But where did all that material come from? Not just out of his head, no matter how large his hat size: in Wodehouse's case, much of arrived courtesy of his voracious reading habits, everything from Shakespeare to W.S. Gilbert via the Bible, Tennyson, Sherlock Holmes, gung-ho schoolboy fiction, gory pulp thrillers, the gloopiest romances and literally hundreds of other writers – even T.S. Eliot, who rubs shoulders with a host of authors whose names are now largely forgotten. No other writer had a broader range of influences.

In his latest groundbreaking study, Paul Kent, author of the *Pelham Grenville Wodehouse* trilogy of literary biographies (also available from TSB) teases out Plum's literary roots, and how he expertly blended elements from all these writers and genres into the heady cocktail that keeps the world laughing over a hundred years on from when he first created it. It's an alternative history of English Literature that will also make you laugh out loud.

SHOWBIZ WODEHOUSE

P. G. Wodehouse's love of the American vernacular made him an outstanding lyricist, and along with Jerome Kern, Cole Porter, and George Gershwin (all Wodehouse collaborators), he helped to invent a quintessential American art form, the musical comedy. Mark Steyn makes a convincing case ... that had Wodehouse died in 1918, he would be remembered not as a novelist, but as "the first great lyricist of the American musical." (Cheryl Miller, Claremont Review of Books)

For many years the toast of Broadway and London's West End, P. G. Wodehouse was bitten by the theatre bug at an early age and stayed bit until the last day of his long life, an influence that also helped to shape his matchless writing style and mighty prose legacy. Former BBC Drama director and commissioning editor Paul Kent lifts the lid on this lesser-known body of Wodehouse's Work, looking at the glittering theatrical worlds of 19th and 20th-century musical comedy, Plum's deep roots in Shakespearean and Classical comedy, and his comprehensive knowledge and understanding of the performing arts.

PELHAM GRENVILLE WODEHOUSE

ALSO AVAILABLE from Paul Kent

PELHAM GRENVILLE WODEHOUSE
VOLUME 1: "This is jolly old Fame"

P. G. "Plum" Wodehouse is widely acknowledged as the greatest English comic writer of the 20th century. The creator of Jeeves & Wooster, Lord Emsworth and Blandings, Ukridge, Mr. Mulliner, the Oldest Member and the Eggs, Beans and Crumpets of the Drones Club, the consistently upbeat tone of his 100 or so books represents one of the largest-ever literary bequests to human happiness by one man. He is one of the few writers we can rely on to increase the number of sunshine hours in the day, helping us to joke melancholy and seriousness back down to their proper size. Granted unprecedented access to Wodehouse's papers and library, lifelong enthusiast Paul Kent takes us on a comprehensive tour of Wodehouse's unique comic world and the imagination that created it. Volume 1 focuses on where that world came from and how Wodehouse shaped it, covering the full range of his achievements – not only his novels and stories but his musical comedies, song lyrics, poetry, journalism. and dramas.

PELHAM GRENVILLE WODEHOUSE
VOLUME 2: "Mid-Season Form"

In 1915, and for the next decade or so, P. G. Wodehouse's fictional world mushroomed within his imagination. His best-known creations, Jeeves and Bertie Wooster, arrived in 1915 as did Lord Emsworth and many of the Blandings circle; the Oldest Member teed off in 1919; the Drones Club threw open its doors in 1921; a new, improved Stanley Featherstonehaugh Ukridge returned to the fold in 1923 and Mr Mulliner sipped his first hot scotch and lemon at the bar parlour of the Angler's Rest in 1926. It's no coincidence that by 1922, Cosmopolitan magazine had dubbed Wodehouse "Contributor to the Gaiety of Nations". In Volume 2 of his brilliantly-reviewed and ground-breaking trilogy, Paul Kent explores the golden years of Wodehouse World, when 'Plum' was writing at the height of what he called his "mid-season form". Packed with fresh research and original insights, this book is an invaluable companion to the best of Wodehouse, taking us on a backstage tour of this great and well-loved writer's imagination.

P. G. Wodehouse in the 21st Century

WHAT HO!: P. G. Wodehouse on . . .

In addition to Paul Kent's 3-volume tour of P. G. Wodehouse's creative imagination, TSB Books is launching a series of Plum-related pamphlets by the same author featuring subjects that complement the main trilogy. The series currently includes – 'Food', 'Love', 'Sport', 'Money', 'Class', 'Cats & Dogs', 'Hollywood', 'Fashion', 'Childhood', and 'Faith'. The pamphlets are 64 pages each, attractively-priced and written in Kent's breezy, no-nonsense style, they are perfect partners to the main books and ideal for gifting.

Find out more at www.canofworms.net/whatho

INDEX TO VOLUME 3: "THE HAPPINESS OF THE WORLD"

Novels and Non-Fiction

Index to Volume 3: "The Happiness of the World"

Short Stories and Serials

Lyrics, Musicals, Plays, Revues and Poems

INDEX TO VOLUME 3: "THE HAPPINESS OF THE WORLD"

Printed in the USA
CPSIA information can be obtained
at www.ICGtesting.com
JSHW020737100824
67865JS00004B/1